HTML Quick Reference

Structure Tags

`<!--...-->`	Creates a comment
`<HTML>...</HTML>`	Encloses the entire HTML document
`<HEAD>...</HEAD>`	Encloses the head of the HTML document
`<ISINDEX>`	Indicates the document is a gateway script that allows searches
`<META>`	Provides general information about the document
`<STYLE>...</STYLE>`	Style information
`<SCRIPT>...</SCRIPT>`	Scripting language
`<TITLE>...</TITLE>`	The title of the document
`<BODY>...</BODY>`	Encloses the body (text and tags) of the HTML document

Common Attributes

`id`	Document-wide identifier
`class`	Class values
`lang`	Language value
`dir`	Direction for weak/neutral text
`title`	Title

Headings

`<H1>...</H1>`	Headings 1 through 6
`<H2>...</H2>`	
`<H3>...</H3>`	
`<H4>...</H4>`	
`<H5>...</H5>`	
`<H6>...</H6>`	

Paragraphs

`<P>...</P>`	A plain paragraph; `</P>` is optional

Links

`<A>...</A>`	Creates a link or anchor Includes common attributes
`HREF="..."`	The URL of the document to be linked to this one
`NAME="..."`	The name of the anchor
`TARGET="..."`	Identifies the window or location to open the link in

Links

`REL="..."`	Defines forward link types
`REV="..."`	Defines reverse link types
`ACCESSKEY="..."`	Determines the accessibility character
`SHAPE="..."`	Is for use with object shapes
`COORDS="..."`	Is for use with object shapes
`TABINDEX="..."`	Determines the tabbing order
`onClick`	Is an intrinsic event
`onMouseOver`	Is an intrinsic event
`onMouseOut`	Is an intrinsic event

Lists

`<OL>...</OL>`	An ordered (numbered) list
`<UL>...</UL>`	An unordered (bulleted) list
`<MENU>...</MENU>`	A menu list of items
`<DIR>...</DIR>`	A directory listing
`<LI>`	A list item
`<DL>...</DL>`	A definition or glossary list
`<DT>`	A definition term
`<DD>`	The corresponding definition to a definition term

Character Formatting

`<EM>...</EM>`	Emphasis (usually italic)
`<STRONG>...</STRONG>`	Stronger emphasis (usually bold)
`<CODE>...</CODE>`	Code sample (usually Courier)
`<KBD>...</KBD>`	Text to be typed (usually Courier)
`<VAR>...</VAR>`	A variable or placeholder for some other value
`<SAMP>...</SAMP>`	Sample text
`<DFN>...<DFN>`	(Proposed) A definition of a term
`<CITE>...</CITE>`	A citation
`<B>...</B>`	Boldface text
`<I>...</I>`	Italic text
`<TT>...</TT>`	Typewriter font

Other Elements

`<HR>`	A horizontal rule line
` `	A line break

continues

Other Elements

`<BLOCKQUOTE>...` `</BLOCKQUOTE>`	Used for long quotes or citations
`<ADDRESS>...` `</ADDRESS>`	Signatures or general information about a document's author
`<FONT>...</FONT>`	Change the size of the font for the enclosed text
`SIZE="..."`	The size of the font, from 1 to 7
`<BASEFONT>`	Sets the default size of the font for the current page
`SIZE="..."`	The default size of the font, from 1 to 7

Images

`<IMG>`	Inserts an inline image into the document; includes common attributes
`ISMAP`	This image is a server-side image map
`USEMAP`	This image is a client-side image map
`SRC="..."`	The URL of the image
`ALT="..."`	A text string that will be displayed in browsers that cannot support images
`ALIGN="..."`	Determines the alignment of the given image
`HEIGHT="..."`	Is the suggested height in pixels
`WIDTH="..."`	Is the suggested width in pixels
`VSPACE="..."`	The space between the image and the text above or below it
`HSPACE="..."`	The space between the image and the text to its left or right

Frames

`<FRAMESET>...` `</FRAMESET>`	Defines a frameset
`ROWS="..."`	Number of rows in frame
`COLS="..."`	Number of columns in frame
`onLoad`	Is an intrinsic event
`onUnload`	Is an intrinsic event
`<FRAME>`	Creates a frame
`NAME="..."`	Is the name of target frame
`SRC="..."`	Calls the frame content source
`FRAMEBORDER="..."`	Determines the frame border

Frames

`MARGINWIDTH="..."`	Defines margin widths
`MARGINHEIGHT="..."`	Defines margin heights
`NORESIZE="..."`	Determines ability to resize frames
`SCROLLING="..."`	Determines ability to scroll within frames

Tables

`<TABLE>...</TABLE>`	Creates a table; includes common attributes
`BORDER="..."`	Indicates whether the table should be drawn with or without a border
`<CAPTION>...</CAPTION>`	The caption for the table
`ALIGN="..."`	The position of the caption Possible values are `TOP` and `BOTTOM`
`<TR>...</TR>`	A table row
`ALIGN="..."`	The horizontal alignment of the contents of the cells within this row; possible values are `LEFT`, `RIGHT`, and `CENTER`
`VALIGN="..."`	The vertical alignment of the contents of the cells within this row; possible values are `TOP`, `MIDDLE`, `BOTTOM`, and `BASELINE` (Netscape only)
`<TH>...</TH>`	A table heading cell
`ALIGN="..."`	The horizontal alignment of the contents of the cell
`VALIGN="..."`	The vertical alignment of the contents of the cell
`ROWSPAN="..."`	The number of rows this cell will span
`COLSPAN="..."`	The number of columns this cell will span
`NOWRAP`	Do not automatically wrap the contents of this cell
`<TD>...</TD>`	Defines a table data cell
`ALIGN="..."`	The horizontal alignment of the contents of the cell
`VALIGN="..."`	The vertical alignment of the contents of the cell
`ROWSPAN="..."`	The number of rows this cell will span
`COLSPAN="..."`	The number of columns this cell will span
`NOWRAP`	Do not automatically wrap the contents of this cell

Here's what people are saying about Laura Lemay's *Teach Yourself Web Publishing with HTML*

"There are some good HTML primers on the Web itself, but if you're like me, you'll find it easier to learn by cracking a book. The best I've found is Laura Lemay's *Teach Yourself Web Publishing with HTML.*"

—Marc Frons, *Business Week*

"Laura Lemay delivers on her title's promise. By following her clear sequence of explanations, examples, and exercises, even the absolute Web novice can create serviceable documents within a few days. Better, she moves quickly beyond mechanics to techniques and tools for designing maximally effective and attractive presentations in spite of the medium's limitations."

—Michael K. Stone, *Whole Earth Review*

"Of all the HTML books out right now, I think Lemay's is the best, and I recommend it."

—Nancy McGough, *Infinite Ink*

"If you are looking for an easy-to-read introduction to HTML, this book is for you. Lemay has a clear understanding of what works and what doesn't, and she conveys her thoughts in a concise, orderly fashion."

—Robert Stewart, *The Virtual Mirror*

"If you want to create a Web page, or even if you already have created one, and you want a *great* book to help you understand it all, check out Laura Lemay's *Teach Yourself Web Publishing with HTML.* I've used mine so much I practically know it by heart!"

—Camille Tillman, *Book Stacks Unlimited*

What's New in This Book

With this, the fourth edition of *Teach Yourself Web Publishing with HTML in a Week*, we've added a lot of additional coverage and up-to-the-minute information, including the following:

- [ ] The latest HTML enhancements, including the emerging HTML 4.0 standard, and extensions in Netscape Communicator 4 and Microsoft Internet Explorer 4
- [ ] Updated coverage of frames, tables, and forms
- [ ] Coverage of Dynamic HTML, the latest from Microsoft and Netscape
- [ ] Style sheets: Learn to customize the look and feel of your pages with cascading style sheets
- [ ] Information about the latest tools to help you create stunning and effective Web sites

Teach Yourself

WEB

PUBLISHING

WITH

HTML 4

in a Week

Teach Yourself
WEB PUBLISHING
WITH HTML 4
in a Week

Laura Lemay
With revisions for the Fourth Edition by
Armen Danesh

sams
net

201 West 103rd Street
Indianapolis, Indiana 46290

Copyright © 1997 by Sams.net Publishing

FOURTH EDITION

International Standard Book Number: 1-57521-336-2

Library of Congress Catalog Card Number: 97-67513

2000   99   98   97   4   3   2   1

Interpretation of the printing code: the rightmost double-digit number is the year of the book's printing; the rightmost single-digit, the number of the book's printing. For example, a printing code of 97-1 shows that the first printing of the book occurred in 1997.

Composed in AGaramond and MCPdigital by Macmillan Computer Publishing

Printed in the United States of America

Trademarks

President, Sams Publishing   Richard K. Swadley
Publishing Manager   Mark Taber
Acquisitions Manager   Beverly M. Eppink
Managing Editor   Brice P. Gosnell
Director of Marketing   Kelli S. Spencer
Product Marketing Managers   Wendy Gilbride, Kim Margolius
Assistant Marketing Manager   Jennifer Pock
Marketing Coordinator   Linda Beckwith

Acquisitions Editor
Mark Taber

Development Editors
Kelly Murdock
Fran Hatton

Software Development Specialist
Bob Correll

Copy Editors
Charles Hutchinson
Dana Rhodes Lesh

Indexer
Johnna VanHoose

Technical Edit Coordinator
Lorraine E. Schaffer

Technical Reviewer
Will Kelly

Editorial Coordinators
Katie Wise
Mandie Rowell

Editorial Assistants
Carol Ackerman
Karen M. Flowers
Andi Richter
Rhonda Tinch-Mize

Cover Designer
Sandra Schroeder

Book Designer
Gary Adair

Copy Writer
David Reichwein

Production Team Supervisors
Brad Chinn
Charlotte Clapp

Production
Rick Bond
Michael Dietsch
Chris Livengood
Carl Pierce
Ian A. Smith

Overview

Contents

Acknowledgments

To Sams and Sams.net Publishing for letting me write the kind of HTML book I wanted to see.

To the Coca-Cola Company, for creating Diet Coke and selling so much of it to me.

To all the folks on the `comp.infosystems.www` newsgroups, the `www-talk` mailing list, and the Web conference on the WELL, for answering questions and putting up with my late-night rants.

To innumerable people who helped me with the writing of this book, including Lance Norskog, Ken Tidwell, Steve Krause, Tony Barreca, CJ Silverio, Peter Harrison, Bill Whedon, Jim Graham, Jim Race, Mark Meadows, and many others I'm sure I've forgotten.

And finally, to Eric Murray, the other half of `1ne.com`, for moral support when I was convinced I couldn't possibly finish writing any of this book on time, for setting up all my UNIX and networking equipment and keeping it running, and for writing a whole lot of Perl code on very short notice. (I need a form that calculates the exact weight of the person who submits it based on the phase of the moon, the current gross national debt, and what that person ate for dinner. You can do that in Perl, can't you?) Most of the programs in this book are his work, and, as such, he deserves a good portion of the credit. Thank you, thank you, thank you, thank you, thank you.

—Laura Lemay

First I must acknowledge my wife. She put up with my lack of sleep and late hours as deadlines loomed. I continue to be surprised she still lets me work on these projects.

I also must acknowledge the Sams and Sams.net staff, particularly Mark Taber, Kelly Murdock, and Cindy Morrow for having patience with me, especially when my Internet connection failed me and I found myself disconnected.

Finally, credit must be given where it is due. This really is Laura Lemay's book; I only helped keep it up to date (if that is even possible in this world of the Internet). It is because she wrote such a good book that this one deserves any credit.

—Arman Danesh

About the Authors

Laura Lemay

Laura Lemay is a technical writer and confirmed Web addict. Between spending 12 hours a day in front of a computer and consuming enormous amounts of Diet Coke, she sometimes manages to write a book. She is the author of *Teach Yourself Web Publishing in a Week* and *Teach Yourself Java in a Week*, and specializes in just about anything related to Web page writing, design, programming, and Web-related publications systems. Her goal for the remainder of the year is to try to get one of her motorcycles to actually run.

You can visit her home page at `http://www.lne.com/lemay/`.

Arman Danesh

Arman Danesh (`armand@juxta.com`) is the Editorial Director of Juxta Publishing Limited, based in Hong Kong. He is the author of *Teach Yourself JavaScript in a Week* and co-author of *JavaScript Developer's Guide*. He has worked as a technology journalist and is a regular contributor and Internet columnist for the *South China Morning Post* and *The Dataphile*. Arman lives with his wife, Tahirih, in Switzerland.

Tell Us What You Think!

As a reader, you are the most important critic and commentator of our books. We value your opinion and want to know what we're doing right, what we could do better, what areas you'd like to see us publish in, and any other words of wisdom you're willing to pass our way. You can help us make strong books that meet your needs and give you the computer guidance you require.

Do you have access to the World Wide Web? Then check out our site at http://www.mcp.com.

NOTE

> If you have a technical question about this book, call the technical support line at 317-581-3833 or send e-mail to support@mcp.com.

As the team leader of the group that created this book, I welcome your comments. You can fax, e-mail, or write me directly to let me know what you did or didn't like about this book—as well as what we can do to make our books stronger. Here's the information:

Fax: 317-581-4669

E-mail: newtech_mgr@sams.mcp.com

Mail: Mark Taber
Comments Department
Sams.net Publishing
201 W. 103rd Street
Indianapolis, IN 46290

Introduction

So you've browsed the Web for a while, and you've seen the sort of stuff that people are putting up on the Net. And you're noticing that more and more stuff is going up all the time, and that more and more people are becoming interested in it. "I want to do that," you think. "How can I do that?" If you have the time and you know where to look, you could find out everything you need to know from the information out on the Web. It's all there, it's all available, and it's all free. Or, you could read this book instead. Here, in one volume that you can keep by your desk to read, reference, and squish spiders with, is nearly all the information you need to create your own Web pages—everything from how to write them, to how to link them together, to how to set up your own Web server and use it to manage forms, and to create special programs to process them.

But wait, there's more. This book goes beyond the scope of other books on how to create Web pages, which just teach you the basic technical details such as how to produce a boldface word. In this book, you'll learn why you should be producing a particular effect and when you should use it, as well as how. In addition, this book provides hints, suggestions, and examples of how to structure your overall presentation, not just the words within each page. This book won't just teach you how to create a Web presentation—it'll teach you how to create a good Web presentation.

Also, unlike many other books on this subject, this book doesn't focus on any one computer system. Regardless of whether you're using a PC running Windows, a Macintosh, or some dialect of UNIX (or any other computer system), many of the concepts in this book will be valuable to you, and you'll be able to apply them to your Web pages regardless of your platform of choice.

Sound good? Glad you think so. I thought it was a good idea when I wrote it, and I hope you get as much out of this book reading it as I did writing it.

Who Should Read This Book

Is this book for you? That depends on the following:

- [ ] If you've seen what's out on the Web, and you want to contribute your own content, this book is for you.

- [ ] If you represent a company that wants to create an Internet "presence" and you're not sure where to start, this book is for you.

- [ ] If you're an information developer, such as a technical writer, and you want to learn how the Web can help you present your information online, this book is for you.

- [ ] If you're doing research or polling and you're interested in creating a system that allows people to "register" comments or vote for particular suggestions or items, this book is for you.

- [ ] If you're just curious about how the Web works, some parts of this book are for you, although you might be able to find what you need on the Web itself.

- [ ] If you've never seen the Web before but you've heard that it's really nifty and want to get set up using it, this book isn't for you. You'll need a more general book about getting set up and browsing the Web before moving on to actually producing Web documents yourself.

- [ ] You've done Web presentations before with text and images and links. Maybe you've played with a table or two and set up a few simple forms. In this case, you may be able to skim the first half of the book, but the second half should still offer you a lot of helpful information.

What This Book Contains

This book is intended to be read and absorbed over the course of two weeks (although it may take you more or less time depending on how much you can absorb in a day). On each day you'll read two chapters, which describe one or two concepts related to Web presentation design.

Day 1   Getting Started: The World Wide Web and You

On Day 1, you get a general overview of the World Wide Web and what you can do with it, and then come up with a plan for your Web presentation.

Day 2   Creating Simple Web Pages

On Day 2, you learn about the HTML language and how to write simple documents and link them together using hypertext links.

Day 3   Doing More with HTML

On Day 3, you do more text formatting with HTML, including working with text alignment, rule lines, and character formatting. You'll also get an overview of the various HTML editors available to help you write HTML.

Day 4   Images, Backgrounds, and Multimedia

Day 4 covers everything you ever wanted to know about images, backgrounds, and using color and multimedia on the Web.

Day 5   Designing Effective Web Pages

On Day 5, you get some hints for creating a well-constructed Web presentation, and you explore some examples of Web presentations to get an idea of what sort of work you can do.

Day 6   Advanced HTML Features: Tables and Frames

On Day 6, you learn about some of the advanced features of HTML available in Netscape Navigator and other browsers: tables and frames.

Day 7   Going Live on the Web

On Day 7, you learn how to put your presentation up on the Web, including how to set up a Web server and advertise the work you've done.

Bonus Day 1   Creating Forms and CGI

Just when you thought you were done, there's an extra day. Bonus Day 1 covers adding interactive forms and image maps to your Web page, including client-side image map tags.

Bonus Day 2   Cascading Style Sheets and Dynamic HTML

And finally, another bonus day brings the total number of days to 9. This day covers some of the latest features to make their way into Netscape Communicator and Microsoft Internet Explorer 4—collectively called Dynamic HTML.

What You Need Before You Start

There are seemingly hundreds of books on the market about how to get connected to the Internet, and lots of books about how to use the World Wide Web. This book isn't one of them. I'm assuming that if you're reading this book, you already have a working connection to the Internet, that you have a World Wide Web browser such as Netscape Navigator, Mosaic, or Lynx available to you, and that you've used it at least a couple of times. You should also have at least a passing acquaintance with some other portions of the Internet such as electronic mail, Gopher, and Usenet news, because I may refer to them in general terms in this book. Although you won't need to explicitly use them to work through the content in this book, some parts of the Web may refer to these other concepts.

In other words, you need to have used the Web in order to provide content for the Web. If you have this one simple qualification, read on!

NOTE

To really take advantage of all the concepts and examples in this book, you should seriously consider using a recent version of Netscape Navigator (version 3.0 or above) or Microsoft Internet Explorer (version 3.0 or above).

Conventions Used in This Book

This book uses special typefaces and other graphical elements to highlight different types of information.

Special Elements

Four types of "boxed" elements present pertinent information that relates to the topic being discussed: Note, Tip, Warning, and New Term. Each item has a special icon associated with it, as described here.

NOTE

Notes highlight special details about the current topic.

TIP

It's a good idea to read the Tips because they present shortcuts or trouble-saving ideas for performing specific tasks.

Don't skip the Warnings. They supply you with information to help you avoid making decisions or performing actions that can cause trouble for you.

 Whenever I introduce a new term, I set it off in a box like this one, and define it for you. I use *italic* for new terms.

HTML Input and Output Examples

Throughout the book, I present exercises and examples of HTML input and output. Here are the Input and Output icons:

 An Input icon identifies HTML code that you can type in yourself.

 An Output icon indicates what the HTML input produces in a browser such as Netscape Navigator or Lynx.

Special Fonts

Several items are presented in a monospace font, which can be plain or italic. Here's what each one means:

`plain mono`	Applied to commands, filenames, file extensions, directory names, Internet addresses, URLs, and HTML input. For example, HTML tags such as `<TABLE>` and `<P>` appear in this font.
`mono italic`	Applied to placeholders, which are generic items for which something specific is substituted as part of a command or as part of computer output. For instance, the term represented by `filename` would be the real name of the file, such as `myfile.txt`.

Teach Yourself Web Publishing: The Web Site

To help you get the most out of this book, there is also a Web site. This site contains updated information about where to find tools and hints and source code for many Web tools you might be interested in incorporating into your own presentations. The site is at `http://www.mcp.com/info/1-57521/1-57521-336-2/`—check it out!

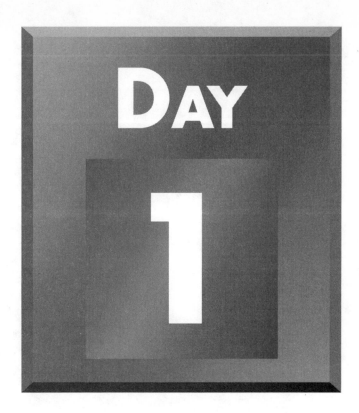

Getting Started: The World Wide Web and You

Chapter **1**

The World of the World Wide Web

A journey of a thousand miles begins with a single step, and here you are at Day 1, Chapter 1, of a journey that will show you how to write, design, and publish pages on the World Wide Web. Before beginning the actual journey, however, you should start with the basics. You'll learn the following:

☐ What the World Wide Web is and why it's really cool

☐ Web browsers: what they do, and a couple popular ones to choose from

☐ What a Web server is and why you need one

☐ Some information about Uniform Resource Locators (URLs)

If you've spent even a small amount time exploring the Web, most, if not all, of this chapter will seem like old news. If so, feel free to skim this chapter and skip ahead to the next chapter, where you'll find an overview of points to think about when you design and organize your own Web documents.

What Is the World Wide Web?

I have a friend who likes to describe things with lots of meaningful words strung together in a chain so that it takes several minutes to sort out what he's just said.

If I were he, I'd describe the World Wide Web as a global, interactive, dynamic, cross-platform, distributed, graphical hypertext information system that runs over the Internet. Whew! Unless you understand each of these words and how they fit together, this description isn't going to make much sense. (My friend often doesn't make much sense, either.)

So let's look at all these words and see what they mean in the context of how you'll be using the Web as a publishing medium.

The Web Is a Hypertext Information System

If you've used any sort of basic online help system, you're already familiar with the primary concept behind the World Wide Web: hypertext.

The idea behind hypertext is that instead of reading text in a rigid, linear structure (such as a book), you can skip easily from one point to another. You can get more information, go back, jump to other topics, and navigate through the text based on what interests you at the time.

 Hypertext enables you to read and navigate text and visual information in a non-linear way based on what you want to know next.

Online help systems or help stacks such as those provided by Microsoft Windows Help or HyperCard on the Macintosh use hypertext to present information. To get more information on a topic, you just click on that topic. The topic might be a link that takes you to a new screen (or window or dialog box) that contains the new information. Perhaps you'll find links on words or phrases that take you to still other screens, and links on those screens that take you even further away from your original topic. Figure 1.1 shows a simple diagram of how this kind of system works.

Figure 1.1.
A simple online help system.

Now imagine that your online help system is linked to another online help system on another application related to yours; for example, your drawing program's help is linked to your word processor's help. Your word processor's help is then linked to an encyclopedia, where you can look up any other concepts that you don't understand. The encyclopedia is hooked into a global index of magazine articles that enables you to get the most recent information on the topics that the encyclopedia covers. The article index is then also linked into information about the writers of those articles, and some pictures of their children. (See Figure 1.2.)

Figure 1.2.

A more complex online help system.

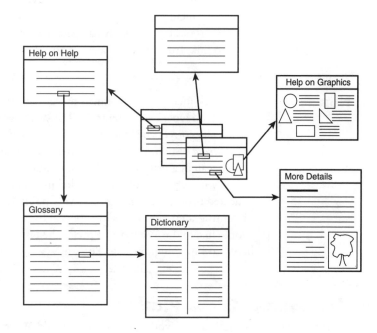

If you had all these interlinked help systems available with every program you bought, you would rapidly run out of disk space. You might also question whether you needed all this information when all you wanted to know was how to do one simple task. All this information could be expensive, too.

But if the information didn't take up much disk space, and if it were freely available, and you could get it reasonably quickly any time you wanted, then the system would be more interesting. In fact, the information system might very well end up more interesting than the software you bought in the first place.

That's just what the World Wide Web is: more information than you could ever digest in a lifetime, linked together in various ways, out there on the Net, available for you to browse whenever you want. It's big and deep and easy to get lost in. But it's also an immense amount of fun.

The Web Is Graphical and Easy to Navigate

One of the best parts of the Web, and arguably the reason it has become so popular, is its capability to display both text and graphics in full color on the same page. Before the Web, using the Internet involved simple text-only connections. You had to navigate the Internet's various services using typed commands and arcane tools. Although plenty of really exciting information was available on the Net, it wasn't necessarily pretty to look at.

The Web provides capabilities for graphics, sound, and video to be incorporated with the text, and newer software includes even more capabilities for multimedia and embedded applications. More important, you can easily navigate the interface to all these capabilities—just jump from link to link, from page to page, across sites and servers.

NOTE

If the Web incorporates so much more than text, why do I keep calling the Web a Hyper *Text* system? Well, if you're going to be absolutely technically correct about it, the Web is not a hypertext system—it's a hyper*media* system. But, on the other hand, you might argue that the Web began as a text-only system, and much of the content is still text-heavy, with extra bits of media added in as emphasis. Many very educated people are arguing these very points at this moment and presenting their arguments in papers and discursive rants as educated people like to do. Whatever. I prefer the term *hypertext*, and it's my book, so I'm going to use it. You know what I mean.

The Web Is Cross-Platform

If you can access the Internet, you can access the World Wide Web regardless of whether you're running on a low-end PC, a fancy expensive graphics workstation, or a multi-million dollar mainframe. You can use a simple text-only modem connection, a small 14-inch black-and-white monitor, or a 21-inch full-color super gamma-corrected graphics accelerated display system. If you think Windows menus buttons look better than Macintosh menus and buttons, or vice versa (or if you think both Mac and Windows people are weenies), it doesn't matter. The World Wide Web is not limited to any one kind of machine or developed by any one company. The Web is entirely cross-platform.

Cross-platform means that you can access Web information equally well from any computer hardware running any operating system using any display.

NOTE

> The whole idea that the Web is—and should be—cross-platform is strongly held to by purists. The reality, though, is changing quickly. With the introduction of new features, technologies, and media types, the Web is losing some of its capability to be truly cross-platform. As Web authors choose to use these newer features, they willingly limit the potential audience for the content of their sites. For example, a site centered around a Java program is essentially unusable on a text-only modem connection. Similarly, some extensions (known as plug-ins) for Netscape Navigator are available only for one platform (either Windows, Mac, or UNIX). Choosing to use one of these extensions makes that portion of your site unavailable to users of other browsers as well as Netscape's browser on the wrong platform.

You gain access to the Web through an application called a *browser*, like Netscape's Navigator or Microsoft's Internet Explorer. You can find lots of browsers out there for most existing computer systems. And after you have a browser and a connection to the Internet, you've got it made. You're on the Web. (I explain more about what the browser actually does later in this chapter.)

 A *browser* is used to view and navigate Web pages and other information on the World Wide Web.

The Web Is Distributed

Information takes up a great deal of space, particularly when you include images and multimedia capabilities. To store all the information that the Web provides, you would need an untold amount of disk space, and managing it would be almost impossible. Imagine if you were interested in finding out more information about alpacas (a Peruvian mammal known for its wool), but when you selected a link in your online encyclopedia, your computer prompted you to insert CD-ROM #456 ALP through ALR. You could be there for a long time just looking for the right CD!

The Web is successful in providing so much information because that information is distributed globally across thousands of Web sites, each of which contributes the space for the information it publishes. You, as a consumer of that information, go to that site to view the information. When you're done, you go somewhere else, and your system reclaims the disk space. You don't have to install it or change disks or do anything other than point your browser at that site.

 A *Web site* is a location on the Web that publishes some kind of information. When you view a Web page, your browser connects to that Web site to get that information.

Each Web site, and each page or bit of information on that site, has a unique address. This address is called a Uniform Resource Locator, or URL. When people tell you to visit a site at http://www.coolsite.com/, they've just given you a URL. You can use your browser (with the Open command, sometimes called Open URL or Go) to enter in the URL (or just copy and paste it).

 A *Uniform Resource Locator (URL)* is a pointer to a specific bit of information on the Internet.

 NOTE

> URLs are alternatively pronounced as if spelled out "You are Ells" or as an actual word ("earls"). Although I prefer the former pronunciation, I've heard the latter used equally often.

You'll learn more about URLs later in this chapter.

The Web Is Dynamic

Because information on the Web is contained on the site that published it, the people who published it in the first place can update it at any time.

If you're browsing that information, you don't have to install a new version of the help system, buy another book, or call technical support to get updated information. Just bring up your browser and check out what's up there.

If you're publishing on the Web, you can make sure your information is up-to-date all the time. You don't have to spend a lot of time re-releasing updated documents. There is no cost of materials. You don't have to get bids on numbers of copies or quality of output. Color is free. And you won't get calls from hapless customers who have a version of the book that was obsolete four years ago.

Consider, for example, the development effort for a Web server called Apache. Apache is being developed and tested through a core of volunteers, has many of the features of the larger commercial servers, and is free. The Apache Web site at http://www.apache.org/ is the central location for information about the Apache software, documentation, and the server software itself. (Figure 1.3 shows its home page.) Because the site can be updated any time, new releases can be distributed quickly and easily. Changes and bug fixes to the documentation, which is all online, can be made directly to the files. And new information and news can be published almost immediately.

Figure 1.3.
The Apache Web site.

NOTE The pictures throughout this book are usually taken from a browser on the Macintosh (Netscape, most often) or using the text-only browser Lynx. The only reason for this use is that I'm writing this book primarily on a Macintosh. If you're using Windows or a UNIX system, don't feel left out. As I noted earlier, the glory of the Web is that you see the same information regardless of the platform you're using. So ignore the buttons and window borders, and focus on what's inside the window.

For some sites, the ability to update the site on the fly at any moment is precisely why the site exists. Figure 1.4 shows the home page for *The Nando Times*, an online newspaper that is updated 24 hours a day to reflect new news as it happens. Because the site is up and available all the time, it has an immediacy that neither hard-copy newspapers nor most television news programs can match. Visit *The Nando Times* at http://www.nando.net/nt/nando.cgi.

Web Browsers Can Access Many Forms of Internet Information

If you've read any of the innumerable books on how to use the Internet, you're aware of the dozens of different ways of getting at information on the Net: FTP, Gopher, Usenet news, WAIS databases, Telnet, and e-mail. Before the Web became as popular as it is now, to get to these different kinds of information you had to use different tools for each one, all of which had to be installed and all of which used different commands. Although all these choices made for a great market for "How to Use the Internet" books, they weren't really very easy to use.

Web browsers change that. Although the Web itself is its own information system, with its own Internet protocol (the HyperText Transfer Protocol, HTTP), Web browsers can also read files from other Internet services. And, even better, you can create links to information on those systems just as you would create links to information on Web pages. This process is all seamless and all available through a single application.

To point your browser to different kinds of information on the Internet, you use different kinds of URLs. Most URLs start with http:, which indicates a file at an actual Web site. To get to a file on the Web using FTP, you would use a URL that looks something like this: ftp://name_of_site/directory/filename. You can also use an ftp: URL ending with a directory name, and your Web server will show you a list of the files, as in Figure 1.5. This particular figure shows a listing of files from Simtel, a repository of Windows software at ftp://oak.oakland.edu/SimTel/win3/winsock/.

Figure 1.4.
The Nando Times.

To use a Gopher server from a Web browser, use a URL that looks something like this: `gopher://name_of_gopher_server/`. For example, Figure 1.6 shows the Gopher server on the WELL, a popular Internet service in San Francisco. Its URL is `gopher://gopher.well.com/`.

You'll learn more about different kinds of URLs in Chapter 4, "All About Links."

Figure 1.5.
The Simtel FTP archive.

Figure 1.6.
*The WELL's
Gopher server.*

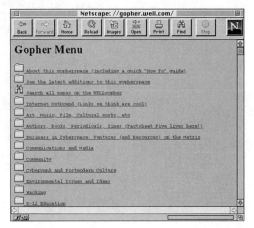

The Web Is Interactive

Interactivity is the ability to "talk back" to the Web server. More traditional media such as television aren't interactive at all; all you do is sit and watch as shows are played at you. Other than changing the channel, you don't have much control over what you see.

The Web is inherently interactive; the act of selecting a link and jumping to another Web page to go somewhere else on the Web is a form of interactivity. In addition to this simple interactivity, however, the Web also enables you to communicate with the publisher of the pages you're reading and with other readers of those pages.

For example, pages can be designed to contain interactive forms that readers can fill out. Forms can contain text-entry areas, radio buttons, or simple menus of items. When the form is "submitted," the information readers type is sent back to the server where the pages originated. Figure 1.7 shows an example of an online form for a rather ridiculous census (a form you'll create later in this book).

Figure 1.7.

The Surrealist Census form.

As a publisher of information on the Web, you can use forms for many different purposes, for example:

☐ To get feedback about your pages.

☐ To get information from your readers (survey, voting, demographic, or any other kind of data). You then can collect statistics on that data, store it in a database, or do anything you want with it.

☐ To provide online order forms for products or services available on the Web.

☐ To create "guestbooks" and conferencing systems that enable your readers to post their own information on your pages. These kinds of systems enable your readers to communicate not only with you, but also with other readers of your pages.

In addition to forms, which provide some of the most popular forms of interactivity on the Web, advanced features of Web development provide even more interactivity. For example, Java and Shockwave enable you to include entire programs and games inside Web pages. Software can run on the Web to enable real-time chat sessions between your readers. Developments in 3D worlds also enable your readers to browse the Web as if they were wandering through real three-dimensional rooms and meeting other people. As time goes on, the Web becomes less of a medium for people passively sitting and digesting information (and becoming "Net potatoes") as it is a medium for reaching and communicating with other people all over the world.

Web Browsers

A Web browser, as I mentioned earlier, is the program you use to view pages on and navigate the World Wide Web. Web browsers are sometimes called Web *clients* or other fancy names ("Internet navigation tools"), but *Web browser* is the most common term.

A wide array of Web browsers is available for just about every platform you can imagine, including graphical-user-interface-based systems (Mac, Windows, X11), and text-only for dial-up UNIX connections. Most browsers are freeware or shareware (try before you buy) or have a lenient licensing policy. (Netscape allows you to evaluate its browser for some time after which you are expected to buy it; it can be kept at no cost for non-commercial use by members of educational institutions and non-profit organizations.) Usually, all you have to do to get a browser is download it from the Net (although downloading is usually easier if you already have a browser you can use to download the new one—sort of a chicken-and-the-egg situation).

If you get your Internet connection through a commercial online service such as America Online or CompuServe, you may have several browsers to choose from. Try a couple and see what works best for you.

Currently, the most popular browser for the World Wide Web is Netscape's Navigator, developed by Netscape Communications Corporation. Netscape has become so popular that using Netscape and using the Web have become synonymous to many people. However, despite the fact that Netscape has the lion's share of the market, it is not the only browser on the Web. This point will become important later when you learn how to design Web pages and learn about the different capabilities of different browsers. Assuming Netscape is the only browser in use on the Web and designing your pages accordingly will limit the audience you can reach with the information you want to present.

NOTE

Choosing to develop for a specific browser, such as Netscape Navigator, is suitable when you know your Web site will be viewed by a limited audience using the targeted browser software. Developing this way is a common practice in corporations implementing intranets, which are internal information systems centered around Internet technology including World Wide Web technology for delivering information to users' desktops within the organization. In these situations, it is a fair assumption that all users in the organization will use the browser supplied to them and, accordingly, it is possible to design the Web component of the intranet to use the specific capabilities of the browser in question.

What the Browser Does

Any Web browser's job is twofold: Given a pointer to a piece of information on the Net (a URL), the browser has to be able to access that information or operate in some way based on the contents of that pointer. For hypertext Web documents, the browser must be able to communicate with the Web server using the HTTP protocol. Because the Web can also manage information contained on FTP and Gopher servers, in Usenet news postings, in e-mail, and so on, browsers can often communicate with those servers or protocols as well.

What the browser does most often, however, is deal with formatting and displaying Web documents. Each Web page is a file written in a language called HyperText Markup Language (HTML) that includes the text of the page, its structure, and links to other documents, images, or other media. (You'll learn all about HTML on Days 2 and 3, because you need to know it so that you can write your own Web pages.) The browser takes the information it gets from the Web server and formats and displays it for your system. Different browsers may format and display the same file differently, depending on the capabilities of that system and the default layout options for the browser itself. You'll learn more about these capabilities tomorrow in Chapter 3, "Begin with the Basics."

Retrieving documents from the Web and formatting them for your system are the two tasks that make up the core of a browser's functionality. However, depending on the browser you use and the features it includes, you may also be able to play multimedia files, view and interact with Java applets, read your mail, or use other advanced features that a particular browser offers.

An Overview of Popular Browsers

This section describes a few of the more popular browsers on the Web currently. They are in no way all the browsers available, and if the browser you're using isn't listed here, don't feel that you have to use one of these browsers. Whatever browser you have is fine as long as it works for you.

You can use the browsers in this section only if you have a direct Internet connection or a dial-up SLIP or PPP Internet connection. Getting your machine connected to the Internet is beyond the scope of this book, but you can find plenty of books to help you do so.

If your connection to the Internet is through a commercial online service (AOL, CompuServe, or Prodigy), you may have a choice of several browsers including the ones in this section and browsers that your provider supplies.

Finally, if the only connection you have to the Internet is through a dial-up text-only UNIX (or other) account, you are limited to using text-only browsers such as Lynx. You cannot view documents in color or view graphics online (although you usually can download them to your system and view them there).

Netscape

By far the most popular browser in use on the Web today is Netscape Navigator, from Netscape Communications Corporation. The Netscape Navigator is most commonly just called Netscape. The Windows 95 version of Netscape is shown in Figure 1.8.

Figure 1.8.

Netscape (for Windows 95).

Netscape is available for Windows, Macintosh, and for many different versions of UNIX running the X Window System. It is well supported and provides up-to-the-minute features including an integrated mail and newsreader, support for Java applets, and the ability to handle plug-ins for more new and interesting features yet to be developed.

The current version of the browser, Netscape Navigator 4, is included in a new suite of Internet tools called Netscape Communicator 4, which is available for downloading at Netscape's site at `http://home.netscape.com/`, or in boxes from your favorite computer software store.

If you're a student, faculty member, or staff member of an educational institution, or if you work for a charitable non-profit organization, you can download and use Netscape for free. Otherwise, you're expected to pay for Netscape after an evaluation period (typically 90 days). If you buy Netscape from a store, you've already paid the license fee.

NCSA Mosaic

At one time, Mosaic held Netscape's place on the Web as the most popular browser. Indeed, Mosaic was the first of the full-color graphical browsers and is usually credited with making the Web as popular as it is today.

Mosaic was developed by NCSA at the University of Illinois, with several supported commercial versions available from companies such as Spry and Spyglass. NCSA Mosaic is free for personal use and comes in versions for Windows, Macintosh, and UNIX (the X Window System); each version is colloquially called WinMosaic, MacMosaic, and XMosaic, respectively. The current version of NCSA Mosaic is 2.01 on the Macintosh, version 2.6 for X Window, and version 3.0 for Windows 95 and NT. For Windows 3.1, development stopped at version 2.1.1. You can find more information and download a copy from `http://www.ncsa.uiuc.edu/SDG/Software/Mosaic/`.

Figure 1.9 shows NCSA Mosaic for Windows 95.

Figure 1.9.

*Mosaic (for
Windows 95).*

Lynx

Lynx ("links," get it?), originally developed by the University of Kansas and now by Foteos Macrides at the Worcester Foundation for Biological Research, is an excellent browser for text-only Internet connections such as dial-up UNIX accounts. It requires VT100 terminal emulation, which most terminal emulation programs should support. You can use arrow keys to select links in Web pages.

Because Lynx runs on systems that lack the capability to display graphics, viewing Web pages using Lynx gives you nothing but the text and the links. Designing pages that work equally well in Lynx and in graphical browsers is one of the more interesting challenges of Web page design (as you'll learn later in this book).

Lynx should be available on the system where you have a dial-up account, or you can download it from `ftp://ftp2.cc.ukans.edu/pub/lynx`. The current version is 2.7FM. (FM are the initials of the author supporting it.) Figure 1.10 shows Lynx running in a Telnet session.

Figure 1.10.

Using Lynx.

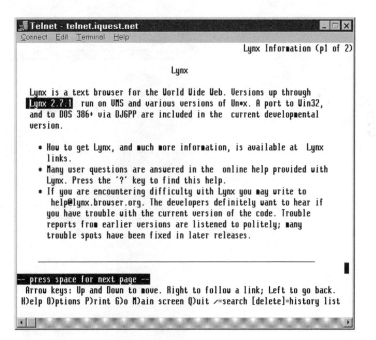

Microsoft Internet Explorer

Microsoft's browser, Internet Explorer, runs on Windows 3.1, Windows 95, Windows NT, and Macintosh, and it is free for downloading from Microsoft's Web site (`http://www.microsoft.com/ie/`). No further license fee is required.

So far, Microsoft has been the only browser developer that has come close to keeping up with Netscape's pace of development, supporting many of Netscape's features and adding a few of its own. In addition, Microsoft has made significant deals with several commercial online services, so its share of the browser market has grown significantly and is a direct challenge to Netscape for control of the browser market. Even with a large number of browsers available today, there are only two in widespread use: Netscape's and Microsoft's.

The current versions of Explorer are 3.02 for Windows 95 and NT 4.0, and 3.01 for Windows NT 3.51, Windows 3.1, and the Macintosh. For more information about all these versions, see the Internet Explorer home page at http://www.microsoft.com/ie/. Currently, preview releases of Internet Explorer 4 for Windows 95 and NT are available for users to try out, but the release version isn't likely to ship until after this book is published.

Figure 1.11 shows Internet Explorer 3.0 running on Windows 95.

Figure 1.11.

Microsoft Internet Explorer (Windows 95).

As with Netscape Navigator, Microsoft is fast at work on version 4 of its browser—initially for Windows 95 and NT 4.0. This new version, slated for release in 1997, promises numerous new features in the emerging Netscape-Microsoft features battle.

NOTE

> With each release of their browsers, Netscape and Microsoft have tried to introduce more new, fancy features. There is no exception with the new versions in preview release. As you see in the second bonus day at the end of the book, these new features include style sheets for providing fine control over the appearance of documents and Dynamic HTML, which encompasses everything from precise layout control to improved scripting of HTML pages.

Web Servers

To view and browse pages on the Web, all you need is a Web browser. To publish pages on the Web, most of the time you'll need a Web server.

NEW TERM A *Web server* is the program that runs on a Web site and is responsible for replying to Web browser requests for files. You need a Web server to publish documents on the Web.

When you use a browser to request a page on a Web site, that browser makes a Web connection to a server (using the HTTP protocol). The server accepts the connection, sends the contents of the files that were requested, and then closes the connection. The browser then formats the information it got from the server.

On the server side, many different browsers may connect to the same server to get the same information. The Web server is responsible for handling all these requests.

Web servers do more than just deposit files. They are also responsible for managing form input and for linking forms and browsers with programs such as databases running on the server.

Just like with browsers, many different servers are available for many different platforms, each with many different features and each ranging in cost from free to very expensive. For now, all you need to know is what the server is there for; you'll learn more about Web servers on Day 7, "Going Live on the Web."

Uniform Resource Locators (URLs)

As you learned earlier, a URL is a pointer to some bit of data on the Web, be it a Web document, a file on FTP or Gopher, a posting on Usenet, or an e-mail address. The URL provides a universal, consistent method for finding and accessing information, not necessarily for you, but mostly for your Web browser. (If URLs were for you, they would be in a format that would make them easier to remember.)

In addition to typing URLs directly into your browser to go to a particular page, you also use URLs when you create a hypertext link within a document to another document. So, any way you look at it, URLs are important to how you and your browser get around on the Web.

URLs contain information about how to get to the information (what protocol to use—FTP, Gopher, HTTP), the Internet host name showing where to look (`www.ncsa.uiuc.edu`, `ftp.apple.com`, `netcom16.netcom.com`, and so on), and the directory or other location on that site to find the file. You also can use special URLs for tasks such as sending mail to people (called Mailto URLs) and for using the Telnet program.

You'll learn all about URLs and what each part means in Chapter 4.

Summary

To publish on the Web, you have to understand the basic concepts that make up the parts of the Web. In this chapter, you learned three major concepts. First, you learned about a few of the more useful features of the Web for publishing information. Second, you learned about Web browsers and servers and how they interact to deliver Web pages. Third, you learned about what a URL is and why it's important to Web browsing and publishing.

Q&A

Q Who runs the Web? Who controls all these protocols? Who's in charge of all this?

A No single entity "owns" or controls the World Wide Web. Given the enormous number of independent sites that supply information to the Web, for any single organization to set rules or guidelines would be impossible. Two groups of organizations, however, have a great influence over the look and feel and direction of the Web itself.

The first is the World Wide Web (W3) Consortium, based at Massachusetts Institute of Technology (MIT) in the United States and INRIA in Europe. The W3 Consortium is made up of individuals and organizations interested in supporting and defining the languages and protocols that make up the Web (HTTP,

HTML, and so on). It also provides products (browsers, servers, and so on) that are freely available to anyone who wants to use them. The W3 Consortium is the closest anyone gets to setting the standards for and enforcing rules about the World Wide Web. You can visit the Consortium's home page at http://www.w3.org/.

The second group of organizations that influences the Web is the browser developers themselves, most notably Netscape Communications Corporation and Microsoft. The competition for most popular and technically advanced browser on the Web is fierce right now, with Netscape and Microsoft as the main combatants. Although both organizations claim to support and adhere to the guidelines proposed by the W3 Consortium, both also include their own new features in new versions of their software—features that often conflict with each other and with the work the W3 Consortium is doing.

Sometimes trying to keep track of all the new and rapidly changing developments feels like being in the middle of a war zone, with Netscape on one side, Microsoft on the other, and the W3 trying to mediate and prevent global thermonuclear war. As a Web designer, you're stuck in the middle, and you'll have to make choices about which side to support, if any, and how to deal with the rapid changes. But that's what the rest of this book is for!

Q Why would anyone use a text-only browser such as Lynx when graphical browsers are available?

A You need a special Internet connection to use a graphical browser on the Web. If your machine isn't directly hooked up to the Internet (for example, on a network at work or school), you'll need to use a modem with a special account to make your system think it's on the Net or an account with a commercial online service. These special accounts can be quite expensive, even in areas that have many Internet service providers. Even then, unless you have a very fast modem, Web pages can take a long time to load, particularly if several graphics appear on the page.

Lynx is the ideal solution for people who either don't have a direct Internet connection or don't want to take the time to use the Web graphically. It's fast and it enables you to get hold of just about everything on the Web—indirectly, yes, but it's there.

Q A lot of the magazine articles I've seen about the Web mention CERN, the European Particle Physics Lab, as having a significant role in Web development. You didn't mention them. Where do they stand in Web development?

A The Web was invented at CERN by Tim Berners-Lee, as I'm sure you know by now from all those magazine articles. And, for several years, CERN was the center for much of the development that went on. In late 1995, however, CERN passed its part in World Wide Web development to INRIA (the Institut National pour la Recherche en Informatique et Automatique), in France. INRIA today is the European leg of the W3 Consortium.

Chapter **2**

Get Organized

When you write a book, a paper, an article, or even a memo, you usually don't just jump right in with the first sentence and then write it through to the end. Same goes with the visual arts—you don't normally start from the top left corner of the canvas or page and work your way down to the bottom right.

A better way to write or draw or design a work is to do some planning beforehand—to know what you're going to do and what you're trying to accomplish, and to have a general idea or rough sketch of the structure of the piece before you jump in and work on it.

Just as with more traditional modes of communication, the process of writing and designing Web pages takes some planning and thought before you start flinging text and graphics around and linking them wildly to each other— perhaps even more so, because trying to apply the rules of traditional writing or design to online hypertext often results in documents that are either difficult to understand and navigate online or that simply don't take advantage of the features that hypertext provides. Poorly organized Web pages are also difficult to revise or to expand.

In this chapter, I describe some of the things you should think about before you begin developing your Web pages. Specifically, you do the following:

- ☐ Learn the differences between a Web presentation, a Web site, a Web page, and a home page
- ☐ Think about the sort of information (content) you want to put on the Web
- ☐ Set the goals for the presentation
- ☐ Organize your content into main topics
- ☐ Come up with a general structure for pages and topics

After you have an overall idea of how you're going to construct your Web pages, you'll be ready to actually start writing and designing those pages tomorrow in Chapter 3, "Begin with the Basics." If you're eager to get started, be patient! You will have more than enough HTML to learn over the next couple of days.

Anatomy of a Web Presentation

First, here's a look at some simple terminology I'll be using throughout this book. You need to know what the following terms mean and how they apply to the body of work you're developing for the Web:

- ☐ The Web presentation
- ☐ The Web site
- ☐ Web pages
- ☐ Home pages

A Web presentation consists of one or more Web pages linked together in a meaningful way, which, as a whole, describes a body of information or creates an overall consistent effect. (See Figure 2.1.)

> **NEW TERM**   A *Web presentation* is a collection of one or more Web pages.

Each Web presentation is stored on a Web site, which is the actual machine on the Web that stores the presentation. Some people refer to the Web presentation and the Web site as the same thing; I like to keep these terms separate because a single Web site can contain many different presentations with very different purposes and be developed by different people. Throughout the first week or so of this book, you'll learn how to develop Web presentations. Later you'll learn how to publish your presentation on an actual Web site.

> **NEW TERM**   A *Web site* is a system on the Internet containing one or more Web presentations.

Figure 2.1.
*Web presentations
and pages.*

The Presentation

Pages within the
Presentation

A Web page is an individual element of a presentation in the same way that a page is a single element of a book or a newspaper (although, unlike paper pages, Web pages can be of any length). Web pages are sometimes called Web documents. Both terms refer to the same thing: a Web page is a single disk file with a single filename that is retrieved from a server and formatted by a Web browser.

NEW TERM   A *Web page* is a single element of a Web presentation and is contained in a single disk file.

The terms *Web presentation, site,* and *page* are pretty easy to grasp, but the term *home page* is a little more problematic because it can have several different meanings.

If you're reading and browsing the Web, you can usually think of the home page as the Web page that loads when you start up your browser or when you choose the Home button. Each browser has its own default home page, which is often the same page for the site that developed the browser. (For example, the Netscape home page is at Netscape's Web site, and the Lynx home page is at the University of Kansas.)

Within your browser, you can change that default home page to start up any page you want—a common tactic I've seen many people use to create a simple page of links to other interesting places or pages that they visit a lot.

If you're publishing pages on the Web, however, the term *home page* has an entirely different meaning. The home page is the first or topmost page in your Web presentation. It's the entry point to the rest of the pages you've created and the first page your readers will see. (See Figure 2.2.)

Figure 2.2.
A home page.

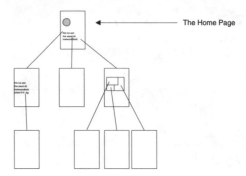

A home page usually contains an overview of the content in the presentation available from that starting point—for example, in the form of a table of contents or a set of icons. If your content is small enough, you might include everything on that single home page—making your home page and your Web presentation the same thing.

NEW TERM A *home page* is the entry or starting point for the rest of your Web presentation.

What Do You Want To Do on the Web?

This question may seem silly. You wouldn't have bought this book if you didn't already have some idea of what you want to put online. But maybe you don't really know what you want to put on the Web, or you have a vague idea but nothing concrete. Maybe your job has suddenly become to put a page for your company on the Web, and someone handed you this book and said, "Here, this will help." Maybe you just want to do something similar to some other Web page you've seen that you thought was particularly cool.

What you want to put on the Web is what I'll refer to throughout this book as your content. *Content* is a general term that can refer to text or graphics or media or interactive forms or anything. If you tell someone what your Web pages are "about," you are describing your content.

NEW TERM Your *content* is the stuff you're putting on the Web. Information, fiction, images, art, programs, humor, diagrams, games—all of this is content.

What sort of content can you put on the Web? Just about anything you want to. Here are some of the kinds of content that are popular on the Web right now:

☐ **Personal information.** You can create pages describing everything anyone could ever want to know about you and how incredibly marvelous you are—your hobbies, your résumé, your picture, things you've done.

☐ **Hobbies or special interests.** A Web page could contain information about a particular topic, hobby, or something you're interested in, for example, music, Star Trek, motorcycles, cult movies, hallucinogenic mushrooms, antique ink bottles, or upcoming jazz concerts in your city.

☐ **Publications**. Newspapers, magazines, and other publications lend themselves particularly well to the Web, and they have the advantage of being more immediate and easier to update than their print counterparts.

☐ **Company profiles.** You could offer information about what a company does, where it is located, job openings, data sheets, white papers, marketing collateral, and whom to contact. Such a page might even present demonstration software, if that's what the company does.

☐ **Online documentation.** The term *online documentation* can refer to everything from quick-reference cards to full reference documentation to interactive tutorials or training modules. And it doesn't have to refer to product documentation; anything task-oriented (changing the oil in your car, making a soufflé, creating landscape portraits in oil, learning HTML) could be described as online documentation.

☐ **Shopping catalogs.** If your company offers items for sale, making your lists available on the Web is a quick and easy way to let your customers know what you have available and your prices. If prices change, you can just update your Web documents to reflect that new information.

☐ **Online stores.** Beyond a simple catalog, the Web can be used to actually sell items to customers. These sites can create a "shopping basket" into which users place and remove items as they browse the catalog. At the end, they can provide a credit card number and shipping information to place the order.

☐ **Polling and opinion gathering.** Interactivity and forms on the Web enable you to get feedback on nearly any topic from your readers, including opinion polls, suggestion boxes, comments on your Web pages or your products, and so on.

☐ **Online education.** The Web's interactivity and low cost of information delivery in many places make it an attractive medium for delivery of distance-learning programs. Already, numerous traditional universities, as well as new online schools and universities, have begun offering distance learning on the Web.

☐ **Anything else that comes to mind.** Hypertext fiction, online toys, media archives, collaborative art…anything!

The Web is limited only by what you want to do with it. In fact, if what you want to do with it isn't in this list, or seems especially wild or half-baked, then that's an excellent reason to try it. The most interesting Web pages are the ones that stretch the boundaries of what the Web is supposed to be capable of.

If you really have no idea of what to put up on the Web, don't feel that you have to stop here. Put this book away, and come up with something before continuing. Maybe by reading through this book you'll get some ideas (and this book will be useful even if you don't have ideas). I've personally found that the best way to come up with ideas is to spend an afternoon browsing on the Web and exploring what other people have done.

Set Your Goals

What do you want people to be able to accomplish in your presentation? Are your readers looking for specific information on how to do something? Are they going to read through each page in turn, going on only when they're done with the page they're reading? Are they just going to start at your home page and wander aimlessly around, exploring your "world" until they get bored and go somewhere else?

As an exercise, come up with a list of several goals that your readers might have for your Web pages. The clearer your goals, the better.

For example, say you're creating a Web presentation describing the company where you work. Some people reading that presentation might want to know about job openings. Others might want to know where you're actually located. Still others may have heard that your company makes technical white papers available over the Net, and they want to download the most recent version of a particular paper. Each of these goals is valid, so you should list each one.

For a shopping catalog Web presentation, you might have only a few goals: to allow your readers to browse the items you have for sale by name or by price, and to order specific items after they're done browsing.

For a personal or special-interest presentation, you may have only a single goal: to allow your readers to browse and explore the information you've provided.

The goals do not have to be lofty ("this Web presentation will bring about world peace") or even make much sense to anyone except you. Still, coming up with goals for your Web documents prepares you to design, organize, and write your Web pages specifically to reach these goals. Goals also help you resist the urge to obscure your content with extra information.

If you're designing Web pages for someone else—for example, if you're creating the Web site for your company or if you've been hired as a consultant—having a set of goals for the site from your employer is definitely one of the most important pieces of information you should have before you create a single page. The ideas you have for the presentation might not be the ideas that other people have for the presentation, and you might end up doing a lot of work that has to be thrown away.

Break Up Your Content into Main Topics

With your goals in mind, now try to organize your content into main topics or sections, chunking related information together under a single topic. Sometimes the goals you came up with in the preceding section and your list of topics will be closely related. For example, if you're putting together a Web page for a bookstore, the goal of being able to order books fits nicely under a topic called, appropriately, "Ordering Books."

You don't have to be exact at this point in development. Your goal here is just to try to come up with an idea of what, specifically, you'll be describing in your Web pages. You can organize the information better later, as you write the actual pages.

For example, say you're designing a Web presentation about how to tune your car. This example is simple because tune-ups consist of a concrete set of steps that fit neatly into topic headings. In this example, your topics might include the following:

- ☐ Change the oil and oil filter
- ☐ Check and adjust engine timing
- ☐ Check and adjust valve clearances
- ☐ Check and replace the spark plugs
- ☐ Check fluid levels, belts, and hoses

Don't worry about the order of the steps or how you're going to get your readers to go from one section to another. Just list the points you want to describe in your presentation.

How about a less task-oriented example? Say you want to create a set of Web pages about a particular rock band because you're a big fan, and you're sure other fans would benefit from your extensive knowledge. Your topics might be as follows:

- ☐ The history of the band
- ☐ Biographies of each of the band members
- ☐ A "discography"—all the albums and singles the band has released
- ☐ Selected lyrics
- ☐ Images of album covers
- ☐ Information about upcoming shows and future albums

You can come up with as many topics as you want, but try to keep each topic reasonably short. If a single topic seems too large, try to break it up into subtopics. If you have too many small topics, try to group them together into some sort of more general topic heading. For example, if you're creating an online encyclopedia of poisonous plants, having individual topics for each plant would be overkill. You can just as easily group each plant name under a letter of the alphabet (A, B, C, and so on) and use each letter as a topic. That's assuming, of course, that your readers will be looking up information in your encyclopedia alphabetically. If they want to look up poisonous plants using some other method, you would have to come up with different topics.

Your goal is to have a set of topics that are roughly the same size and that group together related bits of the information you have to present.

Ideas for Organization and Navigation

At this point, you should have a good idea about what you want to talk about and a list of topics. The next step is to actually start structuring the information you have into a set of Web pages. But before you do that, consider some "standard" structures that have been used in other help systems and online tools. This section describes some of these structures, their various features, and some important considerations, including

☐ The kinds of information that work well for each structure

☐ How readers find their way through the content of each structure type to find what they need

☐ How to make sure readers can figure out where they are within your documents (context) and find their way back to a known position

Think, as you read this section, how your information might fit into one of these structures or how you could combine these structures to create a new structure for your Web presentation.

NOTE

Many of the ideas I describe in this section were drawn from a book called *Designing and Writing Online Documentation* by William K. Horton (John Wiley & Sons, 1994). Although Horton's book was written primarily for technical writers and developers working specifically with online help systems, it's a great book for ideas on structuring documents and for dealing with hypertext information in general. If you start doing a lot of work with the Web, you might want to pick up this book; it provides a lot of insight beyond what I have to offer.

Hierarchies

Probably the easiest and most logical way to structure your Web documents is in a hierarchical or menu fashion, as illustrated in Figure 2.3. Hierarchies and menus lend themselves especially well to online and hypertext documents. Most online help systems, for example, are hierarchical. You start with a list or menu of major topics; selecting one leads you to a list of subtopics, which then leads you to a discussion about a particular topic. Different help systems have different levels, of course, but most follow this simple structure.

Figure 2.3.
Hierarchical organization.

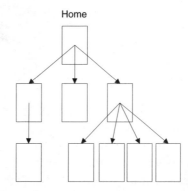

In a hierarchical organization, readers can easily know their position in the structure. Choices are to move up for more general information or down for more specific information. If you provide a link back to the top level, your readers can get back to some known position quickly and easily.

In hierarchies, the home page provides the most general overview to the content below it. The home page also defines the main links for the pages further down in the hierarchy.

For example, a Web presentation about gardening might have a home page with the topics shown in Figure 2.4.

Figure 2.4.
Gardening home page.

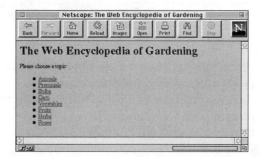

If you select Fruits, you are then linked "down" to a page about fruits (see Figure 2.5). From there, you can go back to the home page, or you can select another link and go further down into more specific information about particular fruits.

Figure 2.5.

Fruits.

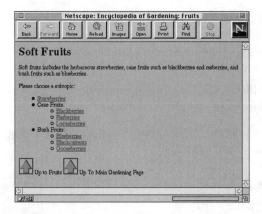

Selecting Soft Fruits takes you to yet another menu-like page, where you have still more categories to choose from (see Figure 2.6). From there, you can go up to Fruits, back to the home page, or down to one of the choices in this menu.

Figure 2.6.

Soft fruits.

Note that each level has a consistent interface (up, down, back to index), and that each level has a limited set of choices for basic navigation. Hierarchies are structured enough that the chance of getting lost is minimal. (This is especially true if you provide clues about where "up" is; for example, a link that says "Up to Soft Fruits" as opposed to just "Up.") Additionally, if you organize each level of the hierarchy and avoid overlap between topics (and the content you have lends itself to a hierarchical organization), using hierarchies can be an easy way to find particular bits of information. If that use is one of your goals for your readers, using a hierarchy may work particularly well.

Avoid including too many levels and too many choices, however, because you can easily annoy your readers. Having too many menu pages results in "voice-mail syndrome." After having to choose from too many menus, readers may forget what it was they originally wanted, and they're too annoyed to care. Try to keep your hierarchy two to three levels deep, combining information on the pages at the lowest levels (or endpoints) of the hierarchy if necessary.

Linear

Another way to organize your documents is to use a linear or sequential organization, much like printed documents are organized. In a linear structure, as illustrated in Figure 2.7, the home page is the title, or introduction, and each page follows sequentially from that structure. In a strict linear structure, links move from one page to another, typically forward and back. You might also want to include a link to "Home" that takes you quickly back to the first page.

Figure 2.7.

Linear organization.

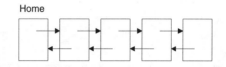

Context is generally easy to figure out in a linear structure simply because there are so few places to go.

A linear organization is very rigid and limits your readers' freedom to explore and your freedom to present information. Linear structures are good for putting material online when the information also has a very linear structure offline (such as short stories, step-by-step instructions, or computer-based training), or when you explicitly want to prevent your readers from skipping around.

For example, consider teaching someone how to make cheese using the Web. Cheese-making is a complex process that involves several steps that must be followed in a specific order.

Describing this process using Web pages lends itself to a linear structure rather well. When navigating a set of Web pages on this subject, you would start with the home page, which might have a summary or an overview of the steps to follow. Then, using the link for "forward," move on to the first step, "Choosing the Right Milk"; to the next step, "Setting and Curdling the Milk"; all the way through to the last step, "Curing and Ripening the Cheese." If you need to review at any time, you could use the link for "back." Because the process is so linear, you would have little need for links that branch off from the main stem or links that join together different steps in the process.

Linear with Alternatives

You can soften the rigidity of a linear structure by allowing the readers to deviate from the main path. For example, you could have a linear structure with alternatives that branch out from a single point (see Figure 2.8). The off-shoots can then rejoin the main branch at some point further down, or they can continue down their separate tracks until they each come to an "end."

For example, say you have an installation procedure for a software package that is similar in most ways, regardless of the computer type, except for one step. At that point in the linear installation, you could branch out to cover each system, as shown in Figure 2.9.

Figure 2.8.

Linear with alternatives.

Figure 2.9.

Different steps for different systems.

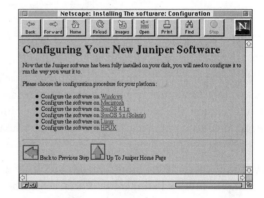

After the system-specific part of the installation, you could then link back to the original branch and continue with the generic installation.

In addition to branching from a linear structure, you could also provide links that allow readers to skip forward or backward in the chain if they need to review a particular step or if they already understand some content (see Figure 2.10).

Figure 2.10.

Skip ahead or back.

Combination of Linear and Hierarchical

A popular form of document organization on the Web is a combination of a linear structure and a hierarchical one, as shown in Figure 2.11. This structure occurs most often when very structured but linear documents are put online; the popular Frequently Asked Questions (FAQ) files use this structure.

Figure 2.11.

Combination of linear and hierarchical organization.

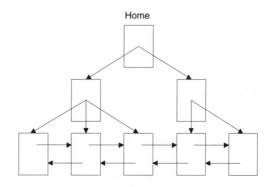

The combination of linear and hierarchical documents works well as long as you have appropriate clues regarding context. Because the readers can either move up and down or forward and backward, they can easily lose their mental positioning in the hierarchy when crossing hierarchical boundaries by moving forward or backward.

For example, say you're putting the Shakespearean play *Macbeth* online as a set of Web pages. In addition to the simple linear structure that the play provides, you can create a hierarchical table of contents and summary of each act linked to appropriate places within the text, something like that shown in Figure 2.12.

Figure 2.12.

Macbeth *hierarchy.*

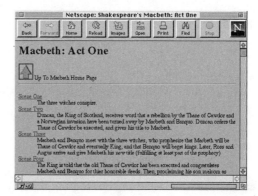

Because this structure is both linear and hierarchical, on each page of the script you provide links to go forward, backward, return to beginning, and up. But what is the context for going up?

If you've just come down into this page from an act summary, the context makes sense. "Up" means go back to the summary you just came from.

But say you go down from a summary and then go forward, crossing an act boundary (say from Act 1 to Act 2). Now what does "up" mean? The fact that you're moving up to a page that you may not have seen before is disorienting given the nature of what you expect from a hierarchy. Up and down are supposed to be consistent.

Consider two possible solutions:

☐ Do not allow "forward" and "back" links across hierarchical boundaries. In this case, to read from Act 1 to Act 2 in *Macbeth*, you have to move up in the hierarchy and then back down into Act 2.

☐ Provide more context in the link text. Instead of just "Up" or an icon for the link that moves up in the hierarchy, include a description as to where you're moving.

Web

A *web* is a set of documents with little or no actual overall structure; the only thing tying each page together is a link (see Figure 2.13). The readers drift from document to document, following the links around.

Figure 2.13.

A web structure.

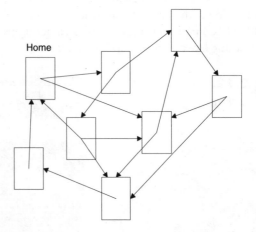

Web structures tend to be free-flowing and allow the readers to wander aimlessly through the content. Web structures are excellent for content that is intended to be meandering or unrelated, or when you want to encourage browsing. The World Wide Web itself is, of course, a giant web structure.

An example of content organized in a web structure might be a set of virtual "rooms" created using Web pages. If you've ever played an old text-adventure game like Zork or Dungeon, or if you've used a Multi-User Dungeon (MUD), you are familiar with this kind of environment.

In the context of a Web presentation, the environment is organized so that each page is a specific location (and usually contains a description of that location). From that location, you can "move" in several different directions, exploring the environment much in the way you would move from room to room in a building in the real world (and getting lost just as easily). For example, the initial home page might look something like the one shown in Figure 2.14.

Figure 2.14.

The home page for a Web-based virtual environment.

From that page, you can then explore one of the links, say, to go into the building, which takes you to the page shown in Figure 2.15.

Figure 2.15.

Another page in the Web environment.

Each room has a set of links to each "adjacent" room in the environment. By following the links, you can explore the rooms in the environment.

The problem with web organizations is that you can get lost in them too easily—just as you might in the "world" you're exploring in the example. Without any overall structure to the content, figuring out the relationship between where you are and where you're going and, often, where you've been is difficult. Context is difficult, and often the only way to find your way back out of a Web structure is to retrace your steps. Web structures can be extremely disorienting and immensely frustrating if you have a specific goal in mind.

To solve the problem of disorientation, you can use clues on each page. Here are two ideas:

☐ Provide a way out. "Return to home page" is an excellent link.

☐ Include a map of the overall structure on each page, with a "you are here" indication somewhere in the map. It doesn't have to be an actual visual map, but providing some sort of context will go a long way toward preventing your readers from getting lost.

Storyboarding Your Web Presentation

The next step in planning your Web presentation is to figure out what content goes on what page and to come up with some simple links for navigation between those pages.

If you're using one of the structures described in the preceding section, much of the organization may arise from that structure, in which case this section will be easy. If you want to combine different kinds of structures, however, or if you have a lot of content that needs to be linked together in sophisticated ways, sitting down and making a specific plan of what goes where will be incredibly useful later as you develop and link each individual page.

What Is Storyboarding and Why Do I Need It?

Storyboarding a presentation is a concept borrowed from filmmaking in which each scene and each individual camera shot is sketched and roughed out in the order in which it occurs in the movie. Storyboarding provides an overall structure and plan to the film that allows the director and staff to have a distinct idea of where each individual shot fits into the overall movie.

NEW TERM *Storyboarding*, borrowed from filmmaking, is the process of creating a rough outline and sketch of what your presentation will look like before you actually write any pages. Storyboarding helps you visualize the entire presentation and how it will look when it's complete.

The storyboarding concept works quite well for developing Web pages as well. The storyboard provides an overall rough outline of what the presentation will look like when it's done, including which topics go on which pages, the primary links, maybe even some conceptual idea of what sort of graphics you'll be using and where they will go. With that representation in hand, you can develop each page without trying to remember exactly where that page fits into the overall presentation and its often complex relationships to other pages.

In the case of really large sets of documents, a storyboard enables different people to develop different portions of the same Web presentation. With a clear storyboard, you can minimize duplication of work and reduce the amount of contextual information each person needs to remember.

For smaller or simpler Web presentations, or presentations with a simple logical structure, storyboarding may be unnecessary. But for larger and more complex projects, the existence of a storyboard can save enormous amounts of time and frustration. If you can't keep all the parts of your content and their relationships in your head, consider creating a storyboard.

So what does a storyboard for a Web presentation look like? It can be as simple as a couple of sheets of paper. Each sheet can represent a page, with a list of topics that each page will describe and some thoughts about the links that page will include. I've seen storyboards for very complex hypertext systems that involved a really large bulletin board, index cards, and string. Each index card had a topic written on it, and the links were represented by string tied on pins from card to card (see Figure 2.16).

Figure 2.16.

A complex storyboard.

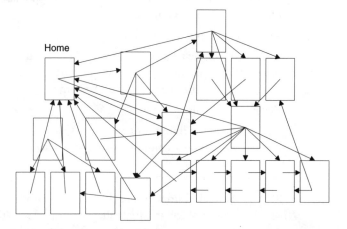

The point of a storyboard is that it organizes your Web pages in a way that works for you. If you like index cards and string, work with these tools. If a simple outline on paper or on the computer works better, use that instead.

Hints for Storyboarding

Some things to think about when developing your storyboard are as follows:

☐ Which topics will go on each page?

A simple rule of thumb is to have each topic represented by a single page. But if you have several topics, maintaining and linking them can be a daunting task.

Consider combining smaller, related topics onto a single page instead. However, don't go overboard and put everything on one page; your readers still have to download your document over the Net. Having several medium-sized pages (say, the size of 2 to 10 pages in your word processor) is better than having one monolithic page or hundreds of little tiny pages.

☐ What are the primary forms of navigation between pages?

What links will you need for your readers to navigate from page to page? They are the main links in your document that enable your readers to accomplish the goals you defined in the first section. Links for forward, back, up, down, or home all fall under the category of primary navigation.

☐ What alternative forms of navigation are you going to provide?

In addition to the simple navigation links, some Web presentations contain extra information that is parallel to the main Web content, such as a glossary of terms, an alphabetical index of concepts, or a credits page. Consider these extra forms of information when designing your plan, and think about how you're going to link them into the main content.

☐ What will you put on your home page?

Because the home page is the starting point for the rest of the information in your presentation, consider what sort of information you're going to put on the home page. A general summary of what's to come? A list of links to other topics?

☐ Review your goals.

As you design the framework for your Web presentation, keep your goals in mind, and make sure you are not obscuring your goals with extra information or content.

NOTE

Several utilities and packages can assist you in storyboarding. Foremost among them are site management packages that can help you manage links in a site, view a graphical representation of the relationship of documents in your site, and even move documents around and automatically update all relevant links in and to the documents.

Summary

Designing a Web presentation, like designing a book outline, a building plan, or a painting, can sometimes be a complex and involved process. Having a plan before beginning can help you keep the details straight and help you develop the finished product with fewer false starts.

In this chapter, you've learned how to put together a simple plan and structure for creating a set of Web pages, including

☐ Deciding what sort of content to present

☐ Coming up with a set of goals for that content

☐ Deciding on a set of topics

☐ Organizing and storyboarding the presentation

With that plan in place, you can now move on to the next few chapters and learn the specifics of how to write individual Web pages, create links between them, and add graphics and media to enhance the presentation for your audience.

Q&A

Q Getting organized seems like an awful lot of work. All I want to do is make something simple, and you're telling me I have to have goals and topics and storyboards.

A If you're doing something simple, then no, you won't need to do much, if any, of the stuff I recommend in this chapter. But if you're talking about developing two or three interlinked pages or more, having a plan before you start really helps. If you just dive in, you may discover that keeping everything straight in your head is too difficult. And the result may not be what you expected, making it hard for people to get the information they need out of your presentation as well as making it difficult for you to reorganize it so that it makes sense. Having a plan before you start can't hurt, and it may save you time in the long run.

Q You've talked a lot in this chapter about organizing topics and pages, but you've said nothing about the design and layout of individual pages.

A I discuss design and layout later in this book, after you've learned more about the sorts of layout HTML (the language used for Web pages) can do, and the stuff that it just can't do. You'll find a whole chapter and more about page layout and design on Day 5, in Chapter 9, "Writing and Designing Web Pages: Dos and Don'ts."

Q What if I don't like any of the basic structures you talked about in this chapter?

A Then design your own. As long as your readers can find what they want or do what you want them to do, no rules say you *must* use a hierarchy or a linear structure. I presented these structures only as potential ideas for organizing your Web pages.

Creating Simple Web Pages

Chapter **3**

Begin with the Basics

After finishing up yesterday's discussion, with lots of text to read and concepts to digest, you're probably wondering when you're actually going to get to write a Web page. That is, after all, why you bought the book. Welcome to Day 2! Today you'll get to create Web pages, learn about HTML (the language for writing Web pages), and learn about the following:

- ☐ What HTML is and why you have to use it
- ☐ What you can and cannot do when you design HTML pages
- ☐ HTML tags: what they are and how to use them
- ☐ Tags for overall page structure: `<HTML>`, `<HEAD>`, and `<BODY>`
- ☐ Tags for titles, headings, and paragraphs: `<TITLE>`, `<H1>`...`<H6>`, and `<P>`
- ☐ Tags for comments
- ☐ Tags for lists

What HTML Is...and What It Isn't

Take note of just one more thing before you dive into actually writing Web pages: You should know what HTML is, what it can do, and most importantly what it can't do.

HTML stands for HyperText Markup Language. HTML is based on the Standard Generalized Markup Language (SGML), a much bigger document-processing system. To write HTML pages, you won't need to know a whole lot about SGML, but knowing that one of the main features of SGML is that it describes the general *structure* of the content inside documents, not that content's actual appearance on the page or on the screen, does help. This concept might be a bit foreign to you if you're used to working with WYSIWYG (What You See Is What You Get) editors, so let's go over the information slowly.

HTML Describes the Structure of a Page

HTML, by virtue of its SGML heritage, is a language for describing the structure of a document, not its actual presentation. The idea here is that most documents have common elements—for example, titles, paragraphs, or lists. Before you start writing, therefore, you can identify and define the set of elements in that document and give them appropriate names (see Figure 3.1).

Figure 3.1.

Document elements.

If you've worked with word processing programs that use style sheets (such as Microsoft Word) or paragraph catalogs (such as FrameMaker), then you've done something similar; each section of text conforms to one of a set of styles that are predefined before you start working.

HTML defines a set of common styles for Web pages: headings, paragraphs, lists, and tables. It also defines character styles such as boldface and code examples. Each element has a name and is contained in what's called a tag. When you write a Web page in HTML, you label the different elements of your page with these tags that say "this is a heading" or "this is a list item." This process is like if you're working for a newspaper or a magazine where you do the writing but someone else does the layout; you might explain to the layout person that this line is the title, this line is a figure caption, or this line is a heading. You do the same with HTML.

HTML Does Not Describe Page Layout

When you're working with a word processor or page layout program, styles are not just named elements of a page—they also include formatting information such as the font size and style, indentation, underlining, and so on. So when you write some text that's supposed to be a heading, you can apply the Heading style to it, and the program automatically formats that paragraph for you in the correct style.

HTML doesn't go this far. For the most part, HTML doesn't say anything about how a page looks when it's viewed. HTML tags just indicate that an element is a heading or a list; they say nothing about how that heading or list is to be formatted. So, as with the magazine example and the layout person who formats your article, the layout person's job is to decide how big the heading should be and what font it should be in. The only thing you have to worry about is marking which section is supposed to be a heading.

Web browsers, in addition to providing the networking functions to retrieve pages from the Web, double as HTML formatters. When you read an HTML page into a browser such as Netscape or Lynx, the browser reads, or parses, the HTML tags and formats the text and images on the screen. The browser has mappings between the names of page elements and actual styles on the screen; for example, headings might be in a larger font than the text on the rest of the page. The browser also wraps all the text so that it fits into the current width of the window.

Different browsers, running on different platforms, may have different style mappings for each page element. Some browsers may use different font styles than others. So, for example, one browser might display italics as italics, whereas another might use reverse text or underlining on systems that don't have italic fonts. Or it might put a heading in all capital letters instead of a larger font. What this means to you as a Web page designer is that the pages you create using HTML may look radically different from system to system and from browser to browser. The actual information and links inside those pages will still be there, but the appearance on the screen will change. You can design a Web page so that it looks perfect on your computer system, but when someone else reads it on a different system, it may look entirely different (and it may very well be entirely unreadable).

Why It Works This Way

If you're used to writing and designing on paper, this concept may seem almost perverse. No control over the layout of a page? The whole design can vary depending on where the page is viewed? This is awful! Why on earth would a system work like this?

Remember in Chapter 1, "The World of the World Wide Web," when I mentioned that one of the cool things about the Web is that it is cross-platform and that Web pages can be viewed on any computer system, on any size screen, with any graphics display? If the final goal of Web publishing is for your pages to be readable by anyone in the world, you can't count on your readers having the same computer systems, the same size screens, the same number of colors, or the same fonts as you. The Web takes into account all these differences and allows all browsers and all computer systems to be on equal ground.

The Web, as a design medium, is not a new form of paper. The Web is an entirely new medium, with new constraints and goals that are very different from working with paper. The most important rules of Web page design, as I'll keep harping on throughout this book, are these:

> *Don't* design your pages based on what they look like on your computer system and on your browser. *Do* design your pages so they work in most browsers. *Do* focus on clear, well-structured content that is easy to read and understand.

Throughout this book, I'll show you examples of HTML code and what they look like when displayed. In many examples, I'll give you a comparison of how a snippet of code looks in two very different browsers: Netscape, probably the most popular browser on the market today, and Lynx, a browser that works on text-only terminals, although it is less popular but still is in common use. Through these examples, you'll get an idea for how different the same page can look from browser to browser.

NOTE Although this rule of designing by structure and not by appearance is the way to produce good HTML, when you surf the Web, you might be surprised that the vast majority of Web sites seem to have been designed with appearance in mind—usually appearance in a particular browser such as Netscape Navigator or Microsoft's Internet Explorer. Don't be swayed by these designs. If you stick to the rules I suggested, in the end your Web pages and Web sites will be all the more successful simply because more people can easily read and use them.

HTML Is a Markup Language

HTML is a *markup language.* Writing in a markup language means that you start with the text of your page and add special tags around words and paragraphs. If you've ever worked with other markup languages such as troff or LaTeX, or even older DOS-based word processors where you put in special codes for things such as "turn on boldface," this language won't seem all that unusual.

3

The tags indicate the different parts of the page and produce different effects in the browser. You'll learn more about tags and how they're used in the next section.

HTML has a defined set of tags you can use. You can't make up your own tags to create new appearances or features. And, just to make sure that things are really confusing, different browsers support different sets of tags.

The base set of HTML tags, the lowest common denominator, is referred to as HTML 2.0. HTML 2.0 is the old standard for HTML (a written specification for it is developed and maintained by the W3 consortium) and the set of tags that all browsers must support. For the next couple of chapters, you'll learn primarily about HTML 2.0 tags that you can use anywhere.

HTML 4.0 is considered the "current generation" of HTML and a catchall for lots of new features that give you flexibility over HTML 2.0 and 3.2 for how you design your pages.

HTML 4.0 is now fairly complete. HTML 4.0 adds some of the elements that have emerged out of the feature war between the two leading browsers: Netscape Navigator and Microsoft Internet Explorer. HTML 4.0 includes support for cascading style sheets, absolute positioning, scripting, and frames, along with other new features.

Some HTML 4.0 features are not yet supported by any browsers. Like HTML 2.0 and 3.2, the HTML 4.0 standard is maintained by the W3 Consortium.

NOTE   If you're interested in how HTML development is working and just exactly what's going on at the W3 Consortium, check out the pages for HTML at the Consortium's site at `http://www.w3.org/MarkUp/`.

Confused yet? You're not alone. Even Web designers with years of experience and hundreds of pages under their belts have to struggle with the problem of which set of tags to choose in order to strike a balance between wide support for a design (using HTML 2.0 and 3.2) or having more flexibility in layout but less consistency across browsers (HTML 4.0 or the browser extensions). Keeping track of all this information can be really confusing. Through-out this book, as I introduce each tag, I'll let you know which version of HTML the tag belongs to, how widely supported it is, and how to use it to best effect in a wide variety of browsers. Later in this book, I'll give you hints on how to deal with the different HTML tags to make sure that your pages are readable and still look good in all kinds of browsers.

Even with all these different tags to choose from, HTML is an especially small and simple-to-learn markup language—far smaller than other languages such as PostScript or troff on UNIX. Those languages are so large and complex that learning enough to write even simple documents often takes ages. With HTML, you can get started right away.

With that note, let's get started.

What HTML Files Look Like

Pages written in HTML are plain text files (ASCII), which means they contain no platform- or program-specific information. They can be read by any editor that supports text (which should be just about any editor—more about this subject later). HTML files contain the following:

- ☐ The text of the page itself
- ☐ HTML tags that indicate page elements, structure, formatting, and hypertext links to other pages or to included media

Most HTML tags look something like this:

```
<TheTagName> affected text </TheTagName>
```

The tag name itself (here, `TheTagName`) is enclosed in brackets (<>).

HTML tags generally have a beginning and an ending tag surrounding the text that they affect. The beginning tag "turns on" a feature (such as headings, bold, and so on), and the ending tag turns it off. Closing tags have the tag name preceded by a slash (/).

 HTML tags are the information inside brackets (<>) that indicate features or elements of a page.

 Just a warning: Be careful of the difference between the forward slash (/) mentioned above and backslashes (\), which are used by DOS and Windows in directory references on hard drives (as in `c:\window` or other directory paths). If you accidentally use the backslash in place of a forward slash in HTML, the browser won't recognize ending tags.

Not all HTML tags have a beginning and an end. Some tags are only one-sided, and still other tags are "containers" that hold extra information and text inside the brackets. You'll learn about these tags as the book progresses.

HTML tags are not case sensitive; that is, you can specify them in uppercase, lowercase, or in any mixture. So, <HTML> is the same as <html> is the same as <HtMl>. I like to put my tags in all caps (<HTML>) so that I can pick them out from the text better. I show them that way in the examples in this book.

Exercise 3.1: Looking at HTML sources.

Before you actually start writing your own HTML pages, getting a feel for what an HTML page looks like certainly helps. Luckily, you can find plenty of source material to look at. Every page that comes over the wire to your browser is in HTML format. (You almost never see the codes in your browser; all you see is the final result.)

Most Web browsers have a way of letting you see the HTML source of a Web page. You may have a menu item or a button for View Document Source or View HTML. In Lynx, the \ (backslash) command toggles between source view and formatted view.

> **TIP**
>
> In some browsers, you cannot directly view the source of a Web page, but you can save the current page as a file to your local disk. In a dialog box for saving the file, you might find a menu of formats—for example, Text, PostScript, or HTML. You can save the current page as HTML and then open that file in a text editor or word processor to see the HTML source.

Try going to a typical home page and then viewing the source for that page. For example, Figure 3.2 shows the home page for AltaVista, a popular search page at http://www.altavista.digital.com/.

The HTML source of the AltaVista home page looks something like Figure 3.3.

Try viewing the source of your own favorite Web pages. You should start seeing some similarities in the way pages are organized and get a feel for the kinds of tags that HTML uses. You can learn a lot about HTML by comparing the text on the screen with the source for that text.

Figure 3.2.
AltaVista home page.

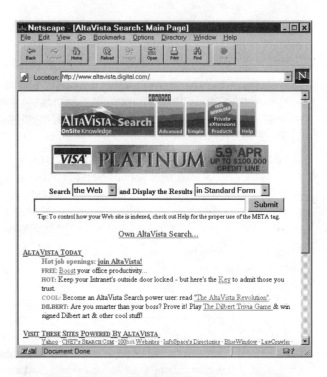

Figure 3.3.
Some HTML source.

Exercise 3.2: Creating an HTML page.

Now that you've seen what HTML looks like, it's your turn to create your own Web page. Start with a simple example so that you can get a basic feel for HTML.

To get started writing HTML, you don't need a Web server, a Web provider, or even a connection to the Web itself. All you really need is something to create your HTML files and at least one browser to view them. You can write, link, and test whole suites of Web pages without even touching a network. In fact, that's what you're going to do for the majority of this book. I'll talk later about publishing everything on the Web so other people can see.

First, you'll need a text editor. A text editor is a program that saves files in ASCII format. ASCII format is just plain text, with no font formatting or special characters. On UNIX, vi, emacs, and pico are all text editors. On Windows, Notepad, Microsoft Write, and DOS Edit are good basic text editors (and free with your system!); a shareware editor such as WED or WinEdit will work as well. On the Macintosh, you can use the SimpleText application that came with your system or a more powerful text editor such as BBedit or Alpha (both of which are shareware).

If you have only a word processor such as Microsoft Word, don't panic. You can still write pages in word processors just as you would in text editors, although doing so is more complicated. When you use the Save or Save As command, you'll see a menu of formats you can use to save the file. One of them should be Text Only, Text Only with Line Breaks, or DOS Text. All these options will save your file as plain ASCII text, just as if you were using a text editor. For HTML files, if you have a choice between DOS Text and just Text, use DOS Text, and use the Line Breaks option if you have it.

NOTE

> If you do use a word processor for your HTML development, be very careful. Many recent word processors are including HTML modes or mechanisms for creating HTML code. The word processor may decide to take over your HTML coding for you or mysteriously put you into that mode without telling you first. This feature may produce unusual results or files that simply don't behave as you expect. If you run into trouble with a word processor, try using a text editor and see whether it helps.

What about the plethora of free and commercial HTML editors that claim to help you write HTML more easily? Most of them are actually simple text editors with some buttons that stick the tags in for you. If you've got one of these editors, go ahead and use it. If you've got a fancier editor that claims to hide all the HTML for you, put it aside for the next couple of days, and try using a plain text editor just for a little while. I'll talk more about HTML editors after this example.

Open your text editor, and type the following code. You don't have to understand what any of it means at this point. You'll learn about it later in this chapter. This simple example is just to get you started.

```
<HTML><HEAD>
<TITLE>My Sample HTML page</TITLE></HEAD>
<BODY>
<H1>This is an HTML Page</H1>
</BODY></HTML>
```

NOTE

> For this example, try typing it in to get a feel for it, but for future examples you might want to use the online versions to prevent having to retype everything.

After you create your HTML file, save it to disk. Remember that if you're using a word processor, choose Save As and make sure you're saving it as text only. When you pick a name for the file, follow these two rules:

☐ The filename should have an extension of `.html` (`.htm` on DOS or Windows systems that have only three-character extensions)—for example, `myfile.html` or `text.html` or `index.htm`. Most Web software will require your files to have this extension, so get into the habit of using it now.

☐ Use small, simple names. Don't include spaces or special characters (bullets, accented characters)—just letters and numbers are fine.

Exercise 3.3: Viewing the result.

Now that you have an HTML file, start up your Web browser. You don't have to be connected to the network because you're not going to be opening pages at any other site. Your browser or network connection software may complain about the lack of a network connection, but usually it will give up and let you use it anyway.

TIP

> If you're using a Web browser from Windows 3.1, using that browser without a network is unfortunately more complicated than on other systems. Many Windows 3.1 browsers (including some versions of Netscape) cannot run without a network, preventing you from looking at your local files without running up online charges. Try starting up your browser while not online to see if this is the case. If your browser has this problem, you can try several workarounds. Depending on your

network software, you might be able to start your network package (Trumpet or Chameleon) but not actually dial the network. This solution often is sufficient for many browsers.

If this solution doesn't work, you'll have to replace the file `winsock.dll` in your Windows directory with a "null sock"—a special file that makes your system think it's on a network when it's not. If you use Netscape, use `mozock.dll` instead.

First, put your original `winsock.dll` in a safe place; you'll need to put everything back the way it was to get back onto the Web. Next, rename the null sock file to `winsock.dll`, and copy it to your Windows directory. With the fake `winsock` file installed, you should be able to use your Windows browser without a network. (It may still give you errors, but it should work.)

After your browser is running, look for a menu item or button labeled Open Local, Open File, or maybe just Open. Choosing it will let you browse your local disk. (If you're using Lynx, use the `cd` command to change to the directory that contains your HTML file and enter the command `lynx myfile.html` to start Lynx.) The Open File command (or its equivalent) tells the browser to read an HTML file from your disk, parse it, and display it, just as if it were a page on the Web. Using your browser and the Open Local command, you can write and test your HTML files on your computer in the privacy of your own home.

If you don't see something like what's in Figure 3.4 (for example, if parts are missing or if everything looks like a heading), go back into your text editor and compare your file to the example. Make sure that all your tags have closing tags and that all your < characters are matched by > characters. You don't have to quit your browser to do so; just fix the file and save it again under the same name.

Next, go back to your browser. Locate and choose a menu item or button called Reload. (In Lynx, you press Ctrl+R.) The browser will read the new version of your file, and voilà, you can edit and preview and edit and preview until you get the file right.

If you're getting the actual HTML text repeated in your browser rather than what's shown in Figure 3.4, make sure your HTML file has an `.html` or `.htm` extension. This file extension tells your browser that it is an HTML file. The extension is important.

If things are going really wrong—if you're getting a blank screen or you're getting some really strange characters—something is wrong with your original file. If you've been using a word processor to edit your files, try opening your saved HTML file in a plain text editor (again Notepad or SimpleText will work just fine). If the text editor can't read the file, or if the result is garbled, you haven't saved the original file in the right format. Go back into your original editor, and try saving the file as text only again. Then try viewing the file again in your browser until you get it right.

Figure 3.4.

The sample HTML file.

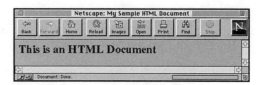

A Note About Formatting

When an HTML page is parsed by a browser, any formatting you may have done by hand—that is, any extra spaces, tabs, returns, and so on—are all ignored. The only thing that formats an HTML page is an HTML tag. If you spend hours carefully editing a plain text file to have nicely formatted paragraphs and columns of numbers, but you don't include any tags, when you read the page into an HTML browser, all the text will flow into one paragraph. All your work will have been in vain.

NOTE

> The one exception to this rule is a tag called <PRE>. You'll learn about this tag tomorrow in Chapter 5, "More Text Formatting with HTML."

The advantage of having all white space (spaces, tabs, returns) ignored is that you can put your tags wherever you want.

The following examples all produce the same output. Try them!

```
<H1>If music be the food of love, play on.</H1>

<H1>
If music be the food of love, play on.
</H1>

<H1>
If music be the food of love, play on.            </H1>

<H1>    If    music    be    the    food    of    love,
play    on. </H1>
```

Programs to Help You Write HTML

You may be thinking that all this tag stuff is a real pain, especially if you didn't get that small example right the first time. (Don't fret about it; I didn't get that example right the first time, and I created it.) You have to remember all the tags, and you have to type them in right and close each one. What a hassle!

Many freeware and shareware programs are available for editing HTML files. Most of these programs are essentially text editors with extra menu items or buttons that insert the appropriate HTML tags into your text. HTML-based text editors are particularly nice for two reasons: You don't have to remember all the tags, and you don't have to take the time to type them all.

I'll discuss some of the available HTML-based editors in Chapter 6, "HTML Assistants: Editors and Converters." For now, if you have a simple HTML editor, feel free to use it for the examples in this book. If all you have is a text editor, no problem; you'll just have to do a little more typing.

What about WYSIWYG editors? Lots of editors on the market purport to be WYSIWYG. The problem is that, as you learned earlier in this chapter, there's really no such thing as WYSIWYG when you're dealing with HTML because WYG can vary wildly based on the browser that someone is using to read your page. With that said, as long as you're aware that the result of working in those editors may vary, using WYSIWYG editors can be a quick way to create simple HTML files. However, for professional Web development and for using many of the very advanced features, WYSIWYG editors usually fall short, and you'll need to go "under the hood" to play with the HTML code anyhow. Even if you intend to use a WYSIWYG editor for the bulk of your HTML work, I recommend you bear with me for the next couple of days and try these examples in text editors so that you get a feel for what HTML really is before you decide to move on to an editor that hides the tags.

In addition to the HTML editors, you also can use converters, which take files from many popular word processing programs and convert them to HTML. With a simple set of templates, you can write your pages entirely in your favorite program and then convert the result when you're done.

In many cases, converters can be extremely useful, particularly for putting existing documents on the Web as fast as possible. However, converters suffer from many of the same problems as WYSIWYG editors: The result can vary from browser to browser, and many newer or advanced features aren't available in the converters. Also, most converter programs are fairly limited, not necessarily by their own features, but mostly by the limitations in HTML itself. No amount of fancy converting is going to make HTML do things that it can't yet do. If a particular capability doesn't exist in HTML, the converter cannot do anything to solve that problem. (In fact, the converter may end up doing strange things to your HTML files, causing you more work than if you just did all the formatting yourself.)

Structuring Your HTML

HTML defines three tags that are used to describe the page's overall structure and provide some simple "header" information. These three tags identify your page to browsers or HTML tools. They also provide simple information about the page (such as its title or its author) before loading the entire thing. The page structure tags don't affect what the page looks like when it's displayed; they're only there to help tools that interpret or filter HTML files.

According to the strict HTML definition, these tags are optional. If your page does not contain them, browsers usually can read the page anyway. However, these page structure tags might become required elements in the future. Tools that need these tags may also come along. If you get into the habit of including the page structure tags now, you won't have to worry about updating all your files later.

<HTML>

The first page structure tag in every HTML page is the <HTML> tag. It indicates that the content of this file is in the HTML language.

All the text and HTML commands in your HTML page should go within the beginning and ending HTML tags, like this:

```
<HTML>
...your page...
</HTML>
```

<HEAD>

The <HEAD> tag specifies that the lines within the beginning and ending points of the tag are the prologue to the rest of the file. Generally, only a few tags go into the <HEAD> portion of the page (most notably, the page title, described later). You should never put any of the text of your page into the header.

Here's a typical example of how you properly use the <HEAD> tag (you'll learn about <TITLE> later):

```
<HTML>
<HEAD>
<TITLE>This is the Title.</TITLE>
</HEAD>
....
</HTML>
```

<BODY>

The remainder of your HTML page, including all the text and other content (links, pictures, and so on), is enclosed within a <BODY> tag. In combination with the <HTML> and <HEAD> tags, your code looks like the following:

```
<HTML>
<HEAD>
<TITLE>This is the Title. It will be explained later on</TITLE>
</HEAD>
<BODY>
....
</BODY>
</HTML>
```

You may notice here that each HTML tag is nested. That is, both `<BODY>` and `</BODY>` tags go inside both `<HTML>` tags; the same with both `<HEAD>` tags. All HTML tags work this way, forming individual nested sections of text. You should be careful never to overlap tags, that is, to do something like this:

```
<HTML>
<HEAD>
<BODY>
</HEAD>
</BODY>
</HTML>
```

Whenever you close an HTML tag, make sure that you're closing the most recently opened tag. (You'll learn more about closing tags as you go on.)

The Title

Each HTML page needs a title to indicate what the page describes. The title is used by your browser's bookmarks or hotlist program, and also by other programs that catalog Web pages. To give a page a title, use the `<TITLE>` tag.

 The *title* indicates what your Web page is about and is used to refer to that page in bookmark or hotlist entries. Titles also appear in the title bar of many GUI browsers (including Netscape Navigator and Microsoft Internet Explorer).

`<TITLE>` tags always go inside the page header (the `<HEAD>` tags) and describe the contents of the page, as follows:

```
<HTML>
<HEAD>
<TITLE>The Lion, The Witch, and the Wardrobe</TITLE>
</HEAD>
<BODY>
....
</BODY>
</HTML>
```

You can have only one title in the page, and that title can contain only plain text; that is, no other tags should appear inside the title.

When you pick a title, try to pick one that is both short and descriptive of the content on the page. Additionally, your title should be relevant out of context. If someone browsing on the Web follows a random link and ends up on this page, or if a person finds your title in a friend's browser history list, would he or she have any idea what this page is about? You may not intend the page to be used independently of the pages you specifically linked to it, but because anyone can link to any page at any time, be prepared for that consequence and pick a helpful title.

Also, because many browsers put the title in the title bar of the window, you may have a limited number of words available. (Although the text within the <TITLE> tag can be of any length, it may be cut off by the browser when it's displayed.) The following are some other examples of good titles:

```
<TITLE>Poisonous Plants of North America</TITLE>
<TITLE>Image Editing: A Tutorial</TITLE>
<TITLE>Upcoming Cemetery Tours, Summer 1997</TITLE>
<TITLE>Installing The Software: Opening the CD Case</TITLE>
<TITLE>Laura Lemay's Awesome Home Page</TITLE>
```

Here are some not-so-good titles:

```
<TITLE>Part Two</TITLE>
<TITLE>An Example</TITLE>
<TITLE>Nigel Franklin Hobbes</TITLE>
<TITLE>Minutes of the Second Meeting of the Fourth Conference of the
Committee for the Preservation of English Roses, Day Four, After Lunch</TITLE>
```

The following examples show how titles look in both Netscape and Lynx, as shown in Figures 3.5 and 3.6, respectively.

 `<TITLE>Poisonous Plants of North America</TITLE>`

Figure 3.5.
The output in Netscape.

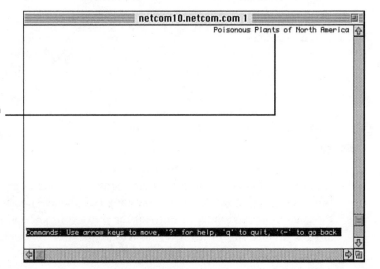

Figure 3.6.
The output in Lynx.

The title is displayed in
the upper-right corner

Headings

Headings are used to divide sections of text, just like this book is divided. ("Headings," above, is a heading.) HTML defines six levels of headings. Heading tags look like the following:

```
<H1>Installing Your Safetee Lock</H1>
```

The numbers indicate heading levels (H1 through H6). The headings, when they're displayed, are not numbered. They are displayed either in bigger or bolder text, or are centered or underlined, or are capitalized—so that they stand out from regular text.

Think of the headings as items in an outline. If the text you're writing has a structure, use the headings to indicate that structure, as shown in the next code lines. (Notice that I've indented the headings in this example to show the hierarchy better. They don't have to be indented in your page; in fact, the indenting will be ignored by the browser.)

```
<H1>Engine Tune-Up</H1>
   <H2>Change The Oil</H2>
   <H2>Adjust the Valves</H2>
   <H2>Change the Spark Plugs</H2>
     <H3>Remove the Old Plugs</H3>
     <H3>Prepare the New Plugs</H3>
        <H4>Remove the Guards</H4>
        <H4>Check the Gap</H4>
        <H4>Apply Anti-Seize Lubricant</H4>
        <H4>Install the Plugs</H4>
   <H2>Adjust the Timing</H2>
```

Unlike titles, headings can be any length, including many lines of text. (Because headings are emphasized, though, having many lines of emphasized text may be tiring to read.)

A common practice is to use a first-level heading at the top of your page to either duplicate the title (which is usually displayed elsewhere), or to provide a shorter or less contextual form of the title. For example, if you have a page that shows several examples of folding bed sheets, part of a long presentation on how to fold bed sheets, the title might look something like this:

```
<TITLE>How to Fold Sheets: Some Examples</TITLE>
```

The topmost heading, however, might just be as follows:

```
<H1>Examples</H1>
```

Don't use headings to display text in boldface type or to make certain parts of your page stand out more. Although the result may look cool on your browser, you don't know what it'll look like when other people use their browsers to read your page. Other browsers may number headings or format them in a manner that you don't expect. Also, tools to create searchable indexes of Web pages may extract your headings to indicate the important parts of a page. By using headings for something other than an actual heading, you may be foiling those search programs and creating strange results.

The following examples show headings. Figure 3.7 shows how they appear in Netscape, and Figure 3.8 shows how they appear in Lynx.

```
<H1>Engine Tune-Up</H1>
    <H2>Change The Oil</H2>
    <H2>Change the Spark Plugs</H2>
        <H3>Prepare the New Plugs</H3>
            <H4>Remove the Guards</H4>
            <H4>Check the Gap</H4>
```

Figure 3.7.
The output in Netscape.

Figure 3.8.
The output in Lynx.

Paragraphs

Now that you have a page title and several headings, you can add some ordinary paragraphs to the page.

The first version of HTML specified the `<P>` tag as a one-sided tag. There was no corresponding `</P>`, and the `<P>` tag was used to indicate the end of a paragraph (a paragraph break), not the beginning. So paragraphs in the first version of HTML looked like this:

```
The blue sweater was reluctant to be worn, and wrestled with her as
she attempted to put it on. The collar was too small, and would not
fit over her head, and the arm holes moved seemingly randomly away
from her searching hands.<P>
Exasperated, she took off the sweater and flung it on the floor.
Then she vindictively stomped on it in revenge for its recalcitrant
behavior.<P>
```

Most browsers that were created early in the history of the Web assume that paragraphs will be formatted this way. When they come across a <P> tag, these browsers start a new line and add some extra vertical space between the line just ended and the next one.

Now the paragraph tags are two-sided (<P>...</P>), but <P> indicates the beginning of the paragraph. Also, the closing tag (</P>) is optional. So the sweater story would look like this in the current versions of HTML:

```
<P>The blue sweater was reluctant to be worn, and wrestled with her as
she attempted to put it on. The collar was too small, and would not
fit over her head, and the arm holes moved seemingly randomly away
from her searching hands.</P>
<P>Exasperated, she took off the sweater and flung it on the floor.
Then she vindictively stomped on it in revenge for its recalcitrant
behavior.</P>
```

Getting into the habit of using <P> at the start of a paragraph is a good idea; it will become important when you learn how to align text left, right, or centered. Older browsers will accept this form of paragraphs just fine. Whether you use the </P> tag or not is up to you; it might help you remember where a paragraph ends, or it might seem unnecessary. I'll use the closing </P> throughout this book.

Some people like to use extra <P> tags between paragraphs to spread out the text on the page. Once again, here's the cardinal reminder: Design for content, not for appearance. Someone with a text-based browser or a small screen is not going to care much about the extra space you so carefully put in, and some browsers may even collapse multiple <P> tags into one, erasing all your careful formatting.

The following example shows a sample paragraph. Figure 3.9 shows how it appears in Netscape, and Figure 3.10 shows how it appears in Lynx.

INPUT
```
<P>The sweater lay quietly on the floor, seething from its ill
treatment. It wasn't its fault that it didn't fit right. It hadn't
wanted to be purchased by this ill-mannered woman.</P>
```

Figure 3.9.
The output in Netscape.

Figure 3.10.
The output in Lynx.

> The sweater lay quietly on the floor, seething from its ill treatment.
> It wasn't its fault that it didn't fit right. It hadn't wanted to be
> purchased by this ill-mannered woman.

Lists, Lists, and More Lists

In addition to headings and paragraphs, probably the most common HTML element you'll
use is the list. After this section, you'll not only know how to create a list in HTML, but also
how to create five different kinds of lists—a list for every occasion!

HTML defines these five kinds of lists:

☐ Numbered, or ordered lists, typically labeled with numbers

☐ Bulleted, or unordered lists, typically labeled with bullets or some other symbol

☐ Glossary lists, in which each item in the list has a term and a definition for that
term, arranged so that the term is somehow highlighted or drawn out from the text

☐ Menu lists, for lists of short paragraphs (typically one line)

☐ Directory lists, for lists of short items that can be arranged vertically or horizontally

List Tags

All the list tags have common elements:

☐ The entire list is surrounded by the appropriate opening and closing tag for the
kind of list (for example, <UL> and </UL>, or <MENU> and </MENU>).

☐ Each list item within the list has its own tag: <DT> and <DD> for the glossary lists,
and <LI> for all the other lists.

Although the tags and the list items can appear in any arrangement in your HTML code, I
prefer to arrange the HTML for producing lists so that the list tags are on their own lines and
each new item starts on a new line. This way, you can easily pick out the whole list as well
as the individual elements. In other words, I find this arrangement

```
<P>Dante's Divine Comedy consists of three books:</P>
<UL>
```

```
<LI>The Inferno
<LI>The Purgatorio
<LI>The Paradiso
</UL>
```

easier to read than this arrangement

```
<P>Dante's Divine Comedy consists of three books:</P>
<UL><LI>The Inferno<LI>The Purgatorio<LI>The Paradiso</UL>
```

even though both result in the same output in the browser.

Numbered Lists

Numbered lists are surrounded by the <OL>...</OL> tags (OL stands for Ordered List), and each item within the list begins with the <LI> (List Item) tag.

The <LI> tag is one-sided; you do not have to specify the closing tag. The existence of the next <LI> (or the closing </OL> tag) indicates the end of that item in the list.

When the browser displays an ordered list, it numbers (and often indents) each of the elements sequentially. You do not have to do the numbering yourself, and if you add or delete items, the browser will renumber them the next time the page is loaded.

NEW TERM   *Ordered lists* are lists in which each item is numbered.

So, for example, the following is an ordered list of steps (a recipe) for creating nachos, with each list item a step in the set of procedures:

```
<P>Laura's Awesome Nachos</P>
<OL>
<LI>Warm up Refried beans with chili powder and cumin.
<LI>Glop refried beans on tortilla chips.
<LI>Grate equal parts Jack and Cheddar cheese, spread on chips.
<LI>Chop one small onion finely, spread on chips.
<LI>Heat under broiler 2 minutes.
<LI>Add guacamole, sour cream, fresh chopped tomatoes, and cilantro.
<LI>Drizzle with hot green salsa.
<LI>Broil another 1 minute.
<LI>Nosh.
</OL>
```

Use numbered lists only when you want to indicate that the elements are ordered—that is, that they must appear or occur in that specific order. Ordered lists are good for steps to follow or instructions to the readers. If you just want to indicate that something has some number of elements that can appear in any order, use an unordered list instead.

The following input and output examples show a simple ordered list. You can see how it appears in Netscape in Figure 3.11 and in Lynx in Figure 3.12.

```
<P>For the best Mango Chutney:</P>
<OL>
<LI>Go to the store
<LI>Buy some mango chutney
<LI>Open the bottle
<LI>Serve
</OL>
```

Figure 3.11.

The output in Netscape.

Figure 3.12.

*The onscreen output
in Lynx.*

Ordered lists have several attributes that you can use to customize how the list is rendered by the browser. These attributes allow you to control several features of ordered lists including what numbering scheme to use and from which number to start counting (if you don't want to start at 1).

NEW TERM *Attributes* are extra parts of HTML tags that contain options or other information about the tag itself.

You can customize ordered lists in two main ways: by how they are numbered and what number the list starts at. HTML provides the TYPE attribute, which can take one of five values to define what type of numbering to use on the list:

☐ "1": Specifies that standard Arabic numerals should be used to number the list (that is, 1, 2, 3, 4, and so on)

☐ `"a"`: Specifies that lowercase letters should be used to number the list (that is, a, b, c, d, and so on)

☐ `"A"`: Specifies that uppercase letters should be used to number the list (that is, A, B, C, D, and so on)

☐ `"i"`: Specifies that lowercase Roman numerals should be used to number the list (that is, i, ii, iii, iv, and so on)

☐ `"I"`: Specifies that uppercase Roman numerals should be used to number the list (that is, I, II, III, IV, and so on)

Types of numbering can be specified in the `<OL>` tag as follows: `<OL TYPE="a">`. By default, `TYPE="1"` is assumed.

NOTE ▶ The nice thing about Web browsers is that they generally ignore attributes they don't understand. For example, if a browser doesn't support the `TYPE` attribute of the `<OL>` tag, it will simply ignore it when it is encountered.

3

As an example, consider the following list:

```
<P>Cheesecake ingredients:</P>
<OL>
<LI>Quark Cheese
<LI>Honey
<LI>Cocoa
<LI>Vanilla Extract
<LI>Flour
<LI>Eggs
<LI>Walnuts
<LI>Margerine
</OL>
```

If you were to add `TYPE="I"` to the `<OL>` tag, as follows, then it would appear in Netscape as shown in Figure 3.13.

```
<P>Cheesecake ingredients:</P>
<OL TYPE="I">
<LI>Quark Cheese
<LI>Honey
<LI>Cocoa
<LI>Vanilla Extract
<LI>Flour
<LI>Eggs
<LI>Walnuts
<LI>Margarine
</OL>
```

Figure 3.13.
*The output in Netscape
(for Windows 95).*

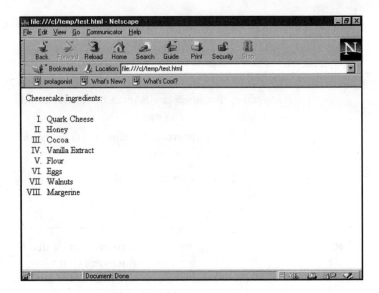

The TYPE attribute can also be applied to the <LI> tag, effectively changing the numbering type in the middle of the list. When the TYPE attribute is used in the <LI> tag, it affects the item in question and all entries following it in the list.

Using another attribute, START, you can specify what number or letter to start your list. The default starting point is 1, of course. Using START, you can change this number. For example, <OL START=4> would start the list at number 4, whereas <OL TYPE="a" START=3> would start the numbering with *c* and move through the alphabet from there.

You can make the preceding example start its numbering with the Roman numeral *V* as follows. The results appear in Figure 3.14.

```
<P>Cheesecake ingredients:</P>
<OL TYPE="I" START=5>
<LI>Quark Cheese
<LI>Honey
<LI>Cocoa
<LI>Vanilla Extract
<LI>Flour
<LI>Eggs
<LI>Walnuts
<LI>Margarine
</OL>
```

OUTPUT

Figure 3.14.
*The output in Netscape
(for Windows 95).*

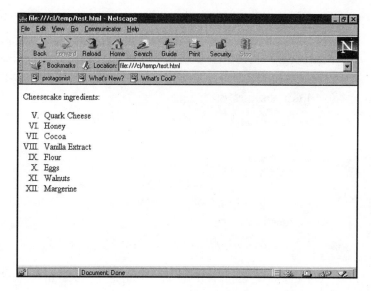

One final attribute—COMPACT—indicates that less space should be used in an ordered list. The attribute is also available for all the other list types discussed in this chapter. You can use the COMPACT attribute in an ordered list like this: <OL COMPACT>.

NOTE

> In HTML 4.0 the COMPACT attribute has been "deprecated," which means it's still supported, but not recommended.

Like with the TYPE attribute, you can change the value of an entry's number at any point in a list. You do so by using the VALUE attribute in the <LI> tag. Assigning a VALUE in an <LI> tag restarts numbering in the list starting with the affected entry.

For instance, what if you wanted the last three items in your list of ingredients to be 10, 11, and 12 instead of 6, 7, and 8. You can reset the numbering at Eggs using the VALUE attribute:

```
<P>Cheesecake ingredients:</P>
<OL TYPE="I">
<LI>Quark Cheese
<LI>Honey
<LI>Cocoa
<LI>Vanilla Extract
<LI>Flour
<LI VALUE=10>Eggs
<LI>Walnuts
<LI>Margarine
</OL>
```

Unordered Lists

In unordered lists, the elements can appear in any order. An unordered list looks just like an ordered list in HTML except that the list is indicated using <UL>...</UL> tags instead of OL. The elements of the list are separated by <LI>, just as with ordered lists. Consider this example:

```
<P>Lists in HTML</P>
<UL>
<LI>Ordered Lists
<LI>Unordered Lists
<LI>Menus
<LI>Directories
<LI>Glossary Lists
</UL>
```

Browsers usually format unordered lists by inserting bullets or some other symbolic marker; Lynx inserts an asterisk (*).

 In *unordered lists,* the items are bulleted or marked with some other symbol.

The following input and output example shows an unordered list. Figure 3.15 shows the results in Netscape, and Figure 3.16 shows the results in Lynx.

```
<P>The three Erinyes, or Furies, were:</P>
<UL>
<LI>Tisiphone
<LI>Megaera
<LI>Alecto
</UL>
```

OUTPUT

Figure 3.15.
The output in Netscape.

OUTPUT

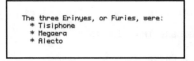

Figure 3.16.
The output in Lynx.

As with ordered lists, unordered lists can be customized. By default, most browsers (Netscape included) use bullets to delineate entries on unordered lists (text browsers such as Lynx generally opt for an asterisk). If you use the TYPE attribute in the <UL> tag, some browsers now can display other types of markers to delineate entries. According to the HTML specification, the TYPE attribute can take three possible values:

☐ `"disc"`: A disc or bullet; this style is generally the default.

☐ `"square"`: Obviously, a square instead of a disc.

☐ `"circle"`: As compared with the `disc`, which most browsers render as a filled circle, this value should generate an unfilled circle on compliant browsers.

In the following input and output example, you see a comparison of these three types as rendered in Netscape Navigator (see Figure 3.17).

```
<UL TYPE="disc">
<LI>DAT - Digital Audio Tapes
<LI>CD - Compact Discs
<LI>Cassettes
</UL>
<UL TYPE="square">
<LI>DAT - Digital Audio Tapes
<LI>CD - Compact Discs
<LI>Cassettes
</UL>
<UL TYPE="circle">
<LI>DAT - Digital Audio Tapes
<LI>CD - Compact Discs
<LI>Cassettes
</UL>
```

OUTPUT

Figure 3.17.
The output in Netscape.

Just as you could change numbering scheme in the middle of an ordered list, you can change the type of bullet mid-stream in a list by using the TYPE attribute in the <LI> tag.

As with ordered lists, you can also use the COMPACT attribute in the <UL> tag, although this setup is effectively ignored in most browsers, and it's no longer recommended in HTML 4.0.

Glossary Lists

Glossary lists are slightly different from other lists. Each list item in a glossary list has two parts:

- [ ] A term
- [ ] The term's definition

Each part of the glossary list has its own tag: <DT> for the term ("definition term"), and <DD> for its definition ("definition definition"). <DT> and <DD> are both one-sided tags, and they usually occur in pairs, although most browsers can handle single terms or definitions. The entire glossary list is indicated by the tags <DL>...</DL> ("definition list").

NEW TERM   In *glossary lists,* each list item has two parts: a term and a definition. Glossary lists are sometimes called definition lists.

The following is a glossary list example with a set of herbs and descriptions of how they grow:

```
<DL>
<DT>Basil<DD>Annual. Can grow four feet high; the scent of its tiny white
flowers is heavenly
<DT>Oregano<DD>Perennial. Sends out underground runners and is difficult
to get rid of once established.
<DT>Coriander<DD>Annual. Also called cilantro, coriander likes cooler
weather of spring and fall.
</DL>
```

Glossary lists are usually formatted in browsers with the terms and definitions on separate lines, and the left margins of the definitions are indented.

You don't have to use glossary lists for terms and definitions, of course. You can use them anywhere that the same sort of list is needed. Here's an example:

```
<DL>
<DT>Macbeth<DD>I'll go no more. I am afraid to think of
what I have done; look on't again I dare not.
<DT>Lady Macbeth<DD>Infirm of purpose! Give me the daggers.
The sleeping and the dead are as but pictures. 'Tis the eye
if childhood that fears a painted devil. If he do bleed, I'll
gild the faces if the grooms withal, for it must seem their
guilt. (Exit. Knocking within)
<DT>Macbeth<DD>Whence is that knocking? How is't wit me when
every noise apalls me? What hands are here? Ha! They pluck out
mine eyes! Will all Neptune's ocean wash this blood clean from
my hand? No. This my hand will rather the multitudinous seas
incarnadine, making the green one red. (Enter Lady Macbeth)
<DT>Lady Macbeth<DD>My hands are of your color, but I shame to
wear a heart so white.
</DL>
```

The following input and output example shows how a glossary list is formatted in Netscape (see Figure 3.18) and Lynx (see Figure 3.19).

```
<DL>
<DT>Basil<DD>Annual. Can grow four feet high; the scent
of its tiny white flowers is heavenly.
<DT>Oregano<DD>Perennial. Sends out underground runners
and is difficult to get rid of once established.
<DT>Coriander<DD>Annual. Also called cilantro, coriander
likes cooler weather of spring and fall.
</DL>
```

Figure 3.18.
The output in Netscape.

Figure 3.19.
The output in Lynx.

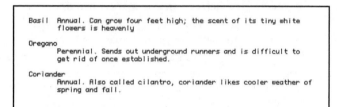

Definition lists don't provide as many attributes to control their appearance as you had in the previous types of lists. The only attribute that the <DL> tag can take is the deprecated COMPACT attribute.

Menu and Directory Lists

Menus are lists of items or short paragraphs with no bullets or numbers or other label-like elements. They are similar to simple lists of paragraphs, except that some browsers may indent them or format them in some way differently from normal paragraphs. Menu lists are surrounded by <MENU> and </MENU> tags, and each list item is indicated using <LI>, as shown in this example:

```
<MENU>
<LI>Go left
<LI>Go right
<LI>Go up
<LI>Go down
</MENU>
```

Directory lists are for items that are even shorter than menu lists, and are intended to be formatted by browsers horizontally in columns—like doing a directory listing on a UNIX system. As with menu lists, directory lists are surrounded by `<DIR>` and `</DIR>`, and with `<LI>` for the individual list items, as shown in this example:

```
<DIR>
<LI>apples
<LI>oranges
<LI>bananas
</DIR>
```

Menu lists are used for short lists of single items. *Directory lists* are even shorter lists of items such as those you would find in a UNIX or DOS directory listing.

NOTE

> Although menu and directory lists exist in the HTML specification, they are not commonly used in Web pages. In HTML 4.0, they are considered different from unordered and glossary lists—to be rendered differently in appearance than unordered or glossary lists—but browsers haven't implemented them differently. Considering that most browsers seem to format menus and directories in similar ways to the glossary lists or as unordered lists, and not in the way they are described in the specification, sticking with the other three forms of lists is probably best.

The following input and output example shows a menu list and a directory list. The result is shown in Netscape in Figure 3.20 and in Lynx in Figure 3.21.

```
<MENU>
<LI>Canto 1: The Dark Wood of Error
<LI>Canto 2: The Descent
<LI>Canto 3: The Vestibule
<LI>Canto 4: Circle One: Limbo
<LI>Canto 5: Circle Two: The Carnal
</MENU>

<DIR>
<LI>files
<LI>applications
<LI>mail
<LI>stuff
<LI>phone_numbers
</DIR>
```

Figure 3.20.
The output in Netscape.

Figure 3.21.
The output in Lynx.

Nesting Lists

What happens if you put a list inside another list? Nesting lists is fine as far as HTML is concerned; just put the entire list structure inside another list as one of its elements. The nested list just becomes another element of the first list, and it is indented from the rest of the list. Lists like this work especially well for menu-like entities in which you want to show hierarchy (for example, in tables of contents) or as outlines.

Indenting nested lists in HTML code itself helps show their relationship to the final layout:

```
<OL>
    <UL>
    <LI>WWW
    <LI>Organization
    <LI>Beginning HTML
    <UL>
        <LI>What HTML is
        <LI>How to Write HTML
        <LI>Doc structure
        <LI>Headings
        <LI>Paragraphs
        <LI>Comments
    </UL>
<LI>Links
<LI>More HTML
</OL>
```

Many browsers format nested ordered lists and nested unordered lists differently from their enclosing lists. For example, they might use a symbol other than a bullet for a nested list, or number the inner list with letters (a, b, c) instead of numbers. Don't assume that this will be the case, however, and refer back to "section 8, subsection b" in your text, because you cannot determine what the exact formatting will be in the final output.

The following input and output example shows a nested list and how it appears in Netscape (see Figure 3.22) and Lynx (see Figure 3.23).

```
<H1>Peppers</H1>
<UL>
<LI>Bell
<LI>Chile
    <UL>
    <LI>Serrano
    <LI>Jalapeno
    <LI>Habanero
    <LI>Anaheim
    </UL>
<LI>Szechuan
<LI>Cayenne
</UL>
```

OUTPUT

Figure 3.22.
The output in Netscape.

Figure 3.23.
The output in Lynx.

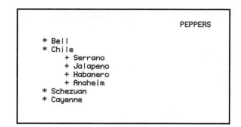

Comments

You can put comments into HTML pages to describe the page itself or to provide some kind of indication of the status of the page. Some source code control programs can put page status into comments, for example. Text in comments is ignored when the HTML file is parsed; comments don't ever show up on screen—that's why they're comments. Comments look like the following:

```
<!-- This is a comment -->
```

Each line of text should be individually commented. Not including other HTML tags within comments is usually a good idea. (Although this practice isn't strictly illegal, many browsers may get confused when they encounter HTML tags within comments and display them anyway.) As a good rule of thumb, don't include <, >, or -- inside an HTML comment.

Here are some examples:

```
<!-- Rewrite this section with less humor -->
<!-- Neil helped with this section -->
<!-- Go Tigers! -->
```

Exercise 3.4: Creating a real HTML page.

At this point, you know enough to get started creating simple HTML pages. You understand what HTML is, you've been introduced to a handful of tags, and you've even tried browsing an HTML file. You haven't created any links yet, but you'll get to that soon enough, in the next chapter.

This exercise shows you how to create an HTML file that uses the tags you've learned about up to this point. It will give you a feel for what the tags look like when they're displayed onscreen and for the sorts of typical mistakes you're going to make. (Everyone makes them, and that's why using an HTML editor that does the typing for you is often helpful. The editor doesn't forget the closing tags, leave off the slash, or misspell the tag itself.)

So, create a simple example in that text editor of yours. Your example doesn't have to say much of anything; in fact, all it needs to include are the structure tags, a title, a couple of headings, and a paragraph or two. Here's an example:

```
<HTML>
<HEAD>
<TITLE>Company Profile, Camembert Incorporated</TITLE>
</HEAD>
<BODY>
<H1>Camembert Incorporated</H1>
<P>"Many's the long night I dreamed of cheese -- toasted, mostly."
-- Robert Louis Stevenson</P>
<H2>What We Do</H2>
<P>We make cheese. Lots of cheese; more than eight tons of cheese
a year.</P>
<H2>Why We Do It</H2>
<P>We are paid an awful lot of money by people who like cheese.
So we make more.</P>
<H2>Our Favorite Cheeses</H2>
<UL>
<LI>Brie
<LI>Havarti
<LI>Camembert
<LI>Mozzarella
</UL>
</BODY>
</HTML>
```

Save the example to an HTML file, open it in your browser, and see how it came out.

If you have access to another browser on your computer or, even better, one on a different computer, I highly recommend opening the same HTML file there so that you can see the differences in appearance between browsers. Sometimes the differences can surprise you; lines that looked fine in one browser might look strange in another browser.

Here's an illustration for you: The cheese factory example looks like Figure 3.24 in Netscape (the Macintosh version) and like Figure 3.25 in Lynx.

See what I mean?

Figure 3.24.

The cheese factory in Netscape.

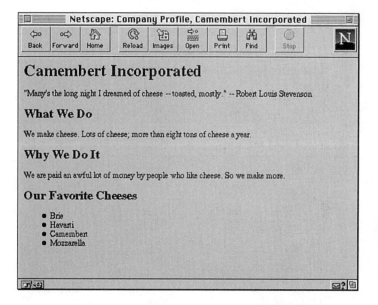

Figure 3.25.

The cheese factory in Lynx.

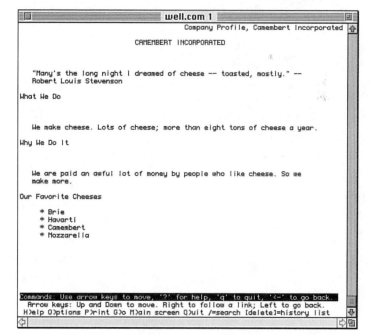

Summary

HTML, a text-only markup language used to describe hypertext pages on the World Wide Web, describes the structure of a page, not its appearance.

In this chapter, you learned what HTML is and how to write and preview simple HTML files. You also learned about the HTML tags shown in Table 3.1.

Table 3.1. HTML tags from this chapter.

Tag	Attribute	Use
`<HTML>` ... `</HTML>`		The entire HTML page.
`<HEAD>` ... `</HEAD>`		The head, or prologue, of the HTML page.
`<BODY>` ... `</BODY>`		All the other content in the HTML page.
`<TITLE>` ... `</TITLE>`		The title of the page.
`<H1>` ... `</H1>`		First-level heading.
`<H2>` ... `</H2>`		Second-level heading.
`<H3>` ... `</H3>`		Third-level heading.
`<H4>` ... `</H4>`		Fourth-level heading.
`<H5>` ... `</H5>`		Fifth-level heading.
`<H6>` ... `</H6>`		Sixth-level heading.
`<P>` ... `</P>`		A paragraph.
`<OL>`...`</OL>`		An ordered (numbered) list. Each of the items in the list begins with `<LI>`.
	TYPE	Specify the numbering scheme to use in the list.
	START	Specify what number to start the list at.
`<UL>`...`</UL>`		An unordered (bulleted or otherwise-marked) list. Each of the items in the list begins with `<LI>`.
	TYPE	Specify the bulleting scheme to use in the list.

3

Tag	Attribute	Use
<MENU>...</MENU>		A menu list (a list of short items or paragraphs).
<DIR>...</DIR>		A list of especially short (one- to two-word) items. Directory lists are not often used in most HTML files.
<LI>		Individual list items in ordered, unordered, menu, or directory lists.
	TYPE	Reset the numbering or bulleting scheme from the current list element.Only applies to <UL> and <OL> lists.
	VALUE	Reset the numbering in the middle of an ordered (<OL>) list.
<DL>...</DL>		A glossary or definition list. Items in the list consist of pairs of elements: a term and its definition.
<DT>		The term part of an item in a glossary list.
<DD>		The definition part of an item in a glossary list.
<!-- ... -->		A comment.

Q&A

Q Can I do *any* formatting of text in HTML?

A You can do some formatting to strings of characters; for example, making a word or two bold. Tags in HTML allow you to change the font size and color of the text in your Web page (for readers using browsers that support the tags—including Netscape and Microsoft Internet Explorer). You'll learn about these features tomorrow, in Chapters 5 and 6.

Q I'm using Windows. My word processor won't let me save a text file with an extension that's anything except .txt. If I type in index.html, my word processor saves the file as index.html.txt. What can I do?

A You can rename your files after you've saved them so they have an html or htm extension, but having to do so can be annoying if you have lots of files. Consider using a text editor or HTML editor for your Web pages.

Q I've noticed in many Web pages that the page structure tags (<HTML>, <HEAD>, <BODY>) aren't used. Do I really need to include them if pages work just fine without them?

A You don't need to, no. Most browsers will handle plain HTML without the page structure tags. But including the tags will allow your pages to be read by more general SGML tools and to take advantage of features of future browsers. And, using these tags is the "correct" thing to do if you want your pages to conform to true HTML format.

Q I've seen comments in some HTML files that look like this:

```
<!-- this is a comment>
```
Is that legal?

A That's the old form of comments used in very early forms of HTML. Although many browsers may still accept it, you should use the new form (and comment each line individually) in your pages.

Q My glossaries came out formatted really strangely! The terms are indented farther in than the definitions!

A Did you mix up the <DD> and <DT> tags? The <DT> tag is always used first (the definition term), and then the <DD> follows (the definition). I mix them up all the time. There are too many D tags in glossary lists.

Q I've seen HTML files that use <LI> outside a list structure, alone on the page, like this:

```
<LI>And then the duck said, "put it on my bill"
```

A Most browsers will at least accept this tag outside a list tag and will format it either as a simple paragraph or as a non-indented bulleted item. However, according to the true HTML definition, using an <LI> outside a list tag is illegal, so "good" HTML pages shouldn't do this. And because you're striving to write good HTML (right?), you shouldn't write your lists this way either. Always put your list items inside lists where they belong.

3

Chapter 4

All About Links

After finishing the preceding chapter, you now have a couple of pages that have some headings, text, and lists in them. These pages are all well and good, but rather boring. The real fun starts when you learn how to create hypertext links and link up your pages to the Web. In this chapter, you'll learn just that. Specifically, you'll learn

- [ ] All about the HTML link tag (<A>) and its various parts
- [ ] How to link to other pages on your local disk using relative and absolute pathnames
- [ ] How to link to other pages on the Web using URLs
- [ ] How to use links and anchors to link to specific places inside pages
- [ ] All about URLs: the various parts of the URL and the kinds of URLs you can use

Creating Links

To create a link in HTML, you need two things:

☐ The name of the file (or the URL of the file) you want to link to

☐ The text that will serve as the "hot spot"—that is, the text that will be highlighted in the browser, which your readers can then select to follow the link

Only the second part is actually visible on your page. When your readers select the text that points to a link, the browser uses the first part as the place to "jump" to.

The Link Tag <A>

To create a link in an HTML page, you use the HTML link tags <A>...</A>. The <A> tag is often called an anchor tag, as it can also be used to create anchors for links. (You'll learn more about creating anchors later in this chapter.) The most common use of the link tag, however, is to create links to other pages.

Unlike the simple tags you learned about in the preceding chapter, the <A> tag has some extra features: the opening tag, <A>, includes both the name of the tag ("A") and extra information about the link itself. The extra features are called attributes of the tag. (You first discovered attributes in Chapter 3, "Begin with the Basics," when you learned about lists.) So instead of the opening <A> tag having just a name inside brackets, it looks something like this:

```
<A NAME="Up" HREF="../menu.html" TITLE="Ostrich Care">
```

The extra attributes (in this example, NAME, HREF, and TITLE) describe the link itself. The attribute you'll probably use most often is the HREF attribute, which is short for "Hypertext REFerence." You use the HREF attribute to specify the name or URL of the file where this link points.

Like most HTML tags, the link tag also has a closing tag, </A>. All the text between the opening and closing tags will become the actual link on the screen and be highlighted, underlined, or colored blue or red when the Web page is displayed. That's the text you or your readers will click on (or select, in browsers that don't use mice) to jump to the place specified by the HREF attribute.

Figure 4.1 shows the parts of a typical link using the <A> tag, including the HREF, the text of the link, and the closing tag.

The following two examples show a simple link and what it looks like in Netscape (see Figure 4.2) and Lynx (see Figure 4.3).

Figure 4.1.
An HTML link using the
<A> tag.

Go back to <A HREF="../menu.html">Main Menu</A>

Figure 4.2.
The output in Netscape.

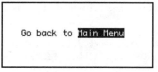

Figure 4.3.
The output in Lynx.

Exercise 4.1: Linking two pages.

Now you can try a simple example, with two HTML pages on your local disk. You'll need your text editor and your Web browser for this exercise. Because both the pages you'll be fooling with are on your local disk, you don't need to be connected to the network. (Be patient; you'll get to do network stuff in the next section of this chapter.)

First, create two HTML pages, and save them in separate files. Here's the code for the two HTML files I created for this section, which I called menu.html and feeding.html. What your two pages look like or what they're called really doesn't matter, but make sure you put in your own filenames if you're following along with this example.

The first file, called menu.html, looks like this:

```
<HTML>
<HEAD>
<TITLE>How To Care For Your Ostrich</TITLE>
</HEAD><BODY>
<H1>Caring for Your New Ostrich</H1>
```

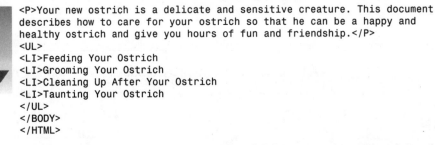

```
<P>Your new ostrich is a delicate and sensitive creature. This document
describes how to care for your ostrich so that he can be a happy and
healthy ostrich and give you hours of fun and friendship.</P>
<UL>
<LI>Feeding Your Ostrich
<LI>Grooming Your Ostrich
<LI>Cleaning Up After Your Ostrich
<LI>Taunting Your Ostrich
</UL>
</BODY>
</HTML>
```

The list of menu items ("Feeding Your Ostrich," "Grooming Your Ostrich," and so on) will be links to other pages. For now, just type them as regular text; you'll turn them into links later.

The second file, `feeding.html`, looks like this:

```
<HTML>
<HEAD>
<TITLE>How To Care For Your Ostrich: Feeding Your Ostrich</TITLE>
</HEAD><BODY>
<H1>Feeding Your Ostrich</H1>
<P>This section describes what, how often, and how to feed your ostrich
</P>
<H2>What to Feed Your Ostrich</H2>
Ostriches benefit best from a balanced diet such as that provided by United
Bird Food's Ostrich Kibble 102. We recommend feeding your ostrich a cup of
kibbles once a day, with ample water.
<H2>How to Feed Your Ostrich</H2>
<P>To feed your ostrich, leave the ostrich kibbles in a container by the
edge of the ostrich's pen.</P>
<P>NOTE: Ostriches do not like being watched while eating, and may attack
you if you stand too close. We recommend leaving your ostrich to eat in peace.
</P>
<P>Go back to Main Menu</P>
</BODY>
</HTML>
```

Make sure that both of your files are in the same directory or folder. If you haven't called them `menu.html` and `feeding.html`, make sure that you take note of the names because you'll need them later.

First, create a link from the menu file to the feeding file. Edit the `menu.html` file, and put the cursor at the following line:

```
<LI>Feeding Your Ostrich
```

Link tags do not define the format of the text itself, so leave in the list item tags and just add the link inside the item. First, put in the link tags themselves (the `<A>` and `</A>` tags) around the text that you want to use as the link:

```
<LI><A>Feeding Your Ostrich</A>
```

Now add the name of the file you want to link to as the HREF part of the opening link tag. Enclose the name of the file in quotation marks (straight quotes ("), not curly or typesetter's quotes (")), with an equals sign between HREF and the name. Note that uppercase and lowercase are different, so make sure you type the filename exactly as you saved it. (Feeding.html is not the same file as feeding.html; it has to be exactly the same case.) Here I've used feeding.html; if you used different files, use those different filenames.

```
<LI><A HREF="feeding.html">Feeding Your Ostrich</A>
```

Now, start your browser, select Open File (or its equivalent in your browser), and open the menu.html file. The paragraph that you used as your link should now show up as a link that is in a different color, underlined, or otherwise highlighted. Figure 4.4 shows how it looked when I opened it in the Windows 95 version of Netscape.

Figure 4.4.

The menu.html
file with link.

Now, when you click on the link, your browser should load in and display the feeding.html page, as shown in Figure 4.5.

If your browser can't find the file when you choose the link, make sure that the name of the file in the HREF part of the link tag is the same as the name of the file on the disk, that uppercase and lowercase match, and that both of the files are in the same directory. Remember to close your link, using the </A> tag, at the end of the text that serves as the link. Also, make sure that you have quotation marks at the end of the filename (sometimes you can easily forget) and that both quotation marks are ordinary straight quotes. All these things can confuse the browser and make it not find the file or display the link properly.

Figure 4.5.
The feeding.html
page.

NOTE

Don't get confused by this issue of case sensitivity. Tags in HTML are not case sensitive. But filenames refer to files on a Web server somewhere, and because most Web servers run on operating systems where filenames are case sensitive (such as UNIX or Windows NT), you should make sure the case of letters in filenames in your links is correct.

Now you can create a link from the feeding page back to the menu page. A paragraph at the end of the feeding.html page is intended for just this purpose:

```
<P>Go back to Main Menu</P>
```

Add the link tag with the appropriate HREF to that line, like this, where menu.html is the original menu file:

```
<P><A HREF="menu.html">Go back to Main Menu</A></P>
```

NOTE

When you include tags inside other tags, make sure that the closing tag closes the tag that you most recently opened. That is, enter

```
<P> <A> ... </A> </P>
```

instead of

`<P> <A> ... </P> </A>`

Some browsers can become confused if you overlap tags in this way, so always make sure that you close the most recently opened tag first.

Now when you reload the "feeding" file, the link will be active, and you can jump between the menu and the feeding file by selecting those links.

Linking Local Pages Using Relative and Absolute Pathnames

The example in the preceding section shows how to link together pages that are contained in the same folder or directory on your local disk (local pages). This section continues that thread, linking pages that are still on the local disk but may be contained in different directories or folders on that disk.

NOTE

Folders and directories are the same, but they're called different names depending on whether you're on Mac, Windows, DOS, or UNIX. I'll simply call them directories from now on to make your life easier.

When you specify just the filename of a linked file within quotation marks, as you did earlier, the browser looks for that file in the same directory as the current file. This is true even if both the current file and the file being linked to are on a server somewhere else on the Net; both files are contained in the same directory on that server. It is the simplest form of a relative pathname.

Relative pathnames can also include directory names, or they can point to the path you would take to navigate to that file if you started at the current directory or folder. A pathname might include directions, for example, to go up two directory levels and then go down two other directories to get to the file.

NEW TERM   *Relative pathnames* point to files based on their locations relative to the current file.

To specify relative pathnames in links, use UNIX-style pathnames regardless of the system you actually have. You therefore separate directory or folder names with forward slashes (/), and you use two dots to refer generically to the directory above the current one (..).

Table 4.1 shows some examples of relative pathnames and what they mean.

Table 4.1. Relative pathnames.

Pathname	Means
HREF="file.html"	file.html is located in the current directory.
HREF="files/file.html"	file.html is located in the directory (or folder) called files (and the files directory is located in the current directory).
HREF="files/morefiles/file.html"	file.html is located in the morefiles directory, which is located in the files directory, which is located in the current directory.
HREF="../file.html"	file.html is located in the directory one level up from the current directory (the "parent" directory).
HREF="../../files/file.html"	file.html is located two directory levels up, in the directory files.

If you're linking files on a personal computer (Mac or PC), and you want to link to a file on a different disk, use the name or letter of the disk as just another directory name in the relative path.

On the Macintosh, the name of the disk is used just as it appears on the disk itself. Assume you have a disk called Hard Disk 2, and your HTML files are contained in a folder called HTML Files. If you want to link to a file called jane.html in a folder called Public on a shared disk called Jane's Mac, you can use the following relative pathname:

HREF="../../Jane's Mac/Public/jane.html"

On DOS systems, you refer to the disks by letter, just as you would expect, but instead of using c:, d:, and so on, substitute a vertical bar (¦) for the colon (the colon has a special meaning in link pathnames), and don't forget to use forward slashes like you do with UNIX. So, if the current file is located in C:\FILES\HTML\, and you want to link to D:\FILES.NEW\HTML\MORE\INDEX.HTM, the relative pathname to that file is as follows:

HREF="../../d¦/files.new/html/more/index.htm"

In most instances, you'll never use the name of a disk in relative pathnames, but I've included it here for completeness. Most of the time, you'll link between files that are reasonably close (only one directory or folder away) in the same presentation.

Absolute Pathnames

You can also specify the link to another page on your local system by using an absolute pathname. Relative pathnames point to the page you want to link by describing its location relative to the current page. Absolute pathnames, on the other hand, point to the page by starting at the top level of your directory hierarchy and working downward through all the intervening directories to reach the file.

NEW TERM   *Absolute pathnames* point to files based on their absolute location on the file system.

Absolute pathnames always begin with a slash, which is the way they are differentiated from relative pathnames. Following the slash are all directories in the path from the top level to the file you are linking.

NOTE   "Top" has different meanings depending on how you're publishing your HTML files. If you're just linking to files on your local disk, the top is the top of your file system (/ on UNIX, or the disk name on a Mac or PC). When you're publishing files using a Web server, the top may or may not be the top of your file system (and generally isn't). You'll learn more about absolute pathnames and Web servers on Day 7, "Putting It All Online."

Table 4.2 shows some examples of absolute pathnames and what they mean.

Table 4.2. Absolute pathnames.

Pathname	Means
HREF="/u1/lemay/file.html"	file.html is located in the directory /u1/lemay (typically on UNIX systems).
HREF="/d¦/files/html/file.htm"	file.htm is located on the D: disk in the directories files/html (on DOS systems).
HREF="/Hard Disk 1/HTML Files/file.html"	file.html is located on the disk Hard Disk 1, in the folder HTML Files (typically on Macintosh systems).

Should You Use Relative or Absolute Pathnames?

To link between your own pages, most of the time you should use relative pathnames instead of the absolute pathnames. Using absolute pathnames may seem easier for complicated links between lots of pages, but absolute pathnames are not portable. If you specify your links as absolute pathnames, and you move your files elsewhere on the disk or rename a directory or a disk listed in that absolute path, then all your links will break, and you'll have to edit all your HTML files laboriously and fix them all. Using absolute pathnames also makes moving your files to a Web server very difficult when you decide to actually make them available on the Web.

Specifying relative pathnames enables you to move your pages around on your own system and to move them to other systems with little or no file modifications to fix the links. Maintaining HTML pages with relative pathnames is much easier, so the extra work of setting them up initially is often well worth the effort.

Links to Other Documents on the Web

So now you have a whole set of pages on your local disk, all linked to each other. In some places in your pages, however, you want to refer to a page somewhere else on the Net—for example, to the Palo Alto Zoo home page for more information on the socialization of ostriches. You can also use the link tag to link those other pages on the Net, which I'll call remote pages.

 Remote pages are contained somewhere on the Web other than the system you're currently working on.

The HTML code you use to link pages on the Web looks exactly the same as the code you use for links between local pages. You still use the <A> tag with an HREF attribute, and you include some text to serve as the link on your Web page. But instead of a filename or a path in the HREF, you use the URL of that page on the Web, as Figure 4.6 shows.

Figure 4.6.

Link to remote files.

Exercise 4.2: Linking your ostrich pages to the Web.

Go back to those two pages you linked together earlier in this chapter, the ones about ostriches. The `menu.html` file contains several links to other local pages that describe how to take care of your ostrich.

Now say you want to add a link to the bottom of the menu file to point to the ostrich archives at the Palo Alto Zoo (the world's leading authority on the care of ostriches), whose URL is `http://www.zoo.palo-alto.ca.us/ostriches/home.html`.

NOTE

I'm making up most of this information as I go along. Although the city of Palo Alto, California, has a Web page (URL `http://www.city.palo-alto.ca.us/home.html`), Palo Alto doesn't have a zoo with ostriches (the city does have a small petting zoo, however). For the purposes of this example, just pretend that you can find a Web page for the Palo Alto Zoo.

First, add the appropriate text for the link to your menu page, as follows:

```
<P>The Palo Alto Zoo has more information on ostriches</P>
```

What if you don't know the URL of the home page for the Palo Alto Zoo (or the page you want to link to), but you do know how to get to it by following several links on several different people's home pages? Not a problem. Use your browser to find the home page for the page you want to link to. Figure 4.7 shows what the home page for the Palo Alto Zoo might look like, if it really existed.

NOTE

If you set up your system (for the preceding chapter) so that it does not connect to the network, you might want to put it back now to follow along with this example.

Most browsers display the URL of the file they're currently looking at in a box somewhere near the top of the page. (In Netscape, this box may be hidden; choose Options|Show Location to see it.) This way, you can easily link to other pages; all you have to do is use your browser to go to the page you want to link to, copy the URL from the window, and paste it into the HTML page you're working on. No typing!

Figure 4.7.

The Palo Alto Zoo home page.

After you have the URL of the zoo, you can construct a link tag in your menu file and paste the appropriate URL into the link, like this:

```
<P>The <A HREF="http://www.zoo.palo-alto.ca.us/ostriches/
home.html">Palo Alto Zoo</A>
has more information on ostriches</P>
```

Of course, if you already know the URL of the page you want to link to, you can just type it into the HREF part of the link. Keep in mind, however, that if you make a mistake, your browser won't be able to find the file on the other end. Most URLs are too complex for normal humans to be able to remember them; I prefer to copy and paste whenever I can to cut down on the chances of typing URLs incorrectly.

Figure 4.8 shows how the menu.html file, with the new link in it, looks when it is displayed in Netscape.

Figure 4.8.

The Palo Alto Zoo link.

Exercise 4.3: Creating a link menu.

EXERCISE

Now that you've learned how to create links in this chapter and lists in the preceding chapter, you can create a link menu. Link menus are links on your Web page that are arranged in list form or in some other short, easy-to-read, and easy-to-understand format. Link menus are terrific for pages that are organized in a hierarchy, for tables of contents, or for navigation among several pages. Web pages that consist of nothing but links often organize the links in menu form.

NEW TERM   *Link menus* are short lists of links on Web pages that give your readers a quick, easy-to-scan overview of the choices they have to jump to from the current page.

The idea of a link menu is that you use short, descriptive terms as the links, with either no text following the link or with a further description following the link itself. Link menus look best in a bulleted or unordered list format, but you can also use glossary lists or just plain paragraphs. Link menus let your readers scan the list of links quickly and easily, a task that may be difficult if you bury your links in body text.

In this exercise, you'll create a Web page for a set of restaurant reviews. This page will serve as the index to the reviews, so the link menu you'll create is essentially a menu of restaurant names.

Start with a simple page framework: a first-level head and some basic explanatory text:

```
<HTML>
<HEAD>
<TITLE>Laura's Restaurant Guide</TITLE>
</HEAD><BODY>
<H1>Laura's Restaurant Reviews</H1>
<P>I spend a lot of time in restaurants in the area, having lunches or dinners
with friends or meeting with potential clients. I've written up several reviews
of many of the restaurants I frequent (and a few I'd rather not go back to).
Here are reviews for the following restaurants:</P>
</BODY></HTML>
```

Now add the list that will become the links, without the link tags themselves. It's always easier to start with link text and then attach actual links afterward. For this list, you'll use a tag to create a bulleted list of individual restaurants. You could use a <MENU> tag here just as easily, but the <OL> tag wouldn't be appropriate because the numbers would imply that you were ranking the restaurants in some way. Here's the HTML list of restaurants; Figure 4.9 shows the page in Netscape as it currently looks with the introduction and the list.

```
<UL>
<LI>Szechuan Supreme
<LI>Mel's Pizza
<LI>Tomi
<LI>The Summit Inn
<LI>Cafe Milieu
</UL>
```

4

Figure 4.9.

A list of restaurants.

Now, modify each of the list items so that they include link tags. You'll need to keep the `<LI>` tag in there because it indicates where the list items begin. Just add the `<A>` tags around the text itself. Here you'll link to filenames on the local disk in the same directory as this file, with each individual file containing the review for the particular restaurant:

```
<UL>
<LI><A HREF="szechuan.html">Szechuan Supreme</A>
<LI><A HREF="mels.html">Mel's Pizza</A>
<LI><A HREF="tomi.html">Tomi</A>
<LI><A HREF="summitinn.html">The Summit Inn</A>
<LI><A HREF="milieu.html">Cafe Milieu</A>
</UL>
```

The menu of restaurants looks fine, although it's a little sparse. Your readers don't know what kinds of food each restaurant serves (although some of the restaurant names indicate the kind of food they serve) or whether the review is good or bad. An improvement would be to add some short explanatory text after the links to provide hints of what is on the other side of the link:

```
<UL>
<LI><A HREF="szechuan.html">Szechuan Supreme</A>. Chinese food. Prices are
excellent, but service is slow
<LI><A HREF="mels.html">Mel's Pizza</A>. Thin-crust New York style pizza.
Awesome, but loud.
<LI><A HREF="tomi.html">Tomi</A>. Sushi. So-so selection, friendly chefs.
<LI><A HREF="summitinn.html">The Summit Inn</A>. California food. Creative
chefs, but you pay extra for originality and appearance.
<LI><A HREF="milieu.html">Cafe Milieu</A>. Lots of atmosphere, sullen
postmodern waitpersons, but an excellent double espresso none the less.
</UL>
```

The final list then looks like Figure 4.10.

You'll use link menus similar to this one throughout this book.

Figure 4.10.
The final menu listing.

Linking to Specific Places Within Documents

The links you've created so far in this chapter have been from one point in a page to another page. But what if, instead of linking to that second page in general, you want to link to a specific place within that page—for example, to the fourth major section down?

You can do so in HTML by creating an anchor within the second page. The anchor creates a special element that you can link to inside the page. The link you create in the first page will contain both the name of the file you're linking to and the name of that anchor. Then, when you follow the link with your browser, the browser will load the second page and then scroll down to the location of the anchor (Figure 4.11 shows an example).

Figure 4.11.
Links and anchors.

Anchors are special places that you can link to inside documents. Links can then jump to those special places inside the page as opposed to jumping just to the top of the page.

You can also use links and anchors within the same page so that if you select one of those links, you jump to different places within that same page.

Creating Links and Anchors

You create an anchor in nearly the same way that you create a link: by using the <A> tag. If you wondered why the link tag uses an <A> instead of an <L>, now you know: A actually stands for Anchor.

When you specify links using <A>, the link has two parts: the HREF attribute in the opening <A> tag, and the text between the opening and closing tags that serve as a hot spot for the link.

You create anchors in much the same way, but instead of using the HREF attribute in the <A> tag, you use the NAME attribute. The NAME attribute takes a keyword (or words) that will be used to name the anchor. Figure 4.12 shows the parts of the <A> tag when used to indicate an anchor.

Figure 4.12.

The <A> tag and anchors.

Anchors also require some amount of text between the opening and closing <A> tags, even though they usually point to a single-character location. The text between the <A> tags is used by the browser when a link that is attached to this anchor is selected. The browser scrolls the page to the text within the anchor so that it is at the top of the screen. Some browsers may also highlight the text inside the <A> tags.

So, for example, to create an anchor at the section of a page labeled Part 4, you might add an anchor called Part4 to the heading, like this:

```
<H1><A NAME="Part4">Part Four: Grapefruit from Heaven</A></H1>
```

Unlike links, anchors do not show up in the final displayed page. Anchors are invisible until you follow a link that points to them.

To point to an anchor in a link, you use the same form of link that you would when linking to the whole page, with the filename or URL of the page in the HREF attribute. After the name of the page, however, include a hash sign (#) and the name of the anchor exactly as it appears in the NAME attribute of that anchor (including the same uppercase and lowercase characters!), like this:

```
<A HREF="mybigdoc.html#Part4">Go to Part 4</A>
```

This link tells the browser to load the page `mybigdoc.html` and then to scroll down to the anchor name `Part4`. The text inside the anchor definition will appear at the top of the screen.

Exercise 4.4: Linking sections between two pages.

Now do an example with two pages. These two pages are part of an online reference to classical music, in which each Web page contains all the references for a particular letter of the alphabet (`A.html`, `B.html`, and so on). The reference could have been organized such that each section is its own page. Organizing it that way, however, would have involved several pages to manage, as well as many pages the readers would have to load if they were exploring the reference. Bunching the related sections together under lettered groupings is more efficient in this case. (Chapter 9, "Writing and Designing Web Pages: Dos and Don'ts," goes into more detail about the trade-offs between short and long pages.)

The first page you'll look at is the one for "M," the first section of which looks like the following in HTML:

```
<HTML>
<HEAD>
<TITLE>Classical Music: M</TITLE>
</HEAD>
<BODY>
<H1>M</H1>
<H2>Madrigals</H2>
<UL>
<LI>William Byrd, <EM>This Sweet and Merry Month of May</EM>
<LI>William Byrd, <EM>Though Amaryllis Dance</EM>
<LI>Orlando Gibbons, <EM>The Silver Swan</EM>
<LI>Roland de Lassus, <EM>Mon Coeur se Recommande &agrave; vous</EM>
<LI>Claudio Monteverdi, <EM>Lamento d'Arianna</EM>
<LI>Thomas Morley, <EM>My Bonny Lass She Smileth</EM>
<LI>Thomas Weelkes, <EM>Thule, the Period of Cosmography</EM>
<LI>John Wilbye, <EM>Sweet Honey-Sucking Bees</EM>
</UL>
<P>Secular vocal music in four, five and six parts, usually a capella.
15th-16th centuries.</P>
<P><EM>See Also</EM>
Byrd, Gibbons, Lassus, Monteverdi, Morley, Weelkes, Wilbye</P>
</BODY>
</HTML>
```

Figure 4.13 shows how this section looks when it's displayed.

In the last line (the `See Also`), linking the composer names to their respective sections elsewhere in the reference would be useful. If you use the procedure you learned previously in this chapter, you can create a link here around the word `Byrd` to the page `B.html`. When your readers select the link to `B.html`, the browser drops them at the top of the Bs. These hapless readers then have to scroll down through all the composers whose names start with

B (and there are lots of them: Bach, Beethoven, Brahms, Bruckner) to get to Byrd—a lot of work for a system that claims to link information so you can find what you want quickly and easily.

Figure 4.13.
Part M of the Online
Music Reference.

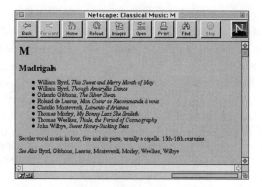

What you want is to be able to link the word Byrd in M.html directly to the section for Byrd in B.html. Here's the relevant part of B.html you want to link. (I've deleted all the Bs before Byrd to make this file shorter for this example. Pretend they're still there.)

NOTE

In this example you will see the use of the <EM> tag. This tag is used to specify text that should be emphasized. In Netscape and Internet Explorer the emphasis is usually done by rendering the text italic.

```
<HTML>
<HEAD>
<TITLE>Classical Music: B</TITLE>
</HEAD>
<BODY>
<H1>B</H1>
<!-- I've deleted all the Bs before Byrd to make things shorter -->
<H2>Byrd, William, 1543-1623</H2>
<UL>
<LI>Madrigals
<UL>
<LI><EM>This Sweet and Merry Month of May</EM>
<LI><EM>Though Amaryllis Dance</EM>
<LI><EM>Lullabye, My Sweet Little Baby</EM>
</UL>
<LI>Masses
<UL>
<LI><EM>Mass for Five Voices</EM>
```

```
<LI><EM>Mass for Four Voices</EM>
<LI><EM>Mass for Three Voices</EM>
</UL>
<LI>Motets
<UL>
<LI><EM>Ave verum corpus a 4</EM>
</UL>
</UL>
<P><EM>See Also</EM>
Madrigals, Masses, Motets</P>
</BODY>
</HTML>
```

You'll need to create an anchor at the section heading for Byrd. You can then link to that anchor from the See Alsos in the file for M.

As I described earlier in this chapter, you need two elements for each anchor: an anchor name and the text inside the link to hold that anchor (which may be highlighted in some browsers). The latter is easy; the section heading itself works well, as it's the element you're actually linking to.

You can choose any name you want for the anchor, but each anchor in the page must be unique. (If you have two or more anchors with the name fred in the same page, how would the browser know which one to choose when a link to that anchor is selected?) A good, unique anchor name for this example is simply Byrd because Byrd can appear only one place in the file, and this is it.

After you've decided on the two parts, you can create the anchor itself in your HTML file. Add the <A> tag to the William Byrd section heading, but be careful here. If you were working with normal text within a paragraph, you'd just surround the whole line with <A>. But when you're adding an anchor to a big section of text that is also contained within an element—such as a heading or paragraph—always put the anchor inside the element. In other words, enter

```
<H2><A NAME="Byrd">Byrd, William, 1543-1623</A></H2>
```

but do not enter

```
<A NAME="Byrd"><H2>Byrd, William, 1543-1623</H2></A>
```

The second example can confuse your browser. Is it an anchor, formatted just like the text before it, with mysteriously placed heading tags? Or is it a heading that also happens to be an anchor? If you use the right code in your HTML file, with the anchor inside the heading, you avoid the confusion.

You can easily forget about this solution—especially if you're like me and you create text first and then add links and anchors. Just surrounding everything with <A> tags makes sense.

Think of the situation this way: If you're linking to just one word, and not to the entire element, you put the `<A>` tag inside the `<H2>`. Working with the whole line of text isn't any different. Keep this rule in mind, and you'll get less confused.

 NOTE

> If you're still confused, refer to Appendix B, "HTML 4.0 Quick Reference," which has a summary of all the HTML tags and rules for which tags can and cannot go inside each one.

So you've added your anchor to the heading, and its name is "Byrd." Now go back to your `M.html` file, to the line with `See Also`:

```
<P><EM>See Also</EM>
Byrd, Gibbons, Lassus, Monteverdi, Morley, Weelkes, Wilbye</P>
```

You're going to create your link here around the word `Byrd`, just as you would for any other link. But what's the URL? As you learned previously, pathnames to anchors look like this:

page_name#anchor_name

If you're creating a link to the `B.html` page itself, the `HREF` is as follows:

```
<A HREF="B.html">
```

Because you're linking to a section inside that page, add the anchor name to link that section so that it looks like this:

```
<A HREF="B.html#Byrd">
```

Note the capital `B` in `Byrd`. Anchor names and links are case sensitive; if you put `#byrd` in your `HREF`, the link might not work properly. Make sure that the anchor name you use in the `NAME` attribute and the anchor name in the link after the `#` are identical.

 TIP

> A common mistake is to put a hash sign in both the anchor name and in the link to that anchor. You use the hash sign only to separate the page and the anchor in the link. Anchor names should never have hash signs in them.

So, with the new link to the new section, the `See Also` line looks like this:

```
<P><EM>See Also</EM>
<A HREF="B.html#Byrd">Byrd</A>,
Gibbons, Lassus, Monteverdi, Morley, Weelkes, Wilbye</P>
```

Of course, you can go ahead and add anchors and links to the other parts of the reference for the remaining composers.

With all your links and anchors in place, test everything. Figure 4.14 shows the Madrigals section with the link to Byrd ready to be selected.

Figure 4.14.
The Madrigals
section with link.

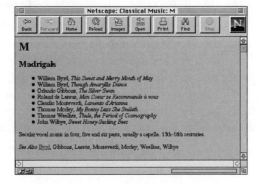

Figure 4.15 shows what pops up when you select the Byrd link.

Figure 4.15.
The Byrd *section.*

Linking to Anchors in the Same Document

What if you have only one large page, and you want to link to sections within that page? You can use anchors for it, too. For larger pages, using anchors can be an easy way to jump around within sections. To link to sections, you just need to set up your anchors at each section the way you usually do. Then, when you link to those anchors, leave off the name of the page itself, but include the hash sign and the name of the anchor. So, if you're linking to an anchor name called Section5 in the same page as the link, the link looks like this:

```
Go to <A HREF=#Section5>The Fifth Section</A>
```

When you leave off the page name, the browser assumes that you're linking with the current page and scrolls to the appropriate section.

Anatomy of a URL

So far in this book you've encountered URLs twice—in Chapter 1, "The World of the World Wide Web," as part of the introduction to the Web, and in this chapter, when you created links to remote pages. If you've ever done much exploring on the Web, you've encountered URLs as a matter of course. You couldn't start exploring without a URL.

As I mentioned in Chapter 1, URLs are Uniform Resource Locators. URLs are effectively street addresses for bits of information on the Internet. Most of the time, you can avoid trying to figure out which URL to put in your links by simply navigating to the bit of information you want with your browser, and then copying and pasting the long string of gobbledygook into your link. But understanding what a URL is all about and why it has to be so long and complex is often useful. Also, when you put your own information up on the Web, knowing something about URLs will be useful so that you can tell people where your Web page is.

In this section, you'll learn what the parts of a URL are, how you can use them to get to information on the Web, and the kinds of URLs you can use (HTTP, FTP, Mailto, and so on).

Parts of URLs

Most URLs contain (roughly) three parts: the protocol, the host name, and the directory or filename (see Figure 4.16).

Figure 4.16.
URL parts.

The protocol is the way in which the page is accessed; that is, the type of protocol or program your browser will use to get the file. If the browser is using HTTP to get to the file, the protocol part is `http`. If the browser uses FTP, the protocol is `ftp`. If you're using Gopher, it's `gopher`, and so on. The protocol matches an information server that must be installed on the system for it to work. You can't use an FTP URL on a machine that does not have an FTP server installed, for example.

The host name is the system on the Internet on which the information is stored, such as `www.netcom.com`, `ftp.apple.com`, or `www.aol.com`. You can have the same host name but have different URLs with different protocols, like this:

```
http://mysystem.com
ftp://mysystem.com
gopher://mysystem.com
```

Same machine, three different information servers, and the browser will use different methods of connecting to that same machine. As long as all three servers are installed on that system and available, you won't have a problem.

The host name part of the URL may include a port number. The port number tells your browser to open a connection of the appropriate protocol on a specific network port other than the default port. The only time you'll need a port number in a URL is if the server handling the information has been explicitly installed on that port. (This issue is covered on Day 7.)

If a port number is necessary, it goes after the host name but before the directory, like this:

```
http://my-public-access-unix.com:1550/pub/file
```

Finally, the directory is the location of the file or other form of information on the host. The directory may be an actual directory and filename, or it may be another indicator that the protocol uses to refer to the location of that information. (For example, Gopher directories are not explicit directories.)

Special Characters in URLs

A *special character* in a URL is anything that is not an upper- or lowercase letter, a number (0–9), or the following symbols: dollar sign ($), dash (-), underscore (_), period (.), or plus sign (+). You might need to specify any other characters using special URL escape codes to keep them from being interpreted as parts of the URL itself.

URL escape codes are indicated by a percent sign (%) and a two-character hexadecimal symbol from the ISO-Latin-1 character set (a superset of standard ASCII). For example, %20 is a space, %3f is a question mark, and %2f is a slash.

Say you have a directory named All My Files, probably on a Macintosh because spaces appear in the filename. Your first pass at a URL with this name in it might look like this:

```
http://myhost.com/harddrive/All My Files/www/file.html
```

If you put this URL in quotation marks in a link tag, it might work (but only if you put it in quotation marks). Because the spaces are considered special characters to the URL, though, some browsers may have problems with them and not recognize the pathname correctly. For full compatibility with all browsers, use %20, as in the following:

```
http://myhost.com/harddrive/All%20My%20Files/www/file.html
```

Most of the time, if you make sure your file and directory names are short and use only alphanumeric characters, you won't need to include special characters in URLs. Keep this point in mind as you write your own pages.

The <A> Tag in HTML 3.2 and 4.0

HTML 3.2 and 4.0 take things further than creating anchors and one-way links using the <A> tag. In particular, they offer the REL and REV attributes, which can be used to define relationships between documents.

Let's consider REL first. REL is used to provide a relationship of the destination of a link with the current document containing the link (or the source document).

For instance,

```
<A REL="parent" HREF="some document">My mom</A>
```

defines the document at the end of the link as holding a parent relationship to the current document. The value of the REL attribute can be a case-insensitive combination of letters and numbers. For instance,

```
<A REL="child">
<A REL="creditor">
<A REL="sponsor">
<A REL="resume">
```

are all valid.

REV is similar to REL in that it defines a relationship. The main difference is that it defines the reverse relationship of REL. That is, REV could be used in our example above like this:

```
<A REV="child" HREF="some document">My mom</A>
```

Whereas the REL example states that the document at the end of the link was the "parent" of the current document, the REV example states the current document is the "child" of the document being linked to.

These sorts of relationship definitions will eventually be used commonly for defining profiles, offering alternate languages to users, and so on. At the moment, they can't be considered commonplace.

Kinds of URLs

Many kinds of URLs are defined by the Uniform Resource Locator specification. (See Appendix A, "Sources for Further Information," for a pointer to the most recent version.) This section describes some of the more popular URLs and some situations to look out for when using them.

HTTP

An HTTP URL is the most popular form of URL on the World Wide Web. HTTP, which stands for HyperText Transfer Protocol, is the protocol that World Wide Web servers use to send HTML pages over the Net.

HTTP URLs follow this basic URL form:

```
http://www.foo.com/home/foo/
```

If the URL ends in a slash, the last part of the URL is considered a directory name. The file that you get using a URL of this type is the "default" file for that directory as defined by the HTTP server, usually a file called index.html. (If the Web page you're designing is the top-level file for all the files in a directory, calling it index.html is a good idea.)

You can also specify the filename directly in the URL. In this case, the file at the end of the URL is the one that is loaded, as in the following examples:

```
http://www.foo.com/home/foo/index.html
http://www.foo.com/home/foo/homepage.html
```

Using HTTP URLs like the following, where foo is a directory, is also usually acceptable:

```
http://www.foo.com/home/foo
```

In this case, because foo is a directory, this URL should have a slash at the end. Most Web servers can figure out that you meant this to be a directory and "redirect" to the appropriate file. Some older servers, however, may have difficulties resolving this URL, so you should always identify directories and files explicitly and make sure that a default file is available if you're indicating a directory.

Anonymous FTP

FTP URLs are used to point to files located on FTP servers—and usually anonymous FTP servers, that is, the ones that you can log into using anonymous as the login ID and your e-mail address as the password. FTP URLs also follow the "standard" URL form, as shown in the following examples:

```
ftp://ftp.foo.com/home/foo
ftp://ftp.foo.com/home/foo/homepage.html
```

Because you can retrieve either a file or a directory list with FTP, the restrictions on whether you need a trailing slash at the end of the URL are not the same as with HTTP. The first URL here retrieves a listing of all the files in the foo directory. The second URL retrieves and parses the file homepage.html in the foo directory.

4

NOTE
Navigating FTP servers using a Web browser can often be much slower than navigating them using FTP itself because the browser does not hold the connection open. Instead, it opens the connection, finds the file or directory listing, displays the listing, and then closes down the FTP connection. If you select a link to open a file or another directory in that listing, the browser will construct a new FTP URL from the items you selected, reopen the FTP connection using the new URL, get the next directory or file, and close it again. For this reason, FTP URLs are best for when you know exactly which file you want to retrieve rather than for when you want to browse an archive.

Although your browser uses FTP to fetch the file, you still can get an HTML file from that server just as if it were an HTTP server, and it will parse and display just fine. Web browsers don't care how they get a hypertext file. As long as they can recognize the file as HTML, either by the servers telling them it's an HTML file (as with HTTP—you'll learn more about it later), or by the extension to the filename, the browsers will parse and display that file as an HTML file. If they don't recognize it as an HTML file, no big deal. The browsers can either display the file if they know what kind of file it is or just save the file to disk.

Non-Anonymous FTP

All the FTP URLs in the preceding section are used for anonymous FTP servers. You can also specify an FTP URL for named accounts on an FTP server, like this:

```
ftp://username:password@ftp.foo.com/home/foo/homepage.html
```

In this form of the URL, the `username` part is your login ID on the server, and `password` is that account's password. Note that no attempt is made to hide the password in the URL. Be very careful that no one is watching you when you're using URLs of this form—and don't put them into links that someone else can find!

File

File URLs are intended to reference files contained on the local disk. In other words, they refer to files that are located on the same system as the browser. For local files, file URLs take one of these two forms: the first with an empty host name (see the three slashes instead of two?) or with the host name as `localhost`:

```
file:///dir1/dir2/file
file://localhost/dir1/dir2/file
```

Depending on your browser, one or the other will usually work.

File URLs are very similar to FTP URLs. In fact, if the host part of a file URL is not empty or `localhost`, your browser will try to find the given file using FTP. Both of the following URLs result in the same file being loaded in the same way:

```
file://somesystem.com/pub/dir/foo/file.html
ftp://somesystem.com/pub/dir/foo/file.html
```

Probably the best use of file URLs is in startup pages for your browser (which are also called "home pages"). In this instance, because you will almost always be referring to a local file, using a file URL makes sense.

The problem with file URLs is that they reference local files, where "local" means on the same system as the browser that is pointing to the file—not the same system that the page was retrieved from! If you use file URLs as links in your page, and then someone from elsewhere on the Net encounters your page and tries to follow those links, that person's browser will attempt to find the file on his or her local disk (and generally will fail). Also, because file URLs use the absolute pathname to the file, if you use file URLs in your page, you cannot move that page elsewhere on the system or to any other system.

If your intention is to refer to files that are on the same file system or directory as the current page, use relative pathnames instead of file URLs. With relative pathnames for local files and other URLs for remote files, you should not need to use a file URL at all.

Mailto

The Mailto URL is used to send electronic mail. If the browser supports Mailto URLs, when a link that contains one is selected, the browser will prompt you for a subject and the body of the mail message, and send that message to the appropriate address when you're done.

Some browsers do not support `mailto` and produce an error if a link with a Mailto URL is selected.

The Mailto URL is different from the standard URL form. It looks like this:

```
mailto:internet_e-mail_address
```

Here's an example:

```
mailto:lemay@lne.com
```

NOTE If your e-mail address includes a percent sign (%), you'll have to use the escape character %25 instead. Percent signs are special characters to URLs.

Gopher

Gopher URLs use the standard URL file format up to and including the host name. After that, they use special Gopher protocols to encode the path to the particular file. The directory in Gopher does not indicate a directory pathname as HTTP and FTP URLs do and is too complex for this chapter. See the URL specification if you're really interested.

Most of the time, you'll probably use a Gopher URL just to point to a Gopher server, which is easy. A URL of this sort looks like the following:

```
gopher://gopher.myhost.com/
```

If you really want to point directly to a specific file on a Gopher server, probably the best way to get the appropriate URL is not to try to build it yourself. Instead, navigate to the appropriate file or collection using your browser, and then copy and paste the appropriate URL into your HTML page.

Usenet

Usenet news URLs have one of two forms:

```
news:name_of_newsgroup
news:message-id
```

The first form is used to read an entire newsgroup, such as `comp.infosystems.www.authoring.html` or `alt.gothic`. If your browser supports Usenet news URLs (either directly or through a newsreader), it will provide you with a list of available articles in that newsgroup.

The second form enables you to retrieve a specific news article. Each news article has a unique ID, called a message ID, which usually looks something like this:

```
<lemayCt76Jq.CwG@netcom.com>
```

To use a message ID in a URL, remove the angle brackets and include the `news:` part:

```
news:lemayCt76Jq.CwG@netcom.com
```

Be aware that news articles do not exist forever—they "expire" and are deleted—so a message ID that was valid at one point may become invalid a short time later. If you want a permanent link to a news article, you should just copy the article to your Web presentation and link it as you would any other file.

Both forms of URL assume that you're reading news from an NNTP server. Both can be used only if you have defined an NNTP server somewhere in an environment variable or preferences file for your browser. Therefore, news URLs are most useful simply for reading specific news articles locally, not necessarily for using in links in pages.

News URLs, like Mailto URLs, might not be supported by all browsers.

Summary

In this chapter, you learned all about links. Links turn the Web from a collection of unrelated pages into an enormous, interrelated information system (there are those big words again).

To create links, you use the <A>...</A> tags, called the link or anchor tag. The anchor tag has several attributes for indicating files to link to (the HREF attribute) and anchor names (the NAME attribute).

When linking pages that are all stored on the local disk, you can specify their pathnames in the HREF attribute as relative or absolute paths. For local links, relative pathnames are preferred because they let you move local pages more easily to another directory or to another system. If you use absolute pathnames, your links will break if you change anything in the hard-coded path.

If you want to link to a page on the Web (a remote page), the value of the HREF attribute is the URL of that page. You can easily copy the URL of the page you want to link. Just go to that page using your favorite Web browser, and then copy and paste the URL from your browser into the appropriate place in your link tag.

To create links to specific parts of a page, first set an anchor at the point you want to link to, use the <A>...</A> tag as you would with a link, but instead of the HREF attribute, you use the NAME attribute to name the anchor. You can then link directly to that anchor name using the name of the page, a hash sign (#), and the anchor name.

Finally, URLs (Uniform Resource Locators) are used to point to pages, files, and other information on the Internet. Depending on the type of information, URLs can contain several parts, but most contain a protocol type and location or address. URLs can be used to point to many kinds of information but are most commonly used to point to Web pages (http), FTP directories or files (ftp), information on Gopher servers (gopher), electronic mail addresses (mailto), or Usenet news (news).

Q&A

Q My links aren't being highlighted in blue or purple at all. They're still just plain text.

A Is the filename in a NAME attribute rather than in an HREF? Did you remember to close the quotation marks around the filename you're linking to? Both of these errors can prevent links from showing up as links.

Q **I put a URL into a link, and it shows up as highlighted in my browser, but when I click on it, the browser says "unable to access page." If it can't find the page, why did it highlight the text?**

A The browser highlights text within a link tag whether or not the link is valid. In fact, you don't even need to be online for links to still show up as highlighted links, even though you cannot get to them. The only way you can tell whether a link is valid is to select it and try to view the page that the link points to.

As to why the browser couldn't find the page you linked to—make sure you're connected to the network and that you entered the URL into the link correctly. Make sure you have both opening and closing quotation marks around the filename, and that those quotation marks are straight quotes. If your browser prints link destinations in the status bar when you move the mouse cursor over a link, watch that status bar and see whether the URL that appears is actually the URL you want.

Finally, try opening that URL directly in your browser and see whether that solution works. If directly opening the link doesn't work either, there might be several reasons why. Two common ones are

☐ The server is overloaded or is not on the Net.

Machines go down, as do network connections. If a particular URL doesn't work for you, perhaps something is wrong with the machine or the network. Or maybe the site is popular, and too many people are trying to access it at once. Try again later or during non-peak hours for that server. If you know the people who run the server, you can try sending them electronic mail or calling them.

☐ The URL itself is bad.

Sometimes URLs become invalid. Because a URL is a form of absolute pathname, if the file to which it refers moves around, or if a machine or directory name gets changed, the URL won't be any good any more. Try contacting the person or site you got the URL from in the first place. See if that person has a more recent link.

Q **Can I put any URL in a link?**

A You bet. If you can get to a URL using your browser, you can put that URL in a link. Note, however, that some browsers support URLs that others don't. For example, Lynx is really good with Mailto URLs (URLs that allow you to send electronic mail to a person's e-mail address). When you select a Mailto URL in Lynx, it prompts you for a subject and the body of the message. When you're done, it sends the mail.

Other browsers, on the other hand, may not handle Mailto URLs, and insist that a link containing the `mailto` URL is invalid. The URL itself may be fine, but the browser can't handle it.

Q **Can I use images as links?**

A Yup. You'll learn how to link images this way in Chapter 7, "Using Images, Color, and Backgrounds."

Q **You've described only two attributes of the `<A>` tag: `HREF` and `NAME`. Aren't there others?**

A Yes. The `<A>` tag has several attributes including `REL`, `REV`, `SHAPE`, `ACCESSKEY`, and `TITLE`. However, most of these attributes can be used only by tools that automatically generate links between pages, or by browsers that can manage links better than most of those now available. Because 99 percent of the people reading this book won't care about (or ever use) those links or browsers, I'm sticking to `HREF` and `NAME` and ignoring the other attributes.

If you're really interested, I've summarized the other attributes in Appendix B, and pointers to the various HTML specifications are listed in Appendix A, as well.

Q **My links are not pointing to my anchors. When I follow a link, I'm always dropped at the top of the page instead of at the anchor. What's going on here?**

A Are you specifying the anchor name in the link after the hash sign the same way that it appears in the anchor itself, with all the uppercase and lowercase letters identical? Anchors are case sensitive, so if your browser cannot find an anchor name with an exact match, the browser may try to select something else in the page that is closer. This is dependent on browser behavior, of course, but if your links and anchors aren't working, the problem is usually that your anchor names and your anchors do not match. Also, remember that anchor names don't contain hash signs—only the links to them do.

Q **It sounds like file URLs aren't overly useful. Is there any reason I'd want to use them?**

A I can think of two. The first one is if you have many users on a single system (for example, on a UNIX system), and you want to give those local users (but nobody else) access to files on that system. By using file URLs, you can point to files on the local system, and anyone on that system can get to them. Readers from outside the system won't have direct access to the disk and won't be able to get to those files.

A second good reason for using file URLs is that you actually want to point to a local disk. For example, you could create a CD-ROM full of information in HTML form and then create a link from a page on the Web to a file on the CD-ROM using a file URL. In this case, because your presentation depends on a disk your readers must have, using a file URL makes sense.

Q Is there any way to indicate a subject in a Mailto URL?

A Not at the moment. According to the current Mailto URL definition, the only thing you can put in a Mailto URL is the address to mail to. If you really need a subject or something in the body of the message, consider using a form instead.

Doing More with HTML

Chapter **5**

More Text Formatting with HTML

Yesterday you learned the basics of HTML, including several basic page elements and links. With that background, you're now ready to learn more about what HTML can do in terms of text formatting and layout. This chapter describes most of the remaining tags in HTML that you'll need to know to construct pages, including tags in standard HTML 2.0 through HTML 4.0 as well as HTML attributes in individual browsers. Today you'll learn how to do the following:

- ☐ Specify the appearance of individual characters (bold, italic, typewriter)
- ☐ Include special characters (characters with accents, copyright and registration marks, and so on)
- ☐ Create preformatted text (text with spaces and tabs retained)
- ☐ Align text left, right, justified, and centered
- ☐ Change the font and font size
- ☐ Create other miscellaneous HTML text elements, including line breaks, rule lines, addresses, and quotations

In addition, you'll learn the differences between standard HTML and HTML extensions, and when to choose which tags to use in your pages. At the end of this chapter, you'll create a complete Web page that uses many of the tags presented in this chapter as well as the information from the preceding four chapters.

This chapter covers several tags and options, so you might find it a bit overwhelming. Don't worry about remembering everything now; just get a grasp of what sorts of formatting you can do in HTML, and then you can look up the specific tags later. In the next chapter, you'll take a significant break and look at some of the tools and programs that help you write HTML so you don't have to remember everything while you're still learning how to put pages together.

Character Styles

When you use HTML tags for paragraphs, headings, or lists, those tags affect that block of text as a whole, changing the font, changing the spacing above and below the line, or adding characters (in the case of bulleted lists). Character styles are tags that affect words or characters within other HTML entities and change the appearance of that text so it is somehow different from the surrounding text—making it bold or underline, for example.

To change the appearance of a set of characters within text, you can use one of two kinds of tags: logical styles or physical styles.

Logical Styles

Logical style tags indicate how the given highlighted text is to be used, not how it is to be displayed. They are similar to the common element tags for paragraphs or headings. They don't indicate how the text is to be formatted, just how it is to be used in a document. Logical style tags might, for example, indicate a definition, a snippet of code, or an emphasized word.

NEW TERM *Logical style* tags indicate the way text is used (emphasis, citation, definition).

Using logical style tags, the browser determines the actual presentation of the text, be it in bold, italic, or any other change in appearance. You cannot guarantee that text highlighted using these tags will always be bold or always be italic (and, therefore, you should not depend on it, either).

NOTE

HTML 4.0 extends HTML's model of physical and logical styles by providing support for style sheets. With style sheets, page authors will be able to define more precisely the appearance (including font family, style and size) of individual elements or entire classes of elements (such as all unordered lists) in a document. Style sheets are covered in Chapters 17 and 18.

Each character style tag has both opening and closing sides and affects the text within those two tags. The following are the eight logical style tags in standard HTML:

<EM>
This tag indicates that the characters are to be emphasized in some way; that is, they are formatted differently from the rest of the text. In graphical browsers, <EM> is typically italic. For example,

```
<P>We'd all get along much better if you'd stop being so
<EM>silly.</EM></P>
```

<STRONG>
With this tag, the characters are to be more strongly emphasized than with <EM>. <STRONG> text is highlighted differently from <EM> text—for example, in bold. Consider this example:

```
<P>You <STRONG>must</STRONG> open the can before drinking</P>
```

<CODE>
This tag indicates a code sample (a fixed-width font such as Courier in graphical displays). For example,

```
<P><CODE>#include "trans.h"</CODE></P>
```

<SAMP>
This tag indicates sample text, similar to <CODE>. For example,

```
<P>The URL for that page is <SAMP>http://www.cern.ch/</SAMP></P>
```

<KBD>
This tag indicates text intended to be typed by a user. Consider this example:

```
<P>Type the following command:
<KBD>find . -name "prune" -print</KBD></P>
```

<VAR>
This tag indicates the name of a variable or some entity to be replaced with an actual value. It is often displayed as italic or underline, as in this example:

```
<P><CODE>chown </CODE><VAR>your_name the_file</VAR></P>
```

<DFN>
This tag indicates a definition. <DFN> is used to highlight a word that will be defined or has just been defined. For example,

```
<P>Styles that are named after how they are actually used are
called
<DFN>logical character styles</DFN></P>
```

5

<CITE>   This tag indicates a short quote or citation, as in this example:

```
<P>Eggplant has been known to cause nausea in many unsuspecting
people<CITE> (Lemay, 1994)</CITE></P>
```

NOTE   Of the tags in this list, all except <DFN> are part of the official HTML
2.0 specification. <DFN> is part of the HTML 3.2 and 4.0 specifications.

Got all these tags memorized now? Good! There will be a pop quiz at the end of the chapter.
The following code snippets demonstrate each of the logical style tags, and Figures 5.1 and
5.2 illustrate how all eight tags are displayed in Netscape and Lynx.

```
<P>We'd all get along much better if you'd stop being so <EM>silly.</EM>
<P>You <STRONG>must</STRONG> open the can before drinking</P>
<P><CODE>#include "trans.h"</CODE></P>
<P>Type the following command:
<KBD>find . -name "prune" -print</KBD></P>
<P><CODE>chown </CODE><VAR>your_name the_file</VAR></P>
<P>The URL for that page is <SAMP>http://www.cern.ch/</SAMP></P>
<P>Styles that are named on how they are used are called <DFN>character
styles</DFN></P>
<P>Eggplant has been known to cause extreme nausea in many unsuspecting
people<CITE> (Lemay, 1994)</CITE></P>
```

OUTPUT

Figure 5.1.
The output in Netscape.

5

Figure 5.2.

The output in Lynx.

```
We'd all get along much better if you'd stop being so silly.

You must open the can before drinking.

#include "trans.h"

Type the following command: find . -name "prune" -print

chown your_name the_file

The URL for that page is http://www.cern.ch/

Styles that are named on how they are used are called character styles


Eggplant has been known to cause extreme nausea in many unsuspecting
people (Lemay, 1994)
```

Physical Styles

In addition to the tags for style in the preceding section, you also can use a set of tags, physical style tags, to change the actual presentation style of the text—to make it bold, italic, or monospace.

 Physical style tags indicate exactly the way text is to be formatted (bold, underline, and so on).

Like the character style tags, each formatting tag has a beginning and ending tag. Standard HTML 2.0 defined three physical style tags:

<B>	Bold
<I>	Italic
<TT>	Monospaced typewriter font

HTML 3.2 defined several other physical style tags, including the following:

<U>	Underline (deprecated in HTML 4.0)
<S>	Strike through (deprecated in HTML 4.0)
<BIG>	Bigger print than the surrounding text
<SMALL>	Smaller print
<SUB>	Subscript
<SUP>	Superscript

If you use the physical style tags, particularly the HTML 3.2 tags, be forewarned that if a browser cannot handle one of the physical styles, it may substitute another style for the one you're using or ignore that formatting altogether. Although the latest versions of browsers such as Netscape Navigator and Internet Explorer are happy with these tags, enough users

5

are using older versions of these browsers that support these tags to varying degrees. On top of all this, in text-based browsers such as Lynx some of these tags can't be rendered visually and other workarounds will be used to get across the idea.

You can nest character tags—for example, use both bold and italic for a set of characters—like this:

```
<B><I>Text that is both bold and italic</I></B>
```

However, the result on the screen, like all HTML tags, is browser dependent. You will not necessarily end up with text that is both bold and italic. You may end up with one style or the other.

The following input and output example shows some of the physical style tags and how they appear in Netscape (see Figure 5.3) and Lynx (see Figure 5.4).

INPUT

```
<P>In Dante's <I>Inferno</I>, malaboge was the eighth circle of hell,
and held the malicious and fraudulent.</P>
<P>All entries must be received by <B>September 26, 1996</B>.</P>
<P>Type <TT>lpr -Pbirch myfile.txt</TT> to print that file.</P>
<P>Sign your name in the spot marked <U>Sign Here</U>:</P>
<P>People who wear orange shirts and plaid pants <S>have no taste</S>
are fashion-challenged.</P>
<P>RCP floor mats give you <BIG>BIG</BIG> savings over the
competition!</P>
<P>Then, from the corner of the room, he heard a <SMALL>tiny voice
</SMALL>.</P>
<P>In heavy trading today. Consolidated Orange Trucking
rose <SUP>1</SUP>/<SUB>4</SUB>
points on volume of 1,457,900 shares.</P>
```

OUTPUT

Figure 5.3.

The output in Netscape.

5

Figure 5.4.
The output in Lynx.

Preformatted Text

Most of the time, text in an HTML file is formatted based on the HTML tags used to mark up that text. As I mentioned in Chapter 3, "Begin with the Basics," any extra white space (spaces, tabs, returns) that you put in your text are stripped out by the browser.

The one exception to this rule is the preformatted text tag <PRE>. Any white space that you put into text surrounded by the <PRE> and </PRE> tags is retained in the final output. With the <PRE> and </PRE> tags, you can format the text the way you want it to look, and it will be presented that way.

The catch is that preformatted text is also displayed (in graphical displays, at least) in a monospaced font such as Courier. Preformatted text is excellent for displays such as code examples, where you want to indent and format lines appropriately. Because you can also use the <PRE> tag to align text by padding it with spaces, you can use it for simple tables. However, the fact that the tables are presented in a monospaced font may make them less than ideal. (You'll learn how to create real tables in Chapter 11, "Tables.") Here's an example of a table created with <PRE>. Figure 5.5 shows how it looks in Netscape.

```
<PRE>
              Diameter    Distance    Time to     Time to
              (miles)     from Sun    Orbit       Rotate
                          (millions
                          of miles)

              ---------------------------------------------------------
Mercury       3100          36        88 days     59 days
Venus         7700          67        225 days    244 days
Earth         7920          93        365 days    24 hrs
Mars          4200         141        687 days    24 hrs 24 mins
Jupiter      88640         483        11.9 years  9 hrs 50 mins
Saturn       74500         886        29.5 years  10 hrs 39 mins
Uranus       32000        1782        84 years    23 hrs
Neptune      31000        2793        165 days    15 hrs 48 mins
Pluto         1500        3670        248 years   6 days 7 hrs
</PRE>
```

OUTPUT

Figure 5.5.

A table created using <PRE>, *shown in Netscape.*

When creating text for the <PRE> tag, you can use link tags and character styles, but not element tags such as headings or paragraphs. You should break your lines using a return and try to keep your lines at 60 characters or fewer. Some browsers may have limited horizontal space in which to display text. Because browsers usually will not reformat preformatted text to fit that space, you should make sure that you keep your text within the boundaries to prevent your readers from having to scroll from side to side.

Be careful with tabs in preformatted text. The actual number of characters for each tab stop varies from browser to browser. One browser may have tab stops at every fourth character, whereas another may have them at every eighth character. If your preformatted text relies on tabs at a certain number of spaces, consider using spaces instead of tabs.

The <PRE> tag is also excellent for converting files that were originally in some sort of text-only form, such as mail messages or Usenet news postings, to HTML quickly and easily. Just surround the entire content of the article within <PRE> tags, and you have instant HTML, as in this example:

```
<PRE>
To: lemay@lne.com
From: jokes@lne.com
```

```
Subject: Tales of the Move From Hell, pt. 1
Date: Fri, 26 Aug 1994 14:13:38 +0800

I spent the day on the phone today with the entire household
services division of northern California, turning off services,
turning on services, transferring services and other such fun
things you have to do when you move.

It used to be you just called these people and got put on hold for
and interminable amount of time, maybe with some nice music, and
then you got a customer representative who was surly and hard of
hearing, but with some work you could actually get your phone
turned off.
</PRE>
```

The following HTML input and output example shows a simple ASCII art cow. Figure 5.6 shows how the cow appears in Netscape, and Figure 5.7 shows how it appears in Lynx.

INPUT

```
<PRE>
        ( )
Moo   (oo)
       \/------\
        ||      | \
        ||--W ||   *
        ||      ||
        ||      ||
</PRE>
```

OUTPUT

Figure 5.6.
The output in Netscape.

OUTPUT

Figure 5.7.
The output in Lynx.

Horizontal Rules

The <HR> tag, which has no closing tag and no text associated with it, creates a horizontal line on the page. Rule lines are excellent for visually separating sections of a Web page—just before headings, for example, or to separate body text from a list of items. Figure 5.8 shows a rule line.

Figure 5.8.

A rule line.

The following input and output example shows a rule line and a list. Figure 5.9 shows how they appear in Netscape, and Figure 5.10 shows how they appear in Lynx.

INPUT

```
<HR>
<H2>To Do on Friday</H2>
<UL>
<LI>Do laundry
<LI>Send Fedex with pictures
<LI>Have lunch with Mollie
<LI>Read Email
<LI>Set up Ethernet
</UL>
<HR>
```

Figure 5.9.
The output in Netscape.

Figure 5.10.
The output in Lynx.

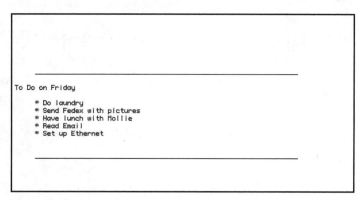

Attributes of the `<HR>` Tag

In HTML, the `<HR>` tag is just as you see it, with no closing tag or attributes. However, HTML 3.2 introduced several attributes to the `<HR>` tag that give you greater control over the appearance of the line drawn by `<HR>`.

The SIZE attribute indicates the thickness, in pixels, of the rule line. The default is 2, and this is also the smallest thickness that you can make the rule line. Figure 5.11 shows some sample rule line thicknesses.

The WIDTH attribute indicates the horizontal width of the rule line. You can specify either the exact width, in pixels, or the value as a percentage of the screen width (for example, 30 percent or 50 percent), which will change if you resize the window. Figure 5.12 shows some sample rule line widths.

If you specify a WIDTH smaller than the actual width of the screen, you can also specify the alignment of that rule line with the ALIGN attribute, making it flush left (ALIGN=LEFT), flush right (ALIGN=RIGHT), or centered (ALIGN=CENTER). By default, rule lines are centered.

Figure 5.11.

Examples of rule line thicknesses.

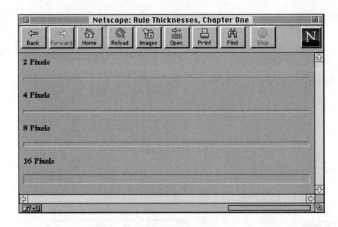

Figure 5.12.

Examples of rule line widths.

A popular trick used by Web designers who use these attributes is to create patterns with several small rule lines, as shown in Figure 5.13.

NOTE

Although presentational attributes such as SIZE, WIDTH, and ALIGN are still supported in HTML 4.0, style sheets will become the recommended way to control appearance.

Finally, the NOSHADE attribute causes the browser to draw the rule line as a plain line in most current browsers, without the three-dimensional shading, as shown in Figure 5.14.

Figure 5.13.

An example of patterns created with several small rule lines.

Figure 5.14.

Rule lines without shading.

Line Break

The `<BR>` tag breaks a line of text at the point where it appears. When a Web browser encounters a `<BR>` tag, it restarts the text after the tag at the left margin (whatever the current left margin happens to be for the current element). You can use `<BR>` within other elements such as paragraphs or list items; `<BR>` will not add extra space above or below the new line or change the font or style of the current entity. All it does is restart the text at the next line.

The following example shows a simple paragraph in which each line ends with a `<BR>`. Figures 5.15 and 5.16 show how it appears in Netscape and Lynx, respectively.

INPUT

```
<P>Tomorrow, and tomorrow, and tomorrow<BR>
Creeps in this petty pace from day to day<BR>
To the last syllable of recorded time;<BR>
And all our yesterdays have lighted fools<BR>
The way to dusty death. Out, out, brief candle!<BR>
Life's but a walking shadow, a poor player,<BR>
That struts and frets his hour upon the stage<BR>
And then is heard no more. It is a tale <BR>
Told by an idiot, full of sound and fury, <BR>
Signifying nothing.</P>
```

5

Figure 5.15.
The output in Netscape.

Figure 5.16.
The output in Lynx.

NOTE

CLEAR is an HTML attribute of the <BR> tag. It is used with images that have text wrapped alongside them. You'll learn about this attribute in Chapter 7, "Using Images, Color, and Backgrounds."

Addresses

The address tag <ADDRESS> is used for signature-like entities on Web pages. Address tags usually go at the bottom of each Web page and are used to indicate who wrote the Web page, who to contact for more information, the date, any copyright notices or other warnings, and anything else that seems appropriate. Addresses are often preceded with a rule line (<HR>), and the <BR> tag can be used to separate the lines, as follows:

```
<HR>
<ADDRESS>
```

```
Laura Lemay lemay@lne.com <BR>
A service of Laura Lemay, Incorporated <BR>
last revised April 30 1997 <BR>
Copyright Laura Lemay 1994 all rights reserved <BR>
Void where prohibited. Keep hands and feet inside the vehicle at all times.
</ADDRESS>
```

Without an address or some other method of "signing" your Web pages, finding out who wrote it or who to contact for more information becomes close to impossible. Signing each of your Web pages using the <ADDRESS> tag is an excellent way to make sure that, if people want to get in touch with you, they can.

The following simple input and output example shows an address. Figure 5.17 shows it in Netscape, and Figure 5.18 shows it in Lynx.

```
<HR>
<ADDRESS>
lemay@lne.com Laura Lemay
</ADDRESS>
```

Figure 5.17.
The output in Netscape.

Figure 5.18.
The output in Lynx.

Quotations

The <BLOCKQUOTE> tag is used to create a quotation. (Unlike the <CITE> tag, which highlights small quotes, <BLOCKQUOTE> is used for longer quotations that should not be nested inside other paragraphs.) Quotations are generally set off from regular text by indentation or some other method. For example, the *Macbeth* soliloquy I used in the example for line breaks would have worked better as a <BLOCKQUOTE> than as a simple paragraph. Here's another example:

```
<BLOCKQUOTE>
"During the whole of a dull, dark, and soundless day in the autumn
of the year, when the clouds hung oppressively low in the heavens,
I had been passing alone, on horseback, through a singularly dreary
tract of country, and at length found myself, as the shades of evening
grew on, within view of the melancholy House of Usher."--Edgar Allen Poe
</BLOCKQUOTE>
```

As in paragraphs, you can separate lines in a <BLOCKQUOTE> using the line break tag <BR>. The following input and output example shows a sample of this use; Figure 5.19 shows how it appears in Netscape.

```
<BLOCKQUOTE>
Guns aren't lawful, <BR>
nooses give.<BR>
gas smells awful.<BR>
You might as well live.<BR>
--Dorothy Parker
</BLOCKQUOTE>
```

Figure 5.19.
The output in Netscape.

Special Characters

As you learned earlier in the week, HTML files are ASCII text and should contain no formatting or fancy characters. In fact, the only characters you should put in your HTML files are characters that are actually printed on your keyboard. If you have to hold down any key other than Shift or type an arcane combination of keys to produce a single character, you can't use that character in your HTML file. That includes characters you may use every day, such as em dashes and curly quotes (and, if your word processor is set up to do automatic curly quotes, you should turn them off when you write your HTML files).

"But wait a minute," you say. "If I can type a character, like a bullet or an accented *a* on my keyboard using a special key sequence, include it in an HTML file, and my browser can display it just fine when I look at that file, what's the problem?"

The problem is that the internal encoding your computer does to produce that character (which allows it to show up properly in your HTML file and in your browser's display) most likely will not translate to other computers. Someone else on the Net reading your HTML file with that funny character in it may very well end up with some other character, or garbage. Or, depending on how your page gets shipped over the Net, the character may be lost before it ever gets to the computer where the file is being viewed.

NOTE

In technical jargon, the characters in HTML files must be from the standard (7-bit) ASCII character set and cannot include any characters from "extended" (8-bit) ASCII, as every platform has a different definition of the characters that are included in the upper ASCII range. HTML browsers interpret codes from upper ASCII as characters in the ISO-Latin-1 (ISO-8859-1) character set, a superset of ASCII.

So what can you do? HTML provides a reasonable solution. It defines a special set of codes, called character entities, which you can include in your HTML files to represent the characters you want to use. When interpreted by a browser, these character entities are displayed as the appropriate special characters for the given platform and font.

Character Entities for Special Characters

Character entities take one of two forms: named entities and numbered entities.

Named entities begin with an ampersand (&) and end with a semicolon (;). In between is the name of the character (or, more likely, a shorthand version of that name like agrave for an *a* with a grave accent or reg for a registered trademark sign). The names, unlike other HTML tags, are case sensitive, so you should make sure to type them exactly. Named entities look something like this:

```
&quot;
&laquo;
&copy;
```

The numbered entities also begin with an ampersand and end with a semicolon, but instead of a name, they have a hash sign and a number. The numbers correspond to character positions in the ISO-Latin-1 (ISO 8859-1) character. Every character for which you can type or use a named entity also has a numbered entity. Numbered entities look like this:

```
&#130;
&#245;
```

You use either numbers or named entities in your HTML file by including them in the same place that the character they represent would go. So, to have the word *resumé* in your HTML file, you would use either

```
resum&eacute;
```

or

```
resum&#233;
```

In Appendix B, "HTML 4.0 Quick Reference," I've included a table that lists the named entities supported by HTML. See that table for specific characters.

NOTE

> HTML's use of the ISO-Latin-1 character set allows it to display most accented characters on most platforms, but it has limitations. For example, common characters such as bullets, em dashes, and curly quotes are simply not available in the ISO-Latin-1 character set. You therefore cannot use these characters at all in your HTML files. Also, many ISO-Latin-1 characters may be entirely unavailable in some browsers, depending on whether those characters exist on that platform and in the current font.
>
> HTML 4.0 takes things a huge leap further by proposing that Unicode should be available as a character set for HTML documents. Unicode is a proposed standard character encoding system that, while backward compatible with our familiar ASCII encoding, offers the capability to encode almost any of the world's characters—including those found in languages such as Chinese and Japanese. This will mean that documents can be easily created in any language but that they can easily contain multiple languages. Browsers have already started supporting Unicode. Netscape Communicator, for instance, supports Unicode and as long as the necessary fonts are available to it, can render documents in many of the scripts provided by Unicode.
>
> This is an important step because Unicode is emerging as a new *de facto* standard for character encoding. Java, for instance, uses Unicode as its default character encoding, and Windows NT supports Unicode character encoding.

5

Character Entities for Reserved Characters

For the most part, character entities exist so you can include special characters that are not part of the standard ASCII character set. Several exceptions do exist, however, for the few characters that have special meaning in HTML itself. You must also use entities for these characters.

For example, say you want to include a line of code that looks something like the following in an HTML file:

```
<P><CODE>if x < 0 do print i</CODE></P>
```

Doesn't look unusual, does it? Unfortunately, HTML cannot display this line as written. Why? The problem is with the < (less-than) character. To an HTML browser, the less-than character means "this is the start of a tag." Because in this context the less-than character is not actually the start of a tag, your browser may get confused. You'll have the same problem with the greater-than character (>) because it means the end of a tag in HTML, and with the ampersand (&), meaning the beginning of a character escape. Written correctly for HTML, the preceding line of code would look like this instead:

```
<P><CODE>if x &lt; 0 do print i</CODE></P>
```

HTML provides named escape codes for each of these characters, and one for the double quotation mark, as well, as shown in Table 5.1.

Table 5.1. Escape codes for characters used by tags.

Entity	Result
<	<
>	>
&	&
"	"

The double quotation mark escape is the mysterious one. Technically, to produce correct HTML files, if you want to include a double quotation mark in text, you should use the escape sequence and not type the quotation mark character. However, I have not noticed any browsers having problems displaying the double quotation mark character when it is typed literally in an HTML file, nor have I seen many HTML files that use it. For the most part, you are probably safe using plain old " in your HTML files rather than the escape code.

Text Alignment

Text alignment is the ability to arrange a block of text such as a heading or a paragraph so that it is aligned against the left margin (left justification, the default), aligned against the right margin (right justification), or centered. Standard HTML 2.0 had no mechanisms for aligning text; the browser was responsible for determining the alignment of the text (which means most of the time it was left-justified).

HTML 3.2 introduced attributes for text and element alignment, and these attributes have been incorporated into all the major browsers. HTML 4.0 still supports alignment attributes, but as more people begin using browsers that support style sheets, that will become the preferred method for controlling text alignment.

Aligning Individual Elements

To align an individual heading or paragraph, use the ALIGN attribute with that HTML element. ALIGN has one of three values: LEFT, RIGHT, or CENTER. Consider these examples:

```
<H1 ALIGN=CENTER>Northridge Paints, Inc.</H2>
<P ALIGN=CENTER >We don't just paint the town red.</P>

<H1 ALIGN=LEFT>Serendipity Products</H1>
<H2 ALIGN=RIGHT><A HREF="who.html">Who We Are</A></H2>
<H2 ALIGN=RIGHT><A HREF="products.html">What We Do</A></H2>
<H2 ALIGN=RIGHT><A HREF="contacts.html">How To Reach Us</A></H2>
```

The following input and output example shows simple alignment of several headings. Figure 5.20 shows the results in Netscape.

```
<H1 ALIGN=LEFT>Serendipity Products</H1>
<H2 ALIGN=RIGHT><A HREF="who.html">Who We Are</A></H2>
<H2 ALIGN=RIGHT><A HREF="products.html">What We Do</A></H2>
<H2 ALIGN=RIGHT><A HREF="contacts.html">How To Reach Us</A></H2>
```

Figure 5.20.

The output in Netscape.

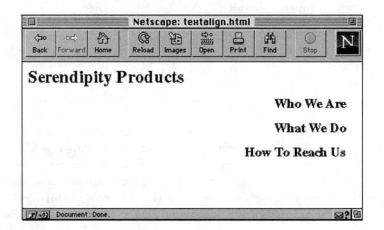

Aligning Blocks of Elements

A slightly more flexible method of aligning text elements is to use the <DIV> tag. <DIV> stands for division and includes the ALIGN attribute just as headings and paragraphs do. Unlike using alignments in individual elements, however, <DIV> is used to surround a block of HTML tags of any kind, and it affects all the tags and text inside the opening and closing tags. Two advantages of DIV over the ALIGN attribute are as follow:

☐ DIV needs to be used only once, rather than including ALIGN repeatedly in several different tags.

☐ DIV can be used to align anything (headings, paragraphs, quotes, images, tables, and so on); the ALIGN attribute is available only on a limited number of tags.

To align a block of HTML code, surround that code by opening and closing <DIV> tags and then include the ALIGN attribute in the opening tag. As in other tags, ALIGN can have the values LEFT, RIGHT, or CENTER, as shown here:

```
<H1 ALIGN=LEFT>Serendipity Products</H1>
<DIV ALIGN=RIGHT>
<H2><A HREF="who.html">Who We Are</A></H2>
<H2><A HREF="products.html">What We Do</A></H2>
<H2><A HREF="contacts.html">How To Reach Us</A></H2>
</DIV>
```

All the HTML between the two <DIV> tags will be aligned according to the value of the ALIGN attribute. If individual ALIGN attributes appear in headings or paragraphs inside the DIV, those values will override the global DIV setting.

Note that <DIV> is not itself a paragraph type. You still need regular element tags (<P>, <H1>, <UL>, <BLOCKQUOTE>, and so on) inside the opening and closing <DIV> tags.

In addition to <DIV>, you also can use the centering tag <CENTER>. The HTML specification defines it as a short version of <DIV ALIGN=CENTER>. The <CENTER> tag acts identically to <DIV ALIGN=CENTER>, centering all the HTML content inside the opening and closing tags. You put the <CENTER> tag before the text you want centered and the </CENTER> tag after you're done, like this:

```
<CENTER>
<H1>Northridge Paints, Inc.</H2>
<P>We don't just paint the town red.</P>
</CENTER>
```

For consistency's sake, you're probably better off using <DIV> and ALIGN to achieve centering.

Fonts and Font Sizes

The <FONT> tag—part of HTML 3.2, but phased out, or deprecated, in HTML 4.0—is used to control the characteristics of a given set of characters not covered by the character styles.

5

Originally, <FONT> was used only to control the font size of the characters it surrounds, but it has since been extended to allow you to change the font itself and the color of those characters.

In this section, I'll discuss fonts and font sizes. On Day 4, "Images, Backgrounds, and Multimedia," when I talk about color in general, you'll learn about changing the font color.

Changing the Font Size

The most common use of the <FONT> tag is to change the size of the font for a character, word, phrase, or on any range of text. The <FONT>...</FONT> tags enclose the text, and the SIZE attribute indicates the size to which the font is to be changed. The values of SIZE are 1 to 7, with 3 being the default size. Consider the following example:

```
<P>Bored with your plain old font?
<FONT SIZE=5>Change it.</FONT></P>
```

Figure 5.21 shows the typical font sizes for each value of SIZE.

Figure 5.21.

Font sizes in Netscape.

You can also specify the size in the <FONT> tag as a relative value using the + or - characters in the value for SIZE. Because the default size is 3, you can change relative font sizes in the range from to -3 to +4, like this:

```
<P>Change the <FONT SIZE=+2>Font</FONT> size again.</P>
```

Here, the word Font (inside the <FONT> tags) will be two size levels larger than the default font when you view that example in a browser that supports this feature.

Relative font sizes are actually based on a value that you can define using the <BASEFONT> tag, another element being phased out in HTML 4.0. The <BASEFONT> tag also has the required attribute SIZE. SIZE can have a value of 1 to 7. All relative font changes in the document after the <BASEFONT> tag will be relative to that value.

Try to avoid using the <FONT> tag to simulate the larger-font effect of the HTML content-based tags such as the heading tags (<H1>, <H2>, and so on) or to emphasize a particular word or phrase. If your documents are viewed in browsers that don't support this feature, you'll lose the font sizes, and your text will appear as if it were any other paragraph. If you stick to the content-based tags, however, a heading is a heading regardless of where you view it. Try to limit your use of the <FONT> tag to small amounts of special effects.

Changing the Font Face

Netscape introduced the <FONT> tag to HTML with its 1.0 browser. Microsoft's Internet Explorer, playing the same game, extended the <FONT> tag to include the FACE attribute. The tag is now part of HTML 3.2, though HTML 4.0 would prefer that you use style sheets.

FACE takes as its value a set of font names, surrounded by quotation marks and separated by commas. When a browser that supports FACE interprets a page with FACE in it, it will search the system for the given font names one at a time. If it can't find the first one, it'll try the second, and then the third, and so on, until it finds a font that is actually installed on the system. If the browser cannot find any of the listed fonts, the default font will be used instead. So, for example, the following text would be rendered in Futura. If Futura is not available, the browser will try Helvetica; then it will fall back on the default if Helvetica is not available.

```
<P><FONT FACE="Futura,Helvetica">Sans Serif fonts are fonts without
the small "ticks" on the strokes of the characters. </FONT></P>
```

If you use the FACE attribute, keep in mind that currently very few browsers support it, so it may be unavailable to most of your audience. Also, many fonts have different names on different systems; for example, plain old Times is Times on some systems, Times Roman on others, and Times New Roman elsewhere. Because of the varying names of fonts and the lack of widespread support for the FACE attribute, changing the font name should be used only as an optional presentation-only feature rather than one to be relied on in your pages.

The Dreaded <BLINK>

You won't find the <BLINK> tag listed in Netscape's official documentation of its attributes. The capability to cause text to blink was included in Netscape as a hidden, undocumented feature, or Easter egg. Still, many pages on the Web seem to use this feature.

The <BLINK>...</BLINK> tags cause the text between the opening and closing tags to have a blinking effect. Depending on the version of Netscape you're using, the text itself can vanish and come back at regular intervals, or an ugly gray or white block may appear and disappear behind the text. Blink is usually used to draw attention to a portion of the page.

The problem with blink is that it provides too much emphasis. Because it repeats, the blink continues to draw attention to that one spot and, in some cases, can be so distracting that it can make absorbing any of the other content of the page nearly impossible. The use of <BLINK> is greatly discouraged by most Web designers (including myself) because many people find it extremely intrusive, ugly, and annoying. Blink is the HTML equivalent of fingernails on a blackboard.

5

If you must use blink, use it sparingly (no more than a few words on a page). Also, be aware that in some versions of Netscape, blinking can be turned off. If you want to emphasize a word or phrase, you should use a more conventional way of doing so, in addition to (or in place of) blink, because you cannot guarantee that blink will be available even if your readers are using Netscape to view your pages.

`<NOBR>` and `<WBR>`

The `<NOBR>`...`</NOBR>` element is the opposite of the `<BR>` tag. The text inside the NOBR tags always remains on one line, even if it would have wrapped to two more lines without the NOBR. NOBR is used for words or phrases that must be kept together on one line, but be careful: Long unbreakable lines can look really strange on your page, and if they are longer than the page width, they might extend beyond the right edge of the screen.

The `<WBR>` tag (word break) indicates an appropriate breaking point within a line (typically one inside a `<NOBR>`...`</NOBR>` sequence). Unlike `<BR>`, which forces a break, `<WBR>` is used only where it is appropriate to do so. If the line will fit on the screen just fine, the `<WBR>` is ignored.

Neither `<NOBR>` nor `<WBR>` are part of HTML 3.2 or HTML 4.0, but they are instead extensions introduced by Netscape but supported in both Netscape Communicator and Internet Explorer 4.

Exercise 5.1: Creating a real HTML page.

Here's your chance to apply what you've learned and create a real Web page. No more disjointed or overly silly examples. The Web page you'll create in this section is a real one, suitable for use in the real world (or the real world of the Web, at least).

Your task for this example is to design and create a home page for a bookstore called The Bookworm, which specializes in old and rare books.

Plan the Page

In Chapter 2, "Get Organized," I mentioned that planning your Web page before writing it usually makes building and maintaining the elements easier. So, first consider the content you want to include on this page. Here are some ideas for topics for this page:

- ☐ The address and phone number of the bookstore
- ☐ A short description of the bookstore and why it is unique
- ☐ Recent titles and authors
- ☐ Upcoming events

Now, come up with some ideas for the content you're going to link from this page. Each title in a list of recently acquired books seems like a logical candidate. You can also create links to more information about each book, its author and publisher, its pricing, maybe even its availability.

The Upcoming Events section might suggest a potential series of links, depending on how much you want to say about each event. If you have only a sentence or two about each one, describing them on this page might make more sense than linking them to another page. Why make your readers wait for each new page to load for just a couple of lines of text?

Other interesting links may arise in the text itself, but for now, starting with the basic link plan will be enough.

Begin with a Framework

Next, create the framework that all HTML files must include: the document structuring commands, a title, and an initial heading. Note that the title is descriptive but short; you can save the longer title for the <H1> element in the body of the text.

```
<HTML>
<HEAD>
<TITLE>The Bookworm Bookshop</TITLE>
</HEAD>
<BODY>
<H1>The Bookworm: A Better Book Store</H1>
</BODY></HTML>
```

Add Content

Now begin adding the content. Because you're undertaking a literary endeavor, starting the page with a nice quote about old books would be a nice touch. Since you're adding a quote, you can use the <BLOCKQUOTE> tag to make it stand out as such. Also, the name of the poem is a citation, so use <CITE> there, too.

```
<BLOCKQUOTE>
"Old books are best--how tale and rhyme<BR>
Float with us down the stream of time!"<BR>
- Clarence Urmy, <CITE>Old Songs are Best</CITE>
</BLOCKQUOTE>
```

The address of the bookstore is a simple paragraph, with the lines separated by line breaks, like this:

```
<P>The Bookworm Bookshop<BR>
1345 Applewood Dr<BR>
Springfield, CA 94325<BR>
(415) 555-0034
</P>
```

After the address comes the description of the bookstore. I've arranged the description to include a list of features, to make the features stand out from the text better:

```
<P>Since 1933, The Bookworm Bookshop has offered
rare and hard-to-find titles for the discerning reader.
Unlike the bigger bookstore chains, the Bookworm offers:</P>
```

5

```
<UL>
<LI>Friendly, knowledgeable, and courteous help
<LI>Free coffee and juice for our customers
<LI>A well-lit reading room so you can "try before you buy"
<LI>Four friendly cats: Esmerelda, Catherine, Dulcinea and Beatrice
</UL>
```

Add one more note about the hours the store is open, and emphasize the actual numbers:

```
<P>Our hours are <STRONG>10am to 9pm</STRONG> weekdays,
<STRONG>noon to 7</STRONG> on weekends.</P>
```

Add More Content

After the description come the other major topics of this home page: the recent titles and upcoming events sections. Because they are topic headings, label them with second-level head tags:

```
<H2>Recent Titles (as of 30-Apr-97)</H2>
<H2>Upcoming Events</H2>
```

The Recent Titles section itself is a classic link menu, as I described earlier in this section. Here you can put the list of titles in an unordered list, with the titles themselves as citations (by using the <CITE> tag):

```
<H2>Recent Titles (30-Apr-97)</H2>
<UL>
<LI>Sandra Bellweather, <CITE>Belladonna</CITE>
<LI>Jonathan Tin, <CITE>20-Minute Meals for One</CITE>
<LI>Maxwell Burgess, <CITE>Legion of Thunder</CITE>
<LI>Alison Caine, <CITE>Banquo's Ghost</CITE>
</UL>
```

Now, add the anchor tags to create the links. How far should the link extend? Should it include the whole line (author and title), or just the title of the book? This decision is a matter of preference, but I like to link only as much as necessary to make sure the link stands out from the text. I prefer this approach to overwhelming the text. Here, I've linked only the titles of the books:

```
<UL>
<LI>Sandra Bellweather, <A HREF="belladonna.html">
<CITE>Belladonna</CITE></A>
<LI>Johnathan Tin, <A HREF="20minmeals.html">
<CITE>20-Minute Meals for One</CITE></A>
<LI>Maxwell Burgess, <A HREF="legion.html">
<CITE>Legion of Thunder</CITE></A>
<LI>Alison Caine, <A HREF="banquo.html">
<CITE>Banquo's Ghost</CITE></A>
</UL>
```

Note that I've put the <CITE> tag inside the link tag <A>. I could have just as easily put it outside the anchor tag; character style tags can go just about anywhere. But as I mentioned once before, be careful not to overlap tags. Your browser may not be able to understand what is going on. In other words, don't do this:

```
<A HREF="banquo.html"><CITE>Banquo's Ghost</A></CITE>
```

Next, move on to the Upcoming Events section. In the planning section, you weren't sure whether this would be another link menu or whether the content would work better solely on this page. Again, this decision is a matter of preference. Here, because the amount of extra information is minimal, creating links for just a couple of sentences doesn't make much sense. So, for this section, create a menu list (by using the <UL> tag), which results in short paragraphs (bulleted in some browsers). I've boldfaced a few phrases near the beginning of each paragraph. These phrases emphasize a summary of the event itself so that each paragraph can be scanned quickly and ignored if the readers aren't interested.

```
<H1>Upcoming Events</H1>
<UL>
<LI><B>The Wednesday Evening Book Review</B> meets, appropriately, on Wednesday
evenings at 7:00 PM for coffee and a round-table discussion. Call the Bookworm
for information on joining the group and this week's reading assignment.
<LI><B>The Children's Hour</B> happens every Saturday at 1pm and includes
reading, games, and other activities. Cookies and milk are served.
<LI><B>Carole Fenney</B> will be at the Bookworm on Friday, September 16, to
read from her book of poems <CITE>Spiders in the Web.</CITE>
<LI><B>The Bookworm will be closed</B> October 1 to remove a family
of bats that has nested in the tower. We like the company, but not
the mess they leave behind!
</UL>
```

Sign the Page

To finish, sign what you have so that your readers know who did the work. Here, I've separated the signature from the text with a rule line. I've also included the most recent revision date, my name as the *Webmaster* (cute Web jargon meaning the person in charge of a Web site), and a basic copyright (with a copyright symbol indicated by the numeric escape ©):

```
<HR>
<ADDRESS>
Last Updated: 30-Apr-97<BR>
WebMaster: Laura Lemay lemay@bookworm.com<BR>
&#169; copyright 1995 the Bookworm<BR>
</ADDRESS>
```

Review What You've Got

Here's the HTML code for the page so far:

```
<HTML>
<HEAD>
<TITLE>The Bookworm Bookshop</TITLE>
</HEAD>
<BODY>
<H1>The Bookworm: A Better Book Store</H1>
```

5

```
<BLOCKQUOTE>
"Old books are best--how tale and rhyme<BR>
Float with us down the stream of time!"<BR>
- Clarence Urmy, <CITE>Old Songs are Best</CITE>
</BLOCKQUOTE>
<P>The Bookworm Bookshop<BR>
1345 Applewood Dr<BR>
Springfield, CA 94325<BR>
 (415) 555-0034
</P>
<P>Since 1933, The Bookworm Bookshop has offered rare
and hard-to-find titles for the discerning reader.
Unlike the bigger bookstore chains, the Bookworm offers:
<UL>
<LI>Friendly, knowledgeable, and courteous help
<LI>Free coffee and juice for our customers
<LI>A well-lit reading room so you can "try before you buy"
<LI>Four friendly cats: Esmerelda, Catherine, Dulcinea and Beatrice
</UL>
<P>Our hours are <STRONG>10am to 9pm</STRONG> weekdays,
<STRONG>noon to 7</STRONG> on weekends.</P>
<H2>Recent Titles (as of 25-Sept-95)</H2>
<UL>
<LI>Sandra Bellweather, <A HREF="belladonna.html">
<CITE>Belladonna</CITE></A>
<LI>Johnathan Tin, <A HREF="20minmeals.html">
<CITE>20-Minute Meals for One</CITE></A>
<LI>Maxwell Burgess, <A HREF="legion.html">
<CITE>Legion of Thunder</CITE></A>
<LI>Alison Caine, <A HREF="banquo.html">
<CITE>Banquo's Ghost</CITE></A>
</UL>
<H2>Upcoming Events</H2>
<UL>
<LI><B>The Wednesday Evening Book Review</B> meets, appropriately, on
Wednesday evenings at 7:00 PM for coffee and a round-table discussion. Call
the Bookworm for information on joining the group and this week's
reading assignment.
<LI><B>The Children's Hour</B> happens every Saturday at 1pm and includes
reading, games, and other activities. Cookies and milk are served.
<LI><B>Carole Fenney</B> will be at the Bookworm on Friday, September 16,
to read from her book of poems <CITE>Spiders in the Web.</CITE>
<LI><B>The Bookworm will be closed</B> October 1 to remove a family
of bats that has nested in the tower. We like the company, but not
the mess they leave behind!
</UL>
<HR>
<ADDRESS>
Last Updated: 30-Apr-97<BR>
WebMaster: Laura Lemay lemay@bookworm.com<BR>
&#169; copyright 1995 the Bookworm<BR>
</ADDRESS>
</BODY></HTML>
```

So, now you have some headings, some text, some topics, and some links, which form the basis for an excellent Web page. At this point, with most of the content in place, consider what else you might want to create links for or what other features you might want to add to this page.

For example, in the introductory section, a note was made of the four cats owned by the bookstore. Although you didn't plan for them in the original organization, you could easily create Web pages describing each cat (and showing pictures), and then link them back to this page, one link (and one page) per cat.

Is describing the cats important? As the designer of the page, that's up to you to decide. You could link all kinds of things from this page if you have interesting reasons to link them (and something to link to). Link the bookstore's address to the local Chamber of Commerce. Link the quote to an online encyclopedia of quotes. Link the note about free coffee to the Coffee Home Page.

I'll talk more about good things to link (and how not to get carried away when you link) on Day 5, "Designing Effective Web Pages," when you learn about Dos and Don'ts for good Web pages. My reason for bringing up this point here is that after you have some content in place in your Web pages, opportunities for extending the pages and linking to other places may arise, opportunities you didn't think of when you created your original plan. So, when you're just about finished with a page, stop and review what you have, both in the plan and in your Web page.

For the purposes of this example, stop here and stick with the links you've got. You're close enough to being done that I don't want to make this chapter longer than it already is!

Test the Result

Now that all the code is in place, you can preview the results in a browser. Figure 5.22 shows how it looks in the Netscape browser. Actually, this figure shows how the page looks after you fix the spelling errors and forgotten closing tags and other strange bugs that always seem to creep into an HTML file the first time you create it. These problems always seem to happen no matter how good you get at creating Web pages. If you use an HTML editor or some other help tool, your job will be easier, but you'll always seem to find mistakes. That's what previewing is for—so you can catch the problems before you actually make the document available to other people.

Looks good so far, but in the browsers I used to test it, the description of the store and the Recent Titles sections tend to run together. They don't have enough distinction between them (see Figure 5.23).

You have two choices for making these sections more distinct:

☐ Add rule lines (<HR>) in between sections.

☐ Change the <H2> tags to <H1> for more emphasis of the individual sections.

Figure 5.22.

The Bookworm home page, almost done.

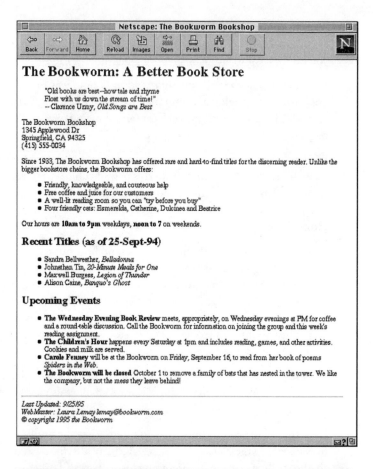

Figure 5.23.

A problem section.

With such design issues, your decision often comes down to a matter of preference and what looks the best in as many browsers as you can get your hands on. Either choice is equally correct, as both are visually interesting, and you don't have to do strange things in HTML to get the design to do what you want.

I settled on a single rule line between the description and the Recent Titles section. Figure 5.24 shows how it came out.

Figure 5.24.

The improved Bookworm home page.

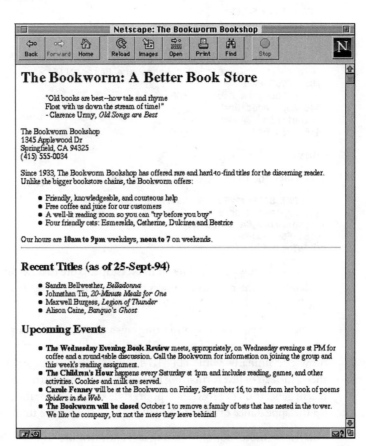

Get Fancy

Everything I've included on the page up to this point has been plain vanilla HTML, so it's readable in all browsers and will look pretty much the same in all browsers. After you get the page to this point, however, you can add some formatting tags and attributes that won't change the page for many readers but might make it look a little fancier in browsers that do support these attributes.

So what attributes do you want to use? I picked two:

☐ Centering the title of the page, the quote, and the bookstore's address

☐ Making a slight font size change to the address itself

To center the topmost part of the page, you can use the <DIV> tag around the heading, the quote, and the bookshop's address, like this:

```
<DIV ALIGN=CENTER>
<H1>The Bookworm: A Better Book Store</H1>
<BLOCKQUOTE>
"Old books are best--how tale and rhyme<BR>
Float with us down the stream of time!"<BR>
- Clarence Urmy, <CITE>Old Songs are Best</CITE>
</BLOCKQUOTE>
<P>The Bookworm Bookshop<BR>
1345 Applewood Dr<BR>
Springfield, CA 94325<BR>
(415) 555-0034
</P>
</DIV>
```

To change the font size of the address, add a <FONT> tag around the lines for the address:

```
<P><FONT SIZE=+1>The Bookworm Bookshop<BR>
1345 Applewood Dr<BR>
Springfield, CA 94325<BR>
(415) 555-0034
</FONT></P>
```

Figure 5.25 shows the final result in Netscape. Note that neither of these changes affects the readability of the page in browsers that don't support <DIV> or <FONT>; the page still works just fine without them. It just looks different.

When should you use text formatting tags and attributes? The general rule that I like to follow is to use these tags only when using them will not interfere with other, generally older, browsers. Similarly, while HTML 4.0 officially encourages Web page authors to use style sheets instead of text formatting tags such as FONT and attributes such as ALIGN, only the most recent generation of browsers support style sheets. So, for the time being, if you want to spiff up the appearance of your text, you'll need to continue to use these tags and attributes.

You'll learn more about formatting tags and attributes as well as how to design well with them in Chapter 9, "Writing and Designing Web Pages: Dos and Don'ts." And we'll talk about how to use style sheets in Chapter 18, "Stylizing Your Pages."

Figure 5.25.

The final Bookworm home page.

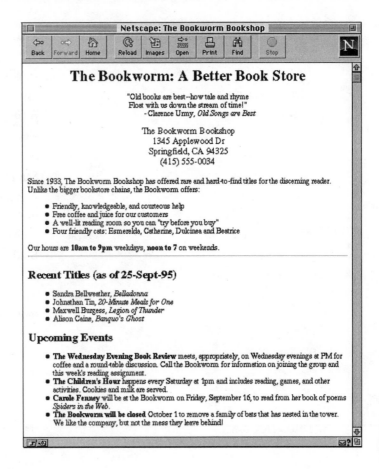

Summary

Tags, tags, and more tags! In this chapter, you learned about most of the remaining tags in the HTML language for presenting text and quite of a few of the tags for additional text formatting and presentation. You also put together a real-life HTML home page. You could stop now and create quite presentable Web pages. But more cool stuff is to come, so don't put down the book yet.

Table 5.2 presents a quick summary of all the tags and attributes you've learned about in this chapter.

Table 5.2. HTML tags from Chapter 5.

Tag	Attribute	Use
`<EM>...</EM>`		Emphasized text.
`<STRONG>...</STRONG>`		Strongly emphasized text.
`<CODE>...</CODE>`		A code sample.
`<KBD>...</KBD>`		Text to be typed in by the user.
`<VAR>...</VAR>`		A variable name.
`<SAMP>...</SAMP>`		Sample text.
`<DFN>...</DFN>`		A definition, or a term about to be defined.
`<CITE>...</CITE>`		A citation.
`<B>...</B>`		Bold text.
`<I>...</I>`		Italic text.
`<TT>...</TT>`		Text in typewriter font (a monospaced font such as Courier).
`<U>...</U>`		(HTML 3.2) Underlined text.
`<S>...</S>`		(HTML 3.2) Strike-through text.
`<BIG>...</BIG>`		(HTML 3.2) Text in a larger font than the text around it.
`<SMALL>...</SMALL>`		(HTML 3.2) Text in a smaller font than the text around it.
`<SUB>...</SUB>`		(HTML 3.2) Subscript text.
`<SUP>...</SUP>`		(HTML 3.2) Superscript text.
`<PRE>...</PRE>`		Preformatted text; all spaces, tabs, and returns are retained. Text is also printed in a monospaced font.
`<HR>`		A horizontal rule line at the given position in the text.
	`SIZE`	The thickness of the rule, in pixels.
	`WIDTH`	The width of the rule, either in exact pixels or as a percentage of page width (for example, 50 percent).

Tag	Attribute	Use
`<HR>`	`ALIGN`	The alignment of the rule on the page. Possible values are `LEFT`, `RIGHT`, and `CENTER`.
	`NOSHADE`	Display the rule without three-dimensional shading.
` `		A line break; start the next character on the next line (but do not create a new paragraph or list item).
`<BLOCKQUOTE>...</BLOCKQUOTE>`		A quotation longer than a few words.
`<ADDRESS>...</ADDRESS>`		A "signature" for each Web page; typically occurs near the bottom of each document and contains contact or copyright information.
`<P>`, `<H1-6>`	`ALIGN=LEFT`	Left-justifies the text within that paragraph or heading.
	`ALIGN=RIGHT`	Right-justifies the text within that paragraph or heading.
	`ALIGN=CENTER`	Centers the text within that paragraph or heading.
`<DIV>...</DIV>`	`ALIGN=LEFT`	Left-justifies all the content between the opening and closing tags.
	`ALIGN=RIGHT`	Right-justifies all the content between the opening and closing tags.
	`ALIGN=CENTER`	Centers all the content between the opening and closing tags.
`<CENTER>...</CENTER>`		Centers all the content between the opening and closing tags.

continues

5

Table 5.2. continued

Tag	Attribute	Use
<FONT>...</FONT>	SIZE	The size of the font to change to, either from 1 to 7 (default is 3) or as a relative number using +N or -N. Relative font sizes are based on the value of <BASEFONT>.
	FACE	The name of the font to change to, as a list of fonts to choose from.
<BASEFONT>	SIZE	The default font size on which relative font size changes are based.
<BLINK>...</BLINK>		(Netscape extension) Causes the enclosed text to have a blinking effect.
<NOBR>...</NOBR>		(Extension) Does not wrap the enclosed text.
<WBR>		(Extension) Wraps the text at this point only if necessary.

NOTE

> The <U>, <S>, <FONT>, and <BASEFONT> tags and the SIZE, WIDTH, and ALIGN attributes are "deprecated"—supported but discouraged—in HTML 4.0 in favor of style sheets.

Q&A

Q **If line breaks appear in HTML, can I also do page breaks?**

A HTML doesn't have a page break tag. Consider what the term "page" means in a Web document. If each document on the Web is a single "page," then the only way to produce a page break is to split your HTML document into separate files and link them.

5

Even within a single document, browsers have no concept of a page; each HTML document simply scrolls by continuously. If you consider a single screen a page, you still cannot have what results in a page break in HTML because the screen size in each browser is different and is based on not only the browser itself but the size of the monitor on which it runs, the number of lines defined, the font being currently used, and other factors that you cannot control from HTML.

When you're designing your Web pages, don't get too hung up on the concept of a "page" the way it exists in paper documents. Remember, HTML's strength is its flexibility for multiple kinds of systems and formats. Think instead in terms of creating small chunks of information and how they link together to form a complete presentation.

Q What about that pop quiz you threatened?

A OK, smarty. Without looking at Table 5.2, list all eight logical style tags and what they're used for. Explain why you should use the logical tags instead of the physical tags. Then create an HTML page that uses each one in a sentence, and test it in several browsers to get a feel for how it looks in each.

Q How can I include em dashes or curly quotes (typesetter's quotes) in my HTML files?

A You can't. Neither em dashes nor curly quotes are defined as part of the ISO-Latin-1 character set, and therefore those characters are not available in HTML at the moment. HTML 4.0 fixes this problem with its support for Unicode, which provides access to a much richer character set.

Q "BLINK is the HTML equivalent of fingernails on a blackboard"? Isn't that a little harsh?

A I couldn't resist. :)

Many people absolutely detest BLINK and will tell you so at a moment's notice, with a passion usually reserved for politics and religion. Some people might ignore your pages simply because you use BLINK. Why alienate your audience and distract from your content for the sake of a cheesy effect?

5

Chapter **6**

HTML Assistants: Editors and Converters

After the bushel of tags and HTML information I've thrown at you over the last couple of chapters, you're probably just the smallest bit overwhelmed. You may be wondering how on earth you're supposed to remember all these tags and all their various attributes, remember which tags go where and which ones have opening and closing tags, and a host of other details.

After you've written a few thousand HTML pages, remembering all these details isn't very difficult. But until you do have that many pages under your belt, sometimes keeping this information in mind can be rough, particularly if you're writing all your HTML files in a plain text editor.

At this point, HTML editors and converters come into play. Both HTML editors and converters make writing HTML files easier—or at least they help you get started and often take away a lot of the drudgery in composing HTML. In this chapter, I'll describe some of the more common editors and converters that claim to make writing HTML easier. These tools fall into the following categories:

☐ Tag editors—text editors that help you create HTML files by inserting tags or managing links

☐ WYSIWYG and near-WYSIWYG editors

☐ Converters—programs that let you convert files created by popular word processing programs or other formats to HTML

This chapter is by no means a complete catalog of the available tools for HTML, only a sample of some of the more popular tools for various platforms. HTML tools sprout like weeds, and by the time you read this chapter, newer, better, and more powerful tools for HTML development are likely to be available. For this reason, Appendix A, "Sources for Further Information," provides some pointers to lists of editors and filters. These lists are constantly updated and are the best sources for finding tools that may not be described in this chapter.

Do You Need an Editor?

Technically you don't need a special HTML editor to create pages for the Web. In fact, it could be argued that one of the reasons the Web became so popular so quickly was that you didn't need any special equipment to publish on the Web. You didn't have to buy a lot of software or upgrade your computer system. Creating pages for publishing on the Web was, and still is, free.

The Web has changed a lot, though. HTML itself has grown a great deal since those days, not only in the number of available tags, but also in complexity. If you're like me and you've been following HTML while it's been changing, the changes haven't been that bad. But if you're just starting out now, you've got a lot of catching up to do.

Editors can help you get over the initial hurdles. They can help you keep track of the tags and create basic pages. If you're interested in learning HTML in depth, these editors can help teach you good HTML coding style and structure so that when you move on to more advanced forms of HTML, you have that baseline to build on. For this reason, you may find that investing a little cash in an editor may pay off in the long run.

Later, after you've created several pages and you understand how HTML works, you might find that the editor you're working with isn't quite as useful as it was when you started out. You might find it fine for creating simple pages or for the first initial pass of a page, but not quite as good for adding advanced stuff. Then you may end up working in a plain text editor after all.

Try a couple of the editors in this chapter. All are available in trial versions for downloading, so you don't face any initial cost or risk.

6

Tag Editors

Tag editor is a term I use to describe a simple stand-alone text editor or an extension to another editor. Tag editors help you write HTML documents by inserting the tags for you. They make no claim to being WYSIWYG—all they do is save you some typing, and they help you remember which tags are which. Instead of trying to remember which tag is which or having to type both the opening and closing parts of a long tag by hand, you can use a tag editor, which usually provides windows or buttons with meaningful names that insert the tag into the text for you at the appropriate spot. You're still working with text, and you're still working directly in HTML, but tag editors take away a lot of the drudgery involved in creating HTML documents.

Most tag editors work best if you already have a document prepared in regular text with none of the tags. Using tag editors as you type a document is slightly more difficult. It's best to type the text and then apply the style after you're done.

HTML Assistant Pro 97 (Windows)

HTML Assistant Pro 97 (shown in Figure 6.1), by Harold Harawitz and distributed by Brooklyn North Software Works, was one of the first HTML editors, and it continues to be one of the best and most popular. Using buttons from a toolbar and various menu commands, you can use HTML Assistant to insert HTML tags as you type and to preview the result with your favorite browser. The interface is simple and intuitive, with all the important tags available on a toolbar.

Figure 6.1.

HTML Assistant.

To get the most use out of HTML Assistant, you'll need to know at least the basics of HTML and preferably have a good idea of which tags go where and what they are used for. If HTML Assistant doesn't currently support a tag, you can add it to a User Tools menu and then insert the tag with the click of a mouse button.

One of its best features is the capability to get URLs from visits to the Web so that you can use them in your pages as links. A form assistant and table assistant help ease the process of designing these more complex HTML structures. Support for ActiveX, Java applets, and scripts brings this version of HTML Assistant Pro right up-to-date.

Visit the home page for HTML Assistant Pro 97 at http://www.brooknorth.com/pro97.html. An electronic version of HTML Assistant Pro 97 sells for $89.95, and the boxed version is $99.95. An older version of the software, HTML Assistant Pro 3 is available at the same price but is a 16-bit application for Windows 3.1, whereas Pro 97 runs on Windows 95.

HotDog (Windows)

HotDog, from Sausage Software, is a full-featured HTML tag editor with support for just about every HTML feature, either existing or proposed—even style sheets. Like HTML Assistant, HotDog has two versions: an original 16-bit version, which should be fine for most people doing basic HTML work, and a professional version, HotDog Pro with more features, that runs on Windows 95. Both cost $99.95. Figure 6.2 shows the HotDog main window.

Figure 6.2.

HotDog Pro.

HotDog is intuitive and powerful, allowing you to insert most of the common tags through well-labeled buttons on a toolbar. HotDog Pro includes templates and wizards for creating default formats for pages including placement of company names, contact information, and more. A resource manager provides easy access to open documents, files on your local system, as well as the Web and collections of favorite text, links, and tags that you use regularly. A tabbed window interface provides access to multiple toolbars for inserting tags without creating a toolbar that is too deep at the top of the window.

Also very nice is the tables editor, which builds tables using spreadsheet-like cells. (You haven't learned about tables in HTML yet; you'll learn about them in Chapter 11, "Tables.") You enter your table data and headings into the table cells in the editor, and when you're done, HotDog inserts all the right HTML tags for the table.

HotDog's biggest drawback is the fact that it tries to support everything nearly equally, from basic HTML tags to the advanced Netscape and Internet Explorer extensions to style sheets. Unless you know exactly what you're doing and which tags you should be using, you can easily become confused about what you can use and the results you expect to see in your favorite browser. Plus, you have that many more tags to search through for the one you really want, even if you do know exactly which tags are supported where. The inclusion of all these extra tags may make HotDog very complete, but it complicates the use of an otherwise terrific editor.

You can get more information about both versions from Sausage Software's Web site at http://www.sausage.com/.

WebEdit (Windows)

Like HotDog, WebEdit (shown in Figure 6.3) purports to support the full suite of HTML and Netscape and Microsoft tags including frames, forms, and tables. With WebEdit, like HotDog, you have dozens of tags and options and alternatives to choose from without any distinction of which tags are actually useful for real-life Web presentations. Having these extra tags needlessly complicates the use of the editor for creating simple pages.

If you know which tags to ignore, however, WebEdit becomes a very nice editor to work in. The toolbar provides immediate access to each element.

WebEdit allows you to preview your work either in the browser of your choice or in a built-in previewer. The previewer is particularly interesting, as it allows you to edit the page on one side of the screen and view the immediate result on the other side. The previewer supports a subset of the tags available in the editor itself.

WebEdit is available as a downloadable 45-day trial version, after which time you must pay for it. The cost is $109.99 for the professional edition. Find out more about WebEdit from http://www.nesbitt.com/.

6

Figure 6.3.
WebEdit.

HTML.edit (Macintosh)

HTML.edit is a HyperCard-based HTML tag editor, but it does not require HyperCard to run. It provides menus and buttons for inserting HTML tags into text files, as well as features for automatic indexing (for creating hyperlinked table of contents lists) and automatic conversion of text files to HTML. Figure 6.4 shows HTML.edit's editing page.

Figure 6.4.
HTML.edit.

HTML.edit's most interesting feature, however, is its Index page, which collects and organizes a set of related HTML documents, sort of like a project in THINK C or a book file in FrameMaker. After a file is listed on the Index page, the file appears in a list of files that you can link between, so you can create navigation links between related files quickly and easily. The Index page allows you to keep track of your entire presentation and the pages inside it.

I found the interface to HTML.edit somewhat confusing to figure out, but a quick read through the online help answered most of my questions. HTML extensions are included as part of a custom tags menu that can be customized to include any new extensions.

HTML.edit, which is freeware, runs on both 68K and PowerPC Macintoshes. You can get information about HTML.edit from `http://ogopogo.nttc.edu/tools/HTMLedit/HTMLedit.html`.

HTML Web Weaver Lite and World Wide Web Weaver (Macintosh)

HTML Web Weaver Lite and World Wide Web Weaver are similar programs with similar interfaces and philosophies. Both were written by Robert C. Best. HTML Web Weaver Lite is shareware ($25, with a 30-day evaluation period) and has fewer features than the commercial World Wide Web Weaver ($59 basic price, cheaper for education, free upgrades to newer versions). Figure 6.5 shows World Wide Web Weaver.

Both Web Weaver programs are basically tag editors with some WYSIWYG capabilities. Unlike other tag editors, in which all the text and tags are in the same font and size, the Web Weaver programs format the tags in a different color from the rest of the text and also format the text itself. (For example, when you apply a heading to a line of text, the Web Weaver programs increase the font size of the heading.) Both allow you to preview the result in your favorite browser.

Both Web Weaver programs work best when you have a base of text to start with and you apply tags to various portions of the text. I found it difficult to apply tags as I was typing (and you don't get the formatting as easily that way, either).

HTML Web Weaver Lite provides basic capabilities for standard HTML, including forms and images. World Wide Web Weaver has many other features including tables and frames and other HTML capabilities as well as Search and Replace. The home page for both programs notes that few new features will be added to HTML Web Weaver Lite, making World Wide Web Weaver most likely the better choice of the two. Get more information and download copies of each from `http://www.MiracleInc.com/`.

6

Figure 6.5.

*World Wide Web
Weaver.*

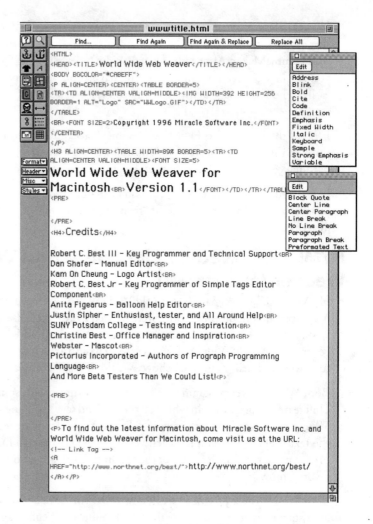

HTML Extensions for Alpha and BBedit (Macintosh)

Alpha and BBedit are two of the more popular shareware text editors available for the Macintosh. Both provide mechanisms to add extensions for working in particular languages and writing text that conforms to a particular style. You can find extensions for both Alpha and BBedit to help with writing HTML pages.

Using a standard text editor with extensions poses significant advantages as opposed to using a dedicated HTML tag editor. For one, general text editors tend to provide more features for writing than simple HTML text editors, including Search and Replace and spell checking. Also, if you're used to working in one of these editors, being able to continue to use it for your HTML development means that you don't have to take the time to learn a new program to do your work.

If you use the Alpha editor, versions after 5.92b (current version is 6.51) include the HTML extensions in the main distribution. You can get Alpha and its HTML extensions from `ftp://cs.rice.edu/public/Alpha/`.

For BBedit, the BBedit HTML extensions are available from most Mac shareware archives or from `http://www.uji.es/bbedit-html-extensions.html`.

tkHTML (UNIX/X11)

tkHTML, by Liem Bahneman, is a simple freeware graphical HTML tag editor for the X11 Windows System that uses the TCL language and the tk toolkit; you don't need to have either installed. Menu items allow you to insert tags into your text, either by inserting the tag and then typing, or by selecting text and choosing the tag the text should have. tkHTML allows you to convert existing text to HTML easily, and a Preview button automatically previews your HTML files using Netscape, Mosaic, or Lynx. (Netscape is the default.) Figure 6.6 shows tkHTML.

Figure 6.6.
tkHTML.

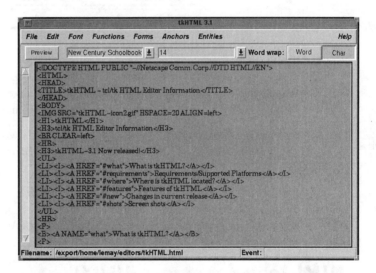

tkHTML supports all of standard HTML and many extensions, including those for tables. You can get more information about tkHTML from `http://www.cobaltgroup.com/~roland/tkHTML/tkHTML.html`.

AsWedit (UNIX)

AsWedit (short for AdvaSoft's Web Editor, presumably, and shown in Figure 6.7), also for the X Window System running Motif and available for many different UNIX flavors, is a context-sensitive HTML editor. Context-sensitive means that different tags and options are available depending on where you've put the cursor in the HTML code. If the cursor is inside a list, for example, the only choice you have is to include a list item.

Figure 6.7.
AsWedit.

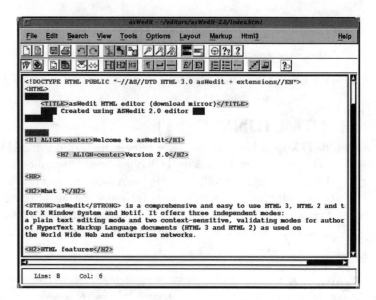

Context sensitivity makes editing using AsWedit interesting, as it forces you to use correct HTML style at all times. Figuring out what was going on was confusing for me when I first tried using it, and if you don't already have a basic idea of what HTML can do and what tags are available in what context, AsWedit can be confusing to use.

AsWedit supports all of standard HTML, as well as most HTML extensions. It also provides an option to disable newer features so that the only available tags are from the standard HTML set.

Two versions of AsWedit are available: a basic version, free for educational users and for evaluation by others, and a $149 commercial version with more features, support, and a manual. You can get information about both versions from AdvaSoft's home page at `http://www.advasoft.com/`.

HTML Tools for emacs (UNIX)

If you prefer to work in emacs, the popular text editor-slash-kitchen sink, you can choose from several emacs packages (modes), including the following:

- [ ] html-mode, the original mode for writing HTML, available at `ftp://archive.cis.ohio-state.edu/pub/gnu/emacs/elisp-archive/modes/html-mode.el.Z`.

- [ ] html-helper-mode, an enhanced version of the preceding. You can get information about it at `http://www.santafe.edu/~nelson/tools/`.

If you use emacs extensively, you might also want to look at William Perry's emacs w3-mode, which turns emacs into a fully featured Web browser with support for most advanced features of HTML. It includes support for HTML 3.2, some Netscape extensions, cascading style sheets and just about anything else you can imagine. Get more information about w3-mode from `http://www.cs.indiana.edu/elisp/w3/docs.html`.

WYSIWYG and Near-WYSIWYG Editors

The concept of a true WYSIWYG (what you see is what you get) editor for HTML files is a bit of a fallacy because (as I've harped on earlier) each browser formats HTML documents in different ways, for different size screens. However, for simple documents, if you have an understanding of what HTML can and cannot do, the editors described in this section can be just fine for creating simple pages and presentations.

In this section, I've made the distinction between WYSIWYG and "near-WYSIWYG" editors. The former are editors that claim to allow you to write HTML files without ever seeing a single tag; everything you need to create an HTML page is available directly in the program.

"Near-WYSIWYG" editors provide a WYSIWYG environment without trying overly hard to hide the tags. They may allow you to toggle between a tag view and a WYSIWYG view, or you might be able to view the tags using a menu item.

Netscape Composer (Windows, Macintosh, UNIX)

Starting with Netscape Communicator, currently in preview release, Netscape is introducing Composer, an upgraded version of the editor found in Netscape Navigator Gold 3.0. (See Figure 6.18.)

If you're used to using Netscape as your browser (as most of you probably are), Navigator Composer will look quite familiar. It enables you to edit documents; you can change the text, add new HTML elements, rearrange formatting, and change colors.

The Netscape HTML editor is very nicely done, with HTML elements all available through toolbar items with well-designed icons and an intuitive layout. The integration with the Communicator environment means that in many cases you can view your pages on a server, make changes to them using the editor, and then upload them back to the server in a few easy steps. In addition, Composer is the editor used in Communicator's Mail and Newsgroup components, thus making it a single editing tool for the whole environment.

Netscape Composer supports many common HTML tags, including, of course, the Netscape HTML extensions. New or unsupported tags can be entered by hand. An obvious omission from Composer's feature set is automatic tools for creating forms, although tables, unsupported in Navigator Gold 3.0, are now in place.

6

Figure 6.8.

Netscape Composer.

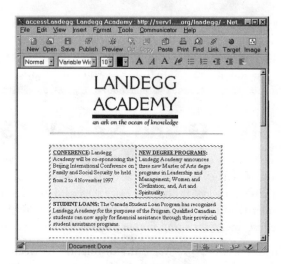

You can download Communicator (which includes Composer) from the Netscape site at
`http://home.netscape.com/`. Communicator is free for educational and nonprofit use, with
an evaluation period for everyone else.

Microsoft FrontPage Express (Windows)

As if to compete with Netscape, which introduced an integrated editor in Navigator 3.0 and
now includes Composer in Communicator, Microsoft has added a page editor to Internet
Explorer 4.0. It's called FrontPage Express, which is derived from its FrontPage site creation
software. (See Figure 6.9.)

Figure 6.9.

FrontPage Express.

FrontPage Express offers the standard features you would expect in a WYSIWYG editor including a toolbar for the most common formatting options. It also provides support for a healthy collection of HTML standard and extension tags including the insertion of ActiveX controls and background sounds.

Noticeably lacking, however, is table support, although you can insert external HTML files into a FrontPage document. You can find more information about the Internet Explorer 4.0 package at `http://www.microsoft.com/ie/ie40/`.

SoftQuad HoTMetaL Pro 3.0 (Windows)

SoftQuad HoTMetaL Pro, as shown in Figure 6.10, is a unique editor that allows very near-WYSIWYG capabilities without trying to hide the fact that you're still working very much in HTML. In HoTMetaL, the tags are represented by flag-type objects that can be inserted only in legal places on the page. So, for example, you can't put regular paragraphs into a <HEAD> section. This is a good thing; it means that if you use HoTMetaL, you cannot write an HTML document that does not conform to correct HTML style.

Figure 6.10.

HoTMetaL Pro 3.0.

The text you type in between the HTML tag objects appears in a font roughly equivalent to what might appear on your screen in a graphical browser. You can also choose to hide the tags so that you can get a better idea of what it'll look like when you're done.

HoTMetaL Professional 3.0, which sells for $159, has all the basic capabilities and support for HTML 2.0, HTML 3.2, and all the Netscape extensions, plus a spell checker, thesaurus, and more (including advanced features such as a dedicated frames editor).

Information about HoTMetaL and SoftQuad's other SGML-based tools is available at http://www.softquad.com/.

PageMill 2.0 (Macintosh, Windows)

Adobe's PageMill, a commercial HTML editor costing $99, bills itself as "The easiest way to create pages for the World Wide Web." Using PageMill is very easy indeed. The main window, shown in Figure 6.11, has a simple toolbar, with most of the main HTML styles (headings, paragraphs, addresses, and character styles) available as menu items. You can enter text and apply styles to the text, or you can choose a style first and then type in the text. For most simple HTML elements, PageMill is indeed WYSIWYG and very easy to use.

Figure 6.11.

PageMill (editing Adobe's Product Pages).

PageMill's handling of images and links is particularly nice, allowing you to drag and drop images onto a page, and drag and drop between open pages to link between them. Double-clicking images brings up an image window with features for applying special image tricks such as transparency and interlacing.

PageMill supports many of the currently popular HTML tags and extensions, including backgrounds, tables, and forms. You can enter raw HTML tags onto the page in the appropriate places for the new features that aren't supported (which defeats the purpose of being WYSIWYG, but at least you're not tied only to what PageMill supports).

One oddity with PageMill is the HTML it generates after you're done creating your pages. Remember the <P> tag, for paragraphs? The common practice now is to close the tag with </P>, but if you don't press Return after the last paragraph of a document, the last <P> tag isn't closed with a </P>.

One nice feature of PageMill 2.0 is the Inspector, which provides a convenient window for accessing properties of pages and elements in your document such as forms and tables.

Overall, PageMill is a great program for simple HTML pages or for putting together a simple program quickly and easily.

Microsoft FrontPage (Windows)

Microsoft's FrontPage, formerly owned by a company called Vermeer, is an integrated Web site construction and maintenance kit that includes a Web site administration tool, a Web server, and various other tools for administering the entire package. The Web page editor (FrontPage Editor, as shown in Figure 6.12) is only a small part of the overall package.

Figure 6.12.

The FrontPage editor.

The editor is easy to work with, although it has a few peculiarities. Although most of the editors let you either select an element and then type, or type first and then change the style, the FrontPage editor separates these two functions. Therefore, you can either insert an element from a menu item and then type in it, or you can select text and change the style using a pull-down menu from the toolbar.

Besides these capabilities, the process of inserting and adding elements is straightforward. Because the editor is tied closely to a browser and a server, you can quickly and easily link between pages and load files and images from the Web.

Part of the FrontPage package is an enormous set of templates and wizards for creating different kinds of Web pages, so you can quickly and easily start and build a Web page or an entire presentation. Because I'm more used to working from scratch, sometimes the many different options were confusing to me, but for beginners, starting from templates might be easier than starting from a blank page.

An integrated Image Composer is designed to make it quick and easy to produce your own graphics for your Web site. In addition, support for database connectivity and scripting (both VBScript and Jscript) makes FrontPage a strong all-around Web development package.

The complete FrontPage package is available for Windows NT and Windows 95. A version of FrontPage is also available for the Macintosh. You can find information about FrontPage at `http://www.microsoft.com/frontpage`.

GNNpress (Windows, Macintosh)

AOLpress, formerly GNNpress, is an integrated browser and HTML editor in much the same vein as Netscape Communicator's Navigator and Composer components. Using AOLpress, you can browse to pages that interest you, edit them in the same window, and then, if you own the pages, save them back to the server where they came from.

AOLpress is right up there with Netscape Composer in terms of ease of use.

One interesting feature of AOLpress is the ability to create miniwebs, which are collections of related pages (what I've been calling Web presentations). When you create a miniweb, you can add pages and link between them fairly easily. In a miniweb window, you can see a graphical representation of your collection of pages.

AOLpress supports most of HTML, including frames. The forms editor is particularly nice, allowing you to insert form elements very quickly and using a dotted line on the page to indicate the current form. (This feature is very useful if you're using pages with multiple forms.)

AOLpress is the client half of an HTML publishing system, the other half being AOLserver. The combination of the two allows you to edit HTML pages anywhere on the Web and then save them back to the server (assuming you have the right access permissions, of course).

AOLpress, which is free, is available for Windows, Macintosh, and is in beta for many flavors of UNIX. Get more information about AOLpress and AOLserver at `http://www.aolpress.com/`.

HTML Editor (Macintosh)

HTML Editor, shown in Figure 6.13, is a freeware editor that lets you insert tags into your file and see the result in a WYSIWYG fashion—at the same time. The tags are shown in a lighter color than the surrounding text, and the text looks like it would look in Netscape or Mosaic, although you can change the appearance of any style and apply it throughout the document. You can choose options to hide the tags in your document to get the full effect, and you can also preview the document using your favorite browser.

Figure 6.13.

HTML Editor.

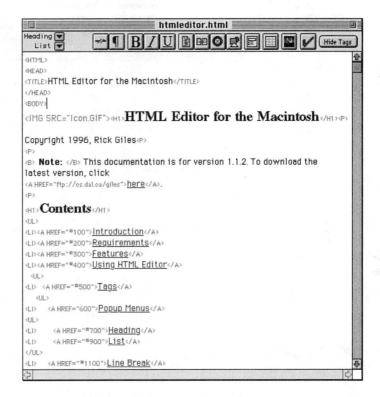

HTML Editor's current version is 1.1.2. It supports only the basic HTML 2.0 tags, not including forms. It does not include any of the Netscape extensions or HTML 3.2 tags. It has a feature for including custom tags, however, so you can customize the application to include these new tags.

The documentation for HTML Editor is available at `http://dragon.acadiau.ca/~giles/HTML_Editor/Documentation.html`. You can get the actual package from `ftp://cs.dal.ca/giles/HTML_Editor_1.0.sit.hqx`.

6

NetObjects Fusion

Fusion, from NetObjects, is a unique site management and page creation tool for developing Web sites (see Figure 6.14). It provides various models for viewing content including styles that define page elements such as banners, navigation bars, and links; pages that allow you to edit individual pages and create and edit common components that appear on all pages; and a site tree viewer that allows you to move pages around in a site's hierarchy of documents.

Figure 6.14.

NetObjects Fusion.

Fusion offers a variety of dynamic components including discussion groups, dynamic Java navigation buttons, and data access components for database publishing. Information is available at NetObjects' Web site at http://www.netobjects.com/.

Converters

What if you prefer not to work in HTML at all—you have your own tool or language that you're familiar with, and you prefer to work with it? Many programs convert different formats into HTML. In this section, I describe some of these converters.

If you use a commercial word processor, and you don't see a converter listed here or among the lists of converters in Appendix A, try calling the vendor of that particular word processor. Conversion to HTML has been a hot topic for most word processing and desktop publishing companies, and the company may have a converter available.

Lists of converters from many formats to HTML are also maintained at Yahoo! at http://www.yahoo.com/Computers_and_Internet/Software/Internet/World_Wide_Web/HTML_Converters/ and at NCSA at http://union.ncsa.uiuc.edu/HyperNews/get/www/html/converters.html.

Plain Text

In many cases, simple HTML editors can add HTML tags quickly to text files, or simply adding <PRE> tags to the beginning and end of a text file is a quick-and-dirty solution. Actual converter programs do, however, exist. For UNIX, two programs, both called text2html, will do the job. See either `http://www.seas.upenn.edu/~mengwong/txt2html.html` or `http://www.cs.wustl.edu/~seth/txt2html/` for more information.

For the Macintosh, two programs called HTML Markup and text2html will create HTML files if you drag and drop a text file onto its icon. You can get either of these programs from various Mac shareware archives; try `http://www.shareware.com/`.

Microsoft Word

You can use Microsoft's Internet Assistant to convert Word documents to HTML easily. You can find it on Microsoft's Web site at `http://www.microsoft.com/sbnmember/download/download.asp`. You can also use QuarterDeck's WebAuthor 2.5 as a conversion tool for Word for Windows files. Find out about WebAuthor from `http://arachnid.qdeck.com/qdeck/products/WebAuthr/`.

Microsoft Word can also export files in RTF (Rich Text Format), which can then be converted into HTML if you use various RTF converters.

RTF (Rich Text Format)

RTF format is output by many popular word processing and page layout programs, and in many cases using it can be the easiest route from many programs to HTML. To convert RTF to HTML on Mac and UNIX, you can get the terrific rtftohtml program, which is the most comprehensive tool out there. Find out more about it at `http://www.sunpack.com/RTF/rtftohtml_overview.html`. For Windows, a version of rtftohtml is promised but is not yet available. However, a package called Tag Perfect, available at most Windows shareware servers (try `http://www.shareware.com/`), also converts RTF to HTML.

Quark XPress

If you use Quark XPress, you can either use the RTF converter mentioned in the preceding section, or you can export your Quark Files to tagged text and then use the Macintosh or UNIX filter described at `http://the-tech.mit.edu/~jeremy/qt2www.html`.

PageMaker

PageMaker 6.5 allows you to create HTML files using its HTML plug-in. If you're using PageMaker, this method may be the quickest way to convert your files to HTML.

You also can use Mitch Cohen's PageMaker Websucker, which is a HyperCard stack that extracts the text from PageMaker files and turns it into HTML. Check `http://www.msystems.com/mcohen/websucker.html` for more information.

6

Working Directly in HTML Versus Using a Converter

With all these converters from word processors to HTML, you can often do most of your HTML development in those programs and deal with converting the files to HTML at the last minute. For many projects, this approach may be the way to go.

Consider the advantages of using a converter:

- ☐ You do not have to keep track of tags. Having to memorize and know the rules of how tags work is a major issue if all you want to do is write.
- ☐ Fewer errors end up in HTML documents (misspellings, missing close tags, overlapping tags). Because the HTML is automatically generated, there's less chance of "operator error" in the final output.
- ☐ You can use a tool you're familiar with. If you know MS Word and live and die by MS Word, you can work in MS Word.

On the other hand, working in a converter is not a panacea. Pitfalls do exist, including the following:

- ☐ No tools can provide all the features of HTML, particularly with links to external documents. Some handworking of the final HTML files will generally be required after you convert.
- ☐ You have to address the split-source issue. After you convert your files from their original form to HTML, you have to monitor two sources. To make changes after the conversion, you will either have to change the original and regenerate the HTML (wiping out any hand-massaging you did to those files), or you'll have to make sure you make the changes to *both* the original source and the HTML documents. For large projects, splitting the source at any time except the very last minute can create enormous headaches for everyone involved.

Working directly in HTML, for all its hideous text-only markup what-you-see-is-nothing-like-what-you-get glory, does have advantages, including the following:

- ☐ All your work is done in one file; no extra step is required to generate the final version.
- ☐ HTML files are text only, making it possible for them to be filtered through programs that can easily perform automatic tasks such as generating tables of contents of major headings (and hyperlinking them back to the headings), or testing for the validity of the links in the files. The files can also easily be put under source code control.

☐ You have the full flexibility of the HTML language, including the ability to code new features as they appear, instead of having to wait for the next revision of the converter.

Summary

To wind down, I've provided some simple lists of HTML editors and converters to help you in your HTML development. After everything you've learned so far, the prospect of tools to help you must come as a welcome relief. Consider using one or more of the tools mentioned in this chapter; they may help you in producing HTML documents.

You know which HTML tag creates a level-three heading and how to create a map file for clickable images. I hope that, somewhere along the line so far, you've picked up some ideas for designing and structuring your documents so that they can be read and navigated quickly and easily and serve the demands of your readers.

Q&A

Q You, as an author of HTML books, probably know HTML pretty well. What HTML editor do you use?

A For the vast majority of my HTML work, I use a plain old text editor: emacs on a UNIX system or Alpha on a Macintosh. However, many of the editors I've reviewed in this chapter have impressed me, HotDog and Netscape Composer in particular, so I might start using an editor for some of the more basic pages. I don't think anything will entirely replace working directly with the tags, however; it's difficult for an editor to be able to keep up with the rapid changes in HTML technology and still be easy to use.

Images, Backgrounds, and Multimedia

Chapter **7**

Using Images, Color, and Backgrounds

If you've been struggling to keep up with all the HTML tags I've been flinging at you over the last couple of days, you can breathe easier: today's chapter will be easier. In fact, today you're going to learn very few new HTML tags. The focus for today is on adding images and color to your Web pages. In this chapter, you'll learn about the HTML codes for adding images, color, and backgrounds. In particular, you'll learn the following:

- ☐ The kinds of images you can use in Web pages
- ☐ How to include images on your Web page, either alone or alongside text
- ☐ How to use images as clickable links
- ☐ How to use external images as a substitute for or in addition to inline images
- ☐ How to provide alternatives for browsers that cannot view images

☐ How to use image dimensions and scaling and how to provide image previews

☐ How to change the font and background colors in your Web page

☐ How to use images for tiled page backgrounds

☐ How (and when) to use images in your Web pages

After this chapter, you'll know all you need to know about adding images to your Web pages.

Images on the Web

Images for Web pages fall into two general classes: inline images and external images. Inline images appear directly on a Web page among the text and links. They are loaded automatically when you load the page itself—assuming, of course, that you have a graphical browser and that you have automatic image loading turned on. External images are not directly displayed when you load a page. They are downloaded only at the request of your readers, usually on the other side of a link. You don't need a graphical browser to view external images; you can download an image file just fine using a text-only browser and then use an image editor or viewer to see that image later on. You'll learn about how to use both inline and external images in this chapter.

 Inline images appear on a Web page along with text and links, and are automatically loaded when the page itself is retrieved.

 External images are stored separate from the Web page and are loaded only on demand, for example, as the result of a link.

Regardless of whether you're using inline or external images, those images must be in a specific format. For inline images, that image has to be in one of two formats: GIF or JPEG. GIF is actually the more popular standard, and more browsers can view inline GIF files than JPEG files. Support for JPEG is becoming more widespread but is still not as popular as GIF, so sticking with GIF is the safest method of making sure your images can be viewed by the widest possible audience. You'll learn more about external images and the formats you can use for them later in this chapter.

For this chapter, assume that you already have an image you want to put on your Web page. How do you get it into GIF or JPEG format so that your page can view it? Most image-editing programs such as Adobe Photoshop, Paint Shop Pro, CorelDraw, or XV provide ways to convert between image formats. You may have to look under an option for Save As or Export in order to find it. Freeware and shareware programs that do nothing but convert between image formats are also available for most platforms.

To save files in GIF format, look for an option called CompuServe GIF, GIF87, GIF89, or just plain GIF. Any of them will work. If you're saving your files as JPEG, usually the option will be simply JPEG.

Remember how your HTML files had to have an `.html` or `.htm` extension for them to work properly? Image files have extensions, too. For GIF files, the extension is `.gif`. For JPEG files, the extension is either `.jpg` or `.jpeg`; either will work fine.

NOTE

> Some image editors will try to save files with extensions in all caps (`.GIF`, `.JPEG`). Although they are the correct extensions, image names, like HTML filenames, are case sensitive, so `GIF` is not the same extension as `gif`. The case of the extension isn't important when you're testing on your local system, but it will be when you move your files to the server, so use lowercase if you possibly can.

Inline Images in HTML: The `<IMG>` Tag

After you have an image in GIF or JPEG format ready to go, you can include it in your Web page. Inline images are indicated in HTML using the `<IMG>` tag. The `<IMG>` tag, like the `<HR>` and `<BR>` tags, has no closing tag. It does, however, have many different attributes that allow different ways of presenting and handling inline images. Many of these attributes are part of HTML 3.2 or HTML 4.0 and might not be available in some older browsers.

The most important attribute to the `<IMG>` tag is `SRC`. The `SRC` attribute indicates the filename or URL of the image you want to include, in quotation marks. The pathname to the file uses the same pathname rules as the `HREF` attribute in links. So, for a GIF file named `image.gif` in the same directory as this file, you can use the following tag:

```
<IMG SRC="image.gif">
```

For an image file one directory up from the current directory, use this tag:

```
<IMG SRC="../image.gif">
```

And so on, using the same rules as for page names in the `HREF` part of the `<A>` tag.

7

EXERCISE

Exercise 7.1: Adding images.

Try a simple example. Here's the Web page for a local haunted house that is open every year
at Halloween. Using all the excellent advice I've given you in the preceding six chapters, you
should be able to create a page like this one fairly easily. Here's the HTML code for this
HTML file, and Figure 7.1 shows how it looks so far.

```
<HTML>
<HEAD>
<TITLE>Welcome to the Halloween House of Terror</TITLE>
</HEAD><BODY>
<H1>Welcome to The Halloween House of Terror!!</H1>
<HR>
<P>Voted the most frightening haunted house three years in a row, the
<STRONG>Halloween House of Terror</STRONG> provides the ultimate in
Halloween thrills. Over <STRONG>20 rooms of thrills and excitement</STRONG> to
make your blood run cold and your hair stand on end!</P>
<P>The Halloween House of Terror is open from <EM>October 20 to November
1st</EM>, with a gala celebration on Halloween night. Our hours are:</P>
<UL>
<LI>Mon-Fri 5PM-midnight
<LI>Sat & Sun 5PM-3AM
<LI><STRONG>Halloween Night (31-Oct)</STRONG>: 3PM-???
</UL>
<P>The Halloween House of Terror is located at:<BR>
The Old Waterfall Shopping Center<BR>
1020 Mirabella Ave<BR>
Springfield, CA 94532</P>
</BODY>
</HTML>
```

Figure 7.1.

*The Halloween House
home page.*

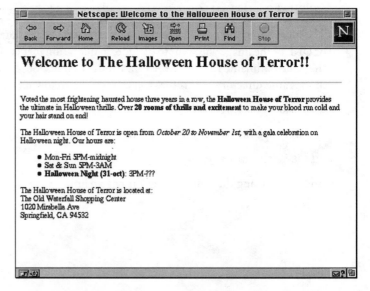

7

So far, so good. Now, you can add an image to the page. I happen to have an image of a spider web (see Figure 7.2) kicking around in a clip art library; it would look excellent at the top of this Web page.

Figure 7.2.
The spider web image.

The image is called `web.gif`, is in GIF format, and is in the same directory as the `halloween.html` page, so it's ready to go into the Web page. Say you want to add this image to this page on its own line so that the heading appears just below it. To do so, add an `<IMG>` tag to the file inside its own paragraph, just before the heading. (Images, like links, don't define their own text elements, so the `<IMG>` tag has to go inside a paragraph or heading element.)

```
<P><IMG SRC="web.gif"></P>
<H1>Welcome to The Halloween House of Terror!!</H1>
```

And now, when you reload the `halloween.html` page, your browser should include the spider web image in the page, as shown in Figure 7.3.

7

Figure 7.3.

The Halloween House home page with the spider web.

If the image doesn't load (if your browser displays a funny-looking icon in its place), first make sure you've specified the name of the file properly in the HTML file. Image filenames are case sensitive, so all the uppercase and lowercase letters have to be the same.

If checking the case doesn't work, double-check the image file to make sure that it is indeed a GIF or JPEG image and that it has the proper file extension.

Finally, make sure that you have image loading turned on in your browser. (The option is called Auto Load Images in both Netscape and Mosaic.)

If one spider is good, two would be really good, right? Try adding another <IMG> tag next to the first one, as follows, and see what happens:

```
<P><IMG SRC="web.gif"><IMG SRC="web.gif"></P>
<H1>Welcome to The Halloween House of Terror!!</H1>
```

Figure 7.4 shows how the page looks in Netscape, with both images adjacent to each other, as you would expect.

And that's all there is to adding images! No matter what the image or how large or small it is, you now know how to include it on a Web page.

Figure 7.4.
Multiple images.

Images and Text

In the preceding exercise, you put an inline image on a page in its own separate paragraph, with text below the image. You can also include an image inside a line of text. (In fact, this is what the phrase "inline image" actually means—in a line of text.)

To include images inside a line of text, just add the `<IMG>` tag at the appropriate point, inside an element tag (`<H1>`, `<P>`, `<ADDRESS>`, and so on), as in the following line. Figure 7.5 shows the difference that putting the image inline with the heading makes. (I've also shortened the title itself.)

```
<H1><IMG SRC="web.gif">The Halloween House of Terror!!</H1>
```

The image doesn't have to be large, and it doesn't have to be at the beginning of the text. You can include an image anywhere in a block of text, like this:

```
<BLOCKQUOTE>
Love, from whom the world <IMG SRC="world.gif"> begun,<BR>
Hath the secret of the sun. <IMG SRC="sun.gif"> <BR>
Love can tell, and love alone,
Whence the million stars <IMG SRC="star.gif"> were strewn <BR>
Why each atom <IMG SRC="atom.gif"> knows its own. <BR>
--Robert Bridges
</BLOCKQUOTE>
```

Figure 7.6 shows how this block looks.

7

Figure 7.5.

The Halloween House page with an image inside the heading.

Figure 7.6.

Images can go anywhere in text.

Text and Image Alignment

Notice that with these examples of including images in text the image is displayed so that the bottom of the image and the bottom of the text match up. The <IMG> tag also includes an ALIGN attribute, which allows you to align the image upward or downward with the surrounding text or other images in the line.

Standard HTML 2.0 defined three basic values for ALIGN:

ALIGN=TOP	Aligns the top of the image with the topmost part of the line (which may be the top of the text or the top of another image).
ALIGN=MIDDLE	Aligns the center of the image with the middle of the line (usually the baseline of the line of text, not the actual middle of the line).
ALIGN=BOTTOM	Aligns the bottom of the image with the bottom of the line of text.

HTML 3.2 provided two other values: LEFT and RIGHT. These values are discussed in the next section, "Wrapping Text Next to Images."

NOTE

The ALIGN attribute for the <IMG> tag is deprecated in HTML 4.0.

In addition to the preceding values, several non-standard values for ALIGN provide greater control over precisely where the image will be aligned within the line. The following values are all supported by Netscape, but were not part of HTML 3.2.

ALIGN=TEXTTTOP	Aligns the top of the image with the top of the tallest text in the line (whereas ALIGN=TOP aligns the image with the topmost item in the line).
ALIGN=ABSMIDDLE	Aligns the middle of the image with the middle of the largest item in the line. (ALIGN=MIDDLE usually aligns the middle of the image with the baseline of the text, not its actual middle.)
ALIGN=BASELINE	Aligns the bottom of the image with the baseline of the text.
ALIGN=ABSBOTTOM	Aligns the bottom of the image with the lowest item in the line (which may be below the baseline of the text).

Figure 7.7 shows examples of all these alignment options. In each case, the line on the left side and the text are aligned to each other, and the arrow varies.

Figure 7.7.

Netscape alignment options.

Wrapping Text Next to Images

Including an image inside a line works fine if you have only one line of text. One aspect of inline images I have sneakily avoided mentioning up to this point is that in HTML 2.0 this alignment worked only with a single line of text. If you had multiple lines of text, and you included an image in the middle of it, all the text around the image (except for the one line) appeared above and below that image. Figure 7.8 shows such an example.

Figure 7.8.

Text does not wrap around images.

What if you wanted to wrap multiple lines of text next to an image so you had text surrounding all sides? Using HTML 2.0, you couldn't. You were restricted to just a single line of text on either side of the image, which limited the kinds of designs you could do.

To get around this limitation in HTML 2.0, Netscape defined two new values for the ALIGN attribute of the <IMG> tag: LEFT and RIGHT. These values were incorporated into HTML 3.2 and are supported now by many browsers other than Netscape.

ALIGN=LEFT and ALIGN=RIGHT

ALIGN=LEFT aligns an image to the left margin, and ALIGN=RIGHT aligns an image to the right margin. But using these attributes also causes any text following the image to be displayed in the space to the right or left of that image, depending on the margin alignment. Figure 7.9 shows an image with some text aligned next to it.

You can put any HTML text (paragraphs, lists, headings, or other images) after an aligned image, and the text will be wrapped into the space between the image and the margin (or you can also have images on both margins and put the text between them). The browser fills in the space with text to the bottom of the image and then continues filling in the text beneath the image.

Figure 7.9.

Text and images aligned.

Stopping Text Wrapping

What if you want to stop filling in the space and start the next line underneath the image? A normal line break won't do it; it'll just break the line to the current margin alongside the image. A new paragraph will also continue wrapping the text alongside the image. To stop wrapping text next to an image, use a line break tag (<BR>) with the attribute CLEAR. With the CLEAR attribute, you can break the line so that the next line of text begins after the end of the image (all the way to the margin). See Figure 7.10 for an example; I've used a smaller image here than the one in the preceding example so that the line break is more visible.

Figure 7.10.

Line break to a clear margin.

The CLEAR attribute can have one of three values:

LEFT	Break to an empty left margin, for left-aligned images
RIGHT	Break to an empty right margin, for right-aligned images
ALL	Break to a line clear to both margins

7

The following code snippet, for example, shows a picture of a tulip with some text wrapped next to it. A line break with CLEAR=LEFT breaks the text wrapping and restarts the text after the image.

```
<P><IMG ALIGN=LEFT SRC="tulipsmall.gif">
<H2>Mystery Tulip Murderer Strikes</H2>
<P>Someone, or something, is killing the tulips of New South Haverford,
Virginia.  Residents of this small town are shocked and dismayed by the
senseless vandalism that has struck their tiny town.</P>
<BR CLEAR=LEFT>
<P>New South Haverford is known for its extravagant displays of tulips
in the springtime, and a good portion of its tourist trade relies on the
people who come from as far as New Hampshire to see what has been estimated
as up to two hundred thousand tulips that bloom in April and May.</P>
```

Text Wrapping in Older Browsers

Given that ALIGN=LEFT and ALIGN=RIGHT are newer features to HTML, take note about what happens if a page that includes these features is viewed in a browser that doesn't support left and right alignment. Usually, you'll just lose the formatting; the text will appear below the image rather than next to it. However, because the first line of text will still appear next to the image, the text may break in odd places. Something as simple as putting a <BR> after the image (which does little in Netscape or other browsers that support text wrapping, but pushes all the text after the image on other browsers) can create an effect that works well both in the browsers that support image and text wrapping and those that don't. Be sure to test your pages in multiple browsers so that you know what the effect will be.

For example, the following input and output example shows the HTML code for a page for Papillon Enterprises, a fictional company that designs Web pages. Figure 7.11 shows the result in Netscape, and Figure 7.12 shows the result in a browser called MacWeb (which does not have image and text wrapping capabilities).

INPUT
```
<H1><IMG SRC="butterfly.gif" ALIGN=RIGHT ALIGN=MIDDLE>
Papillon Enterprises</H1>
<P>Design, Writing, Illustration, and Programming for the
<B>World Wide Web</B></P>
<P>Specializing in:</P>
<UL>
<LI>HTML and Web Page Design
<LI>Illustration
<LI>Forms Design and Programming
<LI>Complete Web Server Installation
</UL>
<HR>
```

Figure 7.11.
The output in Netscape.

Figure 7.12.
*The output in MacWeb
(no image alignment).*

Adjusting the Space Around Images

With the ability to wrap text around an image, you also might want to adjust the amount of space around that image. The VSPACE and HSPACE attributes (introduced in HTML 3.2) allow you to make these adjustments. Both take values in pixels; VSPACE controls the space above and below the image, and HSPACE controls the space to the left and the right.

The following HTML code produces the effect shown in Figure 7.13:

```
<P><IMG SRC="eggplant.gif" VSPACE=30 HSPACE=30 ALIGN=LEFT>
This is an eggplant. We intend to stay a good ways away from it,
because we really don't like eggplant very much.</P>
```

7

Figure 7.13.

Image spacing.

Images and Links

Can an image serve as a link? Sure it can! If you include an `<IMG>` tag inside the opening and closing parts of a link tag (`<A>`), that image serves as a clickable hot spot for the link itself:

```
<A HREF="index.html"><IMG SRC="uparrow.gif"></A>
```

If you include both an image and text in the anchor, the image and the text become hot spots pointing to the same page:

```
<A HREF="index.html"><IMG SRC="uparrow.gif">Up to Index</A>
```

By default, images that are also hot spots for links appear with borders around them to distinguish them from ordinary non-clickable images, as Figure 7.14 shows.

Figure 7.14.

Images that are also links.

You can change the width of the border around the image using the BORDER attribute to `<IMG>`. The BORDER attribute takes a number, which is the width of the border in pixels. BORDER=0 hides the border entirely.

Be careful when setting BORDER to 0 (zero) for images with links. The border provides a visual indication that the image is also a link. By removing that border, you make it difficult for the readers to know which are plain images and which are hot spots without them having to move the mouse around to find them. If you must use borderless image links, make sure that your design provides some indication that the image is selectable and isn't just a plain image. For example, you might design your images so they actually look like buttons, as shown in Figure 7.15.

Figure 7.15.

Images that look like buttons.

Exercise 7.2: Using navigation icons.

Now you can create a simple example of using images as links. When you have a set of related Web pages among which the navigation takes place in a consistent way (for example, moving forward, back, up, home, and so on), providing a menu of navigation options at the top or bottom of each page makes sense so that your readers know exactly how to find their way through your pages.

This example shows you how to create a set of icons that are used to navigate through a linear set of pages. You have three icons in GIF format: one for forward, one for back, and a third to enable the readers to jump to a global index of the entire page structure.

First, you'll write the HTML structure to support the icons. Here, the page itself isn't very important, so you can just include a shell page. Figure 7.16 shows how the page looks at the beginning.

```
<HTML>
<HEAD>
<TITLE>Motorcycle Maintenance: Removing Spark Plugs</TITLE>
<H1>Removing Spark Plugs</H1>
<P>(include some info about spark plugs here)</P>
<HR>
</BODY>
</HTML>
```

Now, at the bottom of the page, add your images using IMG tags. Figure 7.17 shows the result.

```
<IMG SRC="arrowright.gif">
<IMG SRC="arrowleft.gif">
<IMG SRC="arrowup.gif">
```

Figure 7.16.

The basic page, no icons.

Figure 7.17.

The basic page with icons.

Now, add the anchors to the images to activate them. Figure 7.18 shows the result of this addition.

```
<A HREF="replacing.html"><IMG SRC="arrowright.gif"></A>
<A HREF="ready.html"><IMG SRC="arrowleft.gif"></A>
<A HREF="index.html"><IMG SRC="arrowup.gif""></A>
```

Figure 7.18.

The basic page with iconic links.

When you click on the icons now, the browser jumps to the page in the link just as it would have if you had used text links.

Speaking of text, are the icons usable enough as they are? How about adding some text describing exactly what is on the other side of the link? You can add the text inside or outside the anchor, depending on whether you want the text to be a hot spot for the link as well. Here, include it outside the link so that only the icon serves as the hot spot. You can also align the bottoms of the text and the icons using the ALIGN attribute of the <IMG> tag. Finally, because the extra text causes the icons to move onto two lines, arrange each one on its own line instead. See Figure 7.19 for the final menu.

```
<P>
<A HREF="replacing.html"><IMG SRC="arrowright.gif" ALIGN=BOTTOM></A>
On to "Gapping the New Plugs"<BR>
<A HREF="ready.html"><IMG SRC="arrowleft.gif" ALIGN=BOTTOM></A>
Back to "When You Should Replace your Spark Plugs"<BR>
<A HREF="index.html"><IMG SRC="arrowup.gif" ALIGN=BOTTOM></A>
Up To Index
</P>
```

Figure 7.19.
The basic page with iconic links and text.

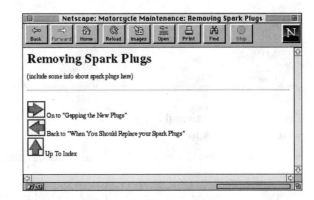

Using External Images

Unlike inline images, external images don't actually appear on your Web page; instead, they're stored separate from the page and linked from that page in much the same way that other HTML pages are.

The reason external images are worth mentioning in this chapter is that external images often can serve a complementary role to inline images. For example,

- ☐ Most Web browsers support inline GIF images, and many of them support inline JPEG images as well. However, most browsers support a much wider array of image formats through the use of external image files and helper applications. So, by using external images, you can use many other image formats besides GIF and JPEG—for example, BMP (Windows bitmaps) or PICT (Macintosh bitmaps).

- ☐ Text-only browsers can't display images inline with Web pages, but you can download external images with a text-only browser and view them with an image-editing or viewing program.

- ☐ You can combine a small inline image on your Web page that loads quickly with a larger, more detailed external image. This way, if readers want to see more, they can choose to load the image themselves.

7

To use external images, you create the image as you would an inline image and then save it with an appropriate filename. As with other files on the Web, the file extension is important. Depending on the image format, use one of the extensions listed in Table 7.1.

Table 7.1. Image formats and extensions.

Format	Extension
GIF	.gif
JPEG	.jpg, .jpeg
XBM	.xbm
TIFF	.tiff, .tif
BMP	.bmp
PICT	.pict

After you have an external image, all you have to do is create a link to it, the same way you would create a link to another HTML page, like this:

```
<P>I grew some really huge <A HREF="bigtomatos.jpeg">tomatoes</A> in
my garden last year</P>
```

For this next exercise, you'll use inline and external images together.

Exercise 7.3: Linking to external GIF and JPEG files.

A common practice in Web pages is to provide a small GIF image (a "thumbnail") inline on the page itself. You can then link that image to its larger external counterpart. Using this approach has two major advantages over including the entire image inline:

☐ It keeps the size of the Web page small so that the page can be downloaded quickly.

☐ It gives your readers a "taste" of the image so they can choose to download the entire image if they want to see more or get a better view.

In this simple example, you'll set up a link between a small image and an external, larger version of that same image. The large image is a photograph of some penguins in GIF format, called `penguinsbig.gif`. It is shown in Figure 7.20.

First, create a thumbnail version of the penguins photograph in your favorite image editor. The thumbnail can be a scaled version of the original file, a clip of that file (say, one penguin out of the group), or anything else you want to use to indicate the larger image.

Here, I've created a picture of one penguin in the group to serve as the inline image. (I've called it `penguinslittle.gif`.) Unlike the large version of the file, which is 100K, the small picture is only 3K. Using the `<IMG>` tag, you can put your image directly on a nearly content-free Web page:

```
<HTML>
<HEAD>
<TITLE>Penguins</TITLE>
</HEAD></BODY>
<H1>Penguins</H1>
<IMG SRC="penguinslittle.gif">
</BODY></HTML>
```

Figure 7.20.

Penguins.

Now, using a link tag, you can link the small icon to the bigger picture by enclosing the <IMG> tag inside an <A> tag:

```
<A HREF="penguinsbig.gif"><IMG SRC="penguinslittle.gif"></A>
```

The final result of the page is shown in Figure 7.21. Now, if you click on the small penguin image, the big image will be downloaded and viewed either by the browser itself or by the helper application defined for GIF files for that browser.

Figure 7.21.

The Penguins home page with link.

An alternative to linking the small image directly to the larger image is to provide the external image in several different formats and then create plain text links to the various different external versions. (You might want to take this approach for readers who have software for one format but not another.) In this part of the example, you'll link to a JPEG version of that same penguins file.

To create the JPEG version of the penguin photograph, you need to use your image editor or converter again to convert the original photograph. Here, I've called it `penguinsbig.jpg`.

To provide both GIF and JPEG forms of the penguin photo, you'll convert the link on the image into a simple link menu to the GIF and JPEG files, providing some information about file size. The result is shown in Figure 7.22.

```
<P><IMG SRC="penguinslittle.gif"></P>
<UL>
<LI>Penguins (<A HREF="pengiunsbig.gif">100K GIF file</A>)
<LI>Penguins (<A HREF="pengiunsbig.jpg">25K JPEG file</A>)
</UL>
```

Figure 7.22.

The Penguins link menu.

 NOTE

Images are not the only types of files you can store externally to your Web page. Sound files, video, zip archives—just about anything can be linked as external files. You'll learn more about this subject in Chapter 8, "External Files, Multimedia, and Animation."

Providing Alternatives to Images

Images can turn a simple text-only Web page into a glorious visual feast. But what happens if someone is reading your Web page from a text-only browser, or what if he or she has image loading turned off so that all your carefully crafted graphics appear as plain generic icons? All of a sudden, that glorious visual feast doesn't look as nice. And, worse, if you haven't taken these possibilities into consideration while designing your Web page, that portion of your audience might not be able to read or use your work.

You can come up with a simple solution to one of these problems. Using the ALT attribute of the <IMG> tag, you can substitute something meaningful in place of the image on browsers that cannot display the image.

Usually, in text-only browsers such as Lynx, graphics that are specified using the <IMG> tag in the original file are "displayed" as the word IMAGE with square brackets around it like this: [IMAGE]. (An example is shown in Figure 7.23.) If the image itself is a link to something else, that link is preserved.

Figure 7.23.

"Images" in Lynx.

```
[IMAGE] Up To Index
```

The ALT attribute in the <IMG> tag provides a more meaningful text alternative to the blank [IMAGE] for your readers who are using text-only Web browsers. The ALT attribute contains a string with the text you want to substitute for the graphic:

```
<IMG SRC="myimage.gif" ALT="[a picture of a cat]">
```

Note that most browsers will interpret the string you include in the ALT attribute as a literal string; that is, if you include any HTML tags in that string, they will be printed as typed instead of being parsed and displayed as HTML code. You therefore can't use whole blocks of HTML code as a replacement for an image—just a few words or phrases.

For example, remember in Exercise 7.2, where you used arrow icons for navigation between pages? Here are two ideas for providing text-only alternatives for those icons:

☐ Use text-only markers to replace the images. Here's the code:

```
<P>
<A HREF="replacing.html"><IMG SRC="arrowright.gif" ALIGN=BOTTOM
ALT="[NEXT]"></A>
On to "Gapping the New Plugs"<BR>
<A HREF="ready.html"><IMG SRC="arrowleft.gif" ALIGN=BOTTOM
ALT="[PREVIOUS]"></A>
Back to "When You Should Replace your Spark Plugs"<BR>
<A HREF="index.html"><IMG SRC="arrowup.gif" ALIGN=BOTTOM ALT="[UP]"></A>
Up To Index</P>
```

Figure 7.24 shows these markers.

☐ Hide the images altogether and make the text the anchor instead. Here's the code:

```
<P>
<A HREF="replacing.html"><IMG SRC="arrowright.gif" ALIGN=BOTTOM ALT="">
On to "Gapping the New Plugs"</A><BR>
<A HREF="ready.html"><IMG SRC="arrowleft.gif" ALIGN=BOTTOM ALT="">
Back to "When You Should Replace your Spark Plugs"</A><BR>
<A HREF="index.html"><IMG SRC="arrowup.gif" ALIGN=BOTTOM ALT="">
Up To Index</A></P>
```

7

Figure 7.24.

Text markers to replace images.

```
[NEXT] On to "Gapping the New Plugs"
[PREVIOUS] Back to "When You Should Replace your Spark Plugs"
[UP] Up To Index
```

Figure 7.25 shows the result of this code.

Figure 7.25.

Hide the images.

```
On to "Gapping the New Plugs"
Back to "When You Should Replace your Spark Plugs"
Up To Index
```

 TIP

A sneaky trick I've seen used for the ALT attribute is to include an ASCII art picture (a picture made up of characters, like the cow in Chapter 5, "More Text Formatting with HTML") in the ALT tag, which then serves as the "picture" in text-only browsers such as Lynx. (Unfortunately, this trick doesn't seem to work in graphical browsers with images turned off.) To accomplish this trick, you'll need the ASCII art prepared ahead of time. Then, in your HTML code, include the entire <IMG> tag inside <PRE>...</PRE> tags, and put the ASCII art inside the ALT attribute, as follows:

```
<PRE>
<IMG SRC="cow.gif" ALT="
        (   )
Moo    (oo)
          \/------\
           ||    | \
           ||----W| |  *
           ||    ||
">
</PRE>
```

In this code, the original image (`cow.gif`) will be replaced by the text version, neatly formatted, in text-only browsers. Note that because the `<PRE>` tags are outside the `<IMG>` tag itself (to get around the fact that you can't put HTML code inside the `ALT` attribute), this trick works best when the image is alone on a line—that is, when no text appears before or after it on the line.

Other Neat Tricks with Images

Now that you've learned about inline and external images, images as links, and how to wrap text around images, you know the majority of what most people do with images in Web pages. But you can play with a few nifty tricks, and they are what this section is all about.

All the attributes in this section were originally Netscape extensions that have since been incorporated into HTML 3.2, and its successor, HTML 4.0.

Image Dimensions and Scaling

Two attributes of the `<IMG>` tag, `HEIGHT` and `WIDTH`, specify the height and width of the image in pixels.

If you use the actual height and width of the image in these values (which you can find out in most image-editing programs), your Web pages will appear to load and display much faster in some browsers than if you do not include these values.

Why? Normally, when a browser parses the HTML code in your file, it has to load and test each image to get its width and height before proceeding so that it can format the text appropriately. Therefore, the browser loads and formats some of your text, waits for the image to load, formats around the image when it gets the dimensions, and then moves on for the rest of the page. If the width and height are already specified in the HTML code itself, the browser can just make a space of the appropriate size for the image and keep formatting all the text around it. This way, your readers can continue reading the text while the images are loading rather than having to wait. And, because `WIDTH` and `HEIGHT` are just ignored in other browsers, there's no reason not to use them for all your images. They neither harm nor affect the image in browsers that don't support them.

TIP

> If you test your page with images in it in Netscape Communicator, try choosing View|Page Info. You'll get a window listing all the images in your page. By selecting each image in turn, you'll get information about that image—including its size, which you can then copy into your HTML file.

If the values for WIDTH and HEIGHT are different from the actual width and height of the image, your browser will automatically scale the image to fit those dimensions. Because smaller images take up less disk space than larger images and therefore take less time to transfer over the network, you can use this sneaky method to get away with using large images on your pages without the additional increase in load time: just create a smaller version, and then scale it to the dimensions you want on your Web page. Note, however, that the pixels will also be scaled, so the bigger version may end up looking grainy or blocky. Experiment with different sizes and scaling factors to get the right effect.

NOTE

> Don't do reverse scaling—creating a large image and then using WIDTH and HEIGHT to scale it down. Smaller file sizes are better because they take less time to load. If you're just going to display a small image, make it smaller to begin with.

More About Image Borders

You learned about the BORDER attribute to the <IMG> tag as part of the section on links, where setting BORDER to a number or to zero determined the width of the image border (or hid it entirely).

Normally, plain images don't have borders; only images that hold links do. You can use the BORDER attribute with plain images, however, to draw a border around the image, like this:

```
<P>Frame the image <IMG SRC="monalisa.gif" BORDER=5></P>
```

Figure 7.26 shows an example of an image with a border around it.

Figure 7.26.
An image border.

Image Previews

One completely optional Netscape extension to images is the use of the LOWSRC attribute to
<IMG>, which provides a sort of preview for the actual image on the page. You use LOWSRC just
like you use SRC, with a pathname to another image file, as follows:

```
<IMG SRC="wall.gif" LOWSRC="wallsmall.gif">
```

When a browser that support LOWSRC encounters a LOWSRC tag, it loads in the LOWSRC image
first, in the first pass for the overall page layout. Then, after all the layout and LOWSRC images
are done loading and displaying, the image specified in SRC is loaded and fades in to replace
the LOWSRC image.

Why would you want this type of preview? The image in LOWSRC is usually a smaller or lower
resolution preview of the actual image, one that can load very quickly and give the readers
an idea of the overall effect of the page. (Make sure your LOWSRC image is indeed a smaller
image; otherwise, there's no point to including it.) Then, after all the layout is done, the
readers can scroll around and read the text while the better images are quietly loaded in the
background. Using LOWSRC is entirely optional; it's simply ignored in older browsers.

Using Color

One way to add color to your Web pages is to add images; images can provide a splash of color
among the black and gray and white. Several HTML 3.2 attributes, however, enable you also
to change the colors of the page itself, including changing the background color of the page,
changing the color of the text and links on that page, and adding "spot color" to individual
characters on that page. In this section, you'll learn how to make all these changes.

NOTE

Although all the HTML 3.2 color and background attributes in this
section are still supported in HTML 4.0, you're now encouraged to
start using style sheets instead.

7

Naming Colors

Before you can change the color of any part of an HTML page, you have to know what color you're going to change it to. You can specify colors using the color extensions to HTML in two ways:

☐ Using a hexadecimal number representing that color

☐ Using one of a set of predefined color names

The most flexible and most widely supported method of indicating color involves finding out the numeric value of the color you want to use. Most image-editing programs have what's called a color picker—some way of choosing a single color from a range of available colors. Most color pickers, in turn, will tell you the value of that color in RGB form, as three numbers (one for red, one for green, and one for blue—that's what RGB stands for). Each number is usually 0 to 255, with 0 0 0 being black and 255 255 255 being white.

After you have your colors as three numbers from 0 to 255, you have to convert those numbers into hexadecimal. You can use any scientific calculator that converts between ASCII and hex to get these numbers. A slew of freeware and shareware color pickers for HTML are available as well, including HTML Color Reference and ColorFinder for Windows, and ColorMeister and ColorSelect for the Macintosh. Alternatively, you can use rgb.html, a form that will do the conversion for you, which you'll learn how to implement later in this book. For now, you can try out the rgb.html form at http://www.lne.com/rgb.html, which will give you the hex for any three numbers. So, for example, the RGB values 0 0 0 convert to 00 00 00, and the RGB values for 255 255 255 convert to FF FF FF.

The final hex number you need is all three numbers put together with a hash sign (#) at the beginning, like the following:

```
#000000
#DE04E4
#FFFF00
```

Netscape and Internet Explorer support a much easier way of indicating colors. Instead of using arcane numbering schemes, you just pick a color name such as Black, White, Green, Maroon, Olive, Navy, Purple, Gray, Red, Yellow, Blue, Teal, Lime, Aqua, Fuchsia, or Silver.

Although color names are easier to remember and to figure out than the numbers, they do offer less flexibility in the kinds of colors you can use, and names are not as widely supported in browsers as the color numbers. Keep in mind that if you do use color names, you may lose the colors in most other browsers.

After you have a color name or number in hand, you can apply that color to various parts of your HTML page.

Changing the Background Color

To change the color of the background on a page, decide what color you want and then add an attribute called BGCOLOR to the <BODY> tag. The <BODY> tag, in case you've forgotten, is the tag that surrounds all the content of your HTML file. <HEAD> contains the title, and <BODY> contains almost everything else. BGCOLOR is an HTML extension introduced by Netscape in the 1.1 version of the browser and incorporated into HTML 3.2.

To use color numbers for backgrounds, you enter the value of the BGCOLOR attribute of the <BODY> tag (the hexadecimal number you found in the preceding section) in quotation marks. They look like the following:

```
<BODY BGCOLOR="#FFFFFF">
<BODY BGCOLOR="#934CE8">
```

To use color names, simply use the name of the color as the value to BGCOLOR:

```
<BODY BGCOLOR=white>
<BODY BGCOLOR=green>
```

NOTE

> Some browsers allow you to indicate color numbers without the leading hash sign (#). Although this method may seem more convenient, given that it is incompatible with many other browsers, the inclusion of the one extra character does not seem like that much of a hardship.

Changing Text Colors

When you can change the background colors, also changing the color of the text itself makes sense. More HTML extensions introduced by Netscape and Internet Explorer, and now part of HTML 3.2, allow you to change the color of the text globally in your pages.

To change the text and link colors, you'll need your color names or numbers just as you did for changing the backgrounds. With a color in hand, you can then add any of the following attributes to the <BODY> tag with either a color number or color name as their values:

TEXT   Controls the color of all the page's body text that isn't a link, including headings, body text, text inside tables, and so on.

LINK   Controls the color of normal, unfollowed links in the page (the ones that are usually blue by default).

VLINK   Controls the color of links you have visited (the ones that are usually purple or red by default).

ALINK   Controls the color of a link that has had the mouse button pressed on it but not released (an activated link). They are often red by default.

For example, to create a page with a black background, white text, and bright purple unfollowed links, you might use the following <BODY> tag:

```
<BODY BGCOLOR="#000000" TEXT="#FFFFFF" LINK="#9805FF">
```

Using the following color names would produce the same effect:

```
<BODY BGCOLOR=black TEXT=white LINK=purple>
```

Both of these links would produce a page that looks something like the one shown in Figure 7.27.

Figure 7.27.

Background and text colors.

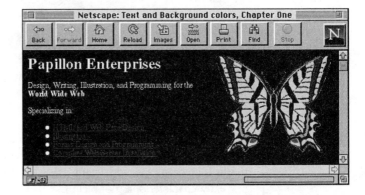

Spot Color

When you change the text colors in a page using attributes to the <BODY> tag, that change affects all the text on the page. Spot color is the ability to change the color of individual characters inside your page, which you can use instead of or in addition to a global text color.

Yesterday you learned about using the HTML tag <FONT> for setting the font size and font name. A third attribute to <FONT>, COLOR, lets you change the color of individual words or phrases. The value of COLOR is either a color name or number:

```
<P>When we go out tonight, we're going to paint the town
<FONT COLOR="#FF0000">RED</FONT>.
```

You can, of course, use font spot colors in addition to font names and sizes.

Image Backgrounds

One last topic for this chapter is the ability to use an image as a background for your pages rather than simply a solid colored background. When you use an image for a background, that image is "tiled"; that is, the image is repeated in rows to fill the browser window.

To create a tiled background, you'll need an image to serve as the tile. Usually, when you create an image for tiling, you need to make sure that the pattern flows smoothly from one tile to the next. You can usually do some careful editing of the image in your favorite image-editing program to make sure the edges line up. The goal is to have the edges meet cleanly so that you don't have a "seam" between the tiles after you've laid them end to end. (See Figure 7.28 for an example of tiles that don't line up very well.) You can also try clip art packages for wallpaper or tile patterns that are often designed specifically to be tiled in this fashion.

Figure 7.28.

Tiled images with "seams."

When you have an image that can be cleanly tiled, all you need to create a tiled image background is the BACKGROUND attribute, part of the <BODY> tag. The value of BACKGROUND is a filename or URL that points to your image file, as in the following example:

```
<BODY BACKGROUND="tiles.gif">
<BODY BACKGROUND="backgrounds/rosemarble.gif">
```

Figure 7.29 shows the result of a simple tiled background.

Figure 7.29.

A tiled background in Netscape.

Internet Explorer offers a twist on the tiled background design: a fixed tile pattern called a *watermark*. The idea here is that when you scroll a page, instead of everything on the page including the background scrolling by, only the page foreground (text and images) scrolls. The tiles in the background stay rooted in one place. To create this effect, use the BGPROPERTIES=FIXED attribute to the body tag, as follows:

```
<BODY BACKGROUND="backgrounds/rosemarble.gif" BGPROPERTIES=FIXED>
```

Hints for Better Use of Images

The use of images in Web pages causes one of the bigger arguments among users and providers of Web pages today. For everyone who wants to design Web pages with more, bigger, and brighter images to take full advantage of the graphical capabilities of the Web, someone on a slow network connection is begging for fewer images so that his or her browser doesn't take three hours to load a page.

As a designer of Web pages, you should consider both of these points of view. Balance the fun of creating a highly visual, colorful Web page with the need to get your information to everyone you want to have it—and that includes people who may not have access to your images at all.

This section offers some hints and compromises you can make in the design of your Web pages so that you can make everyone happy (or everyone unhappy, depending on how you look at it).

Do You Really Need This Image?

For each image you put inline on your Web page, consider why you are putting it there. What does the image add to the design? Does it provide information that could be presented in the text instead? Is it just there because you like how it looks?

Try not to clutter your Web page with pretty but otherwise unnecessary images. A simple Web page with only a few iconic images is often more effective than a page that opens with an enormous graphic and continues the trend with flashy 3D buttons, drop-shadow bullets, and psychedelic line separators.

Keep Your Images Small

A smaller image takes less time to transfer over the Net; therefore, using smaller images makes your Web page load faster and causes less frustration for people trying to read it over a slow link. What could be easier?

To create small images, you can reduce their actual physical dimensions on the screen. You can also create smaller file sizes for your images by reducing the number of colors in an image. Your goal is to reduce the file size of the image so that it transfers faster, but a four-inch by four-inch black-and-white image (two colors) may be smaller in file size than a $1/2$ inch by $1/2$ inch full-color photographic image. With most image-processing programs, you can reduce the number of colors and touch up the result so that it looks good even with fewer colors.

A good rule to follow is that you should try to keep your inline images somewhere under 20K. That size may seem small, but a single 20K file takes nearly 20 seconds to download over a 14.4kbps SLIP connection. Multiply that number by the number of images on your Web page, and the page may take a substantial amount of time to load (even if you're using a browser that can load multiple images at once; the pipe is only so wide). Will people care about what you have in your Web page if they have had to go off and have lunch while it's loading?

NOTE

> The small icons that I used for the arrows in the navigation examples are 300 bytes apiece—less than a third of a kilobyte. The spider web image in the Halloween example is slightly larger than 1K. Small does not mean the image isn't useful.

Reuse Images as Often as Possible

In addition to keeping individual images small, try to reuse the same images as often as you can, on single pages and across multiple pages. For example, if you have images as bullets, use the same image for all the bullets rather than different ones. Reusing images has two significant advantages over using different images:

☐ Reusing images provides a consistency to your design across pages, part of creating an overall "look" for your site.

☐ Even more important, reusing images means that your browser has to download the image only once. After the browser has the image in memory, it can simply draw the image multiple times without having to make lots of connections back to the server.

To reuse an image, you don't have to do anything special; just make sure you refer to each image by the same URL each time you use it. The browser will take care of the rest.

Provide Alternatives to Images

If you're not using the ALT attribute in your images, you should be. The ALT attribute is extremely useful for making your Web page readable by text-only browsers. But what about people who turn off images in their browser because they have a slow link to the Internet? Most browsers do not use the value of ALT in this case. And sometimes ALT isn't enough; because you can specify text only inside an ALT string, you can't substitute HTML code for the image.

To get around all these problems while still keeping your nifty graphical Web page, consider creating alternative text-only versions of your Web pages and putting links to them on the full-graphics versions of the same Web page, like this:

```
<P>A <A HREF="TextVersion.html">text-only</A>
version of this page is available.</P>
```

The link to the text-only page takes up only one small paragraph on the "real" Web page, but it makes the information much more accessible. Providing this version is a courtesy that readers with slow connections will thank you for, and it still allows you to load up your "main" Web page with as many images as you like for those people who have fast connections.

Summary

One of the major features that makes the World Wide Web stand out from other forms of Internet information is that pages on the Web can contain full-color images. It was arguably the existence of those images that allowed the Web to catch on so quickly and to become so popular in so short a time.

To place images on your Web pages, you learned that those images must be in GIF or JPEG format (GIF is more widely supported) and small enough that they can be quickly downloaded over a potentially slow link. In this chapter, you also learned that the HTML tag <IMG> allows you to put an image on the Web page, either inline with text or on a line by itself. The <IMG> tag has three primary attributes:

SRC   The location and filename of the image to include.

ALIGN   How to position the image vertically with its surrounding text. ALIGN can have one of three values: TOP, MIDDLE, or BOTTOM.

ALT   A text string to substitute for the image in text-only browsers.

You can include images inside a link tag (<A>) and have those images serve as hot spots for the links, same as text.

In addition to the standard attributes, several additional attributes to the <IMG> tag provide greater control over images and layout of Web pages. You learned that these attributes, most of which were introduced in HTML 3.2, include the following:

ALIGN=LEFT   Place the image against the appropriate margin, allowing all
and   following text to flow into the space alongside the image. In
ALIGN=RIGHT   addition, a Netscape extension to <BR>, CLEAR, allows you to stop
                wrapping text alongside an image. CLEAR can have three values:
                LEFT, RIGHT, and ALL.

`ALIGN=TEXTTOP`
`ALIGN=ABSMIDDLE`
`ALIGN=BASELINE`
and
`ALIGN=ABSBOTTOM`
	Allow greater control over the alignment of an inline image and the text surrounding it.

`VSPACE`
and
`HSPACE`
	Define the amount of space between an image and the text surrounding it.

`BORDER`	Defines the width of the border around an image (with or without a link). `BORDER=0` hides the border altogether.
`LOWSRC`	Defines an alternative, lower-resolution image that is loaded before the image indicated by SRC.

In addition to images, you can also add color to the background and to the text of a page using attributes to the `<BODY>` tag, or add color to individual characters using the `COLOR` attribute to `<FONT>`. Finally, you also learned that you can add patterned or tiled backgrounds to images by using the `BACKGROUND` attribute to `<BODY>` with an image for the tile.

Q&A

Q How can I create thumbnails of my images so that I can link them to larger external images?

A You'll have to do that with some kind of image-editing program; the Web won't do it for you. Just open up the image, and scale it down to the right size.

Q Can I put HTML tags in the string for the `ALT` attribute?

A That would be nice, wouldn't it? Unfortunately, you can't. All you can do is put an ordinary string in there. Keep it simple, and you should be fine.

Q You discussed a technique for including `LOWSRC` images on a page that are loaded in before regular images are. I've seen an effect on Web pages where an image seems to load in as a really blurry image and then become clearer as time goes on. Is that a `LOWSRC` effect?

A No, actually, that effect is something called an interlaced GIF. Only one image is there; it just displays as it's loading differently from regular GIFs. You'll learn more about interlaced GIFs in the next chapter.

    `LOWSRC` images load in just like regular images (with no special visual effect).

7

Q I've seen some Web pages where you can click on different places in an image and get different link results, such as a map of the United States where each state has a different page. How do you do this in HTML?

A You use something called an image map, which is an advanced form of Web page development. It involves writing code on the server side to interpret the mouse clicks and send back the right result. I describe image maps in Chapter 14, "Image Maps."

Chapter 8

External Files, Multimedia, and Animation

Multimedia is a bit of a high-powered word these days, bringing up images of expensive CD-ROMs with lots of integrated sound and video, textured ray-traced 3D virtual environments, and Doom-like fast-paced action. Multimedia on the Web, primarily because of limitations in network speeds and cross-platform file formats, isn't nearly that much fun. Multimedia on the Web has the potential for being very interesting, but, for the most part, it consists mostly of small sound and video files and simple animation. Yesterday you learned about images and, in particular, about the differences between external and inline images. You can make the same distinction between external and inline multimedia on the Web, and in this chapter, I will.

This chapter consists of two main parts. The first part describes external media files, which are the standard way of creating multimedia on the Web; all browsers support this capability. In this first half of the chapter, you'll learn the following:

- ☐ What external media means
- ☐ How browsers, servers, and helper applications work together to handle external media
- ☐ How to use external sound and video files
- ☐ How to employ external media for uses other than multimedia

In the second part of this chapter, I'll get fancy and talk about how browsers support inline animation and multimedia, including the following:

- ☐ Inline sound and video
- ☐ GIF animation
- ☐ Marquees
- ☐ Animation with Java
- ☐ Netscape's server push and client pull
- ☐ Notes on Shockwave and other plug-ins

What Is External Media?

Yesterday you learned about the difference between inline and external images. Inline images appear directly on a Web page, whereas external images are stored, well, externally and loaded when a reader chooses a link in an HTML Web page. This same distinction between inline and external applies to many other kinds of media besides images. In its most general form, external media is defined as any file that cannot be automatically loaded, played, or displayed by a Web browser on a Web page.

Whereas you're limited when you use inline media to which kinds of files you can use (and, for most browsers, that means only GIF and JPEG images), external files can include just about any kind of file you can create: non-inline GIF files, MPEG video, PostScript files, zipped applications—just about anything you can put on a computer disk can be considered external media.

Using External Media in HTML

To point to an external media file from a Web page, you link to that file just as you would to any other document, by using the <A> tag and the HREF attribute. The path to the external file is a pathname or URL you would use if the file were another HTML document, and the text inside the link describes the file you're linking to. Here's an example:

```
<A HREF="some_external_file">A media file.</A>
```

So what happens when you click on a link to one of these external files? For some files, such as images or text files, your browser may be able to load the file itself into the current browser window. In many cases, however, your browser will download the file and then pass to some other application on your system that is designed to read and handle that file. These other applications are called helper applications, or sometimes viewers, and you can configure your browser to handle different external media types with different applications. If the browser can't figure out what kind of file the external media file is, it'll usually pop up a dialog box asking you what to do (save the file, choose an application, or some other choice).

New Term   A *helper application* is a program on your disk designed to read files that are not directly supported by your browser—for example, unusual image formats, movie formats, compressed or zipped applications, and so on. You can configure your browser to use different helper applications for different files.

How External Media Works in Your Browser

How does the browser figure out whether a given file is readable by the browser itself or whether it needs to be passed on to a helper application? How the browser treats a file is determined by one of two factors: the extension to the filename or the content-type of that file. You've seen the file extension quite a bit up to this point; HTML files must have extensions of `.html` or `.htm`, GIF files must have `.gif` extensions, and so on. When your browser reads and views local files on your disk, it uses the file extension to figure out what kind of file is used.

The content-type comes in when your browser gets files from a Web server. The Web server doesn't send the filename; in some cases, the data it sends back may be automatically generated and not have a filename at all. What the server does send back is a special code called the content-type, which tells the browser what kind of file it is sending. Content-types look something like this: `text/html`, `image/gif`, `video/mpeg`, `application/msword`, and so on.

New Term   A *content-type* is a special code that Web servers use to tell the browser what kinds of files they are sending.

Both the browser and server have lists in their configuration or preferences that map file extensions to content-types. The server uses this list to figure out which content-type to send to the browser with a given file. The browser, in turn, has an additional list that maps content-types to helper applications on the local system. (Figure 8.1 shows Netscape's Helper applications menu.) In this way, regardless of where the browser gets a file, it can figure out what to do with almost every given file it receives.

Figure 8.1.

Netscape's Helper applications.

Allowing Helper applications to deal with most external files works well for browsers, as it means that the browser can remain small and fast (no need to deal with every arcane file format that might be produced on the Web), and the browser is also configurable for new and better helper applications as they are written—or new and better file formats.

With this background in mind, you can actually create some Web pages that link to external media files.

External Sound, Video, and Other Files

Sound and video files are ideal for external media files on a Web page. You can use sound on your Web page for optional annotations to existing text, welcome messages from you or someone important in your organization, or extra information that words and pictures cannot convey. Video can be used to provide even more information that static pictures cannot convey (where the term *video* refers to any digitally encoded motion picture—both animation as well as "real" video files).

Sound Files

To include a link to an external sound on your Web page, you must have the sound file in the right format, just as you would for an image. Currently, the only fully cross-platform sound file format for the Web is Sun Microsystems's AU format. AU allows several different

8

kinds of sound sample encoding, but the most popular one is 8-bit μ-law (that funny character is the Greek letter mu, so μ-law files are pronounced "mew-law"). For this reason, AU files are often called simply μ-law files. AU files are of only barely acceptable quality, as the 8-bit sampling causes them to sound a bit like they are being transmitted over a telephone.

You can use other better quality sound formats for specific platforms. The most popular are AIFF for the Macintosh and Wave (WAV) for Windows, or MPEG audio, which is more cross-platform but even less popular.

Finally, the RealAudio format was developed specifically for playing audio files on the Internet and the World Wide Web. Unlike with most audio files, where you wait for the entire file to download before you can hear it, RealAudio uses streaming, which means that it can play at the same time it's being downloaded; only a small pause occurs as the initial data first arrives on your machine. The one drawback of using RealAudio is that you need to set up a special server to deliver real audio files, and linking to them involves a slightly different process than linking to regular audio files. For both of these reasons, I'm going to postpone talking about RealAudio until later in this book, after you're used to working with servers.

For a browser to recognize your sound file, the file must have the appropriate extension for its file type. Common formats and their extensions are listed in Table 8.1.

Table 8.1. Sound formats and extensions.

Format	Extension
AU/μ-law	.au
AIFF/AIFC	.aiff, .aif
Wave/WAV	.wav
MPEG Audio	.mp2

After you have a file in the right format and with the right extension, you can link to it from your Web page like any other external file:

```
<P>Laurence Olivier's <A HREF="olivier_hamlet.au">"To Be or
Not To Be"</A> soliloquy from the film of the play Hamlet (AIFF
format, 357K)</P>
```

Video Files

Video files, like sound files, must be in one of a handful of formats so that they can be read by the current crop of Web browsers. As I already mentioned, I'll talk extensively about video in the next chapter, but here's a quick format rundown.

For video files that can be read across platforms, the current standard on the Web is MPEG, but both Microsoft's Video for Windows (AVI) and Apple's QuickTime format have been gaining ground as players become more available. QuickTime and AVI files also have the advantage of being able to include an audio track with the video; although MPEG video files can have audio tracks, few existing players can play them.

The file extensions for each of these video files are listed in Table 8.2.

Table 8.2. Video formats and extensions.

Format	Extension
MPEG	`.mpeg, .mpg`
QuickTime	`.mov`
AVI	`.avi`

You simply link the file into your Web page as you would any other external file:

```
<P><A HREF="dumbo3.mov">The "pink elephant" scene</A> from
Disney's <CITE>Dumbo</CITE>.</P>
```

Using External Media for Other Files

External media isn't limited to actual media like sound, video, and images. Any file you can put on your disk with an extension on it can be used as an external media file: text files, PostScript files, Microsoft Word files, ZIP files, Macintosh HQX files, and so on. As long as the file has the right extension and your browser has been configured to be able to handle that file type, you can create a link to this file to download the file when the link is selected.

At least, that's the theory. For many file types, you also might need to configure your server to do the right thing; otherwise, when you try to download the file, you'll get gibberish or nothing at all. You can experiment with linking to different file types for now.

Hints on Using External Media in HTML

If you're going to make use of links to external media files in your Web pages, a very helpful tip for your readers is to include information in the body of the link (or somewhere nearby) about the format of the media (is it AU or AIFF or AVI or MPEG or a ZIP file?) and the file size. All the examples I've used up to this point include this information.

Remember, your readers have no way of knowing what's on the other side of the link. So if they go ahead and select it, downloading the file may take some time—and they may discover after waiting all that time that their systems can't handle the file. By telling your readers what they're selecting, they can make the decision about whether trying to download the file is worth the effort.

8

8

Simply adding a few words as part of the link text is all you really need:

```
<A HREF="bigsnail.jpeg">A 59K JPEG Image of a snail</A>
<A HREF="tacoma.mov">The Fall of the Tacoma Narrows Bridge </A>
 (a 200K QuickTime File)
```

Another useful trick if you use lots of media files on a page is to use small icon images of different media files to indicate a sound or a video clip (or some other media). Figure 8.2 shows some examples. Be sure to include a legend for which formats you're using, and don't forget to include the file sizes, as in the following examples:

```
<A HREF="bigsnail.jpeg"><IMG SRC="earicon.gif"
ALT="[sound]">Whooping Cranes (JPEG, 36K)</A>
```

Figure 8.2.
Media icons.

Exercise 8.1: Creating a media archive.

One of the common types of pages available on the Web is a media archive. A media archive is a Web page that serves no purpose other than to provide quick access to images or other media files for viewing and downloading.

Before the Web became popular, media such as images, sounds, and video were stored in FTP or Gopher archives. The text-only nature of these sorts of archives makes it difficult for people to find what they're looking for, as the filename is usually the only description they have of the content of the file. Even reasonably descriptive filenames, such as `red-bird-in-green-tree.gif` or `verdi-aria.aiff`, aren't very useful when you're talking about images or sounds. Only through the process of actually downloading the file itself can people really decide whether they want it.

By using inline images and icons, and splitting up sound and video files into small clips and larger files, you can create a media archive on the Web that is far more usable than any of the text-only archives.

NOTE

> Keep in mind that this sort of archive, in its heavy use of inline graphics and large media files, is optimally useful in graphical browsers attached to fast networks. However, the Web does provide advantages in this respect over FTP or Gopher servers, even for text-only browsers, simply because more room is available to describe the files on the archive. Instead of having only the filename to describe the file, you can use as many words as you need. Consider this example:
>
> ```
> <P>A <A HREF="orangefish.jpeg">34K JPEG file</A> of
> an orange fish with a bright yellow eye, swimming in
> front of some very pink coral.
> ```

In this exercise, you'll create a simple example of a media archive with several GIF images, AU sounds, and MPEG video.

First, start with the framework for the archive, which includes some introductory text, some inline images explaining the kinds of files, and headings for each file type:

```
<HTML>
<HEAD>
<TITLE>Laura's Way Cool Image Archive</TITLE>
<H1>Laura's Way Cool Image Archive</H1>
<P>Select an image to download the appropriate file.</P>
<P><IMG SRC="penguinslittle.gif">Picture icons indicate GIF images</P>
<P><IMG SRC="earicon.gif">This icon indicates an AU Sound file</P>
<P><IMG SRC="film.gif">This icon indicates an MPEG Video File</P>
<HR>
<H2>Images</H2>
<H2>Sound Files</H2>
<H2>Video Files</H2>
```

Figure 8.3 shows how the framework looks so far.

Figure 8.3.

The framework for the media archive.

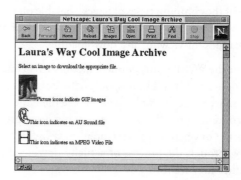

For the archive, use these four large GIF images:

☐ A drawing of a pink orchid

☐ A photograph full of jelly beans

☐ The cougar from the Palo Alto Zoo home page

☐ A biohazard symbol

Using your favorite image editor, you can create thumbnails of each of these pictures to serve as the inline icons and then insert <IMG> links in the appropriate spots in your archive file:

```
<H2>Images</H2>
<IMG SRC="orchidsmall.gif" ALT="a drawing of a pink orchid">
```

```
<IMG SRC="jellybeansmall.gif" ALT="a photograph of some jellybeans">
<IMG SRC="cougarsmall.gif" ALT="a photograph of a cougar">
<IMG SRC="biohazardsmall.gif" ALT="a biohazard symbol">
```

Note that I included values for the ALT attribute to the <IMG> tag, which will be substituted for the images in browsers that cannot view these images. Even though you may not intend for your Web page to be seen by non-graphical browsers, at least offering a clue to people who stumble onto it is polite. This way, everyone can access the media files you're offering on this page.

Now, link the thumbnails of the files to the actual images:

```
<A HREF="orchid.gif">
<IMG SRC="orchidsmall.gif" ALT="a drawing of a pink orchid"></A>
<A HREF="jellybean.gif">
<IMG SRC="jellybeansmall.gif" ALT="a photograph of some jellybeans"> </A>
<A HREF="cougar.gif">
<IMG SRC="cougarsmall.gif" ALT="a photograph of a cougar"> </A>
<A HREF="biohazard.gif">
<IMG SRC="biohazardsmall.gif" ALT="a biohazard symbol"> </A>
```

Figure 8.4 shows the result.

Figure 8.4.

Image links to larger images.

If I leave the archive like this, it looks nice, but I'm breaking one of my own rules: I haven't noted how large the files are. Here, you have several choices for formatting. You could just put the size of the file inline with the image and let the images wrap on the page however they want, as follows:

```
<H2>Images</H2>
<A HREF="orchid.gif">
<IMG SRC="orchidsmall.gif" ALT="a drawing of a pink orchid"></A>(67K)
<A HREF="jellybean.gif">
<IMG SRC="jellybeansmall.gif" ALT="a photograph of some jellybeans"></A>(39K)
```

```
<A HREF="cougar.gif">
<IMG SRC="cougarsmall.gif" ALT="a photograph of a cougar"></A>(122K)
<A HREF="biohazard.gif">
<IMG SRC="biohazardsmall.gif" ALT="a biohazard symbol"></A>(35K)
```

Figure 8.5 shows this result.

Figure 8.5.

Images with text.

Or you could put in line breaks after each image to make sure that they line up along the left edge of the page. I prefer the first method, as it allows a more compact layout of images.

Now, moving on to the sound and video files. You have three sound files and two videos. Because these files can't be reduced to a simple thumbnail image, you can describe them in the text in the archive (including the huge sizes of the files):

```
<H2>Sound and Video Files</H2>
<P>A five-part a capella renaissance madrigal
called "Flora Gave me Fairest Flowers" (650K)</P>
<P>Some lovely wind-chime sounds (79K) </P>
<P>Chicken noises (112K)</P>
<P>The famous Tacoma Narrows bridge accident
(where the bridge twisted and fell down in the wind)(13Meg)</P>
<P>A three-dimensional computer animation of a
flying airplane over a landscape (2.3Meg)</P>
```

Now, add the icon images to each of the descriptions—an ear icon for the sounds and the filmstrip icon for the videos. Here you can also include a value for the ALT attribute to the <IMG> tag, this time providing a simple description that will serve as a placeholder for the link itself in text-only browsers. Note that because you're using icons to indicate what kind of file each one is, you don't have to include text descriptions of that file format in addition to the icon.

Finally, just as you did in the image part of the example, you can link the icons to the external files. Here is the HTML code for the final list:

```
<H2>Sound and Video Files</H2>
<P><A HREF="flora.au">
<IMG SRC="earicon.gif" ALT="[madrigal sound]"> A five-part a capella
renaissance madrigal called "Flora Gave me Fairest Flowers" (650K)</A></P>
```

```
<P><A HREF="windchime.au">
<IMG SRC="earicon.gif" ALT="[windchime sound]"> Some
lovely wind-chime sounds (79K)</A></P>
<P><A HREF="bawkbawk.au">
<IMG SRC="earicon.gif" ALT="[chicken sound]"> Chicken noises (112K)</A></P>
<P><A HREF="tacoma.mpeg">
<IMG SRC="film.gif" ALT="[tacoma video]"> The famous Tacoma
Narrows bridge accident (where the bridge twisted and fell
down in the wind) (13Meg)</A></P>
<P><A HREF="airplane.mpeg">
<IMG SRC="film.gif" ALT="[3D airplane]">A three-dimensional
computer animation of a flying airplane over a landscape (2.3Meg) </A></P>
```

Figure 8.6 shows how this list looks.

Figure 8.6.
Sound and video files.

Et voilà, your media archive. Creating one is simple with the combination of inline images and external files. With the use of the ALT attribute, you can even use it reasonably well in text-only browsers. Figure 8.7 shows how the archive looks in Lynx.

Figure 8.7.
The media archive in Lynx.

The State of Inline Multimedia on the Web

Once upon a time, the only way you could distribute multimedia files over the Web was by using external files as described in the first half of this chapter. However, both Netscape and Microsoft have made many interesting steps toward integrating multimedia more closely into Web pages, either through the use of new HTML tags, through advanced capabilities such as Java, or through the use of "plug-ins"—helper applications that are more closely integrated with the browser and with files viewed within that browser.

For the remainder of this chapter, I'll describe many of the innovations in inline media that different browsers are supporting, including inline sound and video, marquees, and simple animation using GIF files and Java. As you read through this half of the chapter, keep in mind that these capabilities are new and sometimes limited to their respective browsers. If you take advantage of these features, be aware that they may be unavailable for readers not using that particular browser.

Inline Video

One of the earlier mechanisms for handling inline animation was introduced with Microsoft's Internet Explorer browser. Internet Explorer includes an extension to the <IMG> tag that allows AVI (Video for Windows) files to be played inline on Web pages. This HTML extension, called DYNSRC (Dynamic Source), has not yet been supported by any other browsers, but because it is ignored by browsers that don't support it, the new extension does not affect the readability of the page in other browsers. Even the recent release of Netscape Communicator, the fourth version of the company's browser, doesn't support this extension.

To include an AVI video file on a Web page using Internet Explorer, use the <IMG> tag with the DYNSRC attribute. The value of DYNSRC is the path to or URL of the AVI file:

```
<IMG DYNSRC="rainstorm.avi" SRC="rainstorm.gif" ALT="[a rainstorm]">
```

Note that you can still use all the other common attributes to the <IMG> tag for alignment and borders, and you can use them to place the AVI video on the page. Also note that the SRC attribute is still required; this image will be shown in lieu of the AVI file if it cannot be found or in browsers that do not support inline video using DYNSRC.

In addition to DYNSRC, Microsoft added several other attributes to the <IMG> tag to control how the AVI file is played:

☐ The CONTROLS attribute, if included in <IMG>, displays the AVI file with a set of simple controls beneath it for starting, stopping, and replaying the AVI file.

8

☐ The LOOP attribute, whose value is a number, determines how many times the video will play; for example, LOOP=5 will play the video five times. A LOOP value of -1 or INFINITE causes the video to play repeatedly until the reader leaves the page.

☐ The START attribute controls when the video will actually start playing. If you use START=FILEOPEN (the default), the video will begin playing as soon as the page and the video are loaded. If you use START=MOUSEOVER, the video will not start playing until the mouse cursor has been moved over it.

Inline Sounds

In addition to the tags for inline video, Internet Explorer also added a tag for playing inline audio files. These sound files are loaded when the page is loaded without the readers having to press a button or follow a link to play the sound. To add an embedded background sound to a page, use the <BGSOUND> tag, like this:

```
<BGSOUND SRC="trumpet.au">
```

The browser, when it loads the page, will also load and play the background sound. The <BGSOUND> tag does not produce any visual effect on the page.

To repeat the sound multiple times, use the LOOP attribute. If the value of LOOP is a number, the sound is played that number of times. If LOOP is -1 or INFINITE, the sound will be repeated continually until the reader leaves the page.

Explorer supports three different formats for inline sounds: the popular Sun's AU (μ-law) format, Windows WAV files for sound samples, and MIDI files with an .mid extension.

When you're designing Web pages, go easy with background sounds. If you must use one, play it only a short time and then stop. Continually playing sounds is distracting to many readers.

As with the inline video extensions, the <BGSOUND> tag is not supported in Netscape's browsers.

Animated Marquees

A marquee is a line of scrolling text that moves from one side of the Web page to the other. Although you can create a marquee with just about any form of inline animation, Internet Explorer's <MARQUEE> tag allows you to create a marquee quickly and easily (and you don't need to download any other image or animation files). Figure 8.8 shows a scrolling marquee in Internet Explorer (in the process of scrolling).

Figure 8.8.

A scrolling marquee.

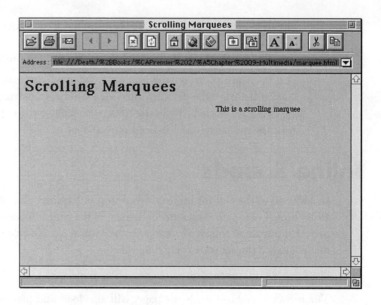

Marquees, which are a feature of Internet Explorer, are not supported in other browsers. Other browsers will still see the text itself; it just won't be animated.

Creating a Marquee

To create a marquee, use the <MARQUEE> tag. The text between the opening and closing <MARQUEE> tags is the text that will scroll:

```
<MARQUEE>I'm scrolling!</MARQUEE>
```

By default, a marquee appears on its own line, in the font and size of the enclosing element. So, for example, by enclosing the marquee inside a heading, you can get a heading-sized marquee:

```
<H1><MARQUEE>I'm scrolling, and large, too!</MARQUEE></H1>
```

This trick doesn't work with all HTML elements; you can't, for example, set the enclosing text to be <FONT COLOR=yellow>. Nor can you include HTML font changes inside the marquee itself; all HTML inside the marquee is ignored.

Changing the Behavior of the Marquee

When you create a simple marquee using just the plain <MARQUEE> tags, the marquee that is created scrolls from the right side of the page to the left, disappearing entirely before reappearing on the right again. It loops continually, just slow enough for you to be able to read it.

8

You can change the behavior, direction, number of times to loop, and the speed of looping with different attributes to the <MARQUEE> tag:

☐ The BEHAVIOR attribute has three values: SCROLL, SLIDE, or ALTERNATE. The default is SCROLL. SLIDE causes the marquee to slide in from the right side of the screen and stop when the text hits the left margin (slide in and "stick"). ALTERNATE starts the text on the left side of the page and bounces it back and forth between the left and right margins.

☐ The DIRECTION attribute, which can have the values LEFT or RIGHT, affects only marquees of type SCROLL and determines which direction the marquee initially moves in. The default is RIGHT (it moves from the right side of the screen to the left); DIRECTION=RIGHT reverses the directions.

☐ The value of the LOOP attribute determines how many times the marquee will scroll by. For example, LOOP=5 will scroll the marquee five times and stop. LOOP=-1 or LOOP=INFINITE will cause the marquee to scroll forever.

☐ Finally, the SCROLLAMOUNT and SCROLLDELAY attributes, which both have number values, determine the speed at which the marquee moves. SCROLLAMOUNT is the number of pixels between each step of the text in the marquee, that is, the number of pixels the text moves to the right or left each time. Higher numbers mean the marquee moves faster. SCROLLDELAY is the number of milliseconds between each step in the animation; higher numbers make the animation work more slowly and less smoothly. By experimenting with SCROLLAMOUNT and SCROLLDELAY, you can find a marquee speed and smoothness that works for your presentation.

Changing the Appearance of the Marquee

A marquee takes up a single vertical line of space on the Web page, and it is transparent to the background color behind it. You can, however, change the appearance of the marquee on the page by using several attributes:

☐ The BGCOLOR attribute determines the background color of the marquee's bounding box and, like all the color specifications in Internet Explorer, can take a hexadecimal RGB number or a color name.

☐ HEIGHT and WIDTH determine the size of the bounding box surrounding the marquee. Both HEIGHT and WIDTH can take a pixel number or a percentage of screen size. For example, HEIGHT=50% takes up half the vertical height of the screen.

☐ HSPACE and VSPACE determine the space between the edges of the marquee's bounding box and the surrounding text. HSPACE determines the space to either side of the marquee, and VSPACE determines the space above and below it.

☐ ALIGN, which can have the values TOP, MIDDLE, or BOTTOM, determines how the text surrounding the marquee will align with the marquee's bounding box (the same as with images). It does not affect the placement of the scrolling text inside the bounding box, which is always aligned at the top.

Figure 8.9 shows the various parts of the marquee's appearance you can change with these attributes.

Figure 8.9.

Marquee parts.

Using Marquees

Using marquees, like the `<BLINK>` tag, is a very intrusive way of getting your readers' attention. Marquees rivet your readers' attention to that one spot, distracting them from reading the rest of the page. As with `<BLINK>`, marquees should be used sparingly, if at all, and with a set number of loops (so the scrolling eventually stops). Small marquees are better than large ones, and marquees without background colors are more subtle than those with background colors.

NOTE

I can't emphasize enough that this is an Internet Explorer tag. If you want to see this type of scrolling text effect in other browsers, consider using a Java applet to do the same thing. You can find many scrolling text applets at the Gamelan Java site: `http://www.gamelan.com/`.

Animation Using GIF Files

Probably the simplest way to create basic animation is by using a feature of the GIF format that allows you to store multiple GIF images in a single GIF file. When these GIF images are loaded into a browser that understands this special format, the individual images are displayed one after the other, creating an animation. Depending on how the GIF file was originally saved, the animation can either play only once, play a number of times, or loop continuously.

Currently, both Internet Explorer and Netscape support animated GIFs as do other browsers.

8

What happens in browsers that don't support GIF animation? The good news is that they'll display only the first image in the series so that you won't lose the image altogether. The bad news is that storing several GIF images as a single animated GIF file means that the size of that file is the combination of all the individual GIF images, making your image files that much larger and more time-consuming to download. So you definitely must consider the trade-offs when deciding whether to use GIF animation in your own Web pages.

To create a GIF animation, you'll need the following:

☐ The set of individual GIF files (frames) that make up your animation

☐ A program that can convert the individual files to an animated GIF file

For the first of these two, you just need to use your favorite image editor to create each individual frame of the animation. Depending on the complexity of the animation you want to create and how artistic you are, this task can be relatively easy or very difficult. (Most impressive animations on the Web these days are done by professional artists.)

When I set out to do a simple GIF animation, I used a black and yellow "Coming Soon" image that I use on some of my Web pages. I simply blocked out some of the lights around the edge for each of the frames (different ones for each frame, of course). The four frames I created are shown in Figure 8.10.

Figure 8.10.
Four Coming Soon frames.

 TIP

> If you use Photoshop for your animation, layers can be really useful. Simply create a background that stays constant throughout the animation, and use different layers to create different frames of the animation. Then, when you want to create the individual frames, save the Photoshop file somewhere safe, flatten the image to the background and one layer, and save it as a GIF file.

After you have your frames, you'll need a program that can convert the images to the special animation format. Unfortunately, this special feature of the GIF format was used very little until the Web discovered it, so most GIF editors do not support it. Some small tools that do are creeping up, however.

☐ For Windows, Alchemy Mindworks's GIF Construction Set is a shareware tool that can create GIF animations, as well as handle many other GIF features (transparency, interlacing, and so on). Find out more from http://www.mindworkshop.com/alchemy/gifcon.html.

☐ For the Macintosh, GIFBuilder is a quick-and-dirty freeware tool that will take a series of GIF, PICT, or TIFF files and output an animated GIF file (and change lots of other GIF options also). You can get GIFBuilder from most popular Macintosh archives (try `http://www.mid.net/INFO-MAC/`), or get more information from `http://iawww.epfl.ch/Staff/Yves.Piguet/clip2gif-home/GifBuilder.html`.

☐ For UNIX systems, the command-line `whirlgGIF` takes a series of GIF files and outputs an animated GIF. WhirlGIF has lots of options for different aspects of the animation. See `http://www.msg.net/utility/whirlgif/` for more information and the source code.

The GIF animation format allows you to specify several different features of the animation, including how many times to loop (0 to infinite), and the delay between individual frames.

After you have an animated GIF file to play with, try it in Netscape or in some other tool that supports animated GIF files. In the case of my Coming Soon image, the "lights" around the edge of the box appear to blink on and off like a movie sign.

Animation Using Java

Java, which is becoming commonplace on the Web, has a lot of people very excited. Java applets are little mini-programs that run on a Web page and can react to user input without having to check back constantly with a Web server (as forms need to do). Indeed, you can do a lot with Java if you know how to program and you're willing to put in the work involved to learn how to use it. (You'll learn more about Java later in this book, in fact.) But even if you don't care about programming, you can use pre-built Java applets on your pages to create animation effects without touching a line of Java code. All you have to do is download a Java applet to your system, include a few lines of HTML on your page, and everything works just fine (assuming, of course, that you and your readers have Java-enabled browsers).

In this section, you'll learn just enough about Java applets to set up animation on your Web page. Later in the week, you'll learn more about Java.

Gathering the Pieces

One pre-built Java animation applet comes directly from Sun; it's called Animator. Animator can do simple animation with and without additional soundtracks, reuse frames, loop an animation, and control the time between each frame. To create animation using Java and the Animator applet, you'll need the following three elements:

☐ A set of image files (GIF or JPEG) that make up your animation, each one usually named with a capital *T* plus a sequential number, like this: `T1.gif`, `T2.gif`, `T3.gif`, and so on. As I've mentioned before, case matters, so make sure that you use a capital *T*. (The Animator applet uses these default names. You can use different names if you want to, but you'll have to configure the applet differently to accept these names. Using the *T* names is therefore the easiest way to go.)

8

☐ Sun's Animator classes. There are three of them: `Animator.class`,
`ParseException.class`, and `DescriptionFrame.class`. You can download all these
classes from the Animator page at `http://www.javasoft.com/applets/applets/`
`Animator/index.html`.

☐ An HTML file that contains the Java applet.

The easiest way to create Java animations without knowing much about Java is to put all your
files into the same directory: all the image files, all the class files, and your HTML file.

So, for example, say I have 12 GIF images of a pocket watch, each of which has the second
hand in a different place on the dial. I've named them `T1.gif`, `T2.gif`, and so on, all the way
up to `T12.gif`. Figure 8.11 shows the first few frames of the animation.

Figure 8.11.
The pocket watch
animation.

After downloading the Animator class files, I put them and the image files into a single
directory called `watch`. Now the last step is to create an HTML file that will contain the Java
animation.

Adding the Applet to Your Web Page

To add Java animation (or any applet) to a Web page, you use the `<APPLET>` and `<PARAM>` tags.
The `<APPLET>` tag contains the applet itself and determines how large the applet's bounding
box will be on the page.

NOTE

> `APPLET` is another tag that HTML 4.0 supports but discourages further
> use. In this case, they want you to use the `OBJECT` tag instead. For the
> broadest compatibility with existing browsers, however, I recommend
> sticking with `APPLET` for now.

To include the Animator applet on your page in a box 100 pixels square, for example, you
would use these lines of code:

```
<APPLET CODE="Animator.class" WIDTH=100 HEIGHT=100>
...
</APPLET>
```

In my watch example, the size of the images is 129×166 pixels, so I'll use those values for the WIDTH and HEIGHT:

```
<APPLET CODE="Animator.class" WIDTH=122 HEIGHT=166>
...
</APPLET>
```

In between the opening and closing <APPLET> tags are several different <PARAM> tags, which indicate different parameters for the Animator applet itself to control the animation. Each <PARAM> tag has two attributes: NAME and VALUE. NAME is used for the parameter name, and VALUE indicates its value. Using different <PARAM> tags, you can include different parameters to pass to the applet—and different applets will require different parameters. The Animator applet has a bunch of parameters to choose from, but I'll mention only a couple here.

STARTIMAGE is the image number to start from, usually 1. If your image filenames start from some other number, you'll use that number. ENDIMAGE, accordingly, is the number of the last image to use in the animation. My watch images are called T1.gif through T12.gif, so the value of STARTIMAGE would be 1 and the value of ENDIMAGE would be 12. You can add these parameters to your HTML file inside <PARAM> tags, which in turn go inside the <APPLET> tag:

```
<APPLET CODE="Animator.class" WIDTH=100 HEIGHT=100>
<PARAM NAME="STARTIMAGE" VALUE="1">
<PARAM NAME="ENDIMAGE" VALUE="12">
</APPLET>
```

The final parameter you'll usually want to include is PAUSE, which determines how many milliseconds the applet will wait between the images in the animation. By default, the pause is set to 3,900 milliseconds (almost four seconds), which is a bit too much of a pause. You can experiment with the pause between frames until you get an animation you like. Here, I picked 1,000 milliseconds, or an even second:

```
<APPLET CODE="Animator.class" WIDTH=100 HEIGHT=100>
<PARAM NAME="STARTIMAGE" VALUE="1">
<PARAM NAME="ENDIMAGE" VALUE="12">
<PARAM NAME="PAUSE" VALUE="1000">
</APPLET>
```

You also can include the REPEAT parameter, which tells the Animator applet to loop the image repeatedly. Clicking on the animation will start and stop it.

```
<APPLET CODE="Animator.class" WIDTH=100 HEIGHT=100>
<PARAM NAME="STARTIMAGE" VALUE="1">
<PARAM NAME="ENDIMAGE" VALUE="12">
<PARAM NAME="PAUSE" VALUE="1000">
<PARAM NAME="REPEAT" VALUE="TRUE">
</APPLET>
```

With all these parameters in place, you can save and load up the HTML file into your favorite Java-enabled browser. The Animator applet will be loaded, and it in turn loads and plays all the images in sequence.

For more information about what you can do with the Animator applet, see the Animator page at http://www.javasoft.com/applets/applets/Animator/index.html.

Multimedia Controls

With the release of Internet Explorer 4, Microsoft has introduced a set of so-called multimedia controls that allow you to use a few lines of HTML code to add multimedia graphics and effects to your pages.

Numerous multimedia controls are available with Internet Explorer 4:

☐ **Behaviors:** Provides special behaviors for controls and other page elements.

☐ **Effects:** Applies a graphics filter to any item on a page.

☐ **Hot Spot:** Makes regions of the screen clickable.

☐ **Mixer:** Mixes multiple WAV audio files.

☐ **Path:** Moves objects on a path.

☐ **Sequencer:** Controls timing of events.

☐ **Sprite:** Creates animations.

☐ **Sprite Buttons:** Creates animated buttons.

☐ **Structured Graphics:** Provides graphics that can be scaled and rotated.

Using these controls can be complicated because they require the use of the Class ID codes needed to include the controls in a page. Microsoft provides a great deal of information about Internet Explorer 4's new features, including the Multimedia controls, at `http://www.microsoft.com/ie/ie40`.

Microsoft provides several demos of Multimedia controls. The demo in Figure 8.12, for example, shows how colors can be blended and faded using ActiveX controls. This demo and others are available at `http://www.microsoft.com/ie/ie40/demos.htm`.

Figure 8.12.

Multimedia controls allow a variety of visual effects.

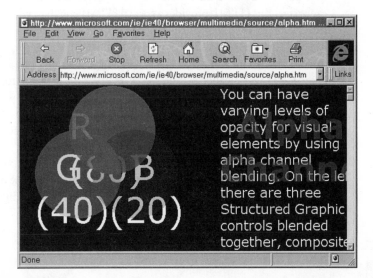

Client Pull and Server Push

One of the earliest and most primitive forms of inline animation in Web pages, client pull and server push, were introduced as part of Netscape 1.1. Client pull causes the browser to load the same page or a different page automatically after a certain amount of time has passed. Server push keeps the connection between the server and the browser open and continues to feed data down the wire.

The concepts behind client pull and server push are similar: They allow a new page or portion of a page to be loaded automatically after a certain amount of time, without the readers' having to select a link or move to a different page. Client pull can be used for automatic slide shows or other slow-moving presentations. For server push, multiple images can load into a single page repeatedly, offering a sort of basic animation.

Server push has fallen out of favor with the Web community, as it requires special setup programs on the server and is complex to set up. Newer forms of animation, such as the GIF animation you learned about in this chapter, have all but replaced the use of server push on the Web. I'll talk more about server push later in this book when you know more about servers.

Client pull, on the other hand, still has uses, not necessarily as an animation technique, but as a mechanism for pages to reload automatically after a certain amount of time has passed, or for a series of pages to load themselves automatically with a pause between them.

Client pull works because of a special HTTP command (called an HTTP header) called Refresh. If a Web server sends the Refresh command to a browser along with a page's data, the browser is supposed to wait a certain amount of time and then reload the page.

Normally, you would have to modify your server to send this special HTTP command with each page. But HTML provides a special HTML tag that, when included inside a Web page, provides a way for the page to "fake" many HTTP headers as if they were sent by the server itself. That special HTML tag is called <META>, a general HTML tag for providing information about an HTML page (meta-information). The attribute of the <META> tag that fakes the HTTP header is called HTTP-EQUIV, and its value for causing a page to reload is Refresh. To indicate the amount of time the browser should wait, use the attribute CONTENT. So, to put it all together, if you want the browser to reload the current page in four seconds, for example, you add the following tag inside the <HEAD> section of your HTML page:

```
<META HTTP-EQUIV="Refresh" CONTENT=4>
```

If the value of CONTENT is 0, the page is refreshed as quickly as the browser can retrieve it (which may not be very fast at all, depending on how fast the connection is—certainly not fast enough for any kind of quality animation).

Note that after you include this header inside your HTML page, the browser will continue to reload that page repeatedly. To get it to stop, you'll have to provide a link on the page to somewhere else that doesn't have a client pull tag inside it.

Client pulls that repeatedly load the same page are useful for pages that are continually being updated—for example, for live data such as stock quotes or sports scores. Another use of client pull is to load a different page after a certain amount of time, instead of loading the same page over and over again—for example, to step automatically through a series of slides or instructions.

To use the <META HTTP-EQUIV> to load a different page from the current one, add the URL of the next page to the value of the CONTENT attribute for the current page, like this:

```
<META HTTP-EQUIV="Refresh"
CONTENT="4;URL=http://mysite.com/page2.html">
```

Note that the URL you put inside CONTENT has to be a full URL; that is, it cannot be a relative pathname. It has to start with http://.

Inside the second page, you can include a pointer to the next page in the series, and inside that page, a pointer to the next page. Using this method, you can have any number of pages load automatically in a sequence. However, just like with the pages that load repeatedly, providing a link out of the automatic reloading is a good idea so that your readers won't be forced to sit through your presentation if they don't want to.

Notes on Shockwave and Other Netscape Plug-Ins

Of all the advances made to support more inline multimedia and animation on the Web, the one that will likely have the most significant effect over the long term is plug-ins.

Plug-ins are sort of like helper applications, except that instead of existing entirely separately from the browser, they add new capabilities to the browser itself. A video plug-in, for example, could allow video files to be played directly inline with the browser. A spreadsheet plug-in could allow editable spreadsheets to be included as elements inside a Web page. The plug-ins can also allow links back to the browser as well. So, for example, the spreadsheet could theoretically contain links that could be activated and followed from inside the plug-in.

Netscape introduced the concept of plug-ins with the 2.0 version of its browser. Plug-ins are available for many forms of sound and video; in fact, newer versions of Netscape Navigator include sound and video plug-ins already installed supporting formats such as AU, AIFF, WAV, MIDI, and QuickTime.

The problem with plug-ins is that if you use plug-in capabilities in your Web pages, all your readers will need to have browsers that support plug-ins (such as Netscape or Microsoft Internet Explorer). They must also have the plug-in installed and available. (Readers who don't have your plug-in will get empty space or broken icons on your page where the media should be.) And many plug-ins are available only for some platforms. For some forms of media, you might also need to configure your server to deliver the new media with the right content-type.

Plug-ins are an advanced Web feature; therefore, I'm going to wait to go into them in detail until later in this book. Because this is the multimedia and animation chapter, though, I do want to mention one significant plug-in for both of these topics: Shockwave from Macromedia.

Shockwave is a plug-in that allows Macromedia Director movies to be played as inline media on a Web page. Macromedia Director is an extremely popular tool among professional multimedia developers for creating multimedia presentations, including synchronized sound and video as well as interactivity. (In fact, many of the CD-ROMs you can buy today were developed using Macromedia Director.) If you're used to working with Director, Shockwave provides an easy way to put Director presentations on the Web. Or, if you're looking to do serious multimedia work on the Web or anywhere else, Director is definitely a tool to check out.

Summary

In this chapter, you learned about two main topics: external media files and inline multimedia and animation.

External media files cannot be read directly by your Web browser. Instead, if you link to an external file, your browser starts up a "helper" application to view or play these files. In this chapter, you learned how external media works, how to use sound and video files as external media, and some hints for designing using external media files.

The second half of this chapter focused on inline multimedia in Netscape and Internet Explorer using new tags and capabilities of these browsers, including tags for inline sound and video, scrolling marquees, inline GIF animation, and Java applets. Table 8.3 shows a summary of the tags you learned about today.

8

8

Table 8.3. Tags for inline media.

Tag	Attribute	Use
`<IMG>`	`DYNSRC`	Includes an AVI file instead of an image. If the AVI file cannot be found or played, the normal image (in SRC) is shown.
	`CONTROLS`	Shows a set of controls under the AVI movie.
	`LOOP`	Indicates the number of times to repeat the AVI movie. If `LOOP` is `-1` or `INFINITE`, the movie loops indefinitely.
	`START`	If `START=FILEOPEN`, the AVI movie begins playing immediately. If `START=MOUSEOVER`, the movie starts playing when the reader moves the mouse cursor over the movie.
`<BGSOUND>`		Plays a background sound.
	`LOOP`	Indicates the number of times to repeat the sound. If `LOOP` is `-1` or `INFINITE`, the sound loops indefinitely.
`<MARQUEE>...</MARQUEE>`		Creates a scrolling text marquee.
	`BEHAVIOR`	If `BEHAVIOR=SCROLL`, the marquee scrolls in from one side of the screen to the other side and then off. If `BEHAVIOR=SLIDE`, the marquee scrolls in from the right and stops at the left margin. If `BEHAVIOR=ALTERNATE`, the marquee bounces from one side of the screen to the other.
	`DIRECTION`	If `BEHAVIOR=SCROLL`, the marquee scrolls in this direction.
	`LOOP`	Indicates the number of times to repeat the marquee. If `LOOP` is `-1` or `INFINITE`, the marquee loops indefinitely.
	`SCROLLAMOUNT`	Indicates the number of pixels to move for each step of the animation; higher numbers mean the marquee moves faster.
	`SCROLLDELAY`	Indicates the number of milliseconds between each step of the animation; higher numbers are slower.

continues

Table 8.3. continued

Tag	Attribute	Use
	BGCOLOR	Indicates the background color of the marquee's bounding box (can be a color number or name).
	HEIGHT	Indicates the height of the marquee's bounding box.
	WIDTH	Indicates the width of the marquee's bounding box.
	HSPACE	Indicates the amount of space between the left and right edges of the marquee and its surrounding text.
	VSPACE	Indicates the amount of space between the upper and lower edges of the marquee and its surrounding text.
	ALIGN	Indicates the alignment of the marquee with the text before or after it. Possible values are TOP, MIDDLE, or BOTTOM.
<APPLET>...</APPLET>		Includes a Java applet on the Web page.
	CODE	Indicates the name of the applet's class.
	WIDTH	Indicates the width of the applet's bounding box.
	HEIGHT	Indicates the height of the applet's bounding box.
<PARAM>...</PARAM>		Specifies parameters to be passed to the applet.
	NAME	Indicates the name of the parameter.
	VALUE	Indicates the value of the parameter.
<META>		Specifies meta-information about the page itself.
	HTTP-EQUIV	Indicates an HTTP header name.
	CONTENT	Indicates the value of any meta-information tags, generally. For client pull, this attribute indicates the number of seconds to wait before reloading the page; you can also include a URL to load.

8

Q&A

Q My browser has a helper application for JPEG images listed in my helper applications list. But when I downloaded a JPEG file, it complained that it couldn't read the document. How can I fix this problem?

A Just because an application is listed in the helper application list (or initialization file) doesn't mean that you have that application available on your system. Browsers are generally shipped with a default listing of helper applications that are most commonly used for the common external file formats available on the Web. You have to locate and install each of those helper applications before your browser can use them. The fact that an application is listed isn't enough.

Q I've been using AU files for my sound samples, but I hear an awful hiss during the quiet parts. What can I do?

A Some sound-editing programs can help remove some of the hiss in AU files, but because of the nature of AU encoding, you'll usually have some amount of noise. If sound quality is that important to you, consider using AIFF or, if you have the converters, MPEG audio.

Q Why don't my MPEG files have sound?

A Maybe they do! The MPEG standard allows for both video and audio tracks, but few players can handle the audio track at this time. You have two choices if you must have sound for your MPEG movies: wait for better players (or bribe a programmer to write one), or convert your movies to QuickTime and show your readers how to install and use QuickTime players.

Q I'm using the Animator applet. I've got a bunch of Java animations that I want to put on different files, but if I put them all in the same directory, I can't name them all T1, T2, and so on, without naming conflicts. What do I do?

A The Animator applet contains lots of parameters I did not include in this chapter. One of them, IMAGESOURCE, takes a directory name relative to the current directory for images. So you can store your images in individual subdirectories and avoid naming problems. Using other Animator parameters, you can also change the names from T1, T2, and so on. See the URL for the Animator applet for details.

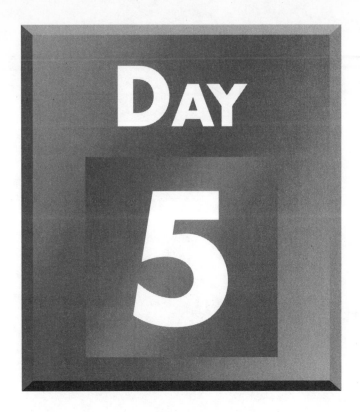

DAY

5

Designing Effective Web Pages

Chapter 9

Writing and Designing Web Pages: Dos and Don'ts

You won't learn about any HTML tags in this chapter or how to convert files from one strange file format to another. You're mostly done with the HTML part of Web page design. Next come the intangibles, the things that separate your pages from those of someone who just knows the tags and can fling text and graphics around and call it a presentation.

Armed with the information from the last five days, you could put this book down now and go off and merrily create Web pages to your heart's content. However, armed with both that information and what you'll learn today, you can create better Web pages. Do you need any more incentive to continue reading?

This chapter includes hints for creating well-written and well-designed Web pages, and it highlights dos and don'ts concerning the following:

☐ How to sort out the tangle of whether to use standard HTML tags or HTML extensions or both

☐ How to write your Web pages so that they can be easily scanned and read

☐ Issues concerning design and layout of your Web pages

☐ When and why you should create links

☐ How to use images effectively

☐ Other miscellaneous tidbits and hints

Using the HTML Extensions

In the past, before every browser company was introducing its own new HTML tags, being a Web designer was easy. The only HTML tags you had to deal with were those from HTML 2.0, and the vast majority of the browsers on the Web could read your pages without a problem. Now being a Web designer is significantly more complicated. Now you have to work with several groups of tags:

☐ The HTML 2.0 tags

☐ HTML 3.2 and 4.0 features, such as frames, tables, divisions, backgrounds, color, and style sheets, which are supported by most but not all browsers

☐ Browser-specific tags (from Netscape or Internet Explorer) that may or may not end up as part of the official HTML specification and whose support varies from browser to browser

☐ Other tags proposed for future HTML specification tags that few to no browsers support

If you're finding all this information rather mind-boggling, you're not alone. Authors and developers just like you are all trying to sort out the mess and make decisions based on how they want their pages to look. The HTML extensions do give you more flexibility with layout, but they limit the audience that can view the pages the way you want them to be viewed.

Choosing a strategy for using HTML extensions is one of the more significant design decisions you'll make as you start creating Web pages. You might find it easier to look at the choices you have as a sort of continuum between the conservative and the experimental Web author (see Figure 9.1).

Figure 9.1.
The Web author continuum.

Conservative		Experimental
HTML 2.0	HTML 3.2	HTML 4.0
Widest Audience	More Layout Control	Advanced Features
Most Browser Support	Accepted Standard	Narrower Audience
		Limited Browser Support

NOTE Don't think of these endpoints as value judgments; conservative isn't worse than experimental, or vice versa. You'll find advantages at both ends and significant advantages in the middle.

The conservative Web developer wants the widest possible audience for Web pages. The conservative Web developer sticks to HTML 2.0 tags as defined by the standard. I'm not saying that the conservative Web developer is boring. You can create magnificent Web content with the HTML 2.0 tags, and that content has the advantage over more advanced content in that it is supported without a hitch by the greatest number of browsers and, therefore, will reach the widest possible audience.

The experimental Web developer, on the other hand, wants the sort of control over layout that the more advanced tags—such as the newest Netscape or Microsoft extensions or the latest additions in HTML 4.0—give him or her and is willing to shut out a portion of the audience to get it. The experimental Web developer's pages are designed for a single browser (or at most two or three), tested only in a single browser, and might even have a big announcement on the pages that says "These Pages Are Best Read Using Browser X." Using other browsers to read those pages may make the design unreadable or at least confusing—or it may be just fine.

The best position, in terms of choosing between interesting design and a wide audience, is probably a balance between the two. With some knowledge beforehand of the effects that HTML extensions will have on your pages, both in browsers that support them and those that don't, you can make slight modifications to your design that will enable you to take advantage of both sides. Your pages are still readable and useful in older browsers over a wider range of platforms, but they can also take advantage of the advanced features in the newer browsers. Today, this generally means adopting the HTML 3.2 and 4.0 standard tags to achieve goals that are difficult or impossible with HTML 2.0, but at the same time, being aware of their effect on browsers that don't yet support the full HTML 3.2 or 4.0 specification.

Throughout this book, I've explained which tags are part of HTML 3.2 and 4.0 and which tags are available in which major browsers. I've also noted for each tag the alternatives you can use in cases in which a browser might not be able to view those tags. With this information in hand, you should be able to experiment with each tag in different browsers to see what the effect of each one is on your design.

The most important strategy I can suggest for using extensions while still trying to retain compatibility with other browsers is to test your files in those other browsers. Most browsers are freeware or shareware and available for downloading, so all you need to do is find them and install them. By testing your pages, you can get an idea of how different browsers interpret different tags, and eventually you'll get a feel for which extensions provide the most flexibility, which ones need special coding for alternatives in older browsers, and which tags can be used freely without complicating matters for other browsers.

Writing for Online

Writing on the Web is no different from writing in the real world. Even though the writing you do on the Web is not sealed in hard copy, it is still "published" and is still a reflection of you and your work. In fact, because your writing is online and therefore more transient to your readers, you'll have to follow the rules of good writing that much more closely because your readers will be less forgiving.

Because of the vast quantities of information available on the Web, your readers are not going to have much patience if your Web page is full of spelling errors or poorly organized. They are much more likely to give up after the first couple of sentences and move on to someone else's page. After all, several million pages are available out there. No one has time to waste on bad pages.

I don't mean that you have to go out and become a professional writer to create a good Web page, but I'll give you a few hints for making your Web page easier to read and understand.

Write Clearly and Be Brief

Unless you're writing the Great American Web Novel, your readers are not going to visit your page to linger lovingly over your words. One of the best ways you can make the writing in your Web pages effective is to write as clearly and concisely as you possibly can, present your points, and then stop. Obscuring what you want to say with extra words just makes figuring out your point more difficult.

If you don't have a copy of Strunk and White's *The Elements of Style*, put down this book right now, and go buy that book and read it. Then re-read it, memorize it, inhale it, sleep with it under your pillow, show it to all your friends, quote it at parties, and make it your life. You'll find no better guide to the art of good, clear writing than *The Elements of Style*.

Organize Your Pages for Quick Scanning

Even if you write the clearest, briefest, most scintillating prose ever seen on the Web, chances are good your readers will not start at the top of your Web page and carefully read every word down to the bottom.

Scanning, in this context, is the first quick look your readers give to each page to get the general gist of the content. Depending on what your users want out of your pages, they may scan the parts that jump out at them (headings, links, other emphasized words), perhaps read a few contextual paragraphs, and then move on. By writing and organizing your pages for easy "scannability," you can help your readers get the information they need as fast as possible.

To improve the scannability of your Web pages, follow these guidelines:

- ☐ **Use headings to summarize topics.** Note how this book has headings and subheadings. You can flip through quickly and find the portions that interest you. The same concept applies to Web pages.

- ☐ **Use lists.** Lists are wonderful for summarizing related items. Every time you find yourself saying something like "each widget has four elements" or "use the following steps to do this," the content after that phrase should be an ordered or unordered list.

- ☐ **Don't forget link menus.** As a form of list, link menus have all the advantages of lists for scannability, and they double as excellent navigation tools.

- ☐ **Don't bury important information in text.** If you have a point to make, make it close to the top of the page or at the beginning of a paragraph. Long paragraphs are harder to read and make gleaning the information more difficult. The further into the paragraph you put your point, the less likely anybody will read it.

Figure 9.2 shows the sort of writing technique that you should avoid.

Figure 9.2.

A Web page that is difficult to scan.

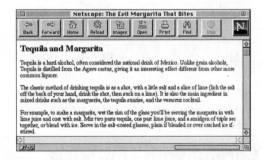

Because all the information on this page is in paragraph form, your readers have to read all three paragraphs to find out what they want and where they want to go next.

How would you improve the example shown in Figure 9.2? Try rewriting this section so that readers can better pick out the main points from the text. Consider the following:

- ☐ These three paragraphs actually contain two discrete topics.
- ☐ The four ingredients of the drink would make an excellent list.

Figure 9.3 shows what an improvement might look like.

Figure 9.3.

An improvement to the
difficult Web page.

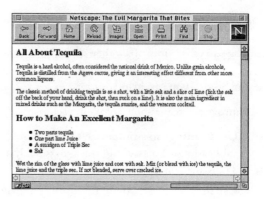

Make Each Page Stand on Its Own

As you write, keep in mind that your readers could jump into any of your Web pages from anywhere. For example, you may structure a page so that section four distinctly follows section three and has no other links to it. Then someone you don't even know might create a link to the page starting section four. From then on, readers could very well find themselves on section four without even being aware that section three exists.

Be careful to write each page so that it stands on its own. These guidelines will help:

☐ **Use descriptive titles.** The title should provide not only the direct subject of this page, but also its relationship to the rest of the pages in the presentation of which it is a part.

☐ **If a page depends on the one before it, provide a navigational link back to the page before it (and preferably also one up to the top level).**

☐ **Avoid initial sentences like the following:** "You can get around these problems by…," "After you're done with that, do…," and "The advantages to this method are…." The information referred to by "these," "that," and "this" are off on some other page. If these sentences are the first words your readers see, they are going to be confused.

Be Careful with Emphasis

Use emphasis sparingly in your text. Paragraphs with a whole lot of boldface and italics or words in ALL CAPS are hard to read—both if you use any of them several times in a paragraph and if you emphasize long strings of text. The best emphasis is used only with small words (such as: AND, THIS, OR, BUT).

Link text is also a form of emphasis. Use single words or short phrases as link text. Do not use entire passages or paragraphs as links.

Figure 9.4 illustrates a particularly bad example of too much emphasis obscuring the rest of the text.

Figure 9.4.

Too much emphasis.

By removing some of the boldface and using less text for your links, you can considerably reduce the amount of distraction in the paragraph, as you can see in Figure 9.5.

Figure 9.5.

Less emphasis.

Be especially careful of emphasis that moves or changes, such as marquees, blinking text, or animation on your pages. Unless the animation is the primary focus of the page, use movement and sound sparingly to prevent distractions from the rest of your page.

Don't Use Browser-Specific Terminology

Avoid references in your text to specific features of specific browsers. For example, don't use the following wording:

- ☐ **"Click Here."** What if your readers are using browsers without a mouse? A more generic phrase is "Select this link." (Of course, you should avoid the "here" syndrome in the first place, which neatly gets around this problem as well.)

- ☐ **"To save this page, pull down the File menu and select Save."** Each browser has a different set of menus and different ways of accomplishing the same action. If at all possible, do not refer to specifics of browser operation in your Web pages.

- ☐ **"Use the Back button to return to the previous page."** As in the preceding note, each browser has a different set of buttons and different methods for going "back." If you want your readers to be able to go back to a previous page or to any specific page, link the pages.

Spell Check and Proofread Your Pages

Spell checking and proofreading may seem like obvious suggestions, but given the number of pages I have seen on the Web that have obviously not had either, this tip bears mentioning.

The process of designing a set of Web pages and making them available on the Web is like publishing a book, producing a magazine, or releasing a product. Publishing Web pages is, of course, considerably easier than publishing books, magazines, or other products, but just because the task is easy does not mean your product can be sloppy.

Thousands of people may be reading and exploring the content you provide. Spelling errors and bad grammar reflect badly on your work, on you, and on the content you're describing. Poor writing may be irritating enough that your readers won't bother to delve any deeper than your home page, even if the subject you're writing about is fascinating.

Proofread and spell check each of your Web pages. If possible, have someone else read them. Other people can often pick up errors that you, the writer, can't see. Even a simple edit can greatly improve many pages and make them easier to read and navigate.

Design and Page Layout

Although the design capabilities of HTML and the Web are quite limited, you still have a lot to work with, and people without a sense of design still have quite a few opportunities to create something that looks simply awful.

Probably the best rule to follow at all times as far as designing each Web page is this: Keep the design as simple as possible. Reduce the number of elements (images, headings, rule lines), and make sure that the readers' eyes are drawn to the most important parts of the page first.

Keep this cardinal rule in mind as you read the next sections, which offer some other suggestions for basic design and layout of Web pages.

Use Headings as Headings

Headings are often rendered in graphical browsers in larger or bolder fonts. Therefore, using a heading tag, as shown in Figure 9.6, to provide some sort of warning, note, or emphasis in regular text is often tempting.

Figure 9.6.

The wrong way to use headings.

Headings work best when they're used as headings because they stand out from the text and signal the start of new topics. If you really want to emphasize a particular section of text, consider using a small image, a rule line, or some other method of emphasis instead. Figure 9.7 shows an example of the same text in Figure 9.6 with a different kind of visual emphasis.

Figure 9.7.

An alternative to the wrong way to use headings.

Group Related Information Visually

Grouping related information within a page is a task for both writing and design. By grouping related information under headings, as I suggested in the "Writing for Online" section earlier in this chapter, you improve the scannability of that information. Visually separating each section from the others helps to make each section distinct and emphasizes the relatedness of the information.

If a Web page contains several sections of information, find a way to separate those sections visually—for example, with a heading or with a rule line <HR>, as shown in Figure 9.8.

Figure 9.8.

Separate sections visually.

Use a Consistent Layout

When you're reading a book or a magazine, each page, each section, usually has the same layout. The page numbers are placed where you expect them, and the first word on each page starts in the same place.

The same sort of consistent layout works equally well in Web pages. A single "look and feel" for each page in your Web presentation is comforting to your readers. After two or three pages, they will know what the elements of each page are and where to find them. If you create a consistent design, your readers can find the information they need and navigate through your pages without having to stop at every page and try to find where elements are located.

Consistent layout can include the following:

☐ **Consistent page elements.** If you use second-level headings (<H2>) on one page to indicate major topics, use second-level headings for major topics on all your pages. If you have a heading and a rule line at the top of your page, use that same layout on all your pages.

☐ **Consistent forms of navigation.** Put your navigation menus in the same place on every page (usually the top or the bottom of the page), and use the same number of them. If you're going to use navigation icons, make sure you use the same icons in the same order for every page.

Using Links

Without links, Web pages would be really dull, and finding anything interesting on the Web would be close to impossible. The quality of your links, in many ways, can be as important as the writing and design of your actual pages. Here's some friendly advice on creating and using links.

Use Link Menus with Descriptive Text

As I've noted in this chapter and frequently in this book, using link menus is a great way of organizing your content and the links on a page. By organizing your links into lists or other menu-like structures, your readers can scan their options for the page quickly and easily.

Just organizing your links into menus, however, often isn't enough. When you arrange your links into menus, make sure that you aren't too short in your descriptions. Using menus of filenames or other marginally descriptive links in menus, like the menu shown in Figure 9.9, is tempting.

Figure 9.9.

A poor link menu.

Well, this figure shows a menu of links, and the links are descriptive of the actual page they point to, but they don't really describe the content of the page. How do readers know what's on the other side of the link, and how can they make decisions about whether they're interested in it from the limited information you've given them? Of these three links, only the last (`pesto.recipe`) gives the readers a hint about what they will see when they jump to that file.

A better plan is either to provide some extra text describing the content of the file, as shown in Figure 9.10, or to avoid the filenames altogether (who cares?). Just describe the contents of the files in the menu, with the appropriate text highlighted, as shown in Figure 9.11.

Figure 9.10.
A better link menu.

Figure 9.11.
Another better link menu.

Either one of these forms is better than the first; both give your readers more clues about what's on the other side of the link.

Use Links in Text

The best way to provide links in text is to first write the text without the links as if the text wasn't going to have links at all—for example, if you were writing it for hard copy. Then you can highlight the appropriate words that will serve as the link text for links to other pages. Make sure that you don't interrupt the flow of the page when you include a link. The idea of using links in text is that the text should stand on its own. That way, the links provide additional or tangential information that your readers can choose to ignore or follow based on their own whims.

Figure 9.12 shows another example of using links in text. Here the text itself isn't overly relevant; it's just there to support the links. If you're using text just to describe links, consider using a link menu instead of a paragraph. Your readers can find the information they want more easily. Instead of having to read the entire paragraph, they can skim for the links that interest them.

Figure 9.12.

*Links in text that
don't work well.*

Probably the easiest way to figure out whether you're creating links within text properly is to print out the formatted Web page from your browser. In hard copy, without hypertext, would the paragraph still make sense? If the page reads funny on paper, it'll read funny online as well. Some simple rephrasing of sentences can often help enormously in making the text on your pages more readable and more usable both online and when printed.

Avoid "Here" Syndrome

A common mistake that many Web authors make in creating links in body text is using the "here" syndrome. The Here syndrome is the tendency to create links with a single highlighted word (here) and to describe the link somewhere else in the text. Look at the following examples (with underlining indicating link text):

```
Information about ostrich socialization is contained here.

Select this link for a tutorial on the internal combustion engine.
```

Because links are highlighted on the Web page, the links visually "pop out" more than the surrounding text (or "draw the eye" in graphic design lingo). Your readers will see the link first, before reading the text. Try creating links this way. Figure 9.13 shows a particularly heinous example of the here syndrome. Close your eyes, open them quickly, pick a "here" at random, and then see how long it takes you to find out what the "here" is for.

Figure 9.13.

Here syndrome.

Now try the same exercise with a well-organized link menu of the same information, as shown in Figure 9.14.

Because "here" says nothing about what the link is used for, your poor readers have to search the text before and after the link itself to find out just what is supposed to be "here." In paragraphs that have lots of "here" or other nondescriptive links, matching up the links with what they are supposed to link to becomes difficult, forcing your readers to work harder to figure out what you mean.

Figure 9.14.

*The same page,
reorganized.*

Instead of this link

    Information about ostrich socialization is contained here.

a much better choice of wording would be something like

    The Palo Alto Zoo has lots of information about ostrich socialization.

or just

    The Palo Alto Zoo has lots of information about ostrich socialization.

To Link or Not To Link

Just as with graphics, every time you create a link, consider why you're linking two pages or sections. Is the link useful? Will it give your readers more information or take them closer to their goal? Is the link relevant in some way to the current content?

Each link should serve a purpose. Link for relevant reasons. Just because you mention the word *coffee* deep in a page about some other topic, you don't have to link that word to the coffee home page. Creating such a link may seem cute, but if a link has no relevance to the current content, it just confuses your readers.

This section describes some of the categories of links that are useful in Web pages. If your links do not fall into one of these categories, consider the reasons that you're including them in your page.

NOTE

> Thanks to Nathan Torkington for his "Taxonomy of Tags," published on the www-talk mailing list, which inspired this section.

Explicit navigation links indicate the specific paths readers can take through your Web pages: forward, back, up, home. These links are often indicated by navigation icons, as shown in Figure 9.15.

Figure 9.15.

Explicit navigation links.

Implicit navigation links, shown in Figure 9.16, are different from explicit navigation links in that the link text implies, but does not directly indicate, navigation between pages. Link menus are the best example of this type of link; from the highlighting of the link text, it is apparent that you will get more information on this topic by selecting the link, but the text itself does not necessarily say so. Note the major difference between explicit and implicit navigation links: If you print a page containing both, you should no longer be able to pick out the implicit links.

Figure 9.16.

Implicit navigation links.

Implicit navigation links can also include table-of-contents-like structures or other overviews made up entirely of links.

Word or concept definitions make excellent links, particularly if you're creating large networks of pages that include glossaries. By linking the first instance of a word to its definition, you can explain the meaning of that word to readers who don't know what it means while not distracting those who do. Figure 9.17 shows an example of this type of link.

Figure 9.17.

Definition links.

Finally, links to tangents and related information are valuable when the text content would distract from the main purpose of the page. Think of tangent links as footnotes or end notes in printed text (see Figure 9.18). They can refer to citations to other works or to additional information that is interesting but not necessarily directly relevant to the point you're trying to make.

Figure 9.18.

Footnote links.

Be careful that you don't get carried away with definitions and tangent links. You might create so many tangents that your readers spend so much time linking elsewhere that they can't follow the point of your original text. Resist the urge to link every time you possibly can, and link only to relevant tangents on your own text. Also, avoid duplicating the same tangent—for example, linking every instance of the letters *WWW* on your page to the WWW Consortium's home page. If you're linking twice or more to the same location on one page, consider removing most of the extra links. Your readers can select one of the other links if they're interested in the information.

Using Images

On Day 4, "Images, Backgrounds, and Multimedia," you learned all about creating and using images in Web pages. This section summarizes many of the hints you learned in those chapters for using images.

Don't Overuse Images

Be careful about including lots of images on your Web page. Besides the fact that each image adds to the amount of time it takes to load the page, including too many images on the same page can make your page look busy and cluttered and distract from the point you're trying to get across. Figure 9.19 shows such an example.

Remember the hints I gave you in Chapter 7, "Using Images, Color, and Backgrounds." Consider the reasons that you need to use each image before you put it on the page. If an image doesn't directly contribute to the content, consider leaving it off.

Figure 9.19.

Too many images.

Use Alternatives to Images

Of course, as soon as I mention images, I have to also mention that not all browsers can view those images. To make your pages accessible to the widest possible audience, you have to take the text-only browsers into account when you design your Web pages. These two possible solutions can help:

☐ Use the ALT attribute of the <IMG> tag to substitute appropriate text strings for the graphics automatically in text-only browsers. Use either a descriptive label to substitute for the default [image] that appears in the place of each inline image, or use an empty string ("") to ignore the image altogether.

☐ If providing a single-source page for both graphical and text-only browsers becomes too much work, and the result is not turning out to be acceptable, consider creating separate pages for each one: a page designed for the full-color full-graphical browsers and a page designed for the text-only browsers. Then provide the option of choosing one or the other from your home page.

Keep Images Small

If you use images, keep in mind that each image is a separate network connection and takes time to load over a network, meaning that each image adds to the total time it takes to view a page. Try to reduce the number of images on a page, and keep your images small both in file size and in actual dimensions. In particular, keep the following hints in mind:

☐ A good rule of thumb for large images is that at a 14.4Kbps modem connection, your page will load at an average of 1K per second. The entire page (text and images) should not take more than 30 seconds to load; otherwise, you risk annoying your readers and having them move on without reading your page. This rule of thumb limits you to 30K total for everything on your page. Strive to achieve that size by keeping your images small.

- [ ] For larger images, consider using thumbnails on your main page and then linking to the larger image rather than putting the larger image inline.

- [ ] Interlace your larger GIF files.

- [ ] Try the tests to see whether JPEG or GIF creates a smaller file for the type of image you're using.

- [ ] In GIF files, the fewer colors you use in the image, the smaller the image will be. You should try to use as few colors as possible to avoid problems with system-specific color allocation.

- [ ] You can reduce the physical size of your images by cropping them (using a smaller portion of the overall image) or by scaling (shrinking) the original image. When you scale the image, you might lose some of the detail from the original image.

- [ ] You can use the WIDTH and HEIGHT attributes to scale the image a larger size than the image actually is. These were originally Netscape-only extensions that were adopted as a part of HTML 3.2. Note the scaled result might not be what you expect. Test this procedure before trying it.

Watch Out for Display Assumptions

Many people create problems for their readers by making a couple of careless assumptions about other people's hardware. When you're developing Web pages, be kind and remember these two guidelines:

- [ ] **Don't assume that everyone has screen or browser dimensions the same as yours.**

    Just because that huge GIF you created is wide enough to fit on your screen in your browser doesn't mean it'll fit someone else's. Coming across an image that is too wide is annoying because it requires the readers to resize their windows all the time or scroll sideways.

    To fit in the width of a majority of browsers' windows, try to keep the width of your images to fewer than 450 pixels (most browsers on the Macintosh have a screen width of about 465).

- [ ] **Don't assume that everyone has full-color displays.**

    Test your images in resolutions other than full color. (You can often test in your image-editing program.) Many of your readers may have display systems that have only 16 colors, only have grayscale, or even just black and white. You may be surprised at the results: colors drop out or dither strangely in grayscale or black and white, and the effect may not be what you intended.

    Make sure your images are visible at all resolutions, or provide alternatives for high- and low-resolution images on the page itself.

Be Careful with Backgrounds and Link Colors

Using HTML extensions, you can use background colors and patterns and change the color of the text on your pages. Using this feature can be very tempting, but be very careful if you decide to do so. The ability to change the page and font colors and to provide fancy backdrops can cause you to quickly and easily make your pages entirely unreadable. Here are some hints for avoiding these problems:

- ☐ **Make sure you have enough contrast between the background and foreground (text) colors.** Low contrast can be hard to read. Also, light-colored text on a dark background is harder to read than dark text on a light background.

- ☐ **Avoid changing link colors at all.** Because your readers have attached semantic meanings to the default colors (blue means unfollowed, purple or red means followed), changing the colors can be very confusing.

- ☐ **Sometimes increasing the font size of all the text in your page using `<BASEFONT>` can make it more readable on a background.** Both the background and the bigger text will be missing in other browsers that don't support the Netscape tags.

- ☐ **If you're using background patterns, make sure the pattern does not interfere with the text.** Some patterns may look interesting on their own but can make it difficult to read the text you put on top of them. Keep in mind that backgrounds are supposed to be in the background. Subtle patterns are always better than wild patterns. Remember, your readers are still visiting your pages for the content on them, not to marvel at your ability to create faux marble in your favorite image editor.

When in doubt, try asking a friend to look at your pages. Because you are familiar with the content and the text, you may not realize how hard your pages are to read. Someone who hasn't read them before will not have your biases and will be able to tell you that your colors are too close or that the pattern is interfering with the text. Of course, you'll have to find a friend who will be honest with you.

Other Good Habits and Hints

In this section, I've gathered several other miscellaneous hints and advice about good habits to get into when you're working with groups of Web pages. They include notes on how big to make each page in your presentation and how to sign your pages.

Link Back to Home

Consider including a link back to the top level or home page on every page of your presentation. Providing this link allows readers a quick escape from the depths of your content. Using a home link is much easier than trying to navigate backward through a hierarchy or trying to use the "back" facility of a browser.

Don't Split Topics Across Pages

Each Web page works best if it covers a single topic in its entirety. Don't split topics across pages; even if you link between them, the transition can be confusing. It will be even more confusing if someone jumps in on the second or third page and wonders what is going on.

If you think that one topic is becoming too large for a single page, consider reorganizing the content so that you can break up that topic into subtopics. This tip works especially well in hierarchical organizations. It allows you to determine exactly to what level of detail each "level" of the hierarchy should go, and exactly how big and complete each page should be.

Don't Create Too Many or Too Few Pages

There are no rules for how many pages you must have in your Web presentation, nor for how large each page should be. You can have one page or several thousand, depending on the amount of content you have and how you have organized it.

With this point in mind, you might decide to go to one extreme or to another, each of which has advantages and disadvantages. For example, say you put all your content in one big page and create links to sections within that page, as illustrated in Figure 9.20.

Figure 9.20.

One big page.

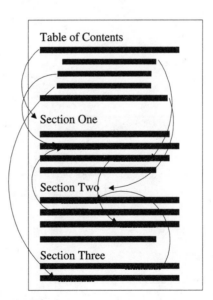

Advantages:

☐ One file is easier to maintain, and links within that file won't ever break if you move elements around or rename files.

☐ This file mirrors real-world document structure. If you're distributing documents both in hard copy and online, having a single document for both makes producing both easier.

Disadvantages:

☐ A large file takes a very long time to download, particularly over slow network connections and especially if the page includes lots of graphics.

☐ Readers must scroll a lot to find what they want. Accessing particular bits of information can become tedious. Navigating at points other than at the top or bottom becomes close to impossible.

☐ The structure is overly rigid. A single page is inherently linear. Although readers can skip around within sections in the page, the structure still mirrors that of the printed page and doesn't take advantage of the flexibility of smaller pages linked in a nonlinear fashion.

On the other extreme, you could create a whole bunch of little pages with links between them, as illustrated in Figure 9.21.

Figure 9.21.

Lots of little pages.

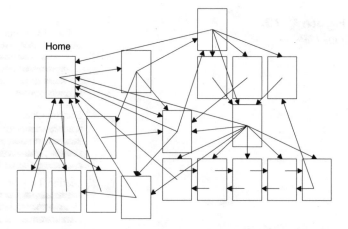

Advantages:

☐ Smaller pages load very quickly.

☐ You can often fit the entire page on one screen, so the information in that page can be scanned very easily.

Disadvantages:

☐ Maintaining all those links will be a nightmare. Just adding some sort of navigational structure to that many pages may create thousands of links.

☐ If you have too many jumps between pages, the jumps may seem jarring. Continuity is difficult when your readers spend more time jumping than actually reading.

What is the solution? Often the content you're describing will determine the size and number of pages you need, especially if you follow the one-topic-per-page suggestion. Testing your Web pages on a variety of platforms and network speeds will let you know whether a single page is too large. If you spend a lot of time scrolling around in it, or if it takes more time to load than you expected, your page may be too large.

Sign Your Pages

Each page should contain some sort of information at the bottom to act as the "signature." I mention this tip briefly in Chapter 5, "More Text Formatting with HTML," as part of the description of the <ADDRESS> tag; that particular tag was intended for just this purpose.

Consider putting the following useful information in the ADDRESS tag on each page:

☐ Contact information for the person who created this Web page or the person responsible for it, colloquially known as the "Webmaster." This information should include at least the person's name and preferably an e-mail address.

☐ The status of the page. Is it complete? Is it a work-in-progress? Is it intentionally left blank?

☐ The date this page was last revised. This information is particularly important for pages that change often. Include a date on each page so that people know how old it is.

☐ Copyright or trademark information, if it applies.

☐ The URL of this page. Including a printed URL of a page that is found at that same URL may seem a bit like overkill, but what happens if someone prints out the page and loses any other reference to it in the stack of papers on his or her desk? Where did it come from? (I've lost URLs many times and often wished for a URL to be typed on the document itself.)

Figure 9.22 shows a nice example of an address block.

Figure 9.22.

A sample address.

A nice touch to include on your Web page is to link a Mailto URL to the text containing the e-mail address of the Webmaster, like this:

```
<ADDRESS>
Laura Lemay <A HREF="mailto:lemay@lne.com">lemay@lne.com</A>
</ADDRESS>
```

This way, the readers of the page who have browsers that support the Mailto URL can simply select the link and send mail to the relevant person responsible for the page without having to retype the address into their mail programs.

NOTE

Linking Mailto URLs will work only in browsers that support Mailto URLs. Even in browsers that don't accept them, the link text will appear as usual, so there's no harm in including the link regardless.

Finally, if you don't want to clutter each page with a lot of personal contact or boilerplate copyright information, a simple solution is to create a separate page for the extra information, and then link the signature to that page. Here's an example:

```
<ADDRESS>
<A HREF="copyright.html">Copyright</A> and
<A HREF="webmaster.html">contact</A> information is available.
</ADDRESS>
```

Provide Non-Hypertext Versions of Hypertext Pages

Even though the Web provides a way to create pages in new and exciting ways, some readers still like to read text offline, on the bus or at the breakfast table. These kinds of readers have real problems with hypertext pages because after you start using hypertext to organize a document, it becomes difficult to tell your browser to "print the whole thing"—the browser knows only the boundaries of individual pages.

If you're using the Web to publish anything that might be readable and usable outside the Web, consider also creating a single text or PostScript version. You can then make it available as an external document for downloading. This way, your readers can both browse the document online and, if they want to, print it out for reading offline. You can even link the location of the hard-copy document to the start of the hypertext version, like this:

```
A <A HREF="ftp://myhome.com/pub/mydir/myfile.ps">PostScript version</A> of
this document is available via ftp at myhome.com in the directory /pub/mydir/
myfile.ps.
```

Of course, a handy cross-reference for the hard-copy version would be to provide the URL for the hypertext version, as follows:

```
This document is also available on hypertext form on
the World Wide Web at the URL:
http://myhome.com/pub/mydir/myfile.index.html.
```

Summary

The main dos and don'ts for Web page design from this chapter are as follow:

☐ Do understand the differences between HTML 2.0, HTML 3.2, HTML 4.0, and browser-specific HTML extensions, and decide which design strategy to follow while using them.

☐ Do use HTML extensions with alternatives, if at all possible.

☐ Do test your pages in multiple browsers.

☐ Do write your pages clearly and concisely.

☐ Do organize the text of your page so that your readers can scan for important information.

☐ Don't write Web pages that are dependent on pages before or after them in the structure. Do write context-independent pages.

☐ Don't overuse emphasis (boldface, italic, all caps, link text, blink, marquees). Do use emphasis sparingly and only when absolutely necessary.

☐ Don't use terminology specific to any one browser (click here, use the back button, and so on).

☐ Do spell check and proofread your pages.

☐ Don't use heading tags to provide emphasis.

☐ Do group related information both semantically (through the organization of the content) and visually (through the use of headings or by separating sections with rule lines).

☐ Do use a consistent layout across all your pages.

☐ Do use link menus to organize your links for quick scanning, and do use descriptive links.

☐ Don't fall victim to the "here" syndrome with your links.

☐ Do have good reasons for using links. Don't link to irrelevant material.

☐ Don't link repeatedly to the same site on the same page.

☐ Do keep your layout simple.

☐ Don't clutter the page with lots of pretty but unnecessary images.

☐ Do provide alternatives to images for text-only browsers.

☐ Do try to keep your images small so that they load faster over the network.

9

☐ Do be careful with backgrounds and colored text so that you do not make your pages flashy but unreadable.

☐ Do always provide a link back to your home page.

☐ Do match topics with pages.

☐ Don't split individual topics across pages.

☐ Do provide a signature block or link to contact information at the bottom of each page.

☐ Do provide single-page, non-hypertext versions of linear documents.

Q&A

Q **I've seen statistics on the Web that say between 60 percent and 90 percent of people on the Web are using Netscape. Why should I continue designing my pages for other browsers and testing my pages in other browsers when most of the world is using Netscape anyhow?**

A You can design explicitly for Netscape if you want to; your pages are your pages, and the decision is yours. But, given how easily you can make small modifications that allow your pages to be viewed and read in other browsers without losing much of the design, why lock out 10 to 40 percent of your audience for the sake of a few tags? Remember, with estimates of the size of the Web growing all the time, 10 percent of your readers could very well be a million people or more.

Q **I'm converting existing documents into Web pages. These documents are very text-heavy and are intended to be read from start to finish instead of being quickly scanned. I can't restructure or redesign the content to better follow the guidelines you've suggested in this chapter—that's not my job. What can I do?**

A Some content is going to be structured this way, particularly when you're converting a document written for paper to online. Ideally, you would be able to rewrite and restructure for online presentation, but realistically you often cannot do anything with the content other than throw it online.

All is not lost, however. You can still improve the overall presentation of these documents by providing reasonable indexes to the content (summaries, tables of contents pages, subject indexes, and so on), and by including standard navigation links back out of the text-heavy pages. In other words, you can create an easily navigable framework around the documents themselves, which can go a long way toward improving content that is otherwise difficult to read online.

Q I have a standard signature block that contains my name and e-mail address, revision information for the page, and a couple of lines of copyright information that my company's lawyers insisted on. It's a little imposing, particularly on small pages, where the signature is bigger than the page itself!

A If your company's lawyers agree, consider putting all your contact and copyright information on a separate page and then linking it on every page instead of duplicating it every time. This way, your pages won't be overwhelmed by the legal stuff, and if the signature changes, you won't have to change it on every single page.

Chapter 10

Examples of Good and Bad Web Design

In this chapter, we'll walk through some simple examples of pages and presentations that you might find out on the Web. (Actually, you won't find these particular pages out on the Web; I developed these examples specifically for this chapter.) Each of these Web presentations is either typical of the kind of information being provided on the Web today or shows some unique method for solving problems you might run into while developing your own presentations. In particular, you'll explore the following Web presentations:

☐ A company profile for the Foozle Sweater Company

☐ An encyclopedia of motorcycles, with images, sounds, and other media clips

☐ The catalog for a small nursery, in which you can both browse and order cacti and succulents

☐ A Web-based book about making bread

In each example, I note some of the more interesting features of the page as well as some of the issues that you might want to consider as you develop your own pages and presentations.

Example One: A Company Profile

Foozle Industries, Inc., makes a wide variety of sweaters for all occasions. (They were responsible for the demon sweater mentioned in Chapter 3, "Begin with the Basics.") Customers visiting the Foozle Industries Web server would first be presented with the Foozle Industries Home Page (see Figure 10.1).

Figure 10.1.

Foozle Industries home page.

From this simple and unpretentious home page, the customer has several choices of pages to visit on Foozle's Web site, arranged in a link menu. I won't describe all of them in this section, just a few that provide interesting features.

What's New at Foozle?

The first link to check out from the Foozle home page is the What's New page. The link to this page has been time stamped, noting the last time it changed. Selecting the What's New link takes you, appropriately, to the What's New page (see Figure 10.2).

Organized in reverse chronological order (from the most recent event backwards), the What's New page contains information about interesting things going on at Foozle Industries, both inside and outside the company. This page is useful for announcing new products to customers on the Web, or just for providing information about the site, the company, and other Foozle information. What's New pages, in general, are useful for sites that are visited repeatedly and frequently, as they allow your readers to find the new information on your site quickly and easily without having to search for it.

10

Figure 10.2.

The Foozle What's New page.

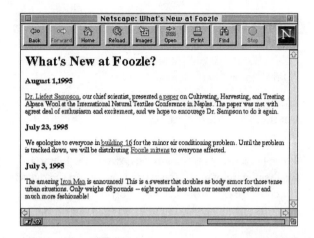

In this What's New page, the topmost item in the list of new things is a note about a paper presented by the Foozle chief scientist at a conference in Naples. That item has a link attached to it, implying that the paper itself is on the other side of that link, and, sure enough, it is (see Figure 10.3).

Figure 10.3.

All about Foozle Alpaca wool.

Alpaca wool is fascinating, but where do you go from here? The links at the top of the page indicate that the reader has two navigation choices: back up to the Foozle home page, or go to an overview of technical papers.

We've visited the home page already, so let's go on to the technical papers.

Technical Papers

The Technical Papers section of the Foozle Web site (see Figure 10.4) provides a list of the papers Foozle has published describing technical issues surrounding the making of sweaters. (Didn't know there were any, did you?)

Each link in the list takes you to the paper it describes. You can't see it in the figure, of course, but the link to the Alpaca wool paper is in a different color, indicating that it has already been visited.

From here, the reader can move down in the hierarchy and read any of the papers, or go back up the hierarchy to the overview page. From the overview page, the reader would then have the choice of exploring the other portions of the Web site: the company overview, the product descriptions, or the listing of open opportunities.

Figure 10.4.

The Technical Papers section.

Features of This Web Site and Issues for Development

This Web presentation for a simple company profile is quite straightforward in terms of design; the structure is a simple hierarchy, with link menus for navigation to the appropriate pages. Extending it is a simple matter of adding additional "limbs" to the hierarchy by adding new links to the top-level page.

However, note the path we took through the few pages in this Web site. In a classic hierarchy the reader visits each "limb" in turn, exploring downward, and then creeping back up levels to visit new pages. However, remember the link between the What's New page and the paper on Alpaca wool? This link caused the reader to move sideways from one limb (the What's New page) to another (the Technical Papers section).

In this example, of course, given its simplicity, there is little confusion. But given a hierarchy much more complicated than this, with multiple levels and sub-trees, having links that cross hierarchical boundaries and allow the reader to break out of the structure can be confusing. After a few lateral links it is difficult to figure out where you are in the hierarchy. This is a common problem with most hypertext systems, and is often referred to as "getting lost in hyperspace."

Few really good solutions exist to the problem of getting lost. I prefer to avoid the problem by trying not to create lateral links across a hierarchy. If you stick with the rigid structure of the hierarchy and provide only navigational links, readers can usually figure out where they are, and if not, they usually have only two main choices: move back up in the hierarchy to a known point, or drill deeper into the hierarchy for more detailed information.

10

Example Two: A Multimedia Encyclopedia

The Multimedia Encyclopedia of Motorcycles is a set of Web pages that provides extensive information about motorcycles and their makers. In addition to text information about each motorcycle maker, the multimedia encyclopedia includes photographs, sounds (engine noises!), and video for many of the motorcycles listed.

The index is organized alphabetically, one page per letter (`A.html`, `B.html`, and so on). To help navigate into the body of the encyclopedia, the home page for this presentation is an overview page.

The Overview Page

The overview page is the main entry point into the body of the encyclopedia (see Figure 10.5).

This page provides two main ways to get into the encyclopedia: by selecting the first letter of the marque or by selecting the name of one of the specific marques mentioned in the list itself.

NOTE

A *marque* is a fancy term used by motorcycle and sports car fanatics to refer to manufacturers of a vehicle.

Figure 10.5.

*The Motorcycle Encyclo-
pedia overview page.*

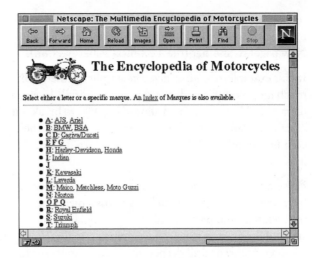

So, for example, if you wanted to find out information about the Norton motorcycle company, you could select N for Norton and then scroll down to the appropriate entry in the N page. But since Norton is one of the major manufacturers listed next to the N link, you could select that link instead and go straight to the entry for Norton.

The Entry for Norton

Each individual page contains entries for all the marques starting with that letter. If the reader has chosen a specific manufacturer, the link points directly to that specific entry (for example, the entry for Norton, shown in Figure 10.6). Each entry contains information about the marque and the various motorcycles it has produced over the years.

Figure 10.6.

Entry for Norton.

So where are the pictures? This was supposed to be a multimedia encyclopedia, wasn't it? In addition to the text describing Norton itself, the entry includes a list of external media files: images of various motorcycles, sound clips of what they sound like, and film of famous riders on their Nortons (see Figure 10.7).

Figure 10.7.

The list of external media.

Each media file is described in text and contains links to those files so you can download them if you want to. For example, selecting the 850 Commando link accesses a JPEG image of the 850 Commando (see Figure 10.8).

Figure 10.8.

The Norton 850 Commando.

Note also that in each point in the text where another manufacturer is mentioned, that manufacturer is linked to its own entry. For example, selecting the word BSA in the last paragraph takes you to the entry for BSA (see Figure 10.9).

Figure 10.9.

Entry for BSA.

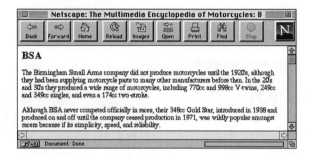

In this way, the reader can jump from link to link and manufacturer to manufacturer, exploring the information the encyclopedia contains based on what interests them. After they're done exploring, however, getting back to a known point is always important. For just this purpose, each entry in the encyclopedia contains a "Back to Overview" link. The duplication of this link in each entry means that the reader never has to scroll far to the top or bottom of the page in order to find the link back to the overview.

The Index of Marques

Back on the main overview page, there's one more feature I'd like to point out: The overview also contains a link to an Index of Marques, an alphabetical listing of all the manufacturers of motorcycles mentioned in the encyclopedia (see Figure 10.10).

Each name in the index is, as you might expect, a link to the entry for that manufacturer in the encyclopedia itself, allowing you yet another way to quickly navigate into the alphabetic listings.

Figure 10.10.

The Index of Marques.

Features of This Web Site and Issues for Development

Probably the best feature of the design of this encyclopedia is the overview page. In many cases, an online encyclopedia of this sort would provide links to each letter in the alphabet, and leave it at that. If you wanted to check out Norton motorcycles, you would select the link for "N" and then scroll down to the entry for Norton. By providing links to some of the more popular motorcycle makers on the overview page itself, the author of this Web page provides a simple quick-reference that shortens the scrolling time and takes its readers directly to where they want to be.

The addition of the Index of Marques is also a nice touch, as it enables readers to jump directly to the entry of a particular manufacturer's name, reducing the amount of scrolling required to find the entry they want. Again, it's the same content in the encyclopedia. The overview page simply provides several different ways to find the information readers might be looking for.

The encyclopedia itself is structured in a loosely based Web pattern, making it possible for readers to jump in just about anywhere and then follow cross-references and graze through the available information, uncovering connections between motorcycles and marques and motorcycle history that might be difficult to uncover in a traditional paper encyclopedia. Also, by providing all the media files external to the pages themselves, the author of this Web presentation not only allows the encyclopedia to be used equally well by graphical and text-only browsers, but also keeps the size of the individual files for each letter small so they can be quickly loaded over the Net.

Finally, note that every listing in each letter has a link back to the overview page. If there were more than a single link, they would clutter the page and look ugly. The only explicit navigation choice is back to the overview, so including a single link enables readers to quickly and easily get back out of the encyclopedia, rather than having to scroll to the top or the bottom of a very long page to get to a set of navigation choices.

The biggest issue with developing a Web presentation of this kind is in setup and maintenance. Depending on the amount of material you have to put online, the task of arranging it all (Do you use exactly 26 files, one for each letter of the alphabet? Or more? Or less?) and creating the links for all the cross-references and all the external media can be daunting indeed. Fortunately, a presentation of this sort does not have to be updated very often, so after the initial work is done, the maintenance is not all that difficult.

Example Three: A Shopping Catalog

Susan's Cactus Gardens is a commercial nursery specializing in growing and shipping cacti and succulents. It offers over 120 species of cacti and succulents as well as books and other cactus-related items. Figure 10.11 shows the home page for Susan's Cactus Gardens.

Figure 10.11.

Susan's Cactus Gardens home page.

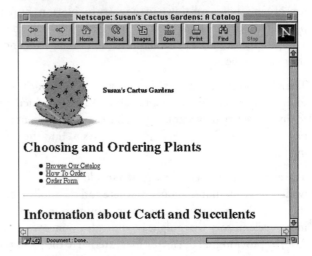

From here, customers have several choices: Read some background about the nursery itself, get information about specials and new plants, browse the catalog, get information about ordering, and actually order the cacti or succulents they have chosen.

Browsing the Catalog

Selecting the Browse Our Catalog link takes customers to another menu page, where they have several choices for how they want to browse the catalog (see Figure 10.12).

By providing several different views of the catalog, the author is serving many different kinds of customers: those who know about cacti and succulents and just want to look up a specific variety, in which case the alphabetic index is most appropriate; those who know they would like, say, an Easter Cactus with pink flowers but are not sure which particular variety they want (the listing by category); as well as those who don't really know or care about the names but would like something that looks nice (the photo gallery).

The alphabetical links (A–F, G–R, S–Z) take customers to an alphabetical listing of the plants available for purchase. Figure 10.13 shows a sample listing from the alphabetical catalog.

Figure 10.12.

How to browse the catalog.

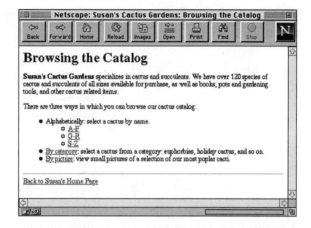

Figure 10.13.

The Cactus Catalog, arranged alphabetically.

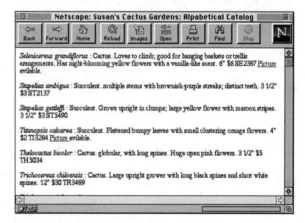

Each item indicates the Latin or scientific name of the cactus, a common name (if any), a simple description, size, order number, and price. If a photograph of this cactus is available in the photo gallery section of the catalog, a link is provided to that photograph so that readers can see what this cactus looks like before they buy it.

The catalog is also cross-referenced by each cactus's common name, if any. The link from the common name takes you back to the primary entry for the cactus. So if you really wanted a plant called Crown of Thorns, selecting that entry would take you to the true entry for that plant, Euphorbia Milii.

Each section of the alphabetical catalog also includes navigation buttons for returning back to the list of catalog views (Browsing the Catalog), or for returning to the home page.

The second view of the catalog (accessible from the Browsing the Catalog page) is the category view. Selecting this link takes the reader to yet another page of menus, listing the available categories (see Figure 10.14).

Figure 10.14.

The category view.

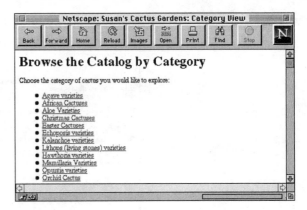

Selecting a particular category—for example, Orchid Cacti—takes customers to a list of the available plants in that category. Each element in the list should look familiar; they're the same elements as in the alphabetical list, sorted in a different order (see Figure 10.15).

Figure 10.15.

The Cactus Catalog by category.

From the category index, customers can go back to the list of categories (one step up), or back to the list of catalog views (two steps up). On the Browsing the Catalog page, there's one more catalog view to examine: the photo gallery.

The photo gallery enables customers to browse many of the cacti available at the nursery by looking at pictures of them, rather than having to know their scientific names. This feature is obviously available only to graphical browsers but provides an excellent way to browse for interesting cacti.

The photo gallery page (shown in Figure 10.16) is organized as a series of icons, with each small picture of the cactus linked to a larger JPEG equivalent. The text description of each picture also takes you back to the appropriate entry in the main catalog.

Figure 10.16.

The Cactus Catalog photo gallery.

Ordering

After customers have finished browsing the catalog and they have an idea of the cacti they want to order, they can jump back up to the home page for Susan's Cactus Gardens and find out how to order. (It's the second bullet in the list shown previously in Figure 10.11.)

The page for ordering is just some simple text (see Figure 10.17): information about where to call or send checks, tables for shipping costs, notes on when they will ship plants, and so on.

Figure 10.17.

Ordering plants.

In the section on ordering by mail, there is a link to an order form. The form itself is a PostScript file that customers will download, print out, and then fill out and send to the nursery. (It's an external file, specified in the HREF attribute to a link tag, just as you would specify any external media file.)

NOTE

> Why not order online? This page could easily have included an HTML form that allows readers to order their cacti online. I didn't include one here because you haven't learned about forms yet; we'll do that later in the book on Day 7, "Going Live on the Web."

And, lastly, note that the third bullet on the Susan's Cactus Gardens home page is a direct link to the order form file; it's provided here so that repeat customers won't have to take the added step of going back to the ordering, shipping, and payment page again.

Features of This Web Site and Issues for Development

In any online shopping service, the goals are to allow the reader to browse the items for sale and then to order those items. Within the browsing goal, there are several subgoals: What if the reader wants a particular item? Can it be found quickly and easily? What if someone just wants to look through the items for sale until he or she finds something interesting?

These two goals for browsing the online inventory may seem conflicting, but in this particular example they've been handled especially well through the use of multiple views of the content of the catalog. The multiple views do provide a level of indirection (an extra menu between the top-level page and the contents of the catalog itself), but that small step provides a branching in the hierarchy structure that helps each different type of customer accomplish his or her goals.

Probably the hardest part of building and maintaining a set of Web pages of this sort is maintaining the catalog itself, particularly if items need to be added or removed, or if prices change frequently. If the nursery had only one catalog view (the alphabetical one), this would not be so bad, as you could make changes directly to the catalog files. With additional views and the links between them, however, maintenance of the catalog becomes significantly more difficult.

Ideally, this sort of information could be stored in a database rather than as individual HTML files. Databases are designed to handle information like this and to be able to generate different views on request. But how do you hook up the database with the Web pages?

The Web has a mechanism for running programs on the server side. This could mean that given enough programming skill (and familiarity with your database), you could create a program to do database queries from a Web page and return a neatly formatted list of items. Then, on the Web page, when someone requested the alphabetical listing, they would get an automatically generated list that was as up to date as the database was. But to do this, you'll need a database that can talk to your Web server, which, depending on the system your Web server runs on, may or may not be technically feasible. And you need the programming skill to make it work.

An alternate solution is to keep the data in the database and then dump it to text and format it in HTML every once in awhile. The primary difficulty with that solution, of course, is how much work it would take to do the conversion each time while still preserving the cross-references to the other pages. Could the process be automated, and how much setup and daily maintenance would that involve?

With this kind of application, these are the kinds of questions and technical challenges you may have to deal with if you create Web presentations. Sometimes the problem involves more than designing, writing, and formatting information on the screen.

Example Four: An Online Book

In this final example, we'll look at an online book called Bread & Circuses. This is a book that might very well have been published in hardcopy and has since been converted to HTML and formatted with few changes—the book-like structure has been retained in HTML, with each chapter a separate page. This is quite common on the Web, not necessarily with books, but with papers, articles, and otherwise linear forms of information. Does it work? Read on.

The home page for Bread & Circuses (shown in Figure 10.18) is, appropriately, a table of contents, just as it might be in a real book. Organized as lists within lists, this table of contents is essentially a large link menu with pointers to the various sections in the book.

Figure 10.18.

The Bread & Circuses table of contents.

Readers who are interested in all the content the book has to offer could simply select the first link (Basics) and read all the way through from start to finish. Or, they could choose a topic and jump directly to that section in the book.

Proofing

Choosing the link for Proofing takes the reader to the file for Chapter 1 and then scrolls down to the appropriate section in that file (shown in Figure 10.19).

Figure 10.19.

The section on proofing.

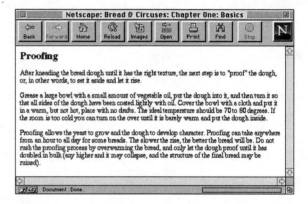

Here, the reader can read all about proofing. At the end of this section is the next section, "Shaping," and following it is the remainder of the chapter. Finally, at the end of the chapter, there are navigation links back to the table of contents, or on to the next chapter (see Figure 10.20).

Figure 10.20.

Navigation links.

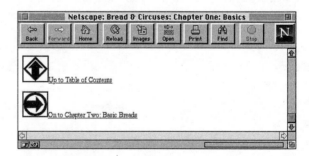

The two navigation links allow you either to progress linearly through the book by selecting the next chapter link, or to go back to the table of contents and choose another section or chapter to read. Note in this example the placement of the navigation links only at the end of each chapter file. The table of contents makes it easy to jump into the middle of the chapter, but to jump back out again you have to scroll all the way to the bottom (or go back using your browser).

The Index

On the table-of-contents page at the bottom of the list, there's a link to an index (the same place it would be in a hardcopy book—at the end). The index is similar to the table of contents in that it provides an overview of the content and links into specific places within the book itself. Like a paper index, the online version contains an alphabetical list of major topics and words, each one linked to the spot in the text where it is mentioned (see Figure 10.21).

Figure 10.21.
The index.

Yeast is mentioned multiple times in the book. Because online books do not (usually) have page numbers, linking index entries to multiple locations becomes more of a chore, as you'll have to construct your index so that each entry includes some kind of location reference (not to mention having to add all those anchors inside the chapters themselves).

So is this index useful? Like the table of contents, it does help readers jump to a specific place within the content. But also like the table of contents, it's harder for readers to get back out again once they're in the book—even more so for the index because the author does not provide a navigation link at the end of the chapter directly back to the index. This makes the index useful only in limited circumstances.

Features of This Web Site and Issues for Development

The biggest problem with putting books or other linear material online is that the material is often more difficult to navigate online than it is on paper. Online, readers can't flip through the pages as quickly and easily as they can on paper, and they can't use hints such as page numbers and chapter headings—both ways in which hardcopy books make finding where you are easy. For this reason, when you convert information intended for hardcopy to HTML, it is crucial to include overview pages, such as the table of contents in this example, to enable readers to jump in and out of the content and to find what they want.

More importantly, however, you have to provide methods of jumping back out again. In this example, the table of contents made it possible to jump into the middle of the content, but jumping back out again was less easy because there were few navigation links except at the end of the chapter. And jumping back to the index involved two links: back to the table of contents and then on to the index. In hardcopy, this isn't an issue. Online, it becomes one.

This example provided both a table of contents and an index. Multiple views of the same contents are usually a good thing, as I pointed out in the previous two examples, because they let your readers choose which way they want to find what they are looking for. Watch out for views that are intended for hardcopy, however, as they might not apply overly well. For example, a typical index, with a word or citations and a list of page numbers, doesn't work overly well in a Web presentation because you don't have page numbers. Consider some other method of linking to information in your document.

When converting a linear document to the Web, there may also be the temptation to add extra non-navigational links as well, for example, to refer to footnotes or citations or just related material. However, keep in mind with linear structures as with hierarchies that the structure can often keep your reader from getting lost or confused in your material. Links to other sections in the book can be confusing and muddle the structure you've tried so hard to preserve by converting the document to HTML.

Limited forms of non-navigational links can work well, however—for example, an explicit reference to another section of the book in the text such as, "For more information about yeast, see 'yeast' in Chapter 1." In this case, it is clear where the link is leading, and readers understand where they are and where they are going so they can reorient their position in the presentation.

Summary

I've presented only a couple ideas for using and structuring Web pages here; the variations on these themes are unlimited for the Web pages you will design.

Probably the best way to find examples of the sort of Web pages you might want to design and how to organize them is to go out on the Web and browse what's out there. While you're browsing, in addition to examining the layout and design of individual pages and the content they describe, keep an eye out for the structures people have used to organize their pages, and try to guess why they might have chosen that organization. ("They didn't think about it" is a common reason for many poorly organized Web pages, unfortunately.) Critique other people's Web pages with an eye for their structure and design: Is it easy to navigate them? Did you get lost? Can you easily get back to a known page from any other location in their presentation? If you had a goal in mind for this presentation, did you achieve that goal, and if not, how would you have reorganized it?

Learning from other people's mistakes and seeing how other people have solved difficult problems can help you make your own Web pages better.

Q&A

Q These Web presentations are really cool. What are their URLs?

A As I noted at the beginning of this chapter, the Web presentations I've described here are mock-ups of potential Web presentations that could exist. Although many of the designs and organizations that I have created here were inspired by existing Web pages, these pages do not actually exist on the Web.

Q Three out of the four examples here used some sort of hierarchical organization. Are hierarchies that common, and do I have to use them? Can't I do something different?

A Hierarchies are extremely common on the Web, but that doesn't mean that they're bad. Hierarchies are an excellent way of organizing your content, especially when the information you're presenting lends itself to a hierarchical organization.

You can certainly do something different to organize your presentation. But the simplicity of hierarchies allows them to be easily structured, easily navigated, and easily maintained. Why make more trouble for yourself and for your reader by trying to force a complicated structure on otherwise simple information?

10

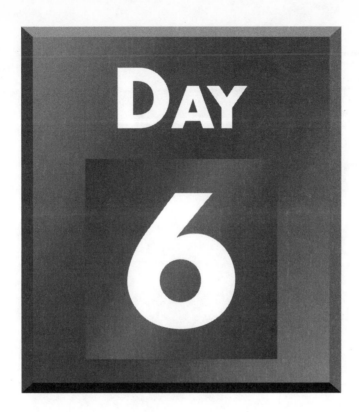

Advanced HTML Features: Tables and Frames

Chapter 11

Tables

Tables are an advanced HTML construct that allows you to arrange text, images, and other HTML content into rows and columns with or without borders. Tables were the first part of what is now HTML to hit the Web, and they've had an enormous influence on how pages are designed and constructed. In this chapter, you'll learn all about tables, including:

☐ The state of table development on the Web

☐ Defining tables in HTML

☐ Creating captions, rows, and heading and data cells

☐ Modifying cell alignment

☐ Creating cells that span multiple rows or columns

☐ Adding color to tables

☐ How to use (or not use) tables in your Web documents

A Note About the Table Definition

Tables were one of the first extensions to HTML that were proposed as part of HTML. In early 1995, Netscape and Mosaic almost simultaneously implemented a simple version of tables in their browsers (with Netscape adding a few extra features). Tables almost immediately revolutionized Web page design because tables can be used not just for presenting data in a tabular form, but also for page layout and control over placement of various HTML elements on a page. Tables have become so popular that most major browsers have now added table support.

At the time tables were originally implemented in Netscape and Mosaic, the actual definition for tables in HTML was still under considerable discussion, as was most of the HTML 3.0 specification. Although the definition of the basic table, as I'll describe in this chapter, is settled, and most browsers that support tables do support this definition, tables are still being discussed and refined by the WWW Consortium and by other interested parties.

Keep the fact that tables are still changing in mind as you design your own tables; although it's unlikely that anything you design now will break in the future, there probably will be changes still to come.

Creating Basic Tables

With that one small warning in mind, let's jump right in. To create tables in HTML, you define the parts of your table and which bits of HTML go where, and then you add HTML table code around those parts. Then you refine the table's appearance with alignments, borders, and colored cells. In this section, you'll learn how to create a basic table with headings, data, and a caption.

One more note, however. Creating tables by hand in HTML is no fun. The code for tables was designed to be easy to generate by programs, not to be written by hand, and as such it can be confusing. You'll do a lot of experimenting, testing, and going back and forth between your browser and your code to get a table to work out right. HTML editors can help a great deal with this, as can working initially in a word processor's table editor or a spreadsheet to get an idea of what goes where. But I suggest doing at least your first bunch of tables the hard way so that you can get an idea how HTML tables work.

Table Parts

Before we get into the actual HTML code to create a table, let me define some terms so we both know what we're talking about:

☐ The *caption* indicates what the table is about—for example, "Voting Statistics, 1950–1994," or "Toy Distribution Per Room at 1564 Elm St." Captions are optional.

☐ The *table headings* label the rows or columns, or both. Table headings are usually in a larger or emphasized font that is different from the rest of the table. Table headings are also optional.

☐ *Table data* is the content of the table itself. The combination of the table headings and table data makes up the sum of the table.

☐ *Table cells* are the individual squares in the table. A cell can contain normal table data or a table heading.

Figure 11.1 shows a typical table and its parts.

Figure 11.1.
The parts of a table.

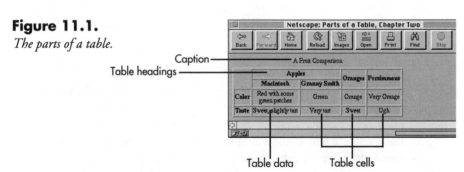

The <TABLE> Tag

To create a table in HTML, you use the <TABLE>...</TABLE> tags, which contain the code for a caption and then the contents of the table itself:

```
<TABLE>
...table contents...
</TABLE>
```

The most common attribute of the <TABLE> tag is the BORDER attribute. In HTML 2.0, BORDER causes the table to be drawn with a border around it, which can be a fancy border in a graphical browser or just a series of dashes and pipes (|) in a text-based browser.

Starting with HTML 3.2, the correct usage of the BORDER attribute is a little different: it indicates the width of a border in pixels. Setting BORDER=0 means the border has no width and is not displayed. BORDER=1 creates a one pixel–wide border, BORDER=2 a two pixel–wide border, and so on.

In addition, if you leave out the BORDER attribute, browsers are expected to not display a border (just like BORDER=0). If you use the old HTML 2.0 form of BORDER with no value (as in <TABLE BORDER>), newer browsers are expected to display a one-pixel border (as with BORDER=1).

Borderless tables are useful when you want to use the table structure for layout purposes, but you don't necessarily want the outline of an actual table on the page.

Rows and Cells

Inside the <TABLE>...</TABLE> tags, you define the actual contents of the table. Tables are specified in HTML row by row, and each row definition contains definitions for all the cells in that row. So, to define a table, you start by defining a top row and each cell in turn, and then you define a second row and its cells, and so on. The columns are automatically calculated based on how many cells there are in each row.

Each table row is indicated by the <TR> tag and ends with the appropriate closing </TR>. Each table row, in turn, has a number of table cells, which are indicated using the <TH>...</TH> (for heading cells) and <TD>...</TD> tags (for data cells). You can have as many rows as you want to and as many cells in each row as you need for your columns, but you should make sure that each row has the same number of cells so that the columns line up.

NOTE

> In early definitions of tables, the closing tags </TR>, </TH>, and </TD> were required for each row and cell. Since then, the table definition has been refined such that each of these closing tags is optional. However, many browsers that support tables still expect the closing tags to be there, and the tables might even break if you don't include the closing tags. Until tables become more consistently implemented across browsers, it's probably a good idea to continue using the closing tags even though they are optional—after all, using them is still correct, so there are no compelling reasons to leave them out.

Here's a simple example: a table with only one row, four cells, and one heading on the left side.

```
<TABLE>
<TR>
    <TH>Heading</TH>
    <TD>Data</TD>
    <TD>Data</TD>
    <TD>Data</TD>
</TR>
</TABLE>
```

The <TH> tag indicates a cell that is also a table heading, and the <TD> tag is a regular cell within the table (TD stands for Table Data). Headings are generally displayed in a different way than table cells, such as in a boldface font. Both <TH> and <TD> should be closed with their respective closing tags </TH> and </TD>.

If it's a heading along the top edge of the table, the <TH> tags for that heading go inside the first row. The HTML for a table with a row of headings along the top and one row of data looks like this:

```
<P>A Table with Headings Across the Top</P>
<TABLE BORDER>
<TR>
    <TH>Drive Plate</TH>
    <TH>Front Cover</TH>
</TR>
<TR>
    <TD>39-49</TD>
    <TD>19-23</TD>
</TR>
</TABLE>
```

If the headings are along the left edge of the table, put each <TH> in the first cell in each row, like this:

```
<P>A Table with Headings Along the Side</P>
<TABLE BORDER>
<TR>
    <TH>Drive Plate</TH>
    <TD>39-49</TD>
</TR>
<TR>
    <TH>Front Cover</TH>
    <TD>19-23</TD>
</TR>
</TABLE>
```

Figure 11.2 shows the results of both these tables.

Figure 11.2.
Small tables and headings.

Both table headings and data can contain either text or HTML code or both, including links, lists, forms, and other tables.

The following input and output example shows a simple table. Figure 11.3 shows its result in Netscape Navigator.

```
<HTML>
<HEAD>
<TITLE>Rows and Cells</TITLE>
</HEAD>
<BODY>
<TABLE BORDER>
<CAPTION>Soup of the Day</CAPTION>
<TR>
    <TH>Monday</TH>
    <TH>Tuesday</TH>
    <TH>Wednesday</TH>
    <TH>Thursday</TH>
    <TH>Friday</TH>
</TR>
<TR>
    <TD>Split Pea</TD>
    <TD>New England<BR>Clam Chowder</TD>
    <TD>Minestrone</TD>
    <TD>Cream of<BR>Broccoli</TD>
    <TD>Chowder</TD>
</TR>
</TABLE>
</BODY>
</HTML>
```

OUTPUT

Figure 11.3.
Rows and cells.

Empty Cells

What if you want a cell with nothing in it? That's easy. Just define a cell with a <TH> or <TD> tag with nothing inside it:

```
<TR>
    <TD></TD>
    <TD>10</TD>
    <TD>20</TD>
</TR>
```

Sometimes, an empty cell of this sort is displayed as if the cell doesn't exist, as shown in Figure 11.4.

Figure 11.4.

Empty cells.

If you want to force a truly empty cell, you can add a line break in that cell by itself with no other text (see Figure 11.5).

```
<TR>
    <TD><BR></TD>
    <TD>10</TD>
    <TD>20</TD>
</TR>
```

Figure 11.5.

Really empty cells.

The following input and output example creates a pattern of empty cells (see Figure 11.6).

INPUT

```
<HTML>
<HEAD>
<TITLE>Empty</TITLE>
</HEAD>
<BODY>
<TABLE BORDER>
<TR>
    <TH></TH><TH><BR></TH><TH></TH><TH></TH>
    <TH><BR></TH><TH></TH><TH><BR></TH><TH></TH>
    <TH></TH><TH><BR></TH><TH></TH><TH></TH>
    <TH><BR></TH><TH></TH><TH><BR></TH><TH></TH>
</TR>
<TR>
    <TH></TH><TH><BR></TH><TH></TH><TH></TH>
    <TH><BR></TH><TH></TH><TH><BR></TH><TH></TH>
    <TH></TH><TH><BR></TH><TH></TH><TH></TH>
    <TH><BR></TH><TH></TH><TH><BR></TH><TH></TH>
</TR>
</TABLE>
</BODY>
</HTML>
```

11

Figure 11.6.
A pattern of empty cells.

Captions

Table captions tell your reader what the table is for. Although you could just use a regular paragraph or a heading as a label for your table, there is a `<CAPTION>` tag for just this purpose. Because the `<CAPTION>` tag labels captions as captions, tools to process HTML files could extract them into a separate file, automatically number them, or treat them in special ways simply because they are captions.

But what if you don't want a caption? You don't have to include one; captions are optional. If you just want a table and don't care about a label, leave the caption off.

The `<CAPTION>` tag goes inside the `<TABLE>` tag just before the table rows, and it contains the title of the table. It closes with the `</CAPTION>` tag.

```
<TABLE>
<CAPTION>Decapitated Tulips in Virginia, 1960-1980</CAPTION>
<TR>
```

The optional `ALIGN` attribute to the caption determines the alignment of the caption. However, depending on which browser you're using, you have different choices for what `ALIGN` means.

In most browsers, `ALIGN` can have one of two values: `TOP` and `BOTTOM`. This is the correct HTML 3.2 use of the `ALIGN` attribute. By default, the caption is placed at the top of the table (`ALIGN=TOP`). You can use the `ALIGN=BOTTOM` attribute to the caption if you want to put the caption at the bottom of the table, like this:

```
<TABLE>
<CAPTION ALIGN=BOTTOM>Torque Limits for Various Fruits</CAPTION>
```

In Internet Explorer, however, captions are different. With Internet Explorer, you use the `VALIGN` attribute to put the caption at the top or the bottom, and `ALIGN` has three different values: `LEFT`, `RIGHT`, and `CENTER`, which align the caption horizontally.

To achieve similar results in Netscape Navigator, use `ALIGN=BOTTOM` or `ALIGN=TOP`, and then use the `<DIV>` tag with its `ALIGN` attribute to align the caption text to the left, right, or center. This also works in Internet Explorer 4.

> **NOTE**
>
> In the HTML 4.0 specification, the `<CAPTION>` tag can take the `ALIGN` attribute with one of four values: `top`, `bottom`, `left`, or `right`. The `VALIGN` attribute used by Microsoft still hasn't found its way into official HTML.

For instance, if you want to place the caption at the bottom of the table, aligned to the right, in Internet Explorer you can use:

```
<CAPTION VALIGN=BOTTOM ALIGN=RIGHT>This is a caption</CAPTION>
```

or you can use the `<DIV>` tag, which also works in Netscape Navigator:

```
<CAPTION ALIGN=BOTTOM><DIV ALIGN=RIGHT>This is a caption</DIV></CAPTION>
```

In general, unless you have a very short table, you should leave the caption in its default position—centered at the top of the table—so that your readers will see the caption first and know what they are about to read, instead of seeing it after they're already done reading the table (at which point they've usually figured out what it's about anyway).

Exercise 11.1: Create a simple table.

Now that you know the basics of how to create a table, let's try a simple example. For this example, we'll create a table that indicates the colors you get when you mix the three primary colors together.

Figure 11.7 shows the table we're going to re-create in this example.

Figure 11.7.
The simple color table.

Here's a quick hint for laying out tables: Because HTML defines tables on a row-by-row basis, it can sometimes be difficult to keep track of the columns, particularly with very complex tables. Before you start actually writing HTML code, it's useful to make a sketch of your table so that you know what the heads are and the values of each cell. You might find that it's easiest to use a word processor with a table editor (such as Microsoft Word) or a spreadsheet to lay out your tables. Then when you have the layout and the cell values, you can write the HTML code for that table.

Let's start with a simple HTML framework for the page that contains a table. Like all HTML files, you can create this file in any text editor:

```
<HTML><HEAD>
<TITLE>Colors</TITLE>
</HEAD>
<BODY>
<TABLE BORDER>
...add table rows and cells here...
</TABLE>
</BODY></HTML>
```

Note that the <TABLE> tag has the BORDER attribute. This draws the highlighted borders around the table.

Now start adding table rows inside the opening and closing <TABLE> tags (where the line "add table rows and cells here" was in the framework). The first row is the three headings along the top of the table. The table row is indicated by <TR>, and each cell by a <TH> tag:

```
<TR>
    <TH>Red</TH>
    <TH>Yellow</TH>
    <TH>Blue</TH>
</TR>
```

NOTE

You can format the HTML code any way you want to; like with all HTML, the browser ignores most extra spaces and returns. I like to format it like this, with the contents of the individual rows indented and the cell tags on separate lines, so I can pick out the rows and columns more easily.

Now add the second row. The first cell in the second row is the Red heading on the left side of the table, so it will be the first cell in this row, followed by the cells for the table data:

```
<TR>
    <TH>Red</TH>
    <TD>Red</TD>
    <TD>Orange</TD>
    <TD>Purple</TD>
</TR>
```

11

Continue by adding the remaining two rows in the table, with the Yellow and Blue headings. Here's what you have so far for the entire table:

```
<TABLE BORDER>
<TR>
    <TH>Red</TH>
    <TH>Yellow</TH>
    <TH>Blue</TH>
</TR>
<TR>
    <TH>Red</TH>
    <TD>Red</TD>
    <TD>Orange</TD>
    <TD>Purple</TD>
</TR>
<TR>
    <TH>Yellow</TH>
    <TD>Orange</TD>
    <TD>Yellow</TD>
    <TD>Green</TD>
</TR>
<TR>
    <TH>Blue</TH>
    <TD>Purple</TD>
    <TD>Green</TD>
    <TD>Blue</TD>
</TR>
</TABLE>
```

Finally, let's add a simple caption. The `<CAPTION>` tag goes just after the `<TABLE BORDER>` tag and just before the first `<TR>` tag:

```
<TABLE BORDER>
<CAPTION><B>Table 1.1:</B> Mixing Colors</CAPTION>
<TR>
```

Now, with a first draft of the code in place, test the HTML file in your favorite browser that supports tables. Figure 11.8 shows how it looks in Netscape Navigator.

Figure 11.8.

The color table.

Oops! What happened with that top row? The headings are all messed up. The answer, of course, is that you need an empty cell at the beginning of that first row to space the headings out over the proper columns. HTML isn't smart enough to match it all up for you (this is exactly the sort of error you're going to find the first time you test your tables).

Let's add an empty table heading cell to that first row (here, the line `<TH><BR></TH>`):

```
<TR>
    <TH><BR></TH>
    <TH>Red</TH>
    <TH>Yellow</TH>
    <TH>Blue</TH>
</TR>
```

NOTE

> I used `<TH>` here, but it could just as easily have been `<TD>`. Because there's nothing in the cell, its formatting doesn't matter.

If you try it again, you should get the right result with all the headings over the right columns.

Table and Cell Alignment

Once you've got your basic table layout with rows, headings, and data, you can start refining how that table looks. The first way to do this is to align the table on the page and to align the contents of the cells inside that table.

Table Alignment

By default, tables are displayed on a line by themselves along the left side of the page, with any text above or below the table.

Using the `ALIGN` attribute, however, you can align tables along the left or right margins and wrap text alongside them the same way you can with images. `ALIGN=LEFT` aligns the table along the left margin, and all text following that table is wrapped in the space between that table and the right side of the page. `ALIGN=RIGHT` does the same thing, with the table aligned to the right side of the page. Figure 11.9 shows an example of a table with text wrapped alongside of it.

As with images, to stop wrapping text alongside an image, you can use the line break tag with the `CLEAR` attribute.

Centering tables is slightly more difficult. Up until the recent release of Internet Explorer 4 and Netscape Navigator 4, no browsers supported `ALIGN=CENTER` on tables. However, you could use the `<CENTER>` or `<DIV ALIGN=CENTER>` tags (both of which you learned about in Chapter 5, "More Text Formatting with HTML") to center tables on the page. Now, with the latest versions of both browsers, `<TABLE ALIGN=CENTER>` is correctly supported.

Figure 11.9.
*A table with text
alongside it.*

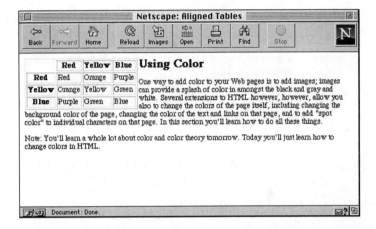

Cell Alignment

When you have your rows and cells in place inside your table and the table properly aligned
on the page, you can align the data within each cell for the best effect based on what your table
contains. HTML tables give you several options for aligning the data within your cells both
horizontally and vertically. Figure 11.10 shows a table (a real HTML one!) of the various
alignment options.

Figure 11.10.
Cell alignment.

Horizontal alignment (the ALIGN attribute) defines whether the data within a cell is aligned
with the left cell margin (LEFT), the right cell margin (RIGHT), or centered within the two
(CENTER).

Vertical alignment (the VALIGN attribute) defines the vertical alignment of the data within the
cell, meaning whether the data is flush with the top of the cell (TOP), flush with the bottom
of the cell (BOTTOM), or vertically centered within the cell (MIDDLE). VALIGN=BASELINE is similar

to VALIGN=TOP, except that it aligns the baseline of the first line of text in each cell (depending on the contents of the cell, this might or might not produce a different result than ALIGN=TOP).

By default, heading cells are centered both horizontally and vertically, and data cells are centered vertically but aligned flush left.

You can override the defaults for an entire row by adding the ALIGN or VALIGN attributes to the <TR> tag, as in this example:

```
<TR ALIGN=CENTER VALIGN=TOP>
```

You can override the row alignment for individual cells by adding ALIGN to the <TD> or <TH> tags:

```
<TR ALIGN=CENTER VALIGN=TOP>
    <TD>14</TD>
    <TD>16</TD>
    <TD ALIGN=LEFT>No Data</TD>
    <TD>15</TD>
</TR>
```

The following input and output example shows the various cell alignments and how they look in Netscape (see Figure 11.11).

INPUT
```
<HTML>
<HEAD>
<TITLE>Cell Alignments</TITLE>
</HEAD>
<BODY>
<TABLE BORDER>
<TR>
    <TH></TH>
    <TH>Left</TH>
    <TH>Centered</TH>
    <TH>Right</TH>
</TR>
<TR>
    <TH>Top</TH>
    <TD ALIGN=LEFT VALIGN=TOP><IMG SRC="button.gif"></TD>
    <TD ALIGN=CENTER VALIGN=TOP><IMG SRC="button.gif"></TD>
    <TD ALIGN=RIGHT VALIGN=TOP><IMG SRC="button.gif"></TD>
</TR>
<TR>
    <TH>Centered</TH>
    <TD ALIGN=LEFT VALIGN=MIDDLE><IMG SRC="button.gif"></TD>
    <TD ALIGN=CENTER VALIGN=MIDDLE><IMG SRC="button.gif"></TD>
    <TD ALIGN=RIGHT VALIGN=MIDDLE><IMG SRC="button.gif"></TD>
</TR>
<TR>
    <TH>Bottom</TH>
    <TD ALIGN=LEFT VALIGN=BOTTOM><IMG SRC="button.gif"></TD>
```

11

```
        <TD ALIGN=CENTER VALIGN=BOTTOM><IMG SRC="button.gif"></TD>
        <TD ALIGN=RIGHT VALIGN=BOTTOM><IMG SRC="button.gif"></TD>
</TR>
</TABLE>
</BODY>
</HTML>
```

Figure 11.11.
Alignment options.

Exercise 11.2: A vegetable planting guide.

Tables are great when you have a lot of information—particularly technical or numeric information—that you want to present in a way that enables your readers to find what they need quickly and easily. Perhaps they're only interested in one bit of that information or a range of it. Presented in a paragraph or in a list, it might be more difficult for your readers to glean what they need.

For example, say you want to summarize information about planting vegetables, which includes the time in the year each vegetable should be planted, how long it takes before you can harvest that vegetable, whether you can transplant an already growing plant, and some common varieties that are known to grow especially well. You can present this information as a list, one paragraph per vegetable, but because the data falls into neat categories, the data will look better and be more accessible as a table.

Figure 11.12 shows the vegetable planting chart, the table you'll be building in this exercise. Like the last example, it's a rather simple table, but it does use links, images, and lists inside the table cells. In addition, it takes advantage of some of the alignment options that I described in the previous section. In this example, we'll start with a basic HTML framework, lay out the rows and the cells, and then adjust and fine-tune the alignment of the data within those cells. You'll find, as you work with more tables, that this plan is the easiest way to develop a table. If you worry about the alignment at the same time that you're constructing the table, it's easy to get confused.

Here's the basic framework for the table, including the caption:

```
<HTML>
<HEAD>
<TITLE>Vegetable Planting Schedule</TITLE>
</HEAD>
<BODY>
<TABLE BORDER>
<CAPTION>Vegetable Planting Schedule</CAPTION>
```

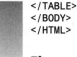

```
</TABLE>
</BODY>
</HTML>
```

Figure 11.12.
*The vegetable
planting schedule.*

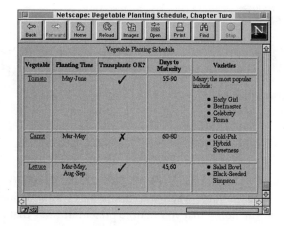

The first row we'll add is the heading for the top table. It's a row with five heading cells, and we'll add it to the table just beneath the <CAPTION> tag:

```
<TR>
    <TH>Vegetable</TH>
    <TH>Planting Time</TH>
    <TH>Transplants OK?</TH>
    <TH>Days to Maturity</TH>
    <TH>Varieties</TH>
</TR>
```

The remaining rows are for the data for the table. Note that within a table cell (a <TH> or <TD> tag), you can put any HTML markup, including links, images, forms, or other tables. In this example, we've used links for each vegetable name (pointing to further information), a checkmark or X image for whether you can plant transplants of that vegetable, and an unordered list for the varieties. Here's the code so far for the headings and the three rows of the table:

```
<TABLE BORDER>
<CAPTION>Vegetable Planting Schedule</CAPTION>
<TR>
    <TH>Vegetable</TH>
    <TH>Planting Time</TH>
    <TH>Transplants OK?</TH>
    <TH>Days to Maturity</TH>
    <TH>Varieties</TH>
</TR>
<TR>
    <TD ><A HREF="tomato.html">Tomato</A></TD>
    <TD>May-June</TD>
    <TD><IMG SRC="check.gif"></TD>
```

```
    <TD>55-90</TD>
    <TD>Many; the most popular include:
        <UL>
        <LI>Early Girl
        <LI>Beefmaster
        <LI>Celebrity
        <LI>Roma
        </UL>
    </TD>
</TR>
<TR>
    <TD><A HREF="carrot.html">Carrot</A></TD>
    <TD>Mar-May</TD>
    <TD><IMG SRC="ex.gif"></TD>
    <TD>60-80</TD>
    <TD>
        <UL>
        <LI>Gold-Pak
        <LI>Hybrid Sweetness
        </UL>
    </TD>
</TR>
<TR>
    <TD><A HREF="lettuce.html">Lettuce</A></TD>
    <TD>Mar-May, Aug-Sep</TD>
    <TD><IMG SRC="check.gif"></TD>
    <TD>45,60</TD>
    <TD>
        <UL>
        <LI>Salad Bowl
        <LI>Black-Seeded Simpson
        </UL>
    </TD>
</TR>
</TABLE>
```

In Netscape, there's one exception to the rule that white space in your original HTML code doesn't matter in the final output. For images in cells, say you've formatted your code with the <IMG> tag on a separate line, like this:

```
<TD>
    <IMG SRC="check.gif">
</TD>
```

With this code, the return between the <TD> and the <IMG> tag is significant; your image will not be properly placed within the cell (this particularly shows up in centered cells). This quirk of the Netscape browser remains the case even in the latest preview release of Netscape Communicator. To correct the problem, just put the <TD> and the <IMG> tags on the same line:

```
<TD><IMG SRC="check.gif"></TD>
```

Figure 11.13 shows what the table looks like so far.

Figure 11.13.

*The vegetable table,
try one.*

 NOTE

Depending on how big your screen and your browser window are, your
table might not look exactly like this one. Browsers reformat tables to
the width of the window as they do with other HTML elements. You'll
learn more about controlling the width of tables in "Defining Table
and Column Widths," later in this chapter.

So far, so good, but the columns would look better centered. We can do this globally for each
row by adding the ALIGN=CENTER attribute to each <TR> tag. (Note that you need to do it only
for the data rows; the headings are already centered.)

```
<TR ALIGN=CENTER>
    <TD ><A HREF="tomato.html">Tomato</A></TD>
    <TD>May-June</TD>
    ...
```

Figure 11.14 shows the new table with the contents of the cells now centered.

Now the table looks much better, except for the bullets in the Varieties column. They were
centered, too, so now they're all out of whack. But that doesn't matter; we can fix that by
adding the ALIGN=LEFT attribute to the <TD> tag for that cell in every row with the following
code. The result is shown in Figure 11.15.

```
<TD ALIGN=LEFT>Many; the most popular include:
    <UL>
    <LI>Early Girl
    ...
```

Figure 11.14.
*The vegetable table,
try two.*

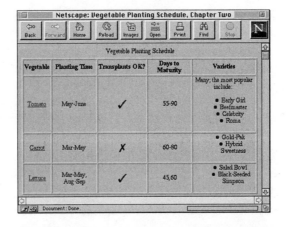

Figure 11.15.
*The vegetable table,
try three.*

NOTE

You could have just kept the default alignment for each row and then added an `ALIGN=CENTER` attribute to every cell that needed to be centered. But that would have been a lot more work. It's usually easier to change the default row alignment to the alignment of the majority of the cells and then change the cell alignment for the individual cells that are left.

We're getting close, but let's try one more thing. Right now, all the cells are vertically centered. Let's add VALIGN=TOP to each data row (next to ALIGN=CENTER) so that the rows will hug the top of the cells.

```
<TR ALIGN=CENTER VALIGN=TOP>
    <TD ><A HREF="tomato.html">Tomato</A></TD>
    <TD>May-June</TD>
```

You're done! Here's the final HTML text for the example:

```
<HTML>
<HEAD>
<TITLE>Vegetable Planting Schedule</TITLE>
</HEAD>
<BODY>
<TABLE BORDER>
<CAPTION>Vegetable Planting Schedule</CAPTION>
<TR>
    <TH>Vegetable</TH>
    <TH>Planting Time</TH>
    <TH>Transplants OK?</TH>
    <TH>Days to Maturity</TH>
    <TH>Varieties</TH>
</TR>
<TR ALIGN=CENTER VALIGN=TOP>
    <TD ><A HREF="tomato.html">Tomato</A></TD>
    <TD>May-June</TD>
    <TD><IMG SRC="check.gif"></TD>
    <TD>55-90</TD>
    <TD ALIGN=LEFT>Many; the most popular include:
        <UL>
        <LI>Early Girl
        <LI>Beefmaster
        <LI>Celebrity
        <LI>Roma
        </UL>
    </TD>
</TR>
<TR ALIGN=CENTER VALIGN=TOP>
    <TD><A HREF="carrot.html">Carrot</A></TD>
    <TD>Mar-May</TD>
    <TD><IMG SRC="ex.gif"></TD>
    <TD>60-80</TD>
    <TD ALIGN=LEFT>
        <UL>
        <LI>Gold-Pak
        <LI>Hybrid Sweetness
        </UL>
    </TD>
</TR>
<TR ALIGN=CENTER VALIGN=TOP>
    <TD><A HREF="lettuce.html">Lettuce</A></TD>
    <TD>Mar-May, Aug-Sep</TD>
    <TD><IMG SRC="check.gif"></TD>
```

```
<TD>45,60</TD>
<TD ALIGN=LEFT>
    <UL>
    <LI>Salad Bowl
    <LI>Black-Seeded Simpson
    </UL>
</TD>
</TR>
</TABLE>
</BODY>
</HTML>
```

Cells That Span Multiple Rows or Columns

The tables we've created up to this point all had one value per cell or had the occasional empty cell. You can also create cells that span multiple rows or columns within the table. Those spanned cells can then hold headings that have subheadings in the next row or column, or you can create other special effects within the table layout. Figure 11.16 shows a table with spanned columns and rows.

Figure 11.16.
Tables with spans.

This cell spans two rows and two columns.

This cell spans two rows.

This cell spans two columns.

To create a cell that spans multiple rows or columns, you add the ROWSPAN or COLSPAN attribute to the <TH> or <TD> tags, along with the number of rows or columns you want the cell to span. The data within that cell then fills the entire width or length of the combined cells, as in the following example:

```
<TR>
    <TH COLSPAN=2>Gender
</TR>
<TR>
    <TH>Male</TH>
    <TH>Female</TH>
</TR>
<TR>
    <TD>15</TD>
    <TD>23</TD>
</TR>
```

Figure 11.17 shows how this table might appear when displayed.

Figure 11.17.

Column spans.

Note that if a cell spans multiple rows, you don't have to redefine that cell as empty in the next row or rows. Just ignore it and move to the next cell in the row; the span will fill in the spot for you.

Cells always span downward and to the right. So to create a cell that spans several columns, you add the COLSPAN attribute to the leftmost cell in the span, and for cells that span rows, you add ROWSPAN to the topmost cell.

The following input and output example shows a cell that spans multiple rows (the cell with the word "Piston" in it). Figure 11.18 shows the result in Netscape.

```
<HTML>
<HEAD>
<TITLE>Ring Clearance</TITLE>
</HEAD>
<BODY>
<TABLE BORDER>
<TR>
    <TH COLSPAN=2></TH>
    <TH>Ring<BR>Clearance</TH>
</TR>
<TR ALIGN=CENTER>
    <TH ROWSPAN=2>Piston</TH>
    <TH>Upper</TH>
    <TD>3mm</TD>
</TR>
<TR ALIGN=CENTER>
    <TH>Lower</TH>
    <TD>3.2mm</TD>
</TR>
</TABLE>
</BODY>
</HTML>
```

Figure 11.18.

Cells that span multiple rows and columns.

Exercise 11.3: A table of service specifications.

Had enough of tables yet? Let's do one more example that takes advantage of everything you've learned here: tables with headings and normal cells, alignments, and column and row spans. This is a very complex table, so we'll go step by step, row by row to build it.

Figure 11.19 shows the table, which indicates service and adjustment specifications from the service manual for a car.

Figure 11.19.

The really complex service specification table.

There are actually five rows and columns in this table. Do you see them? Some of them span columns and rows. Figure 11.20 shows the same table with a grid drawn over it so that you can see where the rows and columns are.

Figure 11.20.

Five columns, five rows.

With tables such as this one that use many spans, it's helpful to draw this sort of grid to figure out where the spans are and in which row they belong. Remember, spans start at the topmost row and the leftmost column.

Ready? Start with the framework, just as you have for the other tables in this chapter:

```
<HTML>
<HEAD>
<TITLE>Service Data</TITLE>
</HEAD>
```

```
<BODY>
<TABLE BORDER>
<CAPTION>Drive Belt Deflection</CAPTION>

</TABLE>
</BODY>
</HTML>
```

Now create the first row. With the grid on your picture, you can see that the first cell is empty and spans two rows and two columns (see Figure 11.21). Therefore, the HTML for that cell would be as follows:

```
<TR>
<TH ROWSPAN=2 COLSPAN=2></TH>
```

Figure 11.21.
The first cell.

The first cell (spans two
columns and two rows)

The second cell in the row is the Used Belt Deflection heading cell, which spans two columns (for the two cells beneath it). So the code for that cell is

```
<TH COLSPAN=2>Used Belt Deflection</TH>
```

Now that you have two cells that span two columns each, there's only the one left in this row. But this one, like the first one, spans the row beneath it:

```
<TH ROWSPAN=2>Set deflection of new belt</TH>
</TR>
```

Now go on to the second row. This isn't the one that starts with the Alternator heading. Remember that the first cell in the previous row has a ROWSPAN and a COLSPAN of two, meaning that it bleeds down to this row and takes up two cells. You don't need to redefine it for this row; you just move on to the next cell in the grid. The first cell in this row is the Limit heading cell, and the second cell is the Adjust Deflection heading cell:

```
<TR>
    <TH>Limit</TH>
    <TH>Adjust Deflection</TH>
</TR>
```

What about the last cell? Just like the first cell, the cell in the row above this one had a ROWSPAN of two, which takes up the space in this row. So the only values you need for this row are the ones you already defined.

Are you with me so far? Now is a great time to try this out in your browser to make sure that everything is lining up. It will look kind of funny because we haven't really put anything on the left side of the table yet, but it's worth a try. Figure 11.22 shows what we've got so far.

Figure 11.22.

The table so far.

Next row! Check your grid if you need to. Here, the first cell is the heading for Alternator, and it spans this row and the one below it. Are you getting the hang of this yet?

```
<TR>
    <TH ROWSPAN=2>Alternator</TH>
```

The next three cells are pretty easy because they don't span anything. Here are their definitions:

```
<TD>Models without AC</TD>
<TD>10mm</TD>
<TD>5-7mm</TD>
```

The last cell in this row is just like the first one:

```
<TD ROWSPAN=2>5-7mm</TD>
</TR>
```

We're up to row number four. In this one, because of the ROWSPANs from the previous row, there are only three cells to define: the cell for Models with AC, and the two cells for the numbers:

```
<TR>
    <TD>Models with AC</TD>
    <TD>12mm</TD>
    <TD>6-8mm</TD>
</TR>
```

NOTE

In this table, I've made the Alternator cell a heading cell and the AC cells plain data. This is mostly an aesthetic decision on my part; I could just as easily have made all three into headings.

Now for the final row—this one should be easy. The first cell (Power Steering Oil Pump) spans two columns (the one with Alternator in it and the with/without AC column). The remaining three are just one cell each:

```
<TR>
    <TH COLSPAN=2>Power Steering Oil Pump</TH>
    <TD>12.5mm</TD>
    <TD>7.9mm</TD>
    <TD>6-8mm</TD>
</TR>
```

That's it. You're done laying out the rows and columns. That was the hard part; the rest is just fine-tuning. Let's try looking at it again to make sure there are no strange errors (see Figure 11.23).

Figure 11.23.

The table: the next step.

Now that you have all the rows and cells laid out, adjust the alignments within the cells. The numbers, at least, should be centered. Because they make up the majority of the table, let's make centered the default alignment for each row:

```
<TR ALIGN=CENTER>
```

But the labels along the left side of the table (Alternator, Models with/without AC, and Power Steering Oil Pump) look funny if they're centered, so let's left-align them:

```
<TH ROWSPAN=2 ALIGN=LEFT>Alternator</TH>
<TD ALIGN=LEFT>Models without AC</TD>

<TD ALIGN=LEFT>Models with AC</TD>

<TH COLSPAN=2 ALIGN=LEFT>Power Steering Oil Pump</TH>
```

Finally, the last bit of fine-tuning I've done is to put some line breaks in the longer headings so that the columns are a little narrower. Because the text in the headings is pretty short to start with, I don't have to worry too much about the table looking funny if it gets too narrow. Here are the lines I modified:

```
<TH ROWSPAN=2>Set<BR>deflection<BR>of new belt</TH>
<TH>Adjust<BR>Deflection</TH>
```

Voilà—the final table, with everything properly laid out and aligned! Figure 11.24 shows the final result.

Figure 11.24.
The final Drive Belt Deflection table.

If you got lost at any time, the best thing you can do is pull out your handy text editor and try it yourself, following along tag by tag. After you've done it a couple of times, it becomes easier.

Here's the full text for the table example:

```
<HTML>
<HEAD>
<TITLE>Service Data</TITLE>
</HEAD>
<BODY>
<TABLE BORDER>
<CAPTION>Drive Belt Deflection</CAPTION>
<TR>
    <TH ROWSPAN=2 COLSPAN=2></TH>
    <TH COLSPAN=2>Used Belt Deflection</TH>
    <TH ROWSPAN=2>Set<BR>deflection<BR>of new belt</TH>
</TR>
<TR>
    <TH>Limit</TH>
    <TH>Adjust<BR>Deflection</TH>
</TR>
<TR ALIGN=CENTER>
    <TH ROWSPAN=2 ALIGN=LEFT>Alternator</TH>
    <TD ALIGN=LEFT>Models without AC</TD>
    <TD>10mm</TD>
    <TD>5-7mm</TD>
    <TD ROWSPAN=2>5-7mm</TD>
</TR>
<TR ALIGN=CENTER>
    <TD ALIGN=LEFT>Models with AC</TD>
    <TD>12mm</TD>
```

```
        <TD>6-8mm</TD>
    </TR>
    <TR ALIGN=CENTER>
        <TH COLSPAN=2 ALIGN=LEFT>Power Steering Oil Pump</TH>
        <TD>12.5mm</TD>
        <TD>7.9mm</TD>
        <TD>6-8mm</TD>
    </TR>
    </TABLE>
    </BODY>
    </HTML>
```

Defining Table and Column Widths

All the tables we've created up to this point relied on the browser itself to decide how wide the table and column widths were going to be. In many cases, this is the best way to make sure your tables are viewable on different browsers with different screen sizes and widths; simply let the browser decide. In other cases, however, you might want to have more control over how wide your tables and columns are, particularly if the defaults the browser comes up with are really strange. In this section you'll learn a couple ways to do just this.

Setting Breaks in Text

Often the easiest way to make small changes to how a table is laid out is by using line breaks (
 tags), using the NOWRAP attribute, or using both <BR> and NOWRAP together.

Line breaks are particularly useful if you have a table in which most of the cells are small and only one or two cells have longer data. As long as the screen width can handle it, the browser generally just creates really long rows, which looks rather odd in some tables (see Figure 11.25).

Figure 11.25.

A table with one long row.

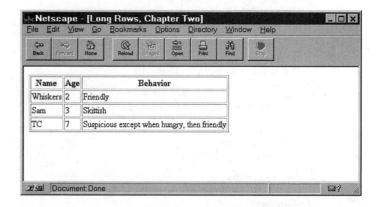

By putting in line breaks, you can wrap that row in a shorter column so that it looks more like the table shown in Figure 11.26.

Figure 11.26.

The long row wraps with <BR>.

Long row now wraps ——

On the other hand, you might have a table in which a cell is being wrapped for which you want all the data on one line. (This can be particularly important for things such as form elements within table cells where you want the label and the input field to stay together.) In this instance, you can add the NOWRAP attribute to the <TH> or <TD> tags, and the browser keeps all the data in that cell on one line. Note that you can always add <BR> tags by hand to that same cell and get line breaks exactly where you want them.

Be careful when you hard-code table cells with line breaks and NOWRAP attributes. Remember, your table might be viewed in many different screen widths. For the most part, you should try to let the browser itself format your table and to make minor adjustments only when necessary In fact, the HTML 4.0 specification recommends using style sheets instead of the NOWRAP attribute.

Table Widths

The WIDTH attribute to the <TABLE> tag defines how wide the table will be on the page. WIDTH can have a value that is either the exact width of the table (in pixels) or a percentage (such as 50 percent or 75 percent) of the current screen width, which can therefore change if the window is resized. If WIDTH is specified, the width of the columns within the table can be compressed or expanded to fit the required width. For example, Figure 11.27 shows a table that would have been quite narrow if it had been left alone. But this table has stretched to fit a 100 percent screen width using the WIDTH attribute, which causes Netscape to spread out all the columns to fit the screen.

Figure 11.27.

Table widths in Netscape.

Note Trying to make the table too narrow for the data it contains might be
impossible, in which case Netscape tries to get as close as it can to your
desired width.

It's always a better idea to specify your table widths as percentages rather than as specific pixel
widths. Because you don't know how wide the browser window will be, using percentages
allows your table to be reformatted to whatever width it is. Using specific pixel widths might
cause your table to run off the page.

Column Widths

The WIDTH attribute can also be used on individual cells (<TH> or <TD>) to indicate the width
of individual columns. As with table width, the WIDTH tag in cells can be an exact pixel width
or a percentage (which is taken as a percentage of the full table width). As with table widths,
using percentages rather than specific pixel widths is a better idea because it allows your table
to be displayed regardless of the window size.

Column widths are useful when you want to have multiple columns of identical widths,
regardless of their contents (for example, for some forms of page layout). Figure 11.28 shows
the same table from the previous example that spans the width of the screen, although this
time the first column is 10 percent of the table width and the remaining three columns are
30 percent. Netscape adjusts the column widths to fit both the width of the screen and the
given percentages.

Figure 11.28.

Column widths.

Other Features of Tables

Sick of tables yet? There are only a few table features left: border widths, cell spacing and cell
padding, and adding color.

11

Border Widths

You can also change the width of the border drawn around the table. If BORDER has a numeric value, the border around the outside of the table is drawn with that pixel width. The default is BORDER=1; BORDER=0 suppresses the border (just as if you had omitted the BORDER attribute altogether).

 NOTE

> The border value applies only to the shaded border along the outside edge of the table, not to the borders around the cells. See the next section for that value.

Figure 11.29 shows an example of a table with a border of 10 pixels.

Figure 11.29.
Table border widths.

Table border —

Cell Spacing

Cell spacing is similar to cell padding except that it affects the amount of space between cells—that is, the width of the shaded lines that separate the cells. The CELLSPACING attribute in the <TABLE> tag affects the spacing for the table. Cell spacing is 2 by default.

Cell spacing also includes the outline around the table, which is just inside the table's border (as set by the BORDER attribute). Experiment with it, and you can see the difference. For example, Figure 11.30 shows a table with cell spacing of 8 and a border of 4.

Figure 11.30.
Cell spacing (and borders).

Cell Padding

Cell padding is the amount of space between the edges of the cells and the cell's contents. By default, Netscape draws its tables with a cell padding of one pixel. You can add more space by adding the CELLPADDING attribute to the <TABLE> tag, with a value in pixels for the amount of cell padding you want. Figure 11.31 shows an example of a table with cell padding of 10 pixels.

Figure 11.31.

Cell padding.

The CELLPADDING attribute with a value of 0 causes the edges of the cells to touch the edges of the cell's contents (which doesn't look very good).

Color in Tables

Just when tables were becoming consistent amongst browsers, someone had to come along and add a whole bunch of new features. That someone was Microsoft, with their Internet Explorer browser, which supports several attributes that allow you to change the color of various parts of the table. Netscape has since included support for background colors in the newest version of its browser. Still, some of the older browsers out there, particularly Netscape 2, don't support these attributes, so keep this in mind if you choose to use these tags. Additionally, the HTML 4.0 specification recommends using style sheets instead of the BGCOLOR attribute.

To change the background color of a table, a row, or a cell inside a row, use the BGCOLOR attribute of the <TABLE>, <TR>, <TH> or <TD> tags. Just like in <BODY>, the value of BGCOLOR is a color specified as a hexadecimal triplet or, in many browsers including Internet Explorer and Netscape Navigator/Communicator, one of the 16 color names: Black, White, Green, Maroon, Olive, Navy, Purple, Gray, Red, Yellow, Blue, Teal, Lime, Aqua, Fuchsia, or Silver.

Each background color overrides the background color of its enclosing element. So, for example, a table background overrides the page background, a row background overrides the table's, and any cell colors override all other colors. If you nest tables inside cells, that nested table has the background color of the cell that encloses it.

11

Also, if you change the color of a cell, don't forget to change the color of the text inside it using <FONT COLOR...> so you can still read it.

Here's an example of changing the background and cell colors in a table. I've created a checkerboard using an HTML table. The table itself is white, with alternating cells in black. The checkers (here, red and black circles) are images. The result in Internet Explorer is shown in Figure 11.32.

NOTE

> In order for table cells to show up with background colors, they have to have some sort of contents. Simply putting a <BR> tag in empty cells works fine.

```
<HTML>
<HEAD>
<TITLE>Checkerboard</TITLE>
</HEAD>
<BODY>
<TABLE BGCOLOR="#FFFFFF" WIDTH=50%>
<TR ALIGN=CENTER>
    <TD BGCOLOR="#000000" WIDTH=33%><IMG SRC="redcircle.gif"></TD>
    <TD BGCOLOR="#000000" WIDTH=33%><IMG SRC="redcircle.gif"></TD>
    <TD BGCOLOR="#000000" WIDTH=33%><IMG SRC="redcircle.gif"></TD>
</TR>
<TR ALIGN=CENTER>
    <TD> <IMG SRC="blackcircle.gif"></TD>
    <TD BGCOLOR="#000000"><BR></TD>
    <TD><BR></TD>
</TR>
<TR ALIGN=CENTER>
    <TD BGCOLOR="#000000"><BR></TD>
    <TD><IMG SRC="blackcircle.gif"><BR></TD>
    <TD BGCOLOR="#000000"><IMG SRC="blackcircle.gif"> </TD>
</TR>
</TABLE>
</BODY>
</HTML>
```

Internet Explorer also allows you to change the colors of the elements of the table's border using the BORDERCOLOR, BORDERCOLORLIGHT, and BORDERCOLORDARK attributes. Each of these attributes takes either a color number or name and can be used in <TABLE>, <TH>, or <TD>. Like background colors, the border colors each override the colors of the enclosing element. All three require the enclosing <TABLE> tag to have the BORDER attribute set.

Figure 11.32.
Table cell colors.

These extensions are only (currently) supported in Internet Explorer with the exception of BORDERCOLOR, which is supported in Netscape Navigator 4.

- ☐ BORDERCOLOR sets the color of the border, overriding the 3D look of the default border.
- ☐ BORDERCOLORDARK sets the dark component of 3D-look borders.
- ☐ BORDERCOLORLIGHT sets the light component of 3D-look borders.

Alternatives to Tables

Tables are great for summarizing large amounts of information in a way that can be quickly and easily scanned. In terms of information design, tables are right up there with link menus (as described earlier in this book) for structuring data so that your reader can get in and out of your pages.

The difficulty with tables is that although most newer browsers do support them, they come out particularly messed up in browsers that don't. You won't lose all the data in the table, but you will lose the formatting, which can make your data just as unreadable as if it hadn't been included at all. For example, Figure 11.33 shows a table that looks pretty nice in Netscape.

Figure 11.33.
A table in Netscape 1.1.

Figure 11.34 shows the same table as viewed by an earlier version of Netscape that didn't support tables.

Figure 11.34.
The same table in Netscape 1.0.

Pretty gross, huh? It's also really confusing for your readers if they're not using a browser that supports tables and you haven't warned them about it.

To work around tables for browsers that don't support them, you have several choices. Figure 11.35 shows a simple HTML table, and each of the following choices shows a method of working around that table.

Figure 11.35.
A simple table.

☐ Don't use a table at all. Some layouts can work just as well as a list or series of lists (see Figure 11.36).

Figure 11.36.
The same table as a definition list.

☐ Use an image of a table rather than an actual table. If the table is small enough and you use only black and white, this can be an excellent workaround to the lack of tables. And, with an image, you can also use preformatted text inside the ALT attribute to mock the effect of the table in browsers that can't view images (see Figure 11.37).

Figure 11.37.

The same table as an image.

☐ Use preformatted text (the <PRE> tag) to line up your information in table-like columns—creating tables without the table tags. Keep in mind that preformatted text is usually displayed in a monospaced font such as Courier, so the appearance of the table will not be as nice as it was in table form (see Figure 11.38).

Figure 11.38.

The same table as preformatted text.

☐ Link the table externally. Instead of putting the table directly on your page, consider putting the table on a separate page by itself and creating a link to it on the original page with a suitable description, for example:

```
<P><A HREF="heights.html">A table</A> of the various
heights, weights and eye colors of people in my group.
Your browser must support tables to be able to view this</P>
```

The most complicated way to create tables that work even in non–table-enabled browsers is to design your tables so that the layout works equally well in both. For example, if you use text elements such as headings and block quotes inside table cells, those elements will end up on their own lines if tables aren't supported. Using trial and error and testing your pages in both kinds of browsers, you can often come up with a layout that works equally well inside and outside tables.

One commonly used trick along those lines is to include <P> or <BR> tags at the end of selected cells. By including them at the end of the cell, they're ignored in browsers that support tables but provide line breaks at the appropriate spots in browsers that don't support tables. So, for example, with the color table you created in Exercise 11.1, add line breaks to the last cell in each row:

```
<TABLE BORDER>
<TR>
    <TH><BR></TH>
    <TH>Red</TH>
    <TH>Yellow</TH>
    <TH>Blue<BR></TH>
</TR>
<TR>
    <TH>Red</TH>
    <TD>Red</TD>
    <TD>Orange</TD>
    <TD>Purple<BR></TD>
</TR>
<TR>
    <TH>Yellow</TH>
    <TD>Orange</TD>
    <TD>Yellow</TD>
    <TD>Green<BR></TD>
</TR>
<TR>
    <TH>Blue</TH>
    <TD>Purple</TD>
    <TD>Green</TD>
    <TD>Blue<BR></TD>
</TR>
</TABLE>
```

The <BR> tags won't make any difference to the layout of the table in browsers that understand tables (because they're at the end of the cell), but they are significant to browsers that don't. The paragraph tags make actual paragraph breaks so that each row is on its own line. It's not a replacement for a table, but it does make it a little less confusing to read.

Summary

In this chapter, you've learned all about tables. Tables allow you to arrange your information in rows and columns so that your readers can scan the table quickly and get to the information they need.

While working with tables in this chapter, you've learned about headings and data, captions, defining rows and cells, aligning information within cells, and creating cells that span multiple rows or columns. With these features you can create tables for most purposes.

As you're constructing tables, it's helpful to keep the following steps in mind:

☐ Sketch your table and where the rows and columns fall. Mark which cells span multiple rows and columns.

☐ Start with a basic framework and lay out the rows, headings, and data row by row and cell by cell in HTML. Include row and column spans as necessary. Test frequently in a browser to make sure it's all working correctly.

☐ Modify the alignment in the rows to reflect the alignment of the majority of the cells.

☐ Modify the alignment for individual cells.

☐ Adjust line breaks, if necessary.

☐ Make other refinements such as cell spacing, padding, or color.

☐ Test your table in multiple browsers. Different browsers can have different ideas of how to lay out your table or be more accepting of errors in your HTML code.

Table 11.1 presents a quick summary of the HTML table-creating tags that you've learned about in this chapter.

Table 11.1. The table tags.

Tag	Attribute	Use
`<TABLE>...</TABLE>`		Indicates a table.
	BORDER	An attribute of the `<TABLE>` tag, indicating whether the table will be drawn with a border. The default is no border. If BORDER has a value, that value is the width of the shaded border around the table.
	CELLSPACING	Defines the amount of space between the cells in the table.
	CELLPADDING	Defines the amount of space between the edges of the cell and its contents.
`<CAPTION>...</CAPTION>`		Creates an optional caption for the table.
`<TR>...</TR>`		Defines a table row, which can contain heading and data cells.

Tag	Attribute	Use
<TH>...</TH>		Defines a table cell containing a heading. Heading cells are usually indicated by boldface and centered both horizontally and vertically within the cell.
<TD>...</TD>		Defines a table cell containing data. Table cells are in a regular font, and are left-justified and vertically centered within the cell.
	ALIGN	When used with <TABLE>, possible values are LEFT and RIGHT. Determines the alignment of the table and indicates that text following the table will be wrapped alongside it.
		When used with <CAPTION>, the possible values for most browsers are TOP and BOTTOM. ALIGN indicates whether the caption will be placed at the top of the table (the default) or the bottom. In Internet Explorer, the possible values are LEFT, RIGHT, and CENTER, and indicate the horizontal alignment of the caption.
		When used with <TR>, the possible values are LEFT, CENTER, and RIGHT, which indicate the horizontal alignment of the cells within that row (overriding the default alignment of heading and table cells).
		When used with <TH> or <TD>, the possible values are also LEFT, CENTER, and RIGHT, which override both the row's alignment and any default cell alignment.

continues

Table 11.1. continued

Tag	Attribute	Use
	VALIGN	When used with captions in Internet Explorer, possible values are TOP and BOTTOM and indicate the positioning of the caption relative to the table (same as ALIGN in most other browsers).
		When used with <TR>, possible values are TOP, MIDDLE, and BOTTOM. VALIGN indicates the vertical alignment of the cells within that row (overriding the defaults).
		When used with <TH> or <TD>, the same possible values are used, and VALIGN overrides both the row's vertical alignment and the default cell alignment.
		In Netscape, VALIGN can also have the value BASELINE.
	ROWSPAN	Used within a <TH> or <TD> tag, ROWSPAN indicates the number of cells below this one that this cell will span.
	COLSPAN	Used within a <TH> or <TD> tag, COLSPAN indicates the number of cells to the right of this one that this cell will span.
	BGCOLOR	Can be used with any of the table tags to change the background color of that table element. Cell colors override row colors, which override table colors. The value can be a hexadecimal color number or a color name.
	BORDERCOLOR	(Internet Explorer and Netscape extension) Can be used with any of the table tags to change the color of the border around that element. The value can be a hexadecimal color number or a color name.

11

Tag	Attribute	Use
	BORDERCOLORLIGHT	(Internet Explorer extension) Same as BORDERCOLOR, except it affects only the light component of a 3D-look border.
	BORDERCOLORDARK	(Internet Explorer extension) Same as BORDERCOLOR, except it affects only the dark component of a 3D-look border.
	NOWRAP	Used within a `<TH>` or `<TD>` tag, NOWRAP prevents the browser from wrapping the contents of the cell.
	WIDTH	When used with `<TABLE>`, indicates the width of the table in exact pixel values or as a percentage of page width (for example, 50 percent).
		When used with `<TH` or `<TD>`, WIDTH indicates the width of the cell in exact pixel values or as a percentage of table width (for example, 50 percent).

Q&A

Q Tables are a real hassle to lay out, especially when you get into row and column spans. That last example was awful.

A You're right. Tables are a tremendous pain to lay out by hand like this. However, if you're writing filters and tools to generate HTML code, having the table defined like this makes more sense because you can programmatically just write out each row in turn. Sooner or later, we'll all be working in HTML filters anyhow (let's hope), so you won't have to do this by hand for long.

Q My tables work fine in Netscape Navigator, but they're all garbled in many other browsers. What did I do wrong?

A Did you remember to close all your `<TR>`, `<TH>`, and `<TD>` tags? Make sure you've put in the matching `</TR>`, `</TH>`, and `</TD>` tags, respectively. The closing tags might be legally optional, but often other browsers need those tags in order to understand table layout.

Q Can you nest tables, putting a table inside a single table cell?

A Sure! As I mentioned in this chapter, you can put any HTML code you want to inside a table cell, and that includes other tables.

Chapter 12

Frames and Linked Windows

Before you learn about the details of setting up your own Web site on Day 7, "Going Live on the Web," you need to cover one final subject: frames. Frames are an advanced feature that provides an entirely different way of looking at Web pages. Frames were first introduced in Netscape Navigator 2 and are supported in all later versions as well as Microsoft Internet Explorer version 3 and higher. Even with a growing number of browsers supporting frames, pages created using frames are not easily backward-compatible with other browsers that don't support frames (such as Lynx).

In this chapter, you'll learn all about the following topics:

- [ ] What frames are, what they give you in terms of layout, and who supports them
- [ ] How to work with linked windows
- [ ] How to work with frames
- [ ] How to create complex framesets

What Are Frames and Who Supports Them?

Most of the features and tags discussed in preceding chapters will, as a rule, work on just about any Web browser. The appearance of the page might not be exactly what you had expected, but at the very least, people with older Web browsers can still view the text and links contained on the page.

In this chapter, however, you'll learn about a newer set of tags—used to create frames. In addition, due to the nature of these tags, Web pages created using frames simply won't display using other browsers. The fact that frames can't be displayed on older Web browsers has made frames one of the most hotly debated topics of the "Netscape versus the rest" debate.

NOTE

Netscape planned to submit its frame tags for recognition as part of the HTML 3.2 standard, but the specification available at the time of publication did not include frames. Frames, however, are now part of the HTML 4.0 specification.

Now that you know this information, if you plan to develop presentations specifically for Netscape or Internet Explorer, the capabilities provided by the use of frames bring an entirely new level of layout control to Web publishing. Consider, for example, the demonstration Web page created by Netscape Communications that is shown in Figure 12.1.

Figure 12.1.

A sample Web page with frames.

In this one screen, Netscape has integrated information that would previously have taken many separate screen loads. In addition, because the information displayed on the page is separated into individual areas or frames, the contents of a single frame can be updated without the contents of any other frame being affected. For example, if you click any of the hotlinks associated with the photos in the left frame, the contents of the large frame on the right are automatically updated to display the personal details of the selected staff member. When this update occurs, the contents of the left frame and the bottom frame are not affected.

Apart from the demonstration pages provided by Netscape, many other sites are now using frames in to their Web pages. Of them, one site you might find handy is the color index page developed by InfiNet located at `http://colors.infi.net/colorindex.html`. This page, shown in Figure 12.2, provides a handy reference for many of the colors you can use for backgrounds and text colors, with the colors in the frame on the left and the results in the frame on the right.

Figure 12.2.
The InfiNet color index.

Working with Linked Windows

Before looking at how frames are added to a page, you first need to learn about a new attribute of the <A> tag. This new attribute, called TARGET, takes the following form:

```
TARGET="window_name"
```

Usually, when you click a hyperlink, the contents of the new page replace the current page in the browser window. In a windowed environment, however, there is technically no reason why the contents of the new page can't be displayed in a new window, leaving the contents of the calling page displayed onscreen in their own window.

The TARGET attribute enables you to tell the Web browser to display the information pointed to by a hyperlink in a window called *window_name*. You can basically call the new window anything you want, with the only proviso being that you not use names that start with an underscore (_). These names are reserved for a set of special TARGET values that you'll learn about later in the section "Magic TARGET Names."

When you use the TARGET attribute inside an <A> tag, Netscape first checks to see whether a window with the name *window_name* exists. If it does, the document pointed to by the hyperlink replaces the current contents of *window_name*. On the other hand, if no window called *window_name* currently exists, a new browser window is opened and given the name *window_name*. The document pointed to by the hyperlink is then loaded into the newly created window.

Exercise 12.1: Working with windows.

In this exercise, you'll create four separate HTML documents that use hyperlinks, including the TARGET attribute. These hyperlinks will be used to open two new windows called first_window and second_window, as shown in Figure 12.3. The top window is the original Web browser window, first_window is on the bottom left, and second_window is on the bottom right.

Figure 12.3.

Hyperlinks can be made to open new windows for each of the pages they point to.

First, create the document to be displayed by the main Web browser window, shown in Figure 12.4, by opening your text editor of choice and entering the following lines of code:

12

```
<HTML>
<HEAD>
<TITLE>Target Parent Window</TITLE>
</HEAD>
<BODY>
<H1>Target Parent Window</H1>
<P>
<A HREF="target2.html" TARGET="first_window">Open</A>
 a new window called first_window.
<BR>
<A HREF="target3.html" TARGET="second_window">Open</A>
 a new window called second_window.
</P>
<P>
<A HREF="target4.html" TARGET="first_window">Load</A>
 some new text into first_window.
</P>
</BODY>
</HTML>
```

OUTPUT

Figure 12.4.
The Target Parent window.

12

Save this HTML source as `target1.html`.

Next, create a document called `target2.html` that looks like the page shown in Figure 12.5, by entering the following code:

INPUT

```
<HTML>
<HEAD>
<TITLE>Target First Window</TITLE>
</HEAD>
<BODY>
<H1>Target First Window</H1>
</BODY>
</HTML>
```

Figure 12.5.
target2.html
*displayed in the
Web browser
window named*
first_window.

After saving target2.html, create another document called target3.html that looks like the page shown in Figure 12.6. Do so by entering the following code:

```
<HTML>
<HEAD>
<TITLE>Target Second Window</TITLE>
</HEAD>
<BODY>
<H1>Target Second Window</H1>
</BODY>
</HTML>
```

Figure 12.6.
target3.html
*displayed in the
Web browser
window named*
second_window.

Next, create a fourth document, called target4.html, that looks like this:

```
<HTML>
<HEAD>
<TITLE>Target First Window</TITLE>
</HEAD>
<BODY>
<H1>Target First Window</H1>
<P>But this time with new text...</P>
</BODY>
</HTML>
```

To complete the exercise, load target1.html into your Web browser, and click the top two hyperlinks. This action opens two new windows with the contents of the targets in each one. Note that the new windows probably won't be laid out like the ones shown in Figure 12.3; instead they'll usually overlap each other.

Finally, click the third hyperlink to replace the contents of first_window with the Web page defined by target4.html, as shown in Figure 12.7.

Figure 12.7.
target4.html *displayed in the Web browser window named* first_window.

The <BASE> Tag

When using the TARGET attribute with links, you'll sometimes encounter a situation in which all or most of the hyperlinks on a Web page point to the same window—especially when using frames, as you'll discover in the following section.

In such cases, instead of including a TARGET attribute for each <A> tag, you can use another tag, <BASE>, to define a global target for all the links of a Web page. The <BASE> tag takes the following form:

```
<BASE TARGET="window_name">
```

If you include the <BASE> tag in the <HEAD>...</HEAD> block of a document, every <A> tag that does not have a corresponding TARGET attribute will display the document it points to in the window specified by <BASE TARGET="window_name">. For example, if the tag <BASE TARGET="first_window"> had been included in the HTML source for target1.html, the three hyperlinks could have been written this way:

```
</HTML>
<HEAD>
<TITLE>Target Parent Window</TITLE>
<BASE TARGET="first_window">        <!-- add BASE TARGET="value" here -->
</HEAD>
<BODY>
<H1>Target Parent Window</H1>
<P>
<A HREF="target2.html">Open</A>        <!-- no need to include a TARGET -->
 a new window called first_window.
```

12

```
<BR>
<A HREF="target3.html" TARGET="second_window">Open</A>
 a new window called second_window.
</P>
<P>
<A HREF="target4.html">Load</A>       <!-- no need to include a TARGET -->
 some new text into first_window.
</P>
</BODY>
</HTML>
```

In this case, `target2.html` and `target4.html` are loaded into the default window assigned by the `<BASE>` tag; `target3.html` overrides the default by defining its own target window.

You can also override the window assigned by the `<BASE>` tag by using one of two special window names. If you use `TARGET="_blank"` in a hyperlink, a new browser window that does not have a name associated with it is opened. Alternatively, if you use `TARGET="_self"`, the current window is used rather than the one defined by the `<BASE>` tag.

NOTE

> A point to remember: If you don't provide a `TARGET` using the `<BASE>` tag, and you don't indicate a target in a link's `<A>` tag, then the link will load the new document in the same frame as the link.

Working with Frames

The introduction of frames in Netscape 2.0 heralded a new era for Web publishers. With frames, you can create Web pages that look and feel entirely different from other Web pages—pages that have tables of tables, banners, footnotes, and sidebars, just to name a few common features that frames can give you.

At the same time, frames change what a "page" means to the browser and to the readers. Unlike all the preceding examples, which use a single HTML page to display a screen of information, when you create Web sites using frames, a single screen actually consists of a number of separate HTML documents that interact with each other. Figure 12.8 shows how a minimum of four separate documents is needed to create the screen shown earlier in Figure 12.1.

The first HTML document you need to create is called the frame definition document. In this document, you enter the HTML code that describes the layout of each frame and indicate the name of the separate HTML document that contains the physical information to be displayed. The three remaining HTML documents contain normal HTML tags that define the physical contents of each separate frame area. These documents are referenced by the frame definition document.

Figure 12.8.

Separate HTML documents must be created for each frame.

 The *frame definition document* is the page that contains the layout of each frame and the names of the HTML documents that will fill that frame.

The <FRAMESET> Tag

To create a frame definition document, you use the <FRAMESET> tag. When used in an HTML document, the <FRAMESET> tag replaces the <BODY> tag, as shown here:

```
<HTML>
<HEAD>
<TITLE>Page Title</TITLE>
</HEAD>
<FRAMESET>
    your frame definition goes here.
</FRAMESET>
</HTML>
```

Understanding upfront how a frame definition document differs from a normal HTML document is important. If you include a <FRAMESET> tag in an HTML document, you cannot also include a <BODY> tag. Basically, the two tags are mutually exclusive. In addition, no other formatting tags, hyperlinks, or document text should be included in a frame definition document, except in one special case (the <NOFRAMES> tag) which you'll learn about in the section called, appropriately, "The <NOFRAMES> Tag," later in this chapter. The <FRAMESET> tags contain only the definitions for the frames in this document: what's called the page's frameset.

The <FRAMESET> tag is supported in the HTML 4.0 specification along with two possible attributes: COLS and ROWS.

A *frameset* is a set of frames defined by <FRAMESET> tags in a frame definition document.

The COLS **Attribute**

When you define a <FRAMESET> tag, you must include one of two attributes as part of the tag definition. The first of these attributes is the COLS attribute, which takes the following form:

```
<FRAMESET COLS="column width, column width, ...">
```

The COLS attribute tells the browser to split the screen into a number of vertical frames whose widths are defined by *column width* values separated by commas. You define the width of each frame in one of three ways: explicitly in pixels, as a percentage of the total width of the <FRAMESET>, or with an asterisk (*). When you use the *, Netscape uses as much space as possible for the specified frame.

When included in a complete frame definition, the following <FRAMESET> tag creates a screen with three vertical frames, as shown in Figure 12.9. The first frame is 100 pixels wide, the second is 50 percent of the width of the screen, and the third uses all the remaining space.

  `<FRAMESET COLS="100,50%,*">`

Figure 12.9.

The COLS *attribute defines the number of vertical frames or columns in a frameset.*

NOTE

Because you're designing Web pages that will be used on various screen sizes, you should use absolute frame sizes sparingly. Whenever you do use an absolute size, ensure that one of the other frames is defined using an * to take up all the remaining screen space.

12

TIP

To define a frameset with three equal-width columns, use COLS="*, *, *". This way, you won't have to mess around with percentages because Netscape automatically gives an equal amount of space to each frame assigned an * width.

The ROWS Attribute

The ROWS attribute works the same as the COLS attribute, except that it splits the screen into horizontal frames rather than vertical ones. For example, to split the screen into two equal-height frames, as shown in Figure 12.10, you would write the following:

 INPUT

```
<FRAMESET ROWS="50%,50%">
```

Alternatively, you could use this line:

INPUT

```
<FRAMESET ROWS="*, *">
```

OUTPUT

Figure 12.10.

The ROWS attribute defines the number of horizontal frames or rows in a frameset.

12

 NOTE

If you try either of the preceding examples for yourself, you'll find that the <FRAMESET> tag does not appear to work. You get this result because currently no contents are defined for the rows or columns in the frameset. To define the contents, you need to use the <FRAME> tag, which is discussed in the next section.

The <FRAME> Tag

After you have your basic frameset laid out, you need to associate an HTML document with each frame. To do so, you use the <FRAME> tag, which takes the following form:

```
<FRAME SRC="document URL">
```

For each frame defined in the <FRAMESET> tag, you must include a corresponding <FRAME> tag, as shown here:

```
<FRAMESET ROWS="*,*,*">
    <FRAME SRC="document1.html">
    <FRAME SRC="document2.html">
    <FRAME SRC="document3.html">
</FRAMESET>
```

In this example, a frameset with three equal-height horizontal frames is defined (see Figure 12.11). The contents of document1.html are displayed in the first frame; the contents of document2.html, in the second frame; and the contents of document3.html, in the third frame.

OUTPUT

Figure 12.11.

The <FRAME> tag is used to define the contents of each frame.

> | **TIP** | When you're creating frame definition documents, you might find it helpful to indent the <FRAME> tags so they're separated from the <FRAMESET> tags in your HTML document. Doing so has no effect on the appearance of the resulting Web pages but does tend to make the HTML source easier to read. |

Additional Attributes

You can assign a few extra attributes to a <FRAME> tag to give you additional control over how the user interacts with your frames. Table 12.1 presents the details about them. All these attributes are supported in HTML 4.0.

Table 12.1. Control attributes for the <FRAME> tag.

Attribute	Value	Description
SCROLLING	AUTO (default)	By default, if the contents of a frame take up more space than the area available to the frame, Netscape automatically adds scrollbars to either the side or the bottom of the frame so that the users can scroll through the document.
SCROLLING	NO	Setting the value of SCROLLING to NO disables the use of scrollbars for the current frame. (Note that if you set SCROLLING="NO", but the document contains more text than can fit inside the frame, the users will not be able to scroll the additional text into view.)
SCROLLING	YES	If you set SCROLLING to YES, the scrollbars are included in the frame regardless of whether they are required.
NORESIZE		By default, the users can move the position of borders around each frame on the current screen by grabbing the border and moving it with the mouse. To lock the borders of a frame and prevent them from being moved, use the NORESIZE attribute.
MARGINHEIGHT	pixels	To adjust the margin that appears above and below a document within a frame, set the MARGINHEIGHT to the number indicated by pixels.
MARGINWIDTH	pixels	The MARGINWIDTH attribute enables you to adjust the margin on the left and right side of a frame to the number indicated by pixels.

12

The <NOFRAMES> Tag

If you load a frame definition document into a Web browser that does not support frames, you get only a blank page. To get around this problem, Netscape created a special tag block called <NOFRAMES>. This tag enables you to include body text as part of the document. The <NOFRAMES> tag takes the following form:

```
<HTML>
<HEAD>
<TITLE>Page Title</TITLE>
</HEAD>
<FRAMESET>
 your frame definition goes here.
<NOFRAMES>
  Include any text, hyperlinks, and tags you want to here.
```

```
</NOFRAMES>
</FRAMESET>
</HTML>
```

None of the text you include inside the <NOFRAMES> block will be displayed by browsers that support frames, but when the page is loaded into a Web browser that does not support frames, it will be displayed. Using both frames' content and tags inside <NOFRAMES>, you can create pages that work well with both kinds of browsers.

Changing Frame Borders

Notice that all the frames in this chapter have thick borders separating them. In the original frames implementation in Netscape 2.0, you could do little about this situation. However, with the introduction of Netscape 3.0 and Internet Explorer 3.0, new attributes of the <FRAME> and <FRAMESET> tags give you some control over the color and width of frame borders.

Start with the <FRAME> tag. By using two attributes, BORDERCOLOR and FRAMEBORDER, you can turn borders on and off and specify their color. BORDERCOLOR can be assigned any valid color value either as a name or a hexadecimal triplet. FRAMEBORDER takes two possible values: YES or NO.

NOTE
If you turn off the border, Netscape will not display its default three-dimensional border, but a space will still be left for the border.

NOTE
HTML 4.0 currently only lists the FRAMEBORDER attribute. The BORDERCOLOR attribute qualifies as an extension.

For example, the following creates a frame with a border colored a dark blue (which is defined by #020A33):

```
<FRAME FRAMEBORDER=YES BORDERCOLOR="#020A33" SRC="somefile.html">
```

Both of these attributes can also be used in the <FRAMESET> tag, defining default values for the entire frameset in Netscape and Microsoft Internet Explorer, although HTML 4.0 doesn't provide either attribute for the <FRAMESET> tag.

Of course, there is room for confusion when colored borders are defined. For example, in the following frameset definition, a conflict arises because the two frames share a single common border, but each frame is defined to have a different border color:

```
<FRAMESET ROWS="*,*" FRAMEBORDER=NO>
   <FRAME FRAMEBORDER=YES BORDERCOLOR=yellow SRC="firstfile.html">
   <FRAME BORDERCOLOR=blue SRC="secondfile.html">
</FRAMESET>
```

In addition, the frameset is defined as having no borders, but the first frame is supposed to have a border. How does this problem get resolved? Netscape has specified three simple rules that will be applied in these situations:

☐ Attributes in the outermost frameset have the lowest priority.

☐ Attributes are overridden by attributes in a nested <FRAMESET> tag.

☐ Any BORDERCOLOR attribute in the current frame overrides previous ones in <FRAMESET> tags.

One more attribute of the <FRAMESET> tag enables you to control the width of a border: The BORDER attribute takes a numeric value indicating the width of all borders in the frameset in pixels. You can use the BORDER attribute only in the outermost frameset in a set of nested framesets. Any other use is ignored. Figures 12.12 and 12.13 highlight the effect of the BORDER attribute.

In Figure 12.12, you see a frameset with the definition <FRAMESET BORDER=6 ROWS="25%,*">. Figure 12.13 shows the following frameset definition: <FRAMESET BORDER=0 ROWS="25$,*">.

NOTE The BORDER attribute is not supported in the current draft for HTML 4.0.

Creating Complex Framesets

The framesets you've learned about so far represent the most basic types of frames that can be displayed. But in day-to-day use, you'll rarely use these basic frame designs. In all but the most simple sites, you'll most likely want to use more complex framesets.

Therefore, to help you understand the possible combinations of frames, links, images, and documents that can be used by a Web site, this section of the chapter explores the topic of complex framesets.

Figure 12.12.

A frameset with a border width of 6 pixels.

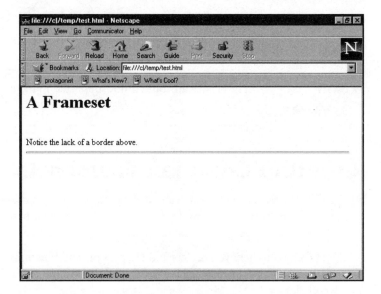

Figure 12.13.

A frameset with a border width of 0 pixels.

Exercise 12.2: Combining ROWS and COLS.

The frame layout presented by Figure 12.1, at the beginning of the chapter, provides a good basis for a simple example that explores how you can combine framesets to create complex designs. To remind you of the basic layout, look at Figure 12.14, which shows a screen that uses a similar design but without any contents.

Figure 12.14.

The "Combining ROWS *and* COLS*" exercise.*

> **TIP**
>
> When you're designing complex frame layouts, a storyboard is an invaluable tool. The storyboard helps you block out the structure of a frameset, and it can also be invaluable when you're adding hyperlinks, as you will see in Exercise 12.3, "Using Named Frames and Hyperlinks."

In Figure 12.14, the top section of the screen is split into two vertical frames, and the third frame, at the bottom of the page, spans the entire width of the screen. To create a frame definition document that describes this layout, open your text editor and enter the following basic HTML structural details:

```
<HTML>
<HEAD>
<TITLE>Complex Frames Exercise</TITLE>
</HEAD>
<FRAMESET>
</FRAMESET>
</HTML>
```

Next, you must decide whether you need to use a ROWS or COLS attribute in your base <FRAMESET>. To do so, look at your storyboard—in this case Figure 12.14—and work out whether any frame areas extend right across the screen or from the top to the bottom of the screen. If any frames extend from the top to the bottom, you need to start with a COLS frameset; otherwise, you need to start with a ROWS frameset. On the other hand, if no frames extend completely across the screen in either direction, you should start with a COLS frameset.

To put it more simply, here are three easily remembered rules:

☐ Left to right, use ROWS

☐ Top to bottom, use COLS

☐ Can't decide, use COLS

NOTE
The reasoning behind the use of the "left to right, use ROWS" rule relates to how Netscape creates frames. Each separate <FRAMESET> definition can split the screen (or a frame) either vertically or horizontally, but not both ways. For this reason, you need to define your framesets in a logical order to ensure that the desired layout is achieved.

In Figure 12.14, the bottom frame extends right across the screen from side to side. As a result, by using the rules mentioned previously, you need to start with a ROWS frameset. To define the base frameset, write the following:

```
<FRAMESET ROWS="*, 80">
    <FRAME SRC="dummy.html">  <!-- this is the frame for row 1 -->
    <FRAME SRC="dummy.html">  <!-- this is the frame for row 2 -->
</FRAMESET>
```

Writing this code splits the screen into two sections: a small frame at the bottom of the screen that is 80 pixels high and a large frame at the top of the screen that uses the rest of the available space. Two <FRAME> tags have also been defined to represent the contents of each frame.

TIP
When laying out the basic structure of a frameset, you normally don't want to be bothered with details such as the actual contents of the frames. However, unless you define <FRAME> tags that include a valid document, your frameset will not be displayed properly when it is loaded into Netscape for testing. To get around this problem, create a small empty HTML document called dummy.html, and use it for all your frame testing.

Nesting <FRAMESET> Tags

The next step in the process is to split the top frame area into two vertical frames. You achieve this effect by placing a second <FRAMESET> block inside the base <FRAMESET> block. When one <FRAMESET> block is nested inside another, the nested block must replace one of the <FRAME> tags in the outside frameset.

Therefore, to split the top frame into two frame areas, you replace the <FRAME> tag for the first frame with an embedded <FRAMESET> block. Doing so embeds the new frameset inside the area defined for the <FRAME> tag it replaces. Inside the <FRAMESET> tag for this new block, you then need to define a COLS attribute as shown here:

```
<FRAMESET ROWS="*, 80">
    <FRAMESET COLS="30%, *">        <!-- the frame for row 1  -->
        <FRAME SRC="dummy.html">    <!--  has been replaced   -->
        <FRAME SRC="dummy.html">    <!--    by an embedded    -->
    </FRAMESET>                     <!--     frameset block    -->
    <FRAME SRC="dummy.html"> <!-- this is the frame for row 2 -->
</FRAMESET>
```

The embedded COLS frameset defines two columns, the first being 30 percent of the width of the embedded frame area and the second taking up all the remaining space in the embedded frame area. In addition, two <FRAME> tags are embedded inside the <FRAMESET> block to define the contents of each column.

NOTE

When used inside an embedded frameset, any percentage sizes are based on a percentage of the total area of the embedded frame and not as a percentage of the total screen.

Finally, save the finished HTML document to your hard drive, and test it by using a frames-compliant browser. Also, if you happen to have a copy of a non-frames-compliant Web browser, try loading the document into it. (You should not see anything when you use the alternative browsers.)

Exercise 12.3: Using named frames and hyperlinks.

As I mentioned earlier in this chapter, the frame definition document itself does not describe the contents of each frame. The documents indicated by the SRC attribute of the <FRAME> actually contain the text, images, and tags displayed by the frameset.

As a result, to turn the frame definition document created in the preceding exercise into a fully working, frame-based Web page, you need to add some valid HTML documents to the definition. The frames are so powerful because any HTML document you've created previously can become the SRC for an individual frame. Therefore, you can easily take the HTML reference documents you've created for each chapter and integrate them into a frameset. But first, so that you understand what you're about to create, Figure 12.15 shows the complete frameset you'll create in this exercise.

Adding Real Documents to Your Frameset

The first step in the process is a simple one. Take the frameset document you created in Exercise 12.2, "Combining ROWS and COLS," and save a copy of it in the same directory as the HTML reference documents you created previously. Name the new file html_frame.html.

Figure 12.15.

The HTML reference document as a frameset.

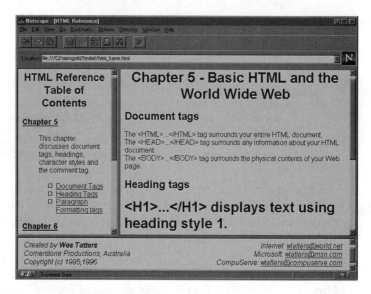

After you create this new file, change the references to the dummy.html file to point to real HTML files (here the changes are highlighted in bold):

```
<FRAMESET ROWS="*, 80">
    <FRAMESET COLS="30%, *">
        <FRAME SRC="html_contents_frame.html">
        <FRAME SRC="05notes_frame.html">
    </FRAMESET>
    <FRAME SRC="html_footer.html">
</FRAMESET>
```

The first <FRAME> tag now points to a file called html_contents_frame.html, which is a copy of the html_contents.html file you've worked with in previous chapters. I just changed the name to protect the original because you need to make some changes to the document. But for now, simply copy the html_contents.html file to html_contents_frame.html.

 TIP

> If you're working on DOS, you'll need to use an alternative naming scheme such as cont_f.htm and 05note_f.htm.

Do the same for 05notes.html by copying it to 05notes_frame.html, and then work through each of the other chapter documents and any other pages they reference.

You next need to make some alterations to 05notes_frame.html. In previous exercises, you have added <ADDRESS> blocks and navigation buttons to each page. With frames, however, you don't need to include either of these elements because, in this exercise, they'll be handled in one way or another by other frames in the frameset. As result, you should remove the signature and navigation buttons from the bottom of `05notes_frame.html`. In addition, remove any other hyperlinks that join the pages together.

Finally, you need to create a new HTML document called `html_footer.html`. In this document, you'll place the information previously shown in the `<ADDRESS>` block of your individual pages. What you place in this document is up to you; however, keep in mind that it will need to fit into the small 80-pixel-high frame at the bottom of the frameset.

To give you some idea about how you might create the contents of `html_footer.html`, here's the partial HTML source used for Figure 12.15:

```
<TABLE WIDTH="100%">
<TR>
    <TD WIDTH="50%">
        <ADDRESS>
        Created by <B>Laura Lemay</B><BR>
        Copyright (c) 1995,1996,1997
        </ADDRESS>
    </TD>
    <TD WIDTH="50%" ALIGN="RIGHT">
        <ADDRESS>
        Email: <A HREF="mailto:lemay@lne.com">lemay@lne.com</A><BR>
        Home Page: <A HREF="http://www.lne.com/lemay/">
            http://www.lne.com/lemay/</A>
        </ADDRESS>
    </TD>
</TR>
</TABLE>
```

This example uses a table without borders to place my name on the left side of the screen and my e-mail addresses on the right.

Naming Individual Frames

If you were to load `html_frame.html` into Netscape at this stage, you would see a screen similar to the one shown in Figure 12.15. Some of the text sizes and spacing might be slightly different, but the general picture would be the same. If, however, you were to click any of the hyperlinks in the left frame, you would most likely get some very strange results. To be more specific, Netscape would attempt to load the contents of the file you select into the left frame, when what you really want it to do is load each document into the right frame.

To make the browser work the way you want, you need to use a slight variation on the `TARGET` attribute discussed at the beginning of this chapter. But instead of the `TARGET` pointing to a new window, you want it to point to one of the frames in the current frameset.

You can achieve this by first giving each frame in your frameset a frame name, or window name. To do so, you include a `NAME` attribute inside the `<FRAME>` tag, which takes the following form:

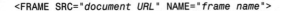

```
<FRAME SRC="document URL" NAME="frame name">
```

Therefore, to assign a name to each of the frames in the `html_frame.html` document, you alter the `<FRAME>` tags to look like this:

```
<FRAMESET ROWS="*, 80">
    <FRAMESET COLS="30%, *">
        <FRAME SRC="html_contents_frame.html"  NAME="Contents">
        <FRAME SRC="05notes_frame.html"  NAME="Chapter">
    </FRAMESET>
    <FRAME SRC="html_footer.html"  NAME="Footer">
</FRAMESET>
```

This source code names the left frame `"Contents"`, the right frame `"Chapter"`, and the bottom frame `"Footer"`. Next, resave the updated `html_frame.html` file, and you're just about finished with the exercise.

Linking Documents to Individual Frames

All you need to do now is make some minor alterations to `html_contents_frame.html` so that each chapter document is loaded into the right-hand frame of the frameset.

You may recall from the beginning of this chapter that the TARGET attribute was used with the `<A>` tag to force a document to load into a specific window. This same attribute is used to control which frame a document is loaded into.

For this exercise, what you want to happen is that, whenever you click a hyperlink in the left frame, the corresponding document is loaded into the right frame. Because you've already assigned the right frame a window name of `"Chapter"`, to load all the documents into the right frame, all you need to do is add TARGET=`"Chapter"` to each tag in the `html_contents_frame.html` document. The following snippet of HTML source demonstrates how to make this change:

```
<DT><A HREF="05notes_frame.html" TARGET="Chapter"><H3>Chapter 5</H3></A>
<DD>
<P>This chapter discusses document tags, headings,
character styles and the comment tag. </P>
<UL>
<LI><A HREF="05notes_frame.html#document_tags" TARGET="Chapter">
    Document tags</A>
<LI><A HREF="05notes_frame.html#heading_tags" TARGET="Chapter">
    Heading tags</A>
<LI><A HREF="05notes_frame.html#paragraph_tags" TARGET="Chapter">
    Paragraph Formatting tags</A>
</UL>
```

NOTE

> If you're using the new naming system set out in this exercise, you need to change the HREF value of each `<A>` tag to point to the new names for each document. For example, `05notes.html` becomes `05notes_frame.html`.

Alternatively, because every tag in the `html_contents_frame.html` document points to the same frame, you could also use the `<BASE TARGET="value">` tag. In this case, you don't need to include TARGET="Chapter" inside each <A> tag. Instead, you place the following inside the <HEAD>...</HEAD> block of the document:

`<BASE TARGET="Chapter">`

The only other change you need to make to html_content_frame.html is purely cosmetic. In the original document, the main heading line uses <H1>; however, this heading size is too large for the small left frame. Therefore, you should replace it with this line:

`<H2 ALIGN="CENTER">HTML Reference Table of Contents</H2>`

With all the changes and new documents created, you should now be able to load html_frame.html into Netscape and view all your HTML reference documents by selecting from the table of contents in the left frame.

TIP

> To get the layout exactly right, you might need to go back and adjust the size of the rows and columns as defined in the <FRAMESET> tags after you get all your links working properly. Remember, the final appearance of a frameset is still determined by the size of the screen and the operating system used by people viewing the documents.

Magic TARGET Names

You can assign four special values to a TARGET attribute, two of which (_blank and _self) you've already encountered. Netscape calls these values Magic TARGET names. Table 12.2 lists the Magic TARGET names and describes their use.

Table 12.2. Magic TARGET names.

TARGET Name	Description
TARGET="_blank"	Forces the document referenced by the <A> tag to be loaded into a new "unnamed" window.
TARGET="_self"	Causes the document referenced by the <A> tag to be loaded into the window or frame that held the <A> tag. This can be useful if the <BASE> tag sets the target to another frame but a specific link needs to load in the current frame.
TARGET="_parent"	Forces the link to load into the <FRAMESET> parent of the current document. If, however, the current document has no parent, TARGET="_self" will be used.
TARGET="_top"	Forces the link to load into the full Web browser window, replacing the current <FRAMESET> entirely. If, however, the current document is already at the top, TARGET="_self" will be used.

12

Floating Frames

With Internet Explorer 3.0, Microsoft introduced a novel variation on frames: floating frames. This concept, which appears in the HTML 4.0 specification, is different from the original frames idea Netscape introduced.

NOTE

The authors of HTML 4.0 have included floating frames but with some hesitation. According to the draft, the same effect as floating frames could be achieved using the `<OBJECT>` tag, so the inclusion of this type of frame is questionable. Still, it is included in the proposal, and Internet Explorer 3 supports the technology, so learning to use floating frames is worthwhile.

You create floating frames by using the `<IFRAME>` tag. Like images, these frames appear inline in the middle of the body of an HTML document (hence the "I" in `<IFRAME>`). The `<IFRAME>` tag allows you to insert an HTML document in a frame anywhere in another HTML document.

`<IFRAME>` takes several key attributes—all of which appear currently in HTML 4.0 except for those indicated as Internet Explorer extensions:

☐ WIDTH: Specifies the width in pixels of the floating frame that will hold the HTML document.

☐ HEIGHT: Specifies the height in pixels of the floating frame that will hold the HTML document.

☐ SRC: Specifies the URL of the HTML document to be displayed in the frame.

☐ NAME: Specifies the name of the frame for the purpose of linking and targeting.

☐ FRAMEBORDER: Indicates whether the frame should display a border. According to the proposal for Cougar, a value of 1 indicates the presence of a border and a value of 0 indicates no border should be displayed.

☐ BORDER: Specifies the thickness of the border in pixels (Internet Explorer extension).

☐ BORDERCOLOR: Specifies the color of the border (Internet Explorer extension).

☐ FRAMESPACING: Specifies the number of additional pixels between frame borders (Internet Explorer extension).

☐ MARGINWIDTH: Specifies the width of the margin in pixels.

☐ MARGINHEIGHT: Specifies the height of the margin in pixels.

☐ NORESIZE: Indicates that the frame should not be resizable by the user (Internet Explorer extension).

☐ SCROLLING: As with the <FRAME> tag, indicates whether the inline frame should include scrollbars. (This attribute can take the values YES, NO, or AUTO; the default is AUTO.)

☐ VSPACE: Specifies the height of the margin (Internet Explorer extension).

☐ HSPACE: Specifies the width of the margin (Internet Explorer extension).

☐ ALIGN: As with the <IMG> tag, specifies the positioning of the frame with respect to the text line in which it occurs. Possible values include LEFT, MIDDLE, RIGHT, TOP, and BOTTOM with the last being the default value. ABSBOTTOM, ABSMIDDLE, BASELINE, and TEXTTOP are available as Internet Explorer extensions.

Because you know how to use both regular frames and inline images, using the <IFRAME> tag is fairly easy. For example, the following HTML code would include a 200-by-200 pixel frame, with a border, and display the document iframe.html in the frame. Figure 12.16 shows the results in Internet Explorer 3.

```
<HTML>
<HEAD>
<TITLE>IFRAME Example</TITLE>
</HEAD>
<BODY>
This is an In-line Frame (also known as a Floating Frame):
<IFRAME SRC="iframe.html" WIDTH=200 HEIGHT=200 FRAMEBORDER=1>
As you can see it just sits there in the middle of the document.
</BODY>
</HTML>
```

Figure 12.16.

An inline (or floating) frame.

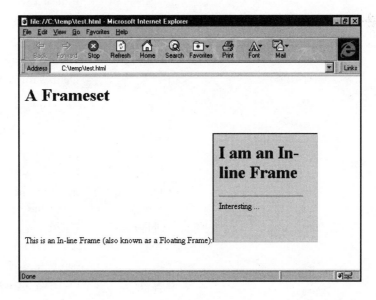

Summary

If your head is hurting after reading this chapter, you're probably not alone. Although the basic concepts behind the use of frames are relatively straightforward, their implementation is somewhat harder to come to grips with. As a result, the best way to learn about frames is by experimenting with them.

In this chapter, you learned how to link a document to a new or an existing window. In addition, you learned how to create framesets and link them together by using the tags listed in Table 12.3.

Table 12.3. New tags discussed in Chapter 12.

Tag	Attribute	Description
`<BASE TARGET="`*`window`*`">`		Sets the global link window for a document.
`<FRAMESET>`		Defines the basic structure of a frameset.
	COLS	Defines the number of frame columns and their width in a frameset.
	ROWS	Defines the number of frame rows and their height in a frameset.
	FRAMEBORDER	Indicates whether the frameset displays borders between frames.
	BORDERCOLOR	Defines the color of borders in a frameset.
	BORDER	Specifies the width of borders in pixels.
`<FRAME>`		Defines the contents of a frame within a frameset.
	SRC	Indicates the URL of the document to be displayed inside the frame.
	MARGINWIDTH	Indicates the size in pixels of the margin on each side of a frame.
	MARGINHEIGHT	Indicates the size in pixels of the margin above and below the contents of a frame.
	SCROLLING	Enables or disables the display of scrollbars for a frame. Values are YES, NO, and AUTO.
	NORESIZE	Prevents the users from resizing frames.
	FRAMEBORDER	Indicates whether the frameset displays borders between frames.

12

Tag	Attribute	Description
	BORDERCOLOR	Defines the color of borders in a frameset.
<IFRAME>		Define an inline or floating frame.
	SRC	Indicates the URL of the document to be displayed in the frame.
	NAME	Indicates the name of the frame for the purpose of linking and targeting.
	WIDTH	Indicates the width of the frame in pixels.
	HEIGHT	Indicates the height of the frame in pixels.
	MARGINWIDTH	Indicates the width of the margin in pixels.
	MARGINHEIGHT	Indicates the height of the margin in pixels.
	SCROLLING	Enables or disables the display of scrollbars in the frame. Values are YES, NO, and AUTO.
	FRAMEBORDER	Enables or disables the display of a border around the frame. Values are 1 or 0.
	BORDER	Indicates the thickness of the border in pixels (Internet Explorer).
	BORDERCOLOR	Indicates the color of the border (Internet Explorer).
	FRAMESPACING	Indicates the space in pixels between frame borders (Internet Explorer).
	VSPACE	Indicates the height of the margin in pixels.
	HSPACE	Indicates the width of the margin in pixels.
	ALIGN	Specifies the alignment of the frame relative to the current line of text. Values are LEFT, RIGHT, MIDDLE, TOP, and BOTTOM (also ABSBOTTOM, ABSMIDDLE, TEXTTOP, and BASELINE in Internet Explorer).
<NOFRAMES>		Defines text to be displayed by Web browsers that don't support the use of frames.

12

If you've made it this far through the book, you should give yourself a pat on the back. With the knowledge you've gained in the last week, you've done just about everything you can do while still working along on a single computer. You're now ready to place your Web pages onto the Internet itself and add more interactive features to those pages such as forms, image maps, and embedded animations.

Q&A

Q Is there any limit to how many levels of `<FRAMESET>` tags I can nest within a single screen?

A No, there isn't a limit. Practically speaking, however, when you get below about four levels, the size of the window space available starts to become unusable.

Q What would happen if I included a reference to a frame definition document within a `<FRAME>` tag?

A Netscape handles such a reference correctly, by treating the nested frame definition document as a nested `<FRAMESET>`. In fact, this technique is used regularly to reduce the complexity of nested frames.

One limitation does exist, however. You cannot include a reference to the current frame definition document in one of its own frames. This situation, called recursion, causes an infinite loop. Netscape Communications has included built-in protection to guard against this type of referencing.

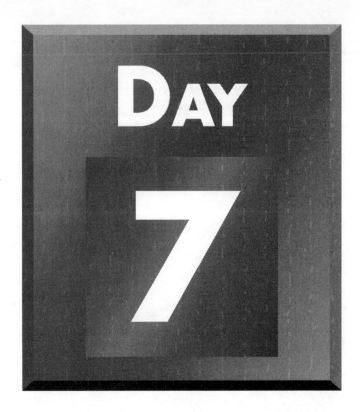

Going Live on the Web

Chapter **13**

Putting It All Online

For the past week, you've been creating and testing your Web pages on your local machine with your own browser. You may not have even had a network connection attached to your machine. At this point, you mostly likely have a Web presentation put together with a well-organized structure and with a reasonable number of meaningful images (each with carefully chosen ALT text). You've also written your text with wit and care, used only relative links, and tested it extensively on your own system.

Now, on Day 7, you're finally ready to publish it, to put it all online so that other people on the Web can see it and link their pages to yours. In this chapter and the next, you'll learn everything you need to get started publishing the work you've done. Today you'll learn about the following topics:

- ☐ What a Web server does and why you need one
- ☐ Where you can find a Web server on which to put your presentation
- ☐ How to install your Web presentation

☐ How to find out your URL
☐ How to test and troubleshoot your Web pages
☐ Methods for advertising your presentation
☐ How to use log files and counters to find out who's viewing your pages

What Does a Web Server Do?

To publish Web pages, you'll need a Web server. The Web server is a program that sits on a machine on the Internet, waiting for a Web browser to connect to it and make a request for a file. After a request comes over the wire, the server locates and sends the file back to the browser. The process is as easy as that.

Web servers and Web browsers communicate using the HyperText Transfer Protocol (HTTP), a special "language" created specifically for the request and transfer of hypertext documents over the Web. Because of this use, Web servers are often called HTTPD servers.

NOTE

> The *D* in *HTTPD* stands for *daemon*. Daemon is a UNIX term for a program that sits in the background and waits for requests. When this program receives a request, it wakes up, processes the request, and then goes back to sleep. You don't have to work in UNIX for a program to act like a daemon, so Web servers on any platform are still called HTTPDs. Most of the time, I call them Web servers.

Other Things Web Servers Do

Although the Web server's primary purpose is to answer requests from browsers, a Web server is responsible for several other tasks. Some of them you'll learn about today; others you'll learn about later this week.

File and Media Types

In Chapter 8, "External Files, Multimedia, and Animation," you learned about content-types and how browsers and servers use file extensions to determine the types of files. Servers are responsible for telling the browsers the kind of content files contain. You can configure a Web server to send different kinds of media or to handle new and different files and extensions. You'll learn more about this subject later in this chapter.

File Management

The Web server is also responsible for very rudimentary file management—mostly in determining where to find a file and keeping track of where it's gone. If a browser requests a file that doesn't exist, the Web server sends back the page with the 404: File Not Found

13

message. Servers can also be configured to create aliases for files (the same file but accessed with a different name), to redirect files to different locations (automatically pointing the browser to a new URL for files that have moved) and to return a default file or a directory listing if a browser requests a URL ending with a directory name.

Finally, servers keep log files for information on how many times each file on the site has been accessed, including the site that accessed it, the date, and, in some servers, the type of browser and the URL of the page they came from.

CGI Scripts, Programs, and Forms Processing

One of the more interesting (and more complex) tasks that a server can perform is to run external programs on the server machine based on input that your readers provide from their browsers. These special programs are most often called CGI scripts and are the basis for creating interactive forms and clickable server-side image maps (images that contain several "hot spots" and perform different operations based on the location within the image that has been selected). CGI scripts can also be used to connect a Web server with a database or other information system on the server side.

Server-Side File Processing

Some servers can process files before they send them along to the browsers. On a simple level are server-side includes, which can insert a date or a chunk of boilerplate text into each page, or run a program. (Many of the access counters you see on pages are run in this way.) Server-side processing can also be used in much more sophisticated ways to modify files on the fly for different browsers or to execute small bits of scripting code.

Authentication and Security

Some Web sites require you to register for their services and make you log in using a name and password every time you visit their sites. This process, called authentication, is a feature most Web servers now include. Using authentication, you can set up users and passwords, and you can restrict access to certain files and directories. You can also restrict access to files or to an entire site based on site names or IP addresses—for example, to prevent anyone outside your company from viewing files that are intended for internal use.

NEW TERM   *Authentication* is the ability to protect files or directories on your Web server so they require your readers to enter names and passwords before the files can be viewed.

For security, some servers now provide a mechanism for secure connections and transactions using Netscape's SSL protocol. SSL provides authentication of the server (to prove that the server is who it says it is) and an encrypted connection between the browser and the server so that sensitive information between the two is kept secret.

13

Locating a Web Server

Before you can put your Web presentation on the Web, you'll need to find a Web server that you can use. Depending on how you get your access to the Internet, locating a Web server may be really easy or not quite so easy.

Using a Web Server Provided by Your School or Work

If you get your Internet connection through school or work, that organization will most likely allow you to publish Web pages on its own Web server. Given that these organizations usually have fast connections to the Internet and people to administer the site for you, this situation is ideal if you have it.

If you're in this situation, you'll have to ask your system administrator, computer consultant, Webmaster, or network provider whether a Web server is available, and, if so, what the procedures are for getting your pages installed. You'll learn more about what to ask later in this chapter.

Using a Commercial Internet or Web Service

If you pay for your access to the Internet through an Internet service provider (ISP) or a commercial online service, you may also be able to publish your Web pages using that service, although doing so may cost you extra, and the service may have restrictions on the kinds of pages you can publish or whether you can run CGI scripts. Ask your provider's help line or online groups or conferences related to Internet services to see how they have set up Web publishing.

In the last few years, several organizations that provide nothing but Web publishing services have popped up. These services usually provide you with some method for transferring your files to their sites (usually FTP), and they provide the disk space and the network connections for access to your files. They also have professional site administrators on site to make sure the servers are running well all the time. Generally, you are charged a flat monthly rate, with some additional cost if you use a large amount of disk space or if you have especially popular pages that take up a lot of network bandwidth. Some services even allow CGI scripts for forms and server-side image maps and will provide consulting to help you set them up; a few will even set up their server with your own host name so that it looks as though you've got your own server running on the Web. These features can make using commercial Web sites an especially attractive option. Appendix A, "Sources for Further Information," includes pointers to lists of these sites.

Note that unlike your main Internet service provider, which you generally want located in your city or somewhere close to minimize phone bills, services that publish Web pages can be located anywhere on the Internet, and you can shop for the cheapest prices and best services without having to worry about geographical location.

Using Anonymous FTP or Gopher

If all else fails and you cannot find a Web server, you do have another option. If your work, school, or ISP doesn't provide a Web server but does provide an anonymous FTP or Gopher server, you can use one of these servers to publish your Web pages. You'll have a different URL (an FTP or Gopher URL), and you won't have nearly the features of a real Web site (forms, scripts, image maps), but if it's all you've got, it'll work well enough for simple pages. And often this option may be cheaper than a dedicated Web server.

Setting Up Your Own Server

For the ultimate in Web publishing, running your own Web site is the way to go. If you run your own site, you can not only publish as much as you want to and include any kind of content you want to, but you also can use forms, CGI scripts, image maps, and many other special options that most other Web publishing services won't let you use. However, the cost, maintenance time, and technical background required to run your own server can be daunting, and running a server is definitely not for everyone. You'll learn more about running your own server in the next chapter.

Organizing and Installing Your HTML Files

After you have access to a Web server, you can publish the Web presentation you've labored so hard to create. But before you actually move it into place on your server, having your files organized is important. You also should have a good idea of what goes where so that you don't lose files or so that your links don't break in the process.

Questions to Ask Your Webmaster

The Webmaster is the person who runs your Web server; this person may also be your system administrator, help desk administrator, or network administrator. Before you can publish your files, you should learn several facts from the Webmaster about how the server is set up. The following list of questions will also help you later in this book when you're ready to figure out what you can and cannot do with your server:

☐ **Where on the server will I put my files?** In many cases, your Webmaster may create a special directory for you. Know where that directory is and how to gain access to it.

In some other cases, particularly on UNIX machines, you may be able to just create a special directory in your home directory and store your files there. If that's the case, your Webmaster will tell you the name of the directory.

☐ **What is the URL of my top-level directory?** This URL may be different from the actual pathname to your files.

13

☐ **What is the name of the system's default index file?** This file is loaded by default when a URL ends with a directory name. Usually, it is `index.html` but may sometimes be `default.html`, `Homepage.html`, or something else.

☐ **Can I run CGI scripts?** Depending on your server, the answer to this question may be a flat-out "no," or you may be limited to certain programs and capabilities. For now, you don't need extensive details about how to create CGI; you'll learn more about this topic later in the book.

☐ **Does my site have limitations on what I can put up or how much?** Some sites restrict pages to specific content (for example, only work-related pages) or allow you only a few pages on the system. They may prevent more than a certain number of people from accessing your pages at once or may have other restrictions on what sort of publishing you can do. Make sure that you understand the limitations of the system and that you can work within these limitations.

Keeping Your Files Organized Using Directories

Probably the easiest way to organize each of your presentations is to include all the files for the presentation in a single directory. If you have many extra files—for your images, for example—you can put them in a subdirectory to that main directory. Your goal is to contain all your files in a single place rather than scatter them around on your disk. After you contain your files, you can set all your links in your files to be relative to that one directory. If you follow these hints, you stand the best chance of being able to move the directory around to different servers without breaking the links.

Having a Default Index File and Correct Filenames

Web servers usually have a default index file that's loaded when a URL ends with a directory name instead of a filename. In the previous section, you learned that one of the questions you should have asked your Webmaster is what the name of this default file is. For most Web servers, this file is usually called `index.html` (`index.htm` for DOS). Your home page or top-level index for each presentation should be called by this name so that the server knows which page to send as the default page. Each subdirectory, in turn, if it contains any HTML files, should also have a default file. If you use this default filename, the URL to that page will be shorter because you don't have to include the actual filename. So, for example, your URL might be `http://www.myserver.com/www/` rather than `http://www.myserver.com/www/index.html`.

Each file should also have an appropriate extension indicating what kind of file it is so that the server can map it to the appropriate file type. If you've been following along in the book so far, all your files should already have this special extension, so you should not have any problems. Table 13.1 shows a list of the common file extensions you should be using for your files and media, in case you've forgotten.

13

Table 13.1. Common file types and extensions.

Format	Extension
HTML	`.html, .htm`
ASCII Text	`.txt`
PostScript	`.ps`
GIF	`.gif`
JPEG	`.jpg, .jpeg`
AU Audio	`.au`
WAV Audio	`.wav`
MPEG Audio	`.mp2`
MPEG Video	`.mpeg, .mpg`
QuickTime Video	`.mov`
AVI Video	`.avi`

If you're using special media in your Web presentation that are not part of this list, you might need to configure your server specially to handle this file type. You'll learn more about this issue later in this chapter.

Installing Your Files

Got everything organized? Then all that's left is to move everything into place on the server. After the server can access your files, you're officially published on the Web. That's all there is to putting your pages online.

But where is the appropriate spot on your server? You should ask your Webmaster for this information. You should also find out how to get to that special spot on the server, whether it's simply copying files, using FTP to put them on the server, or using some other method.

Moving Files Between Systems

If you're using a Web server that has been set up by someone else, usually you'll have to move your Web files from your system to theirs using FTP, Zmodem transfer, or some other method. Although the HTML markup within your files is completely cross-platform, moving the actual files from one type of system to another sometimes has its gotchas. In particular, be careful to do the following:

☐ **Transfer all files as binary.** Your FTP or file-upload program may give you an option to transfer files in binary or text mode (or may give you even different options altogether). Always transfer everything—all your HTML files, all your images, and all your media—in binary format (even the files that are indeed text; you can transfer a text file in binary mode without any problems).

13

If you're working on a Macintosh, your transfer program will most likely give you lots of options with names such as MacBinary, AppleDouble, or other strange names. Avoid all of them. The option you want is flat binary or raw data. If you transfer files in any other format, they may not work when they get to the other side.

☐ **Watch out for filename restrictions.** If you're moving your files to or from DOS systems, you'll have to watch out for the dreaded 8.3—the DOS rule that says filenames must be only eight characters long with three-character extensions. If your server is a PC, and you've been writing your files on some other system, you may have to rename your files and the links to them to have the right file-naming conventions. (Moving files you've created on a PC to some other system is usually not a problem.)

Also, watch out if you're moving files from a Macintosh to other systems; make sure that your filenames do not have spaces or other funny characters in them. Keep your filenames as short as possible, use only letters and numbers, and you'll be fine.

☐ **Be aware of carriage returns and line feeds.** Different systems use different methods for ending a line; the Macintosh uses carriage returns, UNIX uses line feeds, and DOS uses both. When you move files from one system to another, most of the time the end-of-line characters will be converted appropriately, but sometimes they won't. The characters not converting can result in your file coming out double-spaced or all on one single line on the system to which it was moved.

Most of the time, this failure to convert doesn't matter because browsers ignore spurious returns or line feeds in your HTML files. The existence or absence of either one is not terribly important. Where it might be an issue is in sections of text you've marked up with <PRE>; you may find that your well-formatted text that worked so well on one platform doesn't come out well formatted after it's been moved.

If you do have end-of-line problems, you have a couple of options for how to proceed. Many text editors allow you to save ASCII files in a format for another platform. If you know what platform you're moving to, you can prepare your files for that platform before moving them. If you're moving to a UNIX system, small filters for converting line feeds called dos2unix and unix2dos may be available on the UNIX or DOS systems. And, finally, you can convert Macintosh files to UNIX-style files by using the following command line on UNIX:

```
tr '\015' '\012' < oldfile.html > newfile.html
```

In this example, oldfile.html is the original file with end-of-line problems, and newfile.html is the name of the new file.

13

Remote Management Tools

New tools enable you to manage and update the contents of your pages remotely on a remote Web server. Foremost among them are tools from Netscape and Microsoft.

Microsoft's FrontPage is a Web development tool aimed at small- to medium-sized Web sites. FrontPage provides a WYSIWYG page editor, a site manager for managing document trees and links, as well as a variety of server extensions that can be used with a variety of servers ranging from Windows-based Microsoft and Netscape servers to UNIX servers.

These extensions allow Webmasters to include a variety of features in their sites including interactive discussion groups and other interactive features. These extensions also allow you to use FrontPage to upload files into place on the server as you make changes in the content of your site.

Similarly, Netscape's LiveWire includes a tool called SiteManager, which allows you to upload new content to a remote server. Unlike FrontPage, though, LiveWire is really designed for use with Netscape's FastTrack and Enterprise Web servers. LiveWire provides a server-side scripting language using JavaScript that works only with the Netscape servers. Still, the SiteManager tool can be used to manage document trees and links for any site and can be used to upload content via FTP to a server.

Other site development and management tools such as Fusion from NetObjects (`http://www.netobject.com`) provide the capability to develop offline and then update content on a remote server.

What's My URL?

At this point, you have a server, your Web pages are installed and ready to go, and you just need to tell people that your presentation exists. All you need now is a URL.

If you're using a commercial Web server or a server that someone else administers, you might be able to find out easily what your URL is by asking the administrator. (In fact, you were supposed to ask your Webmaster this question, as noted previously.) Otherwise, you'll have to figure it out yourself. Luckily, determining your URL isn't very hard.

As I noted in Chapter 4, "All About Links," URLs are made of three parts: the protocol, the host name, and the path to the file. To determine each of these parts, answer the following questions:

☐ **What am I using to serve the files?** If you're using a real Web server, your protocol is `http`. If you're using FTP or Gopher, the protocol is `ftp` and `gopher`, respectively. (Isn't this easy?)

☐ **What's the name of my server?** This is the network name of the machine your Web server is located on, typically beginning with www—for example, `www.mysite.com`. If the name doesn't start with www, don't worry; having this name

13

doesn't affect whether people can get to your files. Note that the name you'll use is the fully qualified host name—that is, the name that people elsewhere on the Web would use to get to your Web server, which may not be the same name you use to get to your Web server. This name will usually have several parts and end with .com, .edu, or the code for your country (for example, .uk, .fr, and so on).

With some SLIP or PPP connections, you may not even have a network name, just a number—something like 192.123.45.67. You can use it as the network name.

If the server has been installed on a port other than 80, you'll need to know this number, too. Your Webmaster will know this information.

☐ **What's the path to my home page?** The path to your home page most often begins at the root of the directory where Web pages are stored (part of your server configuration), which may or may not be the top level of your file system. For example, if you've put files into the directory /home/www/files/myfiles, your pathname in the URL might just be /myfiles. This is a server-configuration question, so if you can't figure out the answer, you might have to ask your server administrator.

If your Web server has been set up so that you can use your home directory to store Web pages, you can use the UNIX convention of the tilde (~) to refer to the Web pages in your home directory. You don't have to include the name of the directory you created in the URL itself. So, for example, if I have the Web page home.html in a directory called public_html in my home directory (lemay), the path to that file in the URL would be /~lemay/home.html.

After you know these three answers, you can construct a URL. Remember from Chapter 4 that a URL looks like this:

```
protocol://machinename.com:port/path
```

You should be able to plug your values for each of these elements into the appropriate places in the URL structure, as in the following examples:

```
http://www.mymachine.com/www/tutorials/index.html
ftp://ftp.netcom.com/pub/le/lemay/index.html
http://www.commercialweb.com:8080/~lemay/index.html
```

Test, Test, and Test Again

Now that your Web pages are available on the Net, you can take the opportunity to test them on as many platforms using as many browsers as you possibly can. Only after you've seen how your documents look on different platforms will you realize how important it is to design documents that can look good on as many platforms and browsers as possible.

Try looking at your pages now. You might be surprised at the results.

Troubleshooting

What happens if you upload all your files to the server, try to bring up your home page in your browser, and something goes wrong? Here's the first place to look.

Can't Access the Server

If your browser can't even get to your server, this problem is most likely not one that you can fix. Make sure that you have the right server name and that it's a complete host name (usually ending in .com, .edu, .net, or some other common ending name). Make sure that you haven't mistyped your URL and that you're using the right protocol. If your Webmaster told you that your URL included a port number, make sure you're including that port number in the URL after the host name.

Also make sure your network connection is working. Can you get to other Web servers? Can you get to the top-level home page for the site itself?

If none of these ideas solve the problem, perhaps your server is down or not responding. Call your Webmaster to find out whether he or she can help.

Can't Access Files

What if all your files are showing up as Not Found or Forbidden? First, check your URL. If you're using a URL with a directory name at the end, try using an actual filename at the end, and see whether this trick works. Double-check the path to your files; remember that the path in the URL may be different from the path on the actual disk. Also, keep in mind that uppercase and lowercase are significant. If your file is MyFile.html, make sure you're not trying myfile.html or Myfile.html.

If the URL appears to be correct, the next thing to check is file permissions. On UNIX systems, all your directories should be world-executable, and all your files should be world-readable. You can make sure all the permissions are correct by using these commands:

```
chmod 755 filename
chmod 755 directoryname
```

Can't Access Images

You can get to your HTML files just fine, but all your images are coming up as icons or broken icons. First, make sure the references to your images are correct. If you've used relative pathnames, you should not have this problem. If you've used full pathnames or file URLs, the references to your images may very well have broken when you moved the files to the server. (I warned you...)

In some browsers, notably Netscape, if you select an image with the right mouse button (hold down the button on a Mac mouse), you'll get a pop-up menu. Choose the View This Image

13

menu item to try to load the image directly, which will give you the URL of the image where the browser thinks it's supposed to be (which may not be where you think it's supposed to be). You can often track down strange relative pathname problems this way.

If the references all look fine, and the images worked just fine on your local system, the only other place a problem could have occurred is in transferring the files from one system to another. As I mentioned earlier in this chapter, make sure you transfer all your image files in binary format. If you're on the Mac, make sure you transfer the files as raw data or just data. Don't try to use MacBinary or AppleDouble format; otherwise, you'll get problems on the other side.

Links Don't Work

If your HTML and image files are working just fine, but your links don't work, you most likely used pathnames for those links that applied only to your local system. For example, you used absolute pathnames or file URLs to refer to the files you're linking to. As I mentioned for images, if you used relative pathnames and avoided file URLs, you should not have a problem.

Files Are Displaying Wrong

Say you've got an HTML file or a file in some media format that displays or links just fine on your local system. After you upload the file to the server and try to view it, the browser gives you gobbledygook. For example, it displays the HTML code itself instead of the HTML file, or it tries to display an image or media file as text.

This problem could happen in two cases. The first is a situation in which you're not using the right file extensions for your files. Make sure that you're using one of the right file extensions with the right uppercase and lowercase.

In the second case in which this problem could happen, your server is misconfigured to handle your files. For example, if you're working on a DOS system where all your HTML files have extensions of .htm, your server may not understand that .htm is an HTML file. (Most modern servers do, but some older ones don't.) Or you might be using a newer form of media that your server doesn't understand. In either case, your server may be using some default content-type for your files (usually text/plain), which your browser then tries to handle (and doesn't often succeed).

To fix this problem, you'll have to configure your server to handle the file extensions for the media you're working with. If you're working with someone else's server, you'll have to contact your Webmaster and have him or her set up the server correctly. Your Webmaster will need two types of information to make this change: the file extensions you're using and the content-type you want him or her to return. If you don't know the content-type you want, refer to the listing of the most popular types in Appendix D, "MIME Types and File Extensions."

13

Registering and Advertising Your Web Pages

The "build it, and they will come" motto from the movie *Field of Dreams* notwithstanding, people won't simply start to visit your site of their own accord after you've put it online. In fact, with more than 650,000 Web servers online already, and some of these holding thousands of documents, it's highly unlikely that anyone could ever just stumble across your site by accident.

As a result, to get people to visit your Web site, you need to advertise its existence in as many ways as possible. After all, the higher the visibility, the greater the prospect of your site receiving lots of hits.

 Hits is a Web-speak term for the number of visits your Web site receives. This term does not differentiate between people, but instead is simply a record of the number of times a copy of your Web page has been downloaded.

In this section, you'll learn about many of the avenues available for you to promote your site, including the following:

- ☐ Getting your site listed on the major WWW directories
- ☐ Listing your site with the major WWW indexes
- ☐ Using Usenet to announce your site
- ☐ Using business cards, letterheads, and brochures
- ☐ Locating more directories and related Web pages

WWW Site Listings

Many people, when they first start working with the World Wide Web, find it hard to understand that on numerous Web sites out there other people are just itching for the chance to include a hyperlink for your Web pages as part of their own lists. And what they find even harder to understand is that, for the most part, no cost is involved.

There is a simple reason for the existence of so many apparently philanthropic individuals. When the World Wide Web was young and fresh, the best way for a person to promote the existence of his or her site was by approaching other Web developers and asking them to list his or her site on their pages. In return for this favor, this person would also list their sites on his or her pages. Over time, this process has been refined somewhat, but today many sites will still be only too happy to include a link to your site. In fact, don't be surprised if you occasionally receive e-mail from someone asking to be included in your list of sites.

This cooperative nature is a strikingly unique feature of the World Wide Web. Instead of competing for visitors with other similar sites, most Web pages actually include lists of their competitors.

13

Unfortunately, however, a problem still exists with just exchanging hyperlink references with other sites. As was originally the case, people still need to be able to locate a single site as a starting point. To this end, some sort of global Internet directory was needed. Currently, no single site on the World Wide Web can be regarded as the Internet directory, but a few major directories and libraries come very close.

Yahoo!

By far, the most well-known directory of Web sites is the Yahoo! site (see Figure 13.1), created by David File and Jerry Yang, at `http://www.yahoo.com/`. This site started in April 1994 as a small, private list of David's and Jerry's favorite Web sites. But since then, it has grown to be a highly regarded catalog and index of Web sites and is now its own company.

Figure 13.1.

Yahoo!

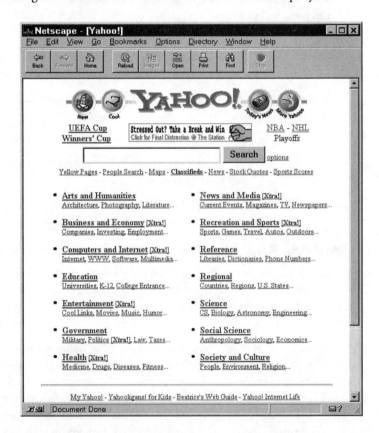

Yahoo! uses an elegant multilevel catalog to organize all the sites it references. To view the contents of any level of the catalog, you select the major category hyperlink that most closely represents the information you are interested in and then follow the chain of associated pages

13

to a list of related Web sites, like the one shown in Figure 13.2. You should definitely take a look at the page shown in this figure. It contains a list of Announcement Services and related Web pages that can help you spread the word about your new Web site.

Figure 13.2.

The Announcement Services category in Yahoo!.

To add your site to the list maintained by Yahoo!, return to the Yahoo! home page at http://www.yahoo.com/, and select the category appropriate to your site. Work your way down the catalog through any subcategories until you locate a list of sites similar to your own. On this page, click the Add URL button (in the banner along the top of the page). Yahoo! then displays a form like the one shown in Figure 13.3, where you can enter the URL and other details about your Web site.

After you submit the form, a new hyperlink is automatically added to the category you selected previously. In addition, your site is also listed in the daily and weekly Yahoo! What's New list, which can be found at http://www.yahoo.com/New/.

13

Figure 13.3.

*The form to add your
URL to Yahoo!.*

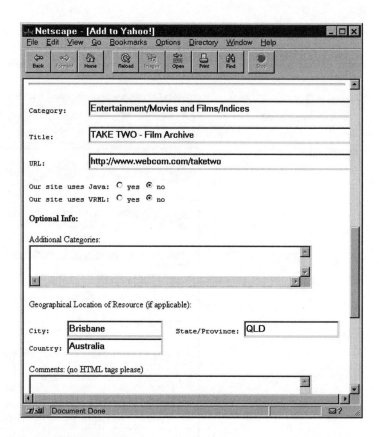

The World Wide Web Virtual Library

The World Wide Web (W3) Virtual Library, located at http://www.w3.org/pub/DataSources/bySubject/Overview.html, is another very popular online catalog. Unlike Yahoo!, which is operated by a single group of people, the W3 Virtual Library is a distributed effort. As such, the contents of each separate category are maintained by different people (all volunteers) and sometimes housed on different computers all over the world.

As a result, to submit your URL for inclusion in a category of the Virtual Library, you need to send an e-mail request to the person maintaining it. To obtain a list of the e-mail addresses for each maintainer, point your Web browser to http://www.w3.org/pub/DataSources/bySubject/Maintainers.html.

The top-level directory, shown in Figure 13.4, maintained by the W3 Consortium also contains a link to the Maintainers page, along with other links that describe the submission process in greater detail. In addition, on this page you'll find information that describes how people can add their own categories to the W3 Virtual Library and become maintainers themselves.

Figure 13.4.

The World Wide Web Virtual Library.

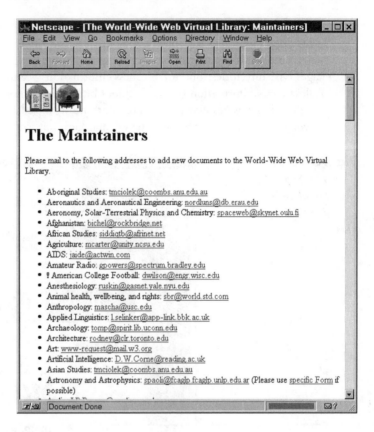

Yellow Pages Listings

Another popular method of promoting your site is by registering it with the growing number of Yellow Pages directories that have begun to spring up on the World Wide Web. You can best think of these sites as the electronic equivalent of your local telephone Yellow Pages directory.

As a rule, Yellow Pages sites are designed specially for commercial and business Web users who want to advertise their services and expertise. For this reason, most of the Yellow Pages sites offer both free and paid advertising space, with the paid listings including graphics, corporate logos, and advanced layout features. A free listing, on the other hand, tends to be little more than a hyperlink and a short comment. When you're starting out, however, free advertising is without a doubt the best advertising. Of the Yellow Pages sites currently in operation, the following are the two most popular:

☐ GTE SuperPages

☐ WWW Business Yellow Pages

13

GTE SuperPages

GTE SuperPages also lists businesses both on and off the Web. The page at http://
www.superpages.com/, which is shown in Figure 13.5, gives you access to two separate Yellow
Pages-type directories: one for business information gleaned from actual United States
Yellow Pages information (which includes businesses without actual Web sites) and one
specifically for businesses with Web sites. Both are organized into categories, and both listings
let you search for specific business names and locations.

Figure 13.5.

*The GTE SuperPages
form for adding or
changing site informa-
tion.*

WWW Business Yellow Pages

The WWW Business Yellow Pages is not as large as the other two mentioned previously, but
because it's free, no harm can be done by including an entry for your business site here. It's
operated as a community service by the University of Houston, College of Business
Administration, at http://www.cba.uh.edu/ylowpges/.

13

As with other Yellow Pages sites, if you want your site included at the WWW Business Yellow Pages, you need to submit an online form. The URL for the application form, as shown in Figure 13.6, is http://www.cba.uh.edu/cgi-bin/autosub.

Figure 13.6.

WWW Business Yellow Pages.

Private Directories

In addition to the broad mainstream Web directories, many private directories on the World Wide Web cater to more specific needs. Some of these directories deal with single issues, whereas others are devoted to areas such as online commerce, education, business, and entertainment.

The best way to locate most of these directories is to use an Internet search tool such as Lycos (http://www.lycos.com/) or WebCrawler (http://www.webcrawler.com/). Alternatively, most of these directories will already be listed in such places as Yahoo! and the W3 Virtual Library, so a few minutes spent visiting relative catalogs at these sites is normally very beneficial.

The Internet Mall

If you who plan to operate an online store via the World Wide Web, a directory such as the Internet Mall—http://www.internet-mall.com/—which is shown in Figure 13.7, is a very

13

good place to start. Listing your Web site on such a mall gives you instant visibility. Having such visibility, however, does not necessarily mean that people will start knocking down your doors immediately, but it does give your store a much greater chance of succeeding.

Figure 13.7.

The Internet Mall.

The main criteria for obtaining a listing on the Internet Mall is that your site must sell tangible products, and people must be able to place an order for them online. Apart from these criteria, only a few types of commerce are not welcome, including the following:

☐ Multilevel marketing schemes

☐ Products available through dealerships

☐ Franchise opportunities

☐ Web publishing or design services

☐ Marketing services

☐ Hotels, restaurants, and non-business sites

13

If you want to make a request for the inclusion of your online store at the Internet Mall, point your Web browser to `http://www.internet-mall.com/howto.htm` for more information.

Netscape Galleria

If you use one of Netscape's Web servers to operate your Web site, you can list your site on Netscape's own shopping mall, called the Netscape Galleria.

In addition, if you rent space from a Web service provider that uses either of the Netscape servers, you might also qualify for a listing. For more information, visit the Netscape Galleria at `http://home.netscape.com/escapes/galleria.html`.

Site Indexes and Search Engines

After you list your new site on the major directories and maybe a few smaller directories, you next need to turn your attention to the indexing and search tools, such as Lycos, WebCrawler, and InfoSeek. Unlike directories, which contain a hierarchical list of Web sites that have been submitted for inclusion to the directory, indexes have search engines (sometimes called "spiders") that prowl the Web and store information about every page and site they find. The indexes then store a database of sites that you can search by using a form.

After you publish your site on the Web and other people link to your site, chances are a search engine will eventually get around to finding and exploring your site. However, you can tell these indexes ahead of time that your site exists and get indexed that much faster. Each of these search engines provides a mechanism that enables you to submit your site for inclusion as part of its index.

Four search engines vie for the title of most popular on the Web: AltaVista, Lycos, WebCrawler, and InfoSeek.

AltaVista

One of the most popular and fastest Web indexes is Digital Equipment's AltaVista index at `http://www.altavista.digital.com/`. AltaVista indexes a good portion of the Web but stands out by having an extremely fast search engine. So, the process of looking up specific search terms on the Web is quick and thorough.

You can submit your page to AltaVista using the form at `http://www.altavista.digital.com/cgi-bin/query?pg=addurl`, as shown in Figure 13.8.

13

Figure 13.8.

AltaVista's Add URL page.

Excite

Excite became known as a search engine and index of the Internet because it offers a unique capability: to search by concept rather than simply by keyword. The software that Excite uses to do this attempts to use a particular algorithm to extract meaning from your concept phrase to find relevant documents. Excite is on the Web at `http://www.excite.com/` and you can submit pages at `http://www.excite.com/Info/add_url.html?a-m-t`.

Lycos

Lycos was one of the earliest search engines and still claims to have the largest overall coverage of the Web. Lycos is located at `http://www.lycos.com/`, and you can find its registration form for asking your site to be visited at `http://www.lycos.com/register.html`. Figure 13.9 shows the registration page.

13

Figure 13.9.

Lycos's registration page.

WebCrawler

Following its relatively recent move onto the Internet, America Online took over the operation of the WebCrawler indexing system located at `http://webcrawler.com/GNN/WebQuery.html` (see Figure 13.10).

WebCrawler does not have as wide a coverage as Lycos or AltaVista, with less than an estimated 40 percent of the World Wide Web index, but it does have the advantage of being the Internet index system of choice for America Online and Global Network Navigator (GNN) users.

The Submit URL form for WebCrawler is located at `http://webcrawler.com/WebCrawler/SubmitURLS.html`.

13

Figure 13.10.

WebCrawler is operated by America Online.

Infoseek

PC Computing magazine voted Infoseek, shown in Figure 13.11 and located at `http://www.infoseek.com/`, the Most Valuable Internet Tool back in 1995, and the service has expanded considerably since then. Like Lycos and WebCrawler, Infoseek is a Web indexing tool, but what makes it even more powerful is its capability to search through many kinds of additional services and databases in addition to the World Wide Web. Such functionality, however, does come at a cost—only the Web search engine can be used without charge.

Submission Tools

Besides the search tools already covered, about 15 other search engines offer differing capabilities. You'll need to make a separate submission to each to ensure that your site is indexed.

Instead of listing the URLs and details for each of these sites, however, I will turn this discussion to two special Web pages that take much of the drudgery out of submitting Web sites to search indexes and directories.

13

Figure 13.11.

Infoseek.

PostMaster2

The PostMaster2 site, shown in Figure 13.12 and located at `http://www.netcreations.com/postmaster/index.html`, is an all-in-one submission page that asks you to fill out all the details required for more than 25 Web indexes and directories, including Yahoo!, Netscape's Escapes, JumpStation, Lycos, Infoseek, WebCrawler, World Wide Web, and the GNN Whole Internet Catalog. After you complete the form, PostMaster2 submits your information to all these sites at once, so you don't have to go to each one individually.

NOTE   PostMaster2 also offers a commercial version of its submission system that delivers announcements about your new site to more than 200 magazines, journals, and other periodicals, in addition to all the sites included in the free version. Using the commercial version, however, is an expensive exercise.

13

Figure 13.12.

PostMaster2.

Submit It!

The Submit It! service provided by Scott Banister is a lot like PostMaster in that it also helps you submit your URL to different directories and search indexes. It supports just about all the same services, but what sets it apart is the way in which you submit your information. Figure 13.13 shows a list of all the search indexes and directories currently supported by Submit It!.

Submit It! doesn't ask you to complete one enormous page, something that many people find daunting. Instead, after you've filled out some general information, you select only the sites you want to submit an entry to and then perform each submission one site at a time.

To learn more about Submit It!, point your Web browser to http://www.submit-it.com/.

13

Figure 13.13.
Submit It!

Announce Your Site via Usenet

The World Wide Web is not the only place on the Internet where you can announce the launch of your new Web site. Many people make use of a small set of Usenet newsgroups that are designed especially for making announcements. To locate these newsgroups, look for newsgroup names that end with .announce. (Refer to the documentation that came with your Usenet newsreader for information about how to find these newsgroups.)

One newsgroup is even devoted just to World Wide Web-related announcements. This newsgroup, named comp.infosystems.www.announce, is shown in Figure 13.14. If your browser supports reading Usenet news, and you've configured it to point to your new server, you can view articles submitted to this newsgroup—and add your own announcements—by entering the following URL into the Document URL field:

```
news:comp.infosystems.www.announce
```

Figure 13.14.

The
`comp.infosystems.`
`www.announce`
newsgroup.

One post in particular to look for in `comp.infosystems.www.announce` is an excellent FAQ called "FAQ: How to Announce Your New Web Site." This FAQ contains an up-to-date list of all the best and most profitable means of promoting your Web site. If you can't locate the FAQ in this newsgroup, you can view an online version at `http://ep.com/faq/webannounce.html`.

NOTE

`comp.infosystems.www.announce` is a moderated newsgroup. As such, any submissions you make to it are approved by a moderator before they appear in the newsgroup listing. To ensure that your announcement is approved, you should read the charter document that outlines the announcement process. You can read this document by pointing your Web browser to `http://boutell.com/%7Egrant/charter.html`.

13

Business Cards, Letterheads, and Brochures

Although the Internet is a wonderful place to promote your new Web site, many people fail to even consider another great advertising method.

Most businesses spend a considerable amount of money each year producing business cards, letterheads, and other promotional material. Very few, however, consider printing their e-mail addresses and home page URLs on them. But why not? With more than 30 million people on the Internet in the U.S. alone, chances are that some of your customers are already on the Internet or will be within a few years.

By printing your e-mail address and home page URL on all your correspondence and promotional material, you can reach an entirely new group of potential site visitors. And who knows, maybe you'll even pick up new clients by spending time explaining to people what all your new address information means.

The bottom line with the promotion of your Web site is lateral thinking. You need to use every tool at your disposal if you want to have a successful and active site.

Finding Out Who's Viewing Your Web Pages

Welcome to being happily published. At this point, you've got your pages up on the Web and ready to be viewed, you've advertised and publicized your site to the world, and people are (hopefully) flocking to your site in droves. Or are they? How can you tell? You can find out in a number of ways, including using log files and access counters.

Log Files

The best way to figure out how often your pages are being seen and by whom is to see whether you can get access to your server's log files. The server keeps track of all this information and, depending on how busy the server is, may keep this information around for weeks or even months. Many commercial Web publishing providers have a mechanism for you to view your own Web logs or to get statistics about how many people are accessing your pages and from where. Ask your Webmaster for help.

If you do get access to the raw log files, you'll most likely see a whole lot of lines that look something like the following. (I've broken this one up onto two lines so that it fits on the page.)

```
vide-gate.coventry.ac.uk - - [17/Apr/1996:12:36:51 -0700]
    "GET /index.html HTTP/1.0" 200 8916
```

What does this information mean? This is the standard look and feel for most log files. The first part of the line is the site that accessed the file. (In this case, it was a site from the United Kingdom.) The two dashes are used for authentication. (If you have login names and passwords set up, the username of the person who logged in and the group that person belonged to will appear here.) The date and time the page was accessed appear inside the brackets. The next part is the actual filename that was accessed; here it's the index.html at the top level of the server. The GET part is the actual HTTP command the browser used; you usually see GET here. Finally, the last two numbers are the HTTP status code and the number of bytes transferred. The status code can be one of many things: 200 means the file was found and transferred correctly; 404 means the file was not found (yes, it's the same status code you get in error pages in your browser). Finally, the number of bytes transferred will usually be the same number of bytes in your actual file; if it's a smaller number, the reader interrupted the load in the middle.

Access Counters

If you don't have access to your server's log files for whatever reason, and you'd like to know at least how many people are looking at your Web pages, you can install an access counter on your page. You've probably seen counters several times in your Web browsing; they look like odometers or little meters that say "Since July 15, 1900, this page has been accessed 5,456,234,432 times."

Lots of Web counters are available, but most of them require you to install something on your server or to have server-side includes set up. A few, including the following sites, provide access counters that don't require server setup (but may cost you some money).

The Web counter at http://www.digits.com/ is easy to set up and very popular. If you have a site without a lot of hits (fewer than 1,000 a day), the counter service is free. Otherwise, you'll need to be part of the commercial plan, with the access counter costing $30 and up.

After you sign up for the digits.com counter service, you'll get a URL that you include on your pages as part of an <IMG> tag. Then, when your page is hit, the browser retrieves that URL at digits.com's server, which generates a new odometer image for you.

For more information about access counters in general (as well as a huge archive of images for access counters), see the Digit Mania home page at http://cervantes.learningco.com/kevin/digits/index.html.

Table 13.2 lists some free counter services.

Table 13.2. Access counter services.

Name	URL
Net-Trak	http://net-trak.netrail.net/
Page Count	http://www.pagecount.com/
Jcount	http://www.jcount.com/
WebTracker	http://www.fxweb.holowww.com/tracker/
Internet Count	http://www.icount.com/
LiveCounter	http://www.chami.com/prog/lc/

Summary

In this chapter, you've reached the final point in creating a Web presentation: publishing your work to the World Wide Web at large through the use of a Web server, either installed by you or available from a network provider. Here you learned what a Web server does and how to get one, how to organize your files and install them on the server, how to find out your URL and use it to test your pages, how to advertise your pages after they're available, and how to find out who's looking at those pages.

From here on, everything you'll learn is icing on an already substantial cake. You'll simply be adding more features (interactivity, forms) to the presentation you already have available on the Web. Congratulations! Have some ice cream.

13

Q&A

Q I have my pages published at an ISP I really like; my URL is something like `http://www.thebestisp.com/users/mypages/`. Instead of this URL, I'd like to have my own host name—something like `http://www.mypages.com/`. How can I do this?

A You have two choices. The easiest way is to ask your ISP if it allows you to have your own domain name. Many ISPs have a method for setting up your domain so that you can still use their services and work with them—only your URL changes. Note that having your own host name may cost more money, but if you really must have that URL, then this may be the way to go.

The other option is to set up your own server with your own domain name. This option could be significantly more expensive than working with an ISP, and it requires at least some background in basic network administration. You'll learn all about this process in the next chapter.

Q I created all my image files on a Mac, uploaded them to my UNIX server using the Fetch FTP program, tested it all, and it all works fine. But now I'm getting e-mail from people saying none of my images are working. What's going on here?

A Usually, when you upload the files using Fetch, you can choose from a pull-down menu where the default is MacBinary. Make sure you change to raw data.

MacBinary files work fine when they're viewed on the Mac. And because I assume you're using a Mac to test your presentation, they'll work fine. But they won't work on any other system. To make sure your images work across platforms, upload them as raw data.

Q I created my files on a DOS system, using the `.htm` extension, like you told me to earlier in the book. Now I've published my files on a UNIX system provided by my job. The problem now is that when I try to get to my pages using my browser, I get the HTML code for those pages—not the formatted result! It all worked on my system at home. What went wrong?

A Some older servers will have this problem. Your server has not been set up to believe that files with an `.htm` extension are actually HTML files, so they send them as the default content-type (`text/plain`) instead. Then, when your browser reads one of your files from a server, it reads that content-type and assumes you have a text file. So your server is messing up everything.

You can fix this problem in several ways. By far the best way to fix it is to tell your Webmaster to change the server configuration so that .htm files are sent as HTML—usually a very simple step that will magically cause all your files to work properly from then on.

If you can't find your Webmaster, or for some strange reason he or she will not make this change, your only other option is to change all your filenames after you upload them to the UNIX system. Note that you'll have to change all the links within those files as well. (Finding a way to convince your Webmaster to fix this problem would be a *much* better solution.)

13

Chapter **14**

Image Maps

Image maps are a special kind of clickable image. Usually, when you embed an image inside a link, clicking anywhere on that image goes to one single location. Using image maps, you can go to different locations based on where inside the image you clicked. In this chapter you'll learn all about image maps and how to create them, including:

- ☐ What an image map is
- ☐ Creating server-side image maps
- ☐ Creating client-side image maps
- ☐ Supporting both types of image maps

What Is an Image Map?

In Chapter 7, "Using Images, Color, and Backgrounds," you learned how to create an image that doubles as a link simply by including the `<IMG>` tag inside a link (`<A>`) tag. In this way, the entire image becomes a link. You can then click the image, the background, or the border, and you get the same effect.

In image maps, different parts of the image activate different links. By using image maps, you can create a visual hyperlinked map that links you to pages describing the regions you click, as in Figure 14.1. Or you can create visual metaphors for the information you're presenting: a set of books on a shelf or a photograph in which each person in the picture is individually described.

Figure 14.1.

Image maps: different places, different links.

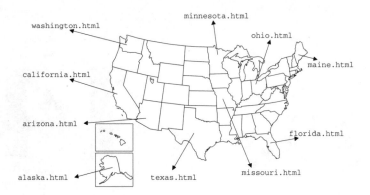

Image maps are special images that have different areas that point to different link locations. Where you go on the site is determined by the place on the image where you click the mouse.

Server-Side Image Maps

Traditionally, image maps are created by using a special program that runs on the server. Such image maps are referred to as server-side image maps.

NEW TERM *Server-side image maps* are implemented using an image displayed by the client and a program that runs on the server.

When a browser activates a link on an image map, it calls a special image map program stored on a Web server. In addition to calling the image map program, the browser also sends the program the x and y coordinates of the position on the image where the mouse was clicked. The image map program then looks up a special map file that matches regions in the image to URLs, does some calculations to figure out which page to load, and then loads the page.

Server-side image maps were one of the earliest Web features and are supported by most, if not all, graphical browsers.

Client-Side Image Maps

Although server-side image maps have been in common use for some time, the problems associated with them have led to the development of a new type of image map called a client-side image map. These are the main problems associated with server-side image maps:

☐ Normally, when you move your cursor over a hyperlink, the URL pointed to by the link is displayed in the Web browser's status bar. Because, however, the Web browser has no idea where the parts of a server-side image map point, all you see when you place your cursor over a server-side image map is either the URL of the image map program itself (not very helpful), or that URL and a set of x,y coordinates (still not very helpful).

☐ You cannot use or test server-side image maps with local files. Image maps require the use of a Web server to run the image map program and process the x and y coordinates.

☐ Because a special program must be run by the server each time a user clicks a page that contains image maps, image maps are much slower to respond to mouse clicks than normal links or images as links. Consequently, the image maps seem to take forever to respond to requests for a new page.

Client-side image maps, on the other hand, remove all these difficulties by removing the need for a special image map program on the server. Instead, they manage all the image-map processing locally on the Web browser itself.

 Client-side image maps work in the same ways as server-side image maps, except there is no program that runs on the server. All the processing of coordinates and pointers to different locations occurs in the browser.

 Client-side image maps are currently supported by the latest Web browsers, including Netscape 2.0 and above. The proposal for client-side image maps made its way into HTML 3.2 and is now official specification.

Image Maps and Text-Only Browsers

Because of the inherently graphical nature of image maps, they can work only in graphical browsers. In fact, if you try to view a document with an image map in a text-only browser such as Lynx, you don't even get an indication that the image exists—unless, of course, the image contains an ALT attribute. But even with the ALT attribute, you won't be able to navigate the presentation without a graphical browser.

If you decide to create a Web page with an image map on it, it's doubly important that you also create a text-only equivalent so that readers with text-only browsers can use your page. The use of image maps can effectively lock out readers using text-only browsers; have sympathy and allow them at least some method for viewing your content.

14

Creating Server-Side Image Maps

In addition to the various disadvantages of using server-side image maps, one other one to put a wrinkle into how I explain them is that some Web servers have different ways of creating them. The methods even vary among servers on the same platform. For example, the W3C (CERN) httpd server and NCSA HTTPd server have incompatible methods of implementing image files. All servers, however, use the same basic ingredients for image maps:

- ☐ Special HTML code to indicate that an image is a map
- ☐ A map file on the server that indicates regions on the image and the Web pages they point to
- ☐ An image-mapping CGI script that links it all together

This section explains how to construct clickable images in general, but its examples focus on the NCSA HTTPd–style servers such as NCSA and Apache. If you need more information for your server, see the documentation that comes with that server or get help from your Web administrator.

Getting an Image

To create an image map, you'll need an image (of course). The image that serves as the map is most useful if it has several discrete visual areas that can be individually selected; for example, images with several symbolic elements, or images that can be easily broken down into polygons. Photographs make difficult image maps because their various "elements" tend to blend together or are of unusual shapes. Figures 14.2 and 14.3 show examples of good and poor images for image maps.

Figure 14.2.

A good image map.

Figure 14.3.

A not-so-good image map.

14

Creating a Map File

The heart of the server-side image map is a map file. Creating a map file involves sketching out the regions in your image that are clickable, determining the coordinates that define those regions, and deciding on the HTML pages where they should point.

NOTE

> The format of the map file depends on the image-mapping program you're using on your server. In this section, I'll talk about image maps on the NCSA HTTPd server and the map files it uses by default. If you're using a different server, you might have several image-mapping programs to choose from with several map formats. Check with your Web administrator or read your server documentation carefully if you're in this situation.

You can create a map file either by sketching regions and noting the coordinates by hand or by using an image map-making program. The latter method is easier because the program will automatically generate a map file based on the regions you draw with the mouse.

The Mapedit and MapThis programs for Windows and WebMap for the Macintosh can all help you create map files in NCSA format. In addition, MapThis also includes support for the creation of client-side image map definitions.

In addition, many of the latest WYSIWYG editors for HTML pages provide facilities for generating image maps.

If you use a UNIX-based system, there is a version of Mapedit available via FTP. (See Appendix A, "Sources for Further Information," for a full list of related FTP sites.)

Table 14.1. provides a list of current tools for generating image maps.

Table 14.1. Image map creation software.

Name	Platform	URL
Web HotSpots	Windows	`http://www.concentric.net/~automata/hotspots.shtml`
Imaptool	Linux/X-Window	`http://www.sci.fi/~uucee/ownprojects/`
MapThis	Windows	`http://galadriel.ecaetc.ohio-state.edu/tc/mt/`

continues

14

Table 14.1. continued

Name	Platform	URL
LiveImage	Windows	`http://www.mediatec.com/`
Mapedit	Windows/UNIX	`http://www.boutell.com/mapedit/`
Poor Person's Image Mapper	Web-based	`http://zenith.berkeley.edu/~seidel/ ClrHlpr/imagemap.html`

If you need your map file in a different format, you can always use these programs to create a basic map and then convert the coordinates you get into the map file format your server needs.

If you must create your map files by hand, here's how to do it. First, make a sketch of the regions you want to make active on your image (see Figure 14.4).

Figure 14.4.

Sketching mappable regions.

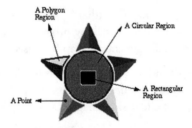

You next need to determine the coordinates for the endpoints of those regions (see Figure 14.5). Most image-editing programs have an option that displays the coordinates of the current mouse position. Use this feature to note the appropriate coordinates. (All the mapping programs mentioned previously will create a map file for you, but for now, following the steps manually will help you better understand the processes involved.)

Figure 14.5.

Getting the coordinates.

For circle regions, note the coordinates of the center point and the radius, in pixels. For rectangle regions, note the upper-left and lower-right corners. For polygon regions, note the coordinates of each corner. For points, note the coordinates of the point.

NOTE

> The 0,0 origin is in the upper-left corner of the image, and positive y is down.

You're more than halfway there. The next step is to come up with a set of URLs to link for each region or point that is selected. You can have multiple regions pointing to the same URL, but each region must have only one link.

With all your regions, coordinates, and URLs noted, you can now write a map file for your server. NCSA HTTPd map files look like this:

```
default URL
circle URL x,y radius
rect URL x,y x,y
poly URL x1,y1 x2,y2 ... xN,yN
point URL x,y
```

The map files for your particular image map program for your server might look different from this, but the essential parts are there. Substitute the values for the coordinates you noted previously in each of the *x* or *y* positions (or *x1*, *y1*, and so on). Note that the *radius* (in the circle line) is the radius for the circle region.

The URLs you specify for either format must be either full URLs (starting with `http`, `ftp`, or some other protocol) or the full pathnames to the files you are linking—that is, everything you could include after the hostname in a URL. You cannot specify relative pathnames in the image map file.

Here's a sample of an NCSA HTTPd map file:

```
circle /www/mapping.html 10,15 20
circle /www/mapping.html 346,23 59
poly /www/test/orange.html 192,3 192,170 115,217
rect /www/pencil.html 57,57 100,210
point /www/pencil.html 100,100
point /www/orange.html 200,200
```

Points enable you to specify that a given mouse click, if it doesn't land directly on a region, will activate the nearest point. Points are useful for photographs or other images with nondiscrete elements, or for a finer granularity than just "everything not in a region."

The order of regions in the map file is relevant; the further up a region is in the file, the higher precedence it has for mouse clicks. If part of the region that occurs on overlapping regions is selected, the first region listed in the map file is the one that is activated.

Finally, the map file includes a "default" region with no coordinates, just a URL. The default is used when a mouse click that is not inside a region is selected; it provides a catch-all for the parts of the image that do not point to a specific link. (Note that if you use an NCSA HTTPd map file and you include `default`, you shouldn't include any points. The existence of point elements precludes that of `default`.)

14

Installing the Map File and the Image Map Program

Creating the map file is the hardest part of making an image map. Once you've got a map file written for your image, you'll have to install both the map file and the image map program on your server and then hook everything up in your HTML files to use the image map.

Save your map file with a descriptive name (say, myimage.map). Where you install the map file on your server isn't important, but I like to put my map files in a central directory called maps at the top level of my Web files.

You'll also need your image map program installed on your server, usually in a special directory called cgi-bin, which has been specially set up to store programs and scripts for your server. (You'll learn more about the cgi-bin directory in Chapter 16, "Beginning CGI Scripting.") Most servers have an image program set up by default, and if you're using someone else's server, that program will most likely be available to you as well. The program to look for is often called htimage or imagemap.

WARNING

Be careful with the NCSA server and the imagemap program. Older versions of imagemap were more difficult to work with and required an extra configuration file; the program that comes with the 1.5 version of the server works much better. If you aren't running the most recent version of the NCSA server, you can get the new image map program from http://hoohoo.ncsa.uiuc.edu/docs/tutorials/imagemap.txt.

Linking It All Together

So now you have an image, a map file, and an image map program. Now let's hook them all up. In your HTML page that contains the image map, you'll use the <A> and <IMG> tags together to create the effect of the clickable image. Here's an example using NCSA's image map program:

```
<A HREF="/cgi-bin/imagemap/maps/myimage.map">
<IMG SRC="image.gif" ISMAP></A>
```

Notice several things about this link. First, the link to the image map script (imagemap) is indicated the way you would expect, but then the path to the map file is appended to the end of it. The path to the map file should be a full pathname from the root of your Web directory (everything after the hostname in your URL), in this case /maps/myimage.map. (This weird-looking form of URL will be described in more detail when you learn more about CGI scripting in Chapter 16.)

The second part of the HTML code that creates a server-side map is the ISMAP attribute to the <IMG> tag. This is a simple attribute with no value that tells the browser to send individual mouse-click coordinates to the image map program on the server side for processing.

And now, with all three parts of the server-side image map in place (the map file, the image map program, and the special HTML code), the image map should work. You should be able to load your HTML file into your browser and use the image map to go to different pages on your server by selecting different parts of the map.

NOTE

If you're running the NCSA HTTPd server and you don't have the newest version of imagemap, you'll get the error Cannot Open Configuration file when you try to select portions of your image. If you get these errors, check with your Web administrator.

Exercise 14.1: A clickable bookshelf.

Image maps can get pretty hairy. The map files are prone to error if you don't have your areas clearly outlined and everything installed in the right place. In this exercise, you'll take a simple image and create a simple map file for it using the NCSA server map file format. This way you can get a feel for what the map files look like and how to create them.

The image you'll use here is a simple color rendering of some books (see Figure 14.6). You can't see the colors here, but from left to right, they are red, blue, yellow, and green.

Figure 14.6.
The bookshelf image.

First, you'll define the regions that will be clickable on this image. Because of the angular nature of the books, it's most appropriate to create polygon-shaped regions. Figure 14.7 shows an example of the sort of region it makes sense to create on the image. This one is for the leftmost (red) book. You can define similar regions for each book in the stack. (Draw on the figure here in this book, if you want to. I won't mind.)

14

Figure 14.7.
*The bookshelf with an
area defined.*

Now that you have an idea of where the various regions are on your image, you'll need to find the exact coordinates of the corners as they appear in your image. To find those coordinates, you can use a mapping program such as Mapedit or WebMap (highly recommended), or you can do it by hand. If you do try it by hand, most image-editing programs should have a way of displaying the x and y coordinates of the image when you move the mouse over it. I used Adobe Photoshop's Info window to come up with the coordinates shown in Figure 14.8.

 TIP

Don't have an image-editing program? Here's a trick if you use Netscape Navigator as your browser: create an HTML file with the image inside a link pointing to a fake file, and include the ISMAP attribute inside the <IMG> tag. You don't actually need a real link; anything will do. The HTML code might look something like this:

```
<A HREF="nothing"><IMG SRC="myimage.gif" ISMAP></A>
```

Now, if you load that HTML file into your browser, the image will be displayed as if it were an image map, and when you move your mouse over it, the x and y coordinates will be displayed in the status line of the browser. Using this trick, you can find the coordinates of any point on that image for the map file.

Figure 14.8.
*The bookshelf with
coordinates.*

With regions and a list of coordinates, you just need the Web pages to jump to when the appropriate book is selected. These can be any documents, or they can be scripts; you can use anything you can call from a browser as a jump destination. For this example, I've created a document called redbook.html and stored it inside the www directory on my Web server. This is the page we'll define as the end-point of the jump when the red book is selected.

Now create the entry in the map file for this area, with the coordinates and the file to link to if that area is clicked on. In NCSA map file, the information looks like this:

```
poly /www/redbook.html 70,0 0,37 0,183 27,192 27,48 103,9
```

Note that the URLs in the map file must be absolute pathnames from the top of the Web root (not from the top of the file system). They cannot be relative URLs from the map file; image maps don't work like that. In this case, my www directory is at the Web root, and the redbook.html file is in that directory, so the URL for the purposes of the map file is /www/redbook.html.

You can now create identical entries for the other books in the image (blue, yellow, and green). Don't forget to include a default line in the map file to map mouse clicks that don't hit any books (here, a file called notabook.html):

```
default /www/notabook.html
```

Save your map file to your map directory on the server (or wherever you keep your maps). Finally, create a Web page that includes the books image, the ISMAP attribute in the <IMG> tag, and the link to the image mapping program. Here's an example that uses the imagemap program on my server:

```
<A HREF="http://www.lne.com/cgi-bin/imagemap/maps/books.map">
<IMG SRC="image.gif" ISMAP></A>
```

And that's it. With everything connected, clicking the image on each book should load the page for that part of the image.

Creating Client-Side Image Maps

When you create a client-side image map, many of the steps for finding the coordinates of each area on the map are exactly the same as they are for creating server-side image maps. Unlike a server-side image map, however, which uses a separate file to store the coordinates and references for each hyperlink, client-side image maps store all the mapping information as part of an HTML document.

14

The `<MAP>` and `<AREA>` Tags

To include client-side image map inside an HTML document, you use the `<MAP>` tag, which looks like this:

```
<MAP NAME="mapname"> coordinates and links  </MAP>
```

The value assigned to the NAME attribute is the name of this map definition. This is the name that will be used later to associate the clickable image with its corresponding coordinates and hyperlink references—so, if you have multiple image maps on the same page, you can have multiple `<MAP>` tags with different names.

Between the `<MAP>` and the `</MAP>` tags, you enter the coordinates for each area in the image map and the destinations of those regions using the same values and links that you determined in the section on server-side image maps. This time, however, the coordinates are defined inside yet another new tag: the `<AREA>` tag. For example, to define the polygon area from Exercise 14.1, you would write this:

```
<AREA SHAPE="POLY" COORDS="70,0, 0,37, 0,183, 27,192, 27,48, 103,9"
    HREF="/www/redbook.html">
```

The type of shape to be used for the region is declared by the SHAPE attribute, which can have the values RECT, POLY, and CIRCLE. The coordinates for each shape are noted using the COORDS attribute. So, for example, the COORDS attribute for the POLY shape is the following, where each x,y combination represents a point on the polygon:

```
<AREA SHAPE="POLY" COORDS="x1,y1,x2,y2,x3,y3,[el],xN,yN" HREF="URL">
```

For RECT shapes, $x1,y1$ is the upper-left corner of the rectangle, and $x2,y2$ is the lower-right corner:

```
<AREA SHAPE="RECT" COORDS="x1,y1,x2,y2" HREF="URL">
```

And for CIRCLE shapes, x,y represents the center of a circular region of size *radius*:

```
<AREA SHAPE="CIRCLE" COORDS="x,y,radius" HREF="URL">
```

The last attribute you need to define for each `<AREA>` tag is the HREF attribute. HREF can be assigned any URL you would usually associate with an `<A>` link, including relative pathnames. In addition, you can assign HREF a value of `"NOHREF"` to define regions of the image that don't contain links to a new page.

NOTE

When using client-side image maps with frames, you can also include the TARGET attribute inside an `<AREA>` tag to open a new page in a specific window, as in this example:

```
<AREA SHAPE="RECT" COORDS="x1,y1,x2,y2" HREF="URL"
TARGET="window_name">.
```

The USEMAP **Attribute**

After your client-side image map has been defined using the <MAP> tag, the last step is to put the image on your Web page. To do this, you use a special form of the <IMG> tag that includes an attribute called USEMAP. (This is different from the ISMAP for server-side image maps.) USEMAP looks like this, where *mapname* is the name of a map defined by the <MAP NAME="*mapname*"> tag:

```
<IMG SRC="image.gif" USEMAP="#mapname">
```

NOTE

Unlike with server-side image maps, you do not need to enclose the <IMG> tag inside an <A> tag. Instead, the USEMAP attribute tells the Web browser that the <IMG> contains a clickable image map.

TIP

The value assigned to USEMAP is a standard URL. This is why *mapname* has a pound (#) symbol in from of it. As with links to anchors inside a Web page, the pound symbol tells the browser to look for *mapname* in the current Web page. However, if you have a very complex image map, it can be stored in a separate HTML file and referenced using a standard URL.

Exercise 14.2: The clickable bookshelf exercise revisited.

To conclude this discussion of image maps, take a look at how the image map example discussed in Exercise 14.1 would be written using client-side image maps. Because we already have the coordinates and the destination, all you really need is to convert the server-side map file into client-side HTML.

So, for the book image, the <MAP> tag and its associated <AREA> tag looks like this:

```
<MAP NAME="books">
<AREA SHAPE="POLY" COORDS="70,0, 0,37, 0,183, 27,192, 27,48, 103,9"
   HREF="/www/redbook.html">
</MAP>
```

The <IMG> tag to refer to the map coordinates is also different. It uses USEMAP instead of ISMAP, and doesn't have a link around it:

```
<IMG SRC="image.gif" USEMAP="#books">
```

Finally, put the whole lot together and test it. Here's a sample HTML file that contains both the <MAP> tag and the image that uses it. The result is shown in Figure 14.9.

```
<HTML><HEAD>
<TITLE>The Virtual Bookshelf</TITLE>
</HEAD><BODY>
<H1>The Virtual Bookshelf</H1>
<P>Please select a book:</P>
<IMG SRC="books.gif" USEMAP="#books">
<MAP NAME="books">
<AREA SHAPE="POLY" COORDS="70,0, 0,37, 0,183, 27,192, 27,48, 103,9"
     HREF="/www/redbook.html" >
</MAP>
</BODY>
</HTML>
```

OUTPUT

Figure 14.9.
*The finished image
map.*

Building Web Pages That Support Both Types of Image Maps

The main problem with using client-side image maps in your Web pages is that although client-side image maps are faster and easier to implement than server-side image maps, they're not supported by all browsers. In particular, a crop of older browsers is still in use that won't work with client-side image maps. Because of this, if you do use client-side image maps, its a good idea to also create a server-side equivalent, and then modify your HTML files so that they support both forms of image map. This way, your pages will work equally well with both image map formats while taking advantage of the newer client-side capabilities in browsers that support them.

To create an image map that uses client-side support, if available, but falls back to server-side support when needed, take the following standard server-side definition:

```
<A HREF="/cgi-bin/imagemap/maps/myimage.map">
<IMG SRC="image.gif" ISMAP>
</A>
```

And add the client-side image map details as part of the `<IMG SRC="image.gif" ISMAP>` text, like this:

```
<A HREF="/cgi-bin/imagemap/maps/myimage.map">
<IMG SRC="image.gif" USEMAP="#books" ISMAP>
</A>
```

You will, of course, need to have installed the `myimage.map` file on your server and to have included the "books" `<MAP>` tag definition somewhere in your HTML document.

Summary

In this chapter you learned how to add image maps to your Web pages. You should now know the difference between server-side and client-side image maps and which ones are available in which browsers. You also learned how to find regions and the coordinates that defined them and to create map files for client-side image maps. You now should know how to connect clickable images, map files, and image map programs on the appropriate servers.

It's been a very full chapter, so to help refresh your memory, Table 14.2 presents a summary of the tags and attributes you learned about in this chapter.

Table 14.2. HTML tags presented in this chapter.

Tag	Attribute	Use
`<MAP>`		Define a map for a client-side image map.
	NAME	An attribute of the `<MAP>` tag used to define the map's name.
	USEMAP	An attribute of the `<IMG>` tag used to associate an image with a client-side image map specified by `<MAP NAME="mapname">`.
`<AREA>`		The individual regions within a `<MAP>` element.
	TYPE	An attribute of the `<AREA>` tag indicating the type of region. Possible values are RECT, POLY, and CIRCLE.
	COORDS	An attribute of the `<AREA>` tag indicating the point bounding the region.
	HREF	An attribute of the `<AREA>` tag indicating the URL of the region.

14

Q&A

Q Do I need a server to create image maps? I want to create and test all of this offline, the same way I did for my regular HTML files.

A If you're using client-side image maps, you can create and test them all on your local system (assuming, of course, that your map destinations all point to files in your local presentation as well). If you're using server-side image maps, however, because you need the image map program on the server, you'll have to be connected to the server for all of this to work.

Q My server-side image maps aren't working. What's wrong?

A Here are a couple things you can look for:

☐ Make sure that the URLs in your map file are absolute pathnames from the top of your root Web directory to the location of the file where you want to link. You cannot use relative pathnames in the map file. If absolute paths aren't working, try full URLs (starting with http).

☐ Make sure that when you append the path of the map file to the image map program, you also use an absolute pathname (as it appears in your URL).

☐ If you're using NCSA, make sure that you're using the newest version of imagemap. Requests to the new imagemap script should not look for configuration files.

Q My client-side image maps aren't working. What's wrong?

A Here are a couple suggestions:

☐ Make sure the pathnames or URLs in your <AREA> tags point to real files.

☐ Make sure the map name in the <MAP> file and the name of the map in the USEMAP attribute in the <IMG> tag match. Only the latter should have a pound sign in front of it.

14

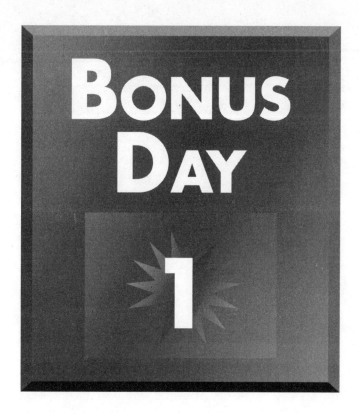

Creating Forms and CGI

Chapter **15**

Basic Forms

Everything you've learned up to this point has involved your giving information to your readers. That information may be text or images, it may be multimedia, or it may be a sophisticated, complex presentation using frames, image maps, and other bits of advanced Web publishing. But basically you're doing all the work, and your readers are simply sitting and reading and following links and digesting the information they've been presented.

Fill-in forms change all that. Forms make it possible for you to transform your Web pages from primarily text and graphics that your readers passively browse to interactive "toys," surveys, and presentations that can provide different options based on the reader's input.

Forms are the last of the major groups of HTML tags you'll learn about in this book. (There are still a few minor tags left after this.) And unlike many of the other tags you've learned about, forms are part of standard HTML and are widely supported by just about every browser on the market. In this chapter you'll learn about the HTML part of forms; tomorrow you'll learn about the server-side programs you need to use in order to do something useful with the information you get back from forms. In particular, today you'll learn about:

☐ Each part of the form on both the browser and server side, and how it all works

☐ The basic form input elements: text fields, radio buttons, and check boxes, as well as buttons for submitting and resetting the form

☐ Other form elements: text areas, menus of options, and hidden fields

☐ Some basic information about form-based file upload, a new feature that allows your readers to send whole files to you via a form

Anatomy of a Form

Creating a form usually involves two independent steps: creating the layout for the form and writing a script program on the server side (called a CGI script or program) to process the information you get back from a form. Today you'll learn about the HTML side of the process, and tomorrow you'll learn all about CGI scripts.

To create a form, you use (guess!) the <FORM> tag. Inside the opening and closing FORM tags are each of the individual form elements plus any other HTML content to create a layout for that form (paragraphs, headings, tables, and so on). You can include as many different forms on a page as you want to, but you can't nest forms—that is, you can't include a <FORM> tag inside another FORM.

The opening tag of the FORM element usually includes two attributes: METHOD and ACTION. The METHOD attribute can be either GET or POST, which determines how your form data is sent to the script to process it. You'll learn more about GET and POST tomorrow.

The ACTION attribute is a pointer to the script that processes the form on the server side. The ACTION can be indicated by a relative path or by a full URL to a script on your server or somewhere else. For example, the following <FORM> tag would call a script called form-name in a cgi-bin directory on the server www.myserver.com:

```
<FORM METHOD=POST ACTION="http://www.myserver.com/cgi-bin/form-name">
...
</FORM>
```

Again, you'll learn more about both of these attributes tomorrow when we delve more into CGI scripts. For today, so that we can test the output of our forms, we're going to be using a boilerplate form template that simply spits back what it gets. In each of the forms today, you'll be using POST as the METHOD, and the action will be the URL of a special script called post-query:

```
<FORM METHOD=POST ACTION="http://www.mcp.com/cgi-bin/post-query">
...
</FORM>
```

NOTE

This particular example uses the post-query script on the server www.mcp.com (the server for the publisher of this book). The post-query script is part of the standard NCSA server distribution and may be available on your own server. Check with your Webmaster to see whether it exists on your server; your forms will work that much faster if you work with a copy closer to you.

Exercise 15.1: Tell me your name.

EXERCISE

Let's try a simple example. In this example, you'll create the form shown in Figure 15.1. This form does absolutely nothing but prompt you for your name. In this form, you would enter your name and press the Submit button (or select the Submit link, in nongraphical browsers). Submit is what sends all the form data back to the server for processing. Then, on the server, a script would do something to that name (store it in a database, mail it to someone for further processing, plaster it across Times square, and so on).

Figure 15.1.

The Tell Me Your Name form.

TIP

Most browsers provide a shortcut: if there is only one text field on the page (besides Submit), you can just press Return to activate the form.

In this chapter we're just going to do the layout. Let's create this form so that you can get the basic idea of how it works. As with all HTML documents, start with a basic framework, with just a single level-two heading that reads Who are you?:

```
<HTML><HEAD>
<TITLE>Tell Me Your Name</TITLE>
</HEAD><BODY>
<H2>Who are you?</H2>
</BODY>
</HTML>
```

Now, add the form. First, add that template for post-query I mentioned earlier:

```
<HTML><HEAD>
<TITLE>Tell Me Your Name</TITLE>
</HEAD><BODY>
```

```
<H2>Who are you?</H2>
<FORM METHOD=POST ACTION="http://www.mcp.com/cgi-bin/post-query">
</FORM>
</BODY>
</HTML>
```

With the form framework in place, we can add the elements of the form. Note that the <FORM> doesn't specify the appearance and layout of the form; you'll have to use other HTML tags for that. (In fact, if you looked at this page in a browser now, you wouldn't see anything on the page that looked like a form.)

The first element inside the form is the text-entry area for the name. First, include the prompt, just as you would any other line of text in HTML:

```
<P>Enter your Name:
```

Then add the HTML code that indicates a text input field:

```
<P>Enter your Name: <INPUT NAME="theName"></P>
```

The <INPUT> tag indicates a simple form element. (There are also several other form elements that use tags other than <INPUT>, but <INPUT> is the most common one.) <INPUT> usually takes at least two attributes: TYPE and NAME.

The TYPE attribute is the kind of form element this is. There are several choices, including "text" for text-entry fields, "radio" for radio buttons, and "check" for check boxes. If you leave the TYPE attribute out, as we've done here, the element will be a text-entry field.

The NAME attribute indicates the name of this element. When your form is submitted to the server, the CGI script that processes it gets the form data as a series of name and value pairs. The value is the actual value your reader enters; the name is the value of this attribute. By including a sensible name for each element, you can easily match up which answer goes with which question.

You can put anything you want as the name of the element, but as with all good programming conventions, it's most useful if you use a descriptive name. Here we've picked the name theName. (Descriptive, yes?)

Now add the final form element: the submit button (or link). Most forms require the use of a submit button; if you have only one text field in the form, however, you can leave it off. The form will be submitted when the reader presses Enter.

```
<P><INPUT TYPE="submit"></P>
```

You'll use the <INPUT> tag for this element as well. The TYPE attribute is set to the special type of "submit," which creates a submit button for the form. The submit button doesn't require a name if there's only one of them; you'll learn how to create forms with multiple submit buttons later on.

It's a good practice to always include a submit button on your form, even if there's only one text field. The submit button is so common that your readers may become confused if it's not there.

Note that each element includes tags for formatting, just as if it were text; form elements follow the same rules as text in terms of how your browser formats them. Without the <P> tags, you'd end up with all the elements in the form on the same line.

You now have a simple form with two elements. The final HTML code to create this form looks like this:

```
<HTML><HEAD>
<TITLE>Tell Me Your Name</TITLE>
</HEAD><BODY>
<H2>Who are you?</H2>
<FORM METHOD=POST ACTION="http://www.mcp.com/cgi-bin/post-query">
<P>Enter your Name: <INPUT NAME="theName"></P>
<P><INPUT TYPE="submit"></P>
</FORM>
</BODY></HTML>
```

So what happens if you do submit the form? The form data is sent back to the server, and the post-query CGI script is called. The post-query script does nothing except return the names and values that you had in the original form. Figure 15.2 shows the output from a form submitted with a name in it.

Figure 15.2.
The output from
post-query.

Simple Form Layout

So now that you have the basics down, I'm sure you want to know exactly what kind of nifty interface elements you can put into a form.

In this section, you'll learn about the <INPUT> tag and the simple form elements you can create with it. There are a few other elements you can use for complex form input; you'll learn about those later in the chapter.

Each of the elements described in this section goes inside a <FORM>...</FORM> tag. In these examples, we'll continue to use the post-query script as the form's ACTION, which returns the name and value pairs it is given.

The Submit Button

Submit buttons (or submit links in nongraphical browsers; for the sake of simplicity, let's just call them buttons) tell the browser to send the form data to the server. You should include at least one submit button on every form even though forms with only one text field don't require them. To create a submit button, use "SUBMIT" as the TYPE attribute in an <INPUT> tag:

```
<INPUT TYPE="SUBMIT">
```

You can change the label text of the button by using the VALUE attribute:

```
<INPUT TYPE="SUBMIT" VALUE="Submit Query">
```

You can have multiple submit buttons in a form by including the NAME attribute inside the <INPUT> tag. Both the NAME and the VALUE of the submit button are then sent to the server for processing; you'll have to test for those name/value pairs when you write your CGI script to see which submit button was pressed. So, for example, you could use submit buttons inside a form for virtual directions, like this:

```
<INPUT TYPE="SUBMIT" NAME="left" VALUE="Left">
<INPUT TYPE="SUBMIT" NAME="right" VALUE="Right">
<INPUT TYPE="SUBMIT" NAME="up" VALUE="Up">
<INPUT TYPE="SUBMIT" NAME="down" VALUE="Down">
<INPUT TYPE="SUBMIT" NAME="forward" VALUE="Forward">
<INPUT TYPE="SUBMIT" NAME="back" VALUE="Back">
```

The following input and output example shows two simple forms with submit buttons: one with a default button and one with a custom label. Figure 15.3 shows the output in Netscape, and Figure 15.4 shows the output in Lynx.

NOTE   These figures show how the buttons appear in Netscape for the Macintosh. The buttons look slightly different in Netscape for other platforms, and may look entirely different in other browsers.

15

INPUT

```
<FORM METHOD=POST ACTION="http://www.mcp.com/cgi-bin/post-query">
<INPUT TYPE="SUBMIT">
</FORM>
<UL>
<FORM METHOD=POST ACTION="http://www.mcp.com/cgi-bin/post-query">
<INPUT TYPE="SUBMIT" VALUE="Press Here">
</FORM>
```

OUTPUT

Figure 15.3.
The output in Netscape.

OUTPUT

Figure 15.4.
The output in Lynx.

Text Input Fields

Text fields enable your reader to type text into a single-line field. For multiple-line fields, use the <TEXTAREA> element, described later in this chapter.

To create a text-entry field, you can either use TYPE="text" in the <INPUT> tag, or leave off the TYPE specification altogether. The default TYPE for the <INPUT> tag is text. You must also include a NAME attribute. NAME indicates the name of this field as passed to the script processing the form.

```
<INPUT TYPE="text" NAME="myText">
```

You can also include the attributes SIZE and MAXLENGTH in the <INPUT> tag. SIZE indicates the length of the text-entry field, in characters; the field is 20 characters by default. Your readers can enter as many characters as they want. The field will scroll horizontally as your reader types. Try to keep the SIZE under 50 characters so that it will fit on most screens.

```
<INPUT TYPE="text" NAME="longText" SIZE="50">
```

MAXLENGTH enables you to limit the number of characters that your reader can type into a text field (refusing any further characters). If MAXLENGTH is less than SIZE, browsers will sometimes draw a text field as large as MAXLENGTH.

In addition to regular text fields, there are also password fields, indicated by TYPE=password. Password text fields are identical to ordinary text fields, except that all the characters typed are echoed back in the browser (masked) as asterisks or bullets (see Figure 15.5).

```
<INPUT TYPE="PASSWORD" NAME="passwd">
```

Figure 15.5.
Password fields.

NOTE

Despite the masking of characters in the browser, password fields are not secure. The password is sent to the server in clear text; that is, anyone could intercept the password and be able to read it while it traverses the Net. The masking is simply a convenience so that users don't have to worry about someone standing next to them reading their passwords.

This input and output example shows several text fields, and their result in Netscape (Figure 15.6) and Lynx (Figure 15.7).

INPUT

```
<FORM METHOD=POST ACTION="http://www.mcp.com/cgi-bin/post-query">
<P>Enter your Name: <INPUT TYPE="TEXT" NAME="theName"><BR>
Enter your Age:
<INPUT TYPE="TEXT" NAME="theAge" SIZE="3" MAXLENGTH="3"><BR>
Enter your Address:
<INPUT TYPE="TEXT" NAME="theAddress" SIZE="80"></P>
</FORM>
```

OUTPUT

Figure 15.6.
The output in Netscape.

Figure 15.7.

The output in Lynx.

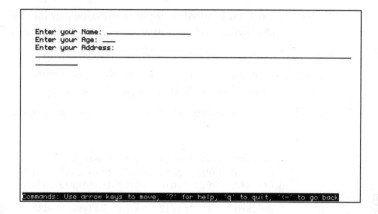

Radio Buttons

Radio buttons indicate a list of items, of which only one can be chosen. If one radio button in a list is selected, all the other radio buttons in the same list are deselected.

Radio buttons use "radio" for their TYPE attribute. You indicate groups of radio buttons using the same NAME for each button in the group. In addition, each radio button in the group must have a unique VALUE attribute, indicating the selection's value.

```
<OL>
<INPUT TYPE="radio" NAME="theType" VALUE="animal">Animal<BR>
<INPUT TYPE="radio" NAME="theType" VALUE="vegetable">Vegetable<BR>
<INPUT TYPE="radio" NAME="theType" VALUE="mineral">Mineral<BR>
</OL>
```

You can use multiple, independent groups of radio buttons by using different names for each group:

```
<OL>
<INPUT TYPE="radio" NAME="theType" VALUE="animal">Animal<BR>
<OL>
<LI><INPUT TYPE="radio" NAME="theAnimal" VALUE="cat">Cat
<LI><INPUT TYPE="radio" NAME="theAnimal" VALUE="dog">Dog
<LI><INPUT TYPE="radio" NAME="theAnimal" VALUE="fish">fish
</OL>
<INPUT TYPE="radio" NAME="theType" VALUE="vegetable">Vegetable<BR>
<INPUT TYPE="radio" NAME="theType" VALUE="mineral">Mineral<BR>
</OL>
```

By default, all radio buttons are off (unselected). You can determine the default radio button in a group using the CHECKED attribute:

```
<OL>
<INPUT TYPE="radio" NAME="theType" VALUE="animal" CHECKED>Animal<BR>
<INPUT TYPE="radio" NAME="theType" VALUE="vegetable">Vegetable<BR>
<INPUT TYPE="radio" NAME="theType" VALUE="mineral">Mineral<BR>
</OL>
```

When the form is submitted, a single name/value pair for the group of buttons is passed to the script. That pair includes the NAME attribute for each group of radio buttons and the VALUE attribute of the button that is currently selected.

Here's an input and output example that shows two groups of radio buttons, and how they look in Netscape (Figure 15.8) and Lynx (Figure 15.9).

```
<FORM METHOD=POST ACTION="http://www.mcp.com/cgi-bin/post-query">
<OL>
<LI><INPUT TYPE="radio" NAME="theType" VALUE="animal" CHECKED>Animal<BR>
<OL>
<LI><INPUT TYPE="radio" NAME="theAnimal" VALUE="cat" CHECKED>Cat
<LI><INPUT TYPE="radio" NAME="theAnimal" VALUE="dog">Dog
<LI><INPUT TYPE="radio" NAME="theAnimal" VALUE="fish">fish
</OL>
<LI><INPUT TYPE="radio" NAME="theType" VALUE="vegetable">Vegetable
<LI><INPUT TYPE="radio" NAME="theType" VALUE="mineral">Mineral
</OL>
</FORM>
```

Figure 15.8.
The output in Netscape.

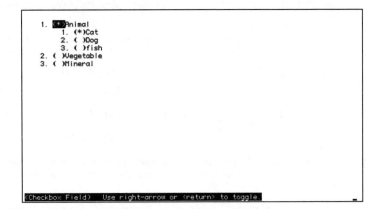

Figure 15.9.
The output in Lynx.

Check Boxes

Check boxes make it possible to choose multiple items in a list. Each check box can be either on or off (the default is off). Check boxes use "checkbox" as their TYPE attribute:

```
<UL>
<LI><INPUT TYPE="checkbox" NAME="red">Red
```

15

```
<LI><INPUT TYPE="checkbox" NAME="green">Green
<LI><INPUT TYPE="checkbox" NAME="blue">Blue
</UL>
```

When the form is submitted, only the name/value pairs for each selected check box are submitted (unselected check boxes are ignored). By default, each name/value pair for a selected check box has a value of ON. You can also use the VALUE attribute to indicate the value you would prefer to see in your script:

```
<UL>
<LI><INPUT TYPE="checkbox" NAME="red" VALUE="chosen">Red
<LI><INPUT TYPE="checkbox" NAME="green" VALUE="chosen">Green
<LI><INPUT TYPE="checkbox" NAME="blue" VALUE="chosen">Blue
</UL>
```

You can also implement check box lists such that elements have the same NAME attribute, similarly to radio buttons. Notice, however, that this means your script will end up with several name/value pairs having the same name (each check box that is selected will be submitted to the script), and you'll have to take that into account when you process the input in your script.

Also, like radio buttons, you can use the CHECKED attribute to indicate that a check box is checked by default.

Here's another one of those input and output examples, with a series of check boxes and how they look in Netscape (Figure 15.10) and Lynx (Figure 15.11).

```
<FORM METHOD=POST ACTION="http://www.mcp.com/cgi-bin/post-query">
<P>Profession (choose all that apply): </P>
<UL>
<LI><INPUT TYPE="checkbox" NAME="doctor" CHECKED>Doctor
<LI><INPUT TYPE="checkbox" NAME="lawyer">Lawyer
<LI><INPUT TYPE="checkbox" NAME="teacher" CHECKED>Teacher
<LI><INPUT TYPE="checkbox" NAME="nerd">Programmer
</UL>
</FORM>
```

OUTPUT

Figure 15.10.
The output in Netscape.

OUTPUT

Figure 15.11.
The output in Lynx.

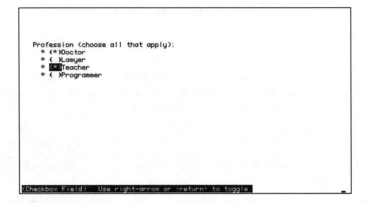

Images

Forms also give you an alternate way of implementing image maps using the TYPE=IMAGE attribute to the <INPUT> tag. Use TYPE=IMAGE with the SRC attribute which, just like SRC in <IMG>, indicates the pathname or URL to an IMAGE:

```
<INPUT TYPE="image" SRC="usamap.gif" NAME="map">
```

Images in forms behave just like image maps; when you click somewhere on the image, the form is submitted back to the server. The coordinates of the point where you clicked are submitted as part of that FORM data, with the value of the NAME attribute included twice with .x and .y appended for each coordinate. So, for example, if this image had the name map, the x coordinate would be contained in the map.x value and the y coordinate would be contained in the map.y value.

In the CGI script to process the form, you'll have to handle those coordinates yourself. Because standard image maps do a much better job of this, TYPE=IMAGE is rarely used to create an image map. It is instead used much more commonly as a replacement submit button. Because the image submits the form when it's selected, you can create an image for the submit button to replace the bland default button for submit.

 NOTE

It is important to remember that some people still use text-based browsers or even speech-based browsers. If you rely on TYPE=IMAGE for a functional part of your forms, the forms are unusable by these people.

Setting and Resetting Default Values

Each form element can have a default value that is entered or selected when the form is viewed:

 15

☐ For text fields, use the VALUE attribute with a string for the default value. The VALUE is entered in the box automatically when the form is displayed.

☐ For check boxes and radio buttons, the attribute CHECKED selects that element by default.

In addition to the default values for each element, you can include a reset button, similar to the submit button, on your form. The reset button clears all selections or entries your reader has made and resets them to their default values. Also like submit, a VALUE attribute indicates the label for the button:

```
<INPUT TYPE="RESET" VALUE="Reset Defaults">
```

Exercise 15.2. The Surrealist census.

Now, let's create a more complicated form example. In this example, the Surrealist Society of America has created a small census via an interactive form on the World Wide Web. Figure 15.12 shows that census.

Figure 15.12.

The Surrealist Society's census form.

The form to create the census falls roughly into three parts: the name field, the radio buttons for choosing the sex, and a set of check boxes for various other options.

Start with the basic structure, as with all HTML documents. We'll use that post-query script as we did in all the previous examples:

```
<HTML><HEAD>
<TITLE>The Surrealist Census</TITLE>
</HEAD><BODY>
<H1>The Surrealist Census</H1>
<P>Welcome to the Surrealist Census. Please fill out the following
form to the best of your abilities.</P>
<P>Use <STRONG>Submit</STRONG> To submit your results.
<HR>
<FORM METHOD=POST ACTION="http://www.mcp.com/cgi-bin/post-query">

</FORM>
<HR>
</BODY></HTML>
```

Note that in this example I've included rule lines before and after the form. Because the form is a discrete element on the page, it makes sense to visually separate it from the other parts of the page. This is especially important if you have multiple forms on the same page; separating them with rule lines or in some other way visually divides them from the other content on the page.

Now, let's add the first element for the reader's name. This is essentially the same element that we used in the previous example, with the name of the element theName:

```
<P><STRONG>Name: </STRONG><INPUT TYPE="TEXT" NAME="theName"></P>
```

The second part of the form is a series of radio buttons for Sex. There are three: Male, Female, and Null (remember, this is the Surrealist Census). Because radio buttons are mutually exclusive (only one can be selected at a time), we'll give all three buttons the same value for NAME (theSex):

```
<P><STRONG>Sex: </STRONG>
<INPUT TYPE="radio" NAME="theSex" VALUE="male">Male
<INPUT TYPE="radio" NAME="theSex" VALUE="female">Female
<INPUT TYPE="radio" NAME="theSex" VALUE="null">Null
</P>
```

Even though each <INPUT> tag is arranged on a separate line, the radio button elements are formatted on a single line. Always remember that form elements do not include formatting; you have to include other HTML tags to arrange them in the right spots.

Now, add the last part of the form: the list of Contains check boxes:

```
<P><STRONG>Contains (Select all that Apply): </STRONG><BR>
<INPUT TYPE="checkbox" NAME="humor">Vitreous Humor<BR>
<INPUT TYPE="checkbox" NAME="fish">Fish<BR>
<INPUT TYPE="checkbox" NAME="glycol">Propylene Glycol<BR>
```

```
<INPUT TYPE="checkbox" NAME="svga">SVGA Support<BR>
<INPUT TYPE="checkbox" NAME="angst">Angst<BR>
<INPUT TYPE="checkbox" NAME="catcon">Catalytic Converter<BR>
<INPUT TYPE="checkbox" NAME="vitamin">Ten Essential Vitamins and Nutrients<BR>
</P>
```

Unlike radio buttons, any number of check boxes can be selected, so each value of NAME is unique.

Finally, add the submit button so that the form can be submitted to the server. A nice touch is to also include a "Clear Form" button. Both buttons have special labels specific to this form:

```
<P><INPUT TYPE="SUBMIT" VALUE="Submit Your Votes">
<INPUT TYPE="RESET" VALUE="Clear Form"></P>
```

Whew! With all the elements in place, here's what the entire HTML file for the form looks like:

```
<HTML><HEAD>
<TITLE>The Surrealist Census</TITLE>
</HEAD><BODY>
<H1>The Surrealist Census</H1>
<P>Welcome to the Surrealist Census. Please fill out the following
form to the best of your abilities.</P>
<P>Use <STRONG>Submit</STRONG> To submit your results.</P>
<HR>
<FORM METHOD="POST" ACTION="http://www.mcp.com/cgi-bin/post-query">
<P><STRONG>Name: </STRONG><INPUT TYPE="TEXT" NAME="theName"></P>
<P><STRONG>Sex: </STRONG>
<INPUT TYPE="radio" NAME="theSex" VALUE="male">Male
<INPUT TYPE="radio" NAME="theSex" VALUE="female">Female
<INPUT TYPE="radio" NAME="theSex" VALUE="null">Null
</P>
<P><STRONG>Contains (Select all that Apply): </STRONG><BR>
<INPUT TYPE="checkbox" NAME="humor">Vitreous Humor<BR>
<INPUT TYPE="checkbox" NAME="fish">Fish<BR>
<INPUT TYPE="checkbox" NAME="glycol">Propylene Glycol<BR>
<INPUT TYPE="checkbox" NAME="svga">SVGA Support<BR>
<INPUT TYPE="checkbox" NAME="angst">Angst<BR>
<INPUT TYPE="checkbox" NAME="catcon">Catalytic Converter<BR>
<INPUT TYPE="checkbox" NAME="vitamin">Ten Essential Vitamins and Nutrients<BR>
</P>
<P><INPUT TYPE="SUBMIT" VALUE="Submit Your Votes">
<INPUT TYPE="RESET" VALUE="Clear Form"></P>
</FORM>
<HR>
</BODY></HTML>
```

Try selecting different parts of the form and seeing what you get back using post-query. Figure 15.13 shows one sample I used; Figure 15.14 shows the result I got back.

Figure 15.13.

A sample surrealist.

Figure 15.14.

The results back from the sample surrealist.

More Forms Layout

In addition to the <INPUT> tag with its many options, there are also two other tags that create form elements: SELECT, which has the ability to create pull-down menus and scrolling lists, and TEXTAREA, for allowing the reader to enter long blocks of text.

This section describes these other two tags. It also explains how to create "hidden" elements—form elements that don't actually show up on the page, but exist in the form nonetheless.

Selections

Selections enable the reader of a form to select one or more items from a menu or a scrolling list. They're similar to radio buttons or check boxes, in a different visual format.

Selections are indicated by the <SELECT> tag, and individual options within the selection are indicated by the <OPTION> tag. The <SELECT> tag also contains a NAME attribute to hold its value when the form is submitted.

<SELECT> and <OPTION> work much like lists do, with the entire selection surrounded by the opening and closing <SELECT> tags. Each option begins with a single-sided <OPTION>, like this:

```
<P>Select a hair color:
<SELECT NAME="hcolor">
<OPTION>Black
<OPTION>Blonde
<OPTION>Brown
<OPTION>Red
<OPTION>Blue
</SELECT></P>
```

When the form is submitted, the value of the entire selection is the text that follows the selected <OPTION> tag—in this case, Brown, Red, Blue, and so on. You can also use the VALUE attribute with each <OPTION> tag to indicate a different value.

Selections of this sort are generally formatted in graphical browsers as popup menus, as shown in Figure 15.15.

Figure 15.15.

Selections.

You can set the default item to be initially selected by using the SELECTED attribute, part of the <OPTION> tag:

```
<P>Select a hair color:
<SELECT NAME="hcolor">
```

```
<OPTION>Black
<OPTION>Blonde
<OPTION SELECTED>Brown
<OPTION>Red
<OPTION>Blue
</SELECT></P>
```

By default, selections act like radio buttons; that is, only one item can be selected at a time.
You can change the behavior of selections to allow multiple options to be selected by using
the MULTIPLE attribute, part of the <SELECT> tag:

```
<P>Shopping List:
<SELECT NAME="shopping" MULTIPLE>
<OPTION>Butter
<OPTION>Milk
<OPTION>Flour
<OPTION>Eggs
<OPTION>Cheese
<OPTION>Beer
<OPTION>Pasta
<OPTION>Mushrooms
</SELECT></P>
```

Be careful when you use MULTIPLE in the script that will process this form. Remember that
each selection list only has one possible NAME. This means that if you have multiple values in
a selection list, all of those values will be submitted to your script, and the program you use
to decode the input might store those in some special way.

NOTE   Each browser determines how the reader makes multiple choices.
Usually, the reader must hold down a key while making multiple
selections, but that particular key may vary from browser to browser.

The optional <SELECT> attribute usually displays the selection as a scrolling list in graphical
browsers, with the number of elements in the SIZE attribute visible on the form itself. (Figure
15.16 shows an example.)

```
<P>Shopping List:
<SELECT NAME="shopping" MULTIPLE SIZE="5">
<OPTION>Butter
<OPTION>Milk
<OPTION>Flour
<OPTION>Eggs
<OPTION>Cheese
<OPTION>Beer
<OPTION>Pasta
<OPTION>Mushrooms
</SELECT></P>
```

15

Figure 15.16.

Selections with SIZE.

Here's an input and output example that shows a simple selection list and how it appears in Netscape for the Mac (Figure 15.17). Note that selection lists may have a different appearance if you're viewing them on a different computer system or in a different browser.

```
<FORM METHOD=POST ACTION="http://www.mcp.com/cgi-bin/post-query">
<P>Select a hair color:
<SELECT NAME="hcolor">
<OPTION>Black
<OPTION>Blonde
<OPTION SELECTED>Brown
<OPTION>Red
<OPTION>Blue
</SELECT></P>
</FORM>
```

Figure 15.17.

The output in Netscape for the Macintosh.

Text Areas

Text areas are input fields in which the reader can type. Unlike regular text-input fields (<INPUT TYPE="text">), text areas can contain many lines of text, making them extremely useful for forms that require extensive input. For example, if you want to create a form that enables readers to compose electronic mail, you might use a text area for the body of the message.

To include a text area element in a form, use the <TEXTAREA> tag. <TEXTAREA> includes three attributes:

NAME   The name to be sent to the CGI script when the form is submitted

ROWS   The height of the text area element, in rows of text

COLS   The width of the text area element in columns (characters)

The <TEXTAREA> tag is a two-sided tag, and both sides must be used. If you have any default text you want to include in the text area, include it in between the opening and closing tags. For example:

```
<TEXTAREA NAME="theBody" ROWS="14" COLS="50">Enter your message here.</TEXTAREA>
```

The text in a text area is generally formatted in a fixed-width font such as Courier, but it's up to the browser to decide how to format it beyond that. Some browsers will allow text wrapping in text areas, others will scroll to the right. Some will allow scrolling if the text area fills up, whereas some others will just stop accepting input.

Netscape provides an extension to HTML that allows you to control text wrapping in the browser. By default in Netscape, text in a text area does not wrap; it simply scrolls to the right. You have to press Enter to get to the next line. Using the WRAP attribute to TEXTAREA, you can change the wrapping behavior:

WRAP=OFF   The default; text will be all on one line, scrolling to the right, until the reader presses Enter.

WRAP=SOFT   Causes the text to wrap automatically in the browser window, but is sent to the server as all one line.

WRAP=HARD   Causes the text to wrap automatically in the browser window. That text is also sent to the server with new-line characters at each point where the text wrapped.

This input and output example shows a simple text area in Netscape (Figure 15.18) and Lynx (Figure 15.19).

INPUT

```
<FORM METHOD=POST ACTION="http://www.mcp.com/cgi-bin/post-query">
<P>Enter any Comments you have about this Web page here:
<TEXTAREA NAME="comment" ROWS="30" COLS="60">
</TEXTAREA>
</P>
</FORM>
```

15

Figure 15.18.
The output in Netscape.

15

Figure 15.19.
The output in Lynx.

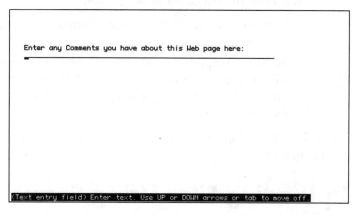

Hidden Fields

One value for the TYPE attribute to the <INPUT> tag I haven't mentioned is "HIDDEN". Hidden fields do not appear on the actual form; they are invisible in the browser display. They will still appear in your HTML code if someone decides to look at the HTML source for your page.

Hidden input elements look like this:

```
<INPUT TYPE="HIDDEN" NAME="theName" VALUE="TheValue">
```

Why would you want to create a hidden form element? If it doesn't appear on the screen and the reader can't do anything with it, what's the point?

Let's take a hypothetical example. You create a simple form. In the script that processes the first form, you create a second form based on the input from the first form. The script to process the second form takes the information from both the first and second forms and creates a reply based on that information. Figure 15.20 shows how all this flows.

Figure 15.20.

Form to form to reply.

How would you pass the information from the first form to the script that processes the second form? You can do one of two things:

- [ ] Write the information from the first form to a temporary file, and then read that file back in again when the second form starts up.
- [ ] In the first script that constructs the second form, create hidden fields in the form with the appropriate information in NAME and VALUE fields. Then those names and values will be passed automatically to the second script when the reader submits the second form.

See? Hidden elements do make sense, particularly when you get involved in generating forms from forms.

Uploading Files Using Forms

A proposal for modifying the standard definition of forms includes allowing forms to be used for uploading whole files full of data to a server. This proposal made its way into HTML 3.2. With forms the way they were until now, you can upload a text file by copying it into a text area, and there's no easy way to upload an image or other binary file.

NOTE

File upload is part of HTML 3.2 and 4.0. At the moment, however, Netscape Navigator 3.0 and 4.0 are the only browsers that fully support form-based file upload, and even then, dealing with the input on the server side is significantly more difficult than dealing with simple form input. The first preview release of Internet Explorer 4, however,

15

doesn't even display the browse button when this type of form element is included. Keep all this in mind as you read this section; file upload is very new indeed.

If you do decide to play with form-based file upload, you'll need to make two simple changes to the HTML code for your form. The first is to include the ENCTYPE="multipart/form-data" attribute inside your <FORM> tag, like this:

```
<FORM METHOD=POST ENCTYPE="multipart/form-data"
ACTION="http://www.myserver.com/cgi-bin/uploadit">

...
</FORM>
```

NOTE

ENCTYPE (short for enclosure type) isn't new; it's actually part of standard HTML 2.0, and its default value is application/x-www-form-urlencoded. Because the vast majority of forms use that default enclosure type, and few browsers or servers know how to deal with any other enclosure type, you don't really need to know anything about ENCTYPE unless you're working with file upload.

The second thing you'll need to add to your form is a new kind of <INPUT> tag. A new value for the TYPE attribute, TYPE="file", inserts a file-upload element (a text field and a button labeled "Browse" that lets you browse the local file system). Here's an example of a form with nothing but a file-upload element in it:

```
<FORM ENCTYPE="multipart/form-data"
ACTION="http://www.myserver.com/cgi-bin/upload" METHOD=POST>
Send this file: <INPUT NAME="userfile" TYPE="file">
<INPUT TYPE="submit" VALUE="Send File">
</FORM>
```

Figure 15.21 shows how this appears in Netscape.

Figure 15.21.
Forms for file upload.

Note that because this is an entirely new kind of form, you won't be able to test this with the post-query program we've been using up to this point. You'll need a special script on the server side to deal with form-based file upload; I'll talk more about this in the next chapter on CGI scripts.

Summary

Text fields, radio buttons, check boxes, submit and reset buttons, selection lists, and text areas—all of these are form elements you can include on your Web pages to get information back from your reader. And in this chapter, you learned all about how to include each of these in your Web page, as well as how to construct the form itself so that when it's submitted it'll call the right programs on the server side to process the information.

Forms are an HTML 2.0 (and, it follows, an HTML 3.2 and HTML 4.0) feature, and the tags for creating forms are widely supported in just about every available browser. Table 15.1 presents a summary of all the tags and attributes you learned about in this chapter.

Table 15.1. HTML tags from this chapter.

Tag	Use
`<FORM>...</FORM>`	A form. You can have multiple forms within a document, but forms cannot be nested.
`ACTION`	An attribute of the `<FORM>` tag indicating the CGI script to process the form input. Contains a relative path or URL to the script.
`METHOD`	An attribute of the `<FORM>` tag, indicating the method with which the form input is given to the script that processes the form. Possible values are GET and POST.

Tag	Use
<INPUT>	A form element.
TYPE	An attribute of the <INPUT> tag indicating the type of form element. Possible values are CHECKBOX, HIDDEN, IMAGE, RADIO, RESET, SUBMIT, and TEXT.

	CHECKBOX	Creates a check box.
	HIDDEN	Creates a form element that is not presented but has a name and a value that can then be passed on to the script that processes the form input.
	IMAGE	Creates a clickable image, similar to an image map, that behaves like a submit button.
	RADIO	Creates a radio button.
	RESET	Creates a button which resets the default values of the form, if any.
	SUBMIT	Creates a button to submit the form to the script which processes the input.
	TEXT	Creates a single-line text field.

Tag	Use
VALUE	An attribute of the <INPUT> tag, indicating the default value for the form element, if any, or the value submitted with the NAME to the script. For SUBMIT and RESET buttons, VALUE indicates the label of the button.
SIZE	An attribute of the <INPUT> tag used only when TYPE is TEXT. Indicates the size of the text field, in characters.
MAXLENGTH	An attribute of the <INPUT> tag used only when TYPE is TEXT. Indicates the maximum number of characters this text field will accept.
CHECKED	An attribute of the <INPUT> tag used only when TYPE is CHECKBOX or RADIO. Indicates that this element is selected by default.
SRC	An attribute of the <INPUT> tag used only when TYPE is IMAGE. Indicates the path or URL to the image file.
<SELECT>	A menu or scrolling list of items. Individual items are indicated by the <OPTION> tag.
MULTIPLE	An attribute of the <SELECT> tag indicating that multiple items in the list can be selected.

continues

Table 15.1. continued

Tag	Use
SIZE	An attribute of the <SELECT> tag which causes the list of items to be displayed as a scrolling list with the number of items indicated by SIZE visible.
<OPTION>	Individual items within a <SELECT> element.
SELECTED	An attribute of the <OPTION> tag indicating that this item is selected by default.
<TEXTAREA>	A text-entry field with multiple lines.
ROWS	An attribute of the <TEXTAREA> tag indicating the height of the text field, in rows.
COLS	An attribute of the <TEXTAREA> tag indicating the width of the text field, in characters.
WRAP	A (Netscape) attribute of the <TEXTAREA> tag indicating how the text inside that text area will behave. Possible values are OFF (the default), in which no wrapping occurs; SOFT, in which wrapping occurs onscreen but the text is send to the server as a single line, or HARD in which wrapping occurs onscreen and new lines are included in the text as submitted to the server.

Q&A

Q **I've got a form with a group of radio buttons, of which one of them has to be selected. When my form first comes up in a browser, none of them are selected, so if my reader doesn't choose one, I don't get any of the values. How can I make it so that one of them is selected?**

A Use the CHECKED attribute to set a default radio button out of the group. If your reader doesn't change it, the value of that radio button will be the one that's submitted.

Q **I'm having a hard time getting my form elements to lay out the way I want them. Nothing lines up right.**

A Form elements, like all HTML elements, lay out based on the size of the screen and the browser's rules for where things go on the screen.

I've seen two ways of affecting how forms are laid out. The first is to use <PRE>; the monospaced text affects the labels for the forms, but not the form elements themselves.

The second solution is to use tables without borders. You can get all your form elements to line up nicely by aligning them inside table cells.

Q I have text areas in my forms. In Netscape, when I type into the text area, the line keeps going and going to the right; it never wraps onto the next line. Do I have to press Enter at the end of every line?

A When you set up your form, include the WRAP attribute to indicate in Netscape how text inside the form will behave. WRAP=SOFT would be a good choice.

Chapter **16**

Beginning CGI Scripting

CGI stands for Common Gateway Interface, a method for running programs on the Web server based on input from a Web browser. CGI scripts enable your readers to interact with your Web pages—to search for an item in a database, to offer comments on what you've written, or to select several items from a form and get a customized reply in return. If you've ever come across a fill-in form or a search dialog on the Web, you've used a CGI script. You may not have realized it at the time because most of the work happens on the Web server, behind the scenes. You see only the result.

As a Web author, you create all the sides of the CGI script: the side the readers see, the programming on the server side to deal with the readers' input, and the results given back to the readers. A CGI script is an extremely powerful feature of Web browser and server interaction that can completely change how you think of a Web presentation.

In this chapter, you'll learn just about everything about CGI scripts, including the following:

- ☐ What a CGI script is and how it works
- ☐ What the output of a CGI script looks like
- ☐ How to create CGI scripts with and without arguments
- ☐ How to create scripts that return special responses
- ☐ How to create scripts to process input from forms
- ☐ Troubleshooting problems with your CGI scripts
- ☐ CGI variables you can use in your scripts
- ☐ Scripts with non-parsed headers
- ☐ Searches using <ISINDEX>

 NOTE

> This chapter and the next one focus primarily on Web servers running on UNIX systems, and most of the examples and instructions will apply only to UNIX. If you run your Web server on a system other than UNIX, the procedures you'll learn in this section for creating CGI scripts may not apply. This chapter will at least give you an idea of how CGI works, and you can combine this information with the documentation of CGI on your specific server.

What Is a CGI Script?

A CGI script, most simply, is a program that is run on a Web server, triggered by input from a browser. The script is usually a link between the server and some other program running on the system—for example, a database.

CGI scripts do not have to be actual scripts. Depending on what your Web server supports, they can be compiled programs or batch files or any other executable entity. For the sake of a simple term for this chapter, however, I'll call them *scripts*.

 NEW TERM A *CGI script* is any program that runs on the Web server. CGI stands for Common Gateway Interface and is a basic set of variables and mechanisms for passing information from the browser to the server.

CGI scripts are usually used in one of two ways: directly or as the ACTION to a form. Scripts to process forms are used slightly differently from regular CGI scripts, but both have similar appearances and behavior. For the first part of this chapter, you'll learn about generic CGI scripts, and then you'll move on to creating scripts that process forms.

16

How Do CGI Scripts Work?

CGI scripts are called by the server, based on information from the browser. Figure 16.1 shows how the process works between the browser, the server, and the script.

Figure 16.1.

Browser to server to script to program and back again.

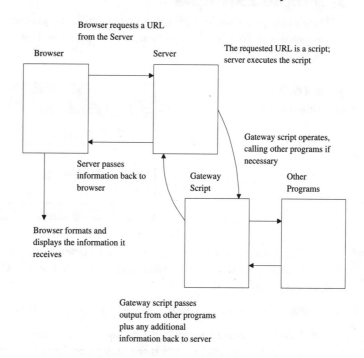

16

Here's a short version of what's actually going on:

1. A URL points to a CGI script. A CGI script URL can appear anywhere that a regular URL can appear—for example, in a link or in an image. Most often, a URL appears as the ACTION to a form. The browser contacts the server with that URL.

2. The server receives the request, notes that the URL points to a script (based on the location of the file or based on its extension, depending on the server), and executes that script.

3. The script performs some action based on the input, if any, from the browser. The action may include querying a database, calculating a value, or simply calling some other program on the system.

4. The script generates some kind of output that the Web server can understand.

5. The Web server receives the output from the script and passes it back to the browser, which formats and displays it for the readers.

Got it? No? Don't worry; this process can be confusing. Read on. The process will become clearer with a couple of examples.

A Simple Example

Here's a simple example, with a step-by-step explanation of what's happening on all sides of the process. In your browser, you encounter a page that looks like the page shown in Figure 16.2.

Figure 16.2.

A page with a script link.

The link to `Display the Date` is a link to a CGI script. It is embedded in the HTML code for the page just like any other link. If you were to look at the HTML code for that page, that link might look like this:

```
<A HREF="http://www.somesite.com/cgi-bin/getdate">Display the Date</A>
```

The fact that `cgi-bin` appears in the pathname is a strong hint that you're looking at a CGI script. In many servers, `cgi-bin` is the only place that CGI scripts can be kept.

When you select the link, your browser requests the URL from the server at the site `www.somesite.com`. The server receives the request and figures out from the configuration that the URL it's been given is a script called `getdate`. The server then executes that script.

The `getdate` script, in this case a shell script to be executed on a UNIX system, looks something like this:

```
#!/bin/sh

echo Content-type: text/plain
echo

/bin/date
```

This script does two things. First, it outputs the line `Content-type: text/plain`, followed by a blank line. Second, it calls the standard UNIX date program, which prints out the date and time. So the complete output of the script looks something like this:

```
Content-type: text/plain

Tue May 25 16:15:57 EDT 1997
```

What's that Content-type thing? It's a special code the Web server passes on to the browser to tell it what kind of document is used. The browser then uses the code to figure out whether it can display the document or whether it needs to load an external viewer. You'll learn specifics about this line later in this chapter.

So, after the script is finished executing, the server gets the result and passes it back to the browser over the Net. The browser has been waiting patiently all this time for some kind of response. When the browser gets the input from the server, it simply displays it, as shown in Figure 16.3.

Figure 16.3.

The result of the date script.

That's the basic idea. Although the process can get much more complicated, this interaction between browser, server, and script is at the heart of how CGI scripts work.

Can I Use CGI Scripts?

Before you can use CGI scripts in your Web presentations, both you and your server must meet several basic conditions. CGI scripting is an advanced Web feature and requires knowledge on your part as well as the cooperation of your Web server provider.

Make sure you can answer all the questions in this section before going on.

Is Your Server Configured to Allow CGI Scripts?

To write and run CGI scripts, you will need a Web server. Unlike with regular HTML files, you cannot write and test CGI scripts on your local system; you have to go through a Web server to do so.

But even if you have a Web server, that server has to be specially configured to run CGI scripts. That usually means that all your scripts will be kept in a special directory called cgi-bin.

Before trying out CGI scripts, ask your server administrator if you are allowed to install and run CGI scripts and, if so, where to put them when you're done writing them. Also, you must have a real Web server to run CGI scripts. If you publish your Web pages on an FTP or Gopher server, you cannot use CGI.

If you run your own server, you'll have to create a `cgi-bin` directory specially and configure your server to recognize that directory as a script directory (part of your server configuration, which, of course, varies from server to server). Also keep in mind the following issues that CGI scripts bring up:

☐ Each script is a program, and it runs on your system when the browser requests it, using CPU time and memory during its execution. What happens to the system if dozens or hundreds or thousands of these scripts are running at the same time? Your system may not be able to handle the load, making it crash or making it unusable for normal work.

☐ Unless you are very careful with the CGI scripts you write, you can potentially open yourself up to someone breaking into or damaging your system by passing arguments to your CGI script that are different from those it expects.

Can You Program?

Beginner beware! To create CGI, process forms, or perform any sort of interactivity on the World Wide Web, you must have a basic grasp of programming concepts and methods, and you should have some familiarity with the system on which you're working. If you don't have this background, I strongly suggest that you consult with someone who does, pick up a book in programming basics, or take a class in programming at your local college. This book is far too short for me to explain both introductory programming and CGI programming at the same time; in this chapter in particular, I am going to assume that you can read and understand the code in these examples.

What Programming Language Should You Use?

You can use just about any programming language you're familiar with to write CGI scripts, as long as your script follows the rules in the next section, and as long as that language can run on the system your Web server runs on. Some servers, however, may support only programs written in a particular language. For example, MacHTTP and WebStar use AppleScript for their CGI scripts; WinHTTPD and WebSite use Visual Basic. To write CGI scripts for your server, you must program in the language the server accepts.

In this chapter and throughout this book, I'll write these CGI scripts in two languages: the UNIX Bourne shell and the Perl language. The Bourne shell is available on nearly any UNIX system and is reasonably easy to learn, but doing anything complicated with it can be difficult. Perl, on the other hand, is freely available, but you'll have to download and compile it on your system. The language itself is extremely flexible and powerful (nearly as powerful as a programming language such as C), but it is also very difficult to learn.

Is Your Server Set Up Right?

To run any CGI scripts, whether they are simple scripts or scripts to process forms, your server must be set up explicitly to run them. You might need to keep your scripts in a special directory, or you might have to use a special file extension, depending on which server you're using and how it's set up.

If you're renting space on a Web server, or if someone else is in charge of administering your Web server, you have to ask the person in charge whether CGI scripts are allowed and, if so, where to put them.

If you run your own server, check with the documentation for the server to see how it handles CGI scripts.

What If You're Not on UNIX?

If you're not on UNIX, stick around. You can still find lots of general information about CGI that might apply to your server. Just for general background, here's some information about CGI on other common Web servers.

WinHTTPD for Windows 3.*x* and WebSite for Windows 95 and NT both include CGI capabilities with which you can manage form and CGI input. Both servers include a DOS and Windows CGI mode, the latter of which allows you to manage CGI through Visual Basic. The DOS mode can be configured to handle CGI scripts using Perl or Tcl (or any other language). WebSite also has a CGI mode for running Perl and Windows shell script CGI programs.

Similarly, Netscape's line of Web servers, including FastTrack and Enterprise Web servers, support a full range of CGI capabilities. Enterprise server, for instance, supports shell CGI, regular CGI, and Windows CGI mode, giving you flexibility to choose the best approach for your needs. Similarly, the latest version of Internet Information Server from Microsoft (version 3.0) supports CGI in many forms.

MacHTTP has CGI capabilities in the form of AppleScript scripts. (MacHTTP is the original shareware version of a commercial Web server named WebStar, which is available from StarNine.) Jon Wiederspan has written an excellent tutorial on using AppleScript CGI, which is included as part of the MacHTTP documentation.

Anatomy of a CGI Script

If you've made it this far, past all the warnings and configurations, congratulations! You can write CGI scripts and create forms for your presentations. In this section, you'll learn about how your scripts should behave so that your server can talk to them and get back the correct response.

The Output Header

Your CGI scripts will generally get some sort of input from the browser by way of the server. You can do anything you want with that information in the body of your script, but the output of the script has to follow a special form.

NOTE

> By "script output," I'm referring to the data your script sends back to the server. On UNIX, the output is sent to the standard output, and the server picks it up from there. On other systems and other servers, your script output may go somewhere else; for example, you might write to a file on the disk or send the output explicitly to another program. Again, you should carefully examine the documentation for your server to see how CGI scripts have been implemented in the server.

The first thing your script should output is a special header that gives the server, and eventually the browser, information about the rest of the data your script is going to create. The header isn't actually part of the document; it's never displayed anywhere. Web servers and browsers actually send information like this back and forth all the time; you just never see it.

You can output three types of headers from scripts: `Content-type`, `Location`, and `Status`. `Content-type` is the most popular, so I'll explain it here; you'll learn about `Location` and `Status` later in this chapter.

You learned about the content-type header earlier in this book; content-types are used by the browser to figure out what kind of data it's receiving. Because script output doesn't have a file extension, you have to explicitly tell the browser what kind of data you're sending back. To do so, you use the content-type header. A content-type header has the words `Content-type`, a special code for describing the kind of file you're sending, and a blank line, like this:

```
Content-type: text/html
```

In this example, the contents of the data to follow are of the type `text/html`; in other words, it's an HTML file. Each file format you work with when you're creating Web presentations has a corresponding content-type, so you should match the format of the output of your script to the appropriate one. Table 16.1 shows some common formats and their equivalent content-types.

Table 16.1. Common formats and content-types.

Format	Content-Type
HTML	`text/html`
Text	`text/plain`
GIF	`image/gif`
JPEG	`image/jpeg`
PostScript	`application/postscript`
MPEG	`video/mpeg`

Note that the content-type line *must* be followed by a blank line. The server cannot figure out where the header ends if you don't include the blank line.

The Output Data

The remainder of your script is the actual data that you want to send back to the browser. The content you output in this part should match the content-type you told the server you were giving it; that is, if you use a content-type of `text/html`, the rest of the output should be in HTML. If you use a content-type of `image/gif`, the remainder of the output should be a binary GIF file, and so on for all the content-types.

Exercise 16.1: Try it.

This exercise is similar to the simple example from earlier in this chapter, the one that printed out the date. This CGI script checks to see whether I'm logged into my Web server and reports back what it finds, as shown in Figure 16.4.

Figure 16.4.

The `pinglaura`
script results.

This example shows the most simple form of a CGI script, which can be called from a Web page by just linking to it like this:

```
<A HREF="http://www.lne.com/cgi-bin/pinglaura">Is Laura Logged in?</A>
```

When you link to a CGI script like this, selecting the link runs the script. There is no input to the script; it just runs and returns data.

First, determine the content-type you'll be outputting. Because it will be an HTML document, the content-type is `text/html`. So the first part of your script, which follows, simply prints out a line containing the content-type and a blank line after that (don't forget that blank line!):

```
#!/bin/sh

echo Content-type: text/html
echo
```

Now, add the remainder of the script: the body of the HTML document, which you had to construct yourself from inside the script. Basically, you're going to do the following:

- ☐ Print out the tags that make up the first part of the HTML document.
- ☐ Test to see whether I'm logged in, and output an appropriate message.
- ☐ Print out the last bit of HTML tags to finish up the document.

Start with the first bit of the HTML. The following commands take care of this job in the UNIX shell:

```
echo "<HTML><HEAD>"
echo "<TITLE>Is Laura There?</TITLE>"
echo "</HEAD><BODY>"
```

Now test to see whether I'm logged into the system using the who command (my login ID is lemay), and store the result in the variable ison. If I'm logged in, the ison variable will have something in it; otherwise, ison will be empty.

```
ison=`who | grep lemay`
```

Test the result and return the appropriate message as part of the script output:

```
if [ ! -z "$ison" ]; then
        echo "<P>Laura is logged in.</P>"
else
        echo "<P>Laura isn't logged in.</P>"
fi
```

Finally, close up the remainder of the HTML tags:

```
echo "</BODY></HTML>"
```

And that's it. If you run the program by itself from a command line to test its output, you get a result something like this:

```
Content-type: text/html

<HTML><HEAD>
<TITLE>Are You There?</TITLE>
</HEAD><BODY>
<P>Laura is not logged in.
</BODY></HTML>
```

Looks like your basic HTML document, doesn't it? That's precisely the point. The output from your script is what is sent back to the server and then out to the browser. So the output of your script should be in a format the server and browser can understand—here, an HTML file.

Now, install this script in the proper place for your server. This step will vary depending on the platform you're using and the server you're using. Most of the time, on UNIX servers, you will find a special cgi-bin directory for scripts. Copy the script there, and make sure it's executable.

NOTE

> If you don't have access to the cgi-bin directory, you must ask your Web server administrator for access. You cannot just create a cgi-bin directory and copy the script there; that won't work. See your Webmaster.

Now that you've got a script ready to go, you can call it from a Web page by linking to it, as I mentioned earlier. Just for reference, here's what the final script looks like:

```sh
#!/bin/sh

echo "Content-type: text/html"
echo
echo "<HTML><HEAD>"
echo "<TITLE>Is Laura There?</TITLE>"
echo "</HEAD><BODY>"

ison=`who | grep lemay`

if [ ! -z "$ison" ]; then
        echo "<P>Laura is logged in.</P>"
else
        echo "<P>Laura isn't logged in.</P>"
fi

echo "</BODY></HTML>"
```

Scripts with Arguments

CGI scripts are most useful if they're written to be as generic as possible. For example, if you want to check whether different people are logged into the system using the script in the preceding example, you might have to write several different scripts (`pinglaura`, `pingeric`, `pingelsa`, and so on). It would make more sense to have a single generic script and then send the name you want to check for as an argument to the script.

To pass arguments to a script, specify those arguments in the script's URL with a question mark (?) separating the name of the script from the arguments and with plus signs (+) separating each individual argument, like this:

```
<A HREF="/cgi-bin/myscript?arg1+arg2+arg3">run my script</A>
```

When the server receives the script request, it passes `arg1`, `arg2`, and `arg3` to the script as arguments. You can then parse and use those arguments in the body of the script.

This method of passing arguments to a script is sometimes called a query because it is how browsers communicated search keys in an earlier version of searches called ISINDEX searches. (You'll learn more about these searches later.) These days, most searches are done using forms, but this form of encoding arguments is still used; you should be familiar with it if you use CGI scripts often.

Exercise 16.2: Check to see whether anyone is logged in.

Now that you know how to pass arguments to a script, you can modify the `pinglaura` script so that it is more generic. Call this script `pinggeneric`.

Start with the beginning of the script you used in the preceding example, with a slightly different title:

```
#!/bin/sh
echo "Content-type: text/html"
echo
echo "<HTML><HEAD>"
echo "<TITLE>Are You There?</TITLE>"
echo "</HEAD><BODY>"
```

In the preceding example, the next step was to test whether I was logged on. Here's the place where the script becomes generic. Instead of the name `lemay` hard-coded into the script, use `${1}` instead, with `${1}` as the first argument, `${2}` as the second, `${3}` as the third, and so on.

```
ison=`who | grep "${1}"`
```

NOTE

> Why the extra quotation marks around the `${1}`? They keep nasty people from passing weird arguments to your script.

All that's left is to modify the rest of the script to use the argument instead of the hard-coded name:

```
if [ ! -z "$ison" ]; then
        echo "<P>$1 is logged in"
else
        echo "<P>$1 isn't logged in"
fi
```

Now finish up with the closing `<HTML>` tag:

```
echo "</BODY></HTML>"
```

With the script complete, you can modify the HTML page that calls the script. The `pinglaura` script was called with an HTML link, like this:

```
<A HREF="http://www.lne.com/cgi-bin/pinglaura">Is Laura Logged in?</A>
```

The generic version is called in a similar way, with the argument at the end of the URL, as in the following line. (This one tests for someone named John.)

```
<A HREF="http://www.lne.com/cgi-bin/pinggeneric?john">Is John Logged in?</A>
```

Try this script on your own server, with your own login ID in the URL for the script to see what kind of result you get.

Passing Other Information to the Script

In addition to passing arguments to a script through query arguments, you can pass information to a CGI script in a second way (that still isn't forms). The second way, called path information, is used for arguments that can't change between invocations of the script, such as the name of a temporary file or the name of the file that called the script itself. As you'll

16

see in the section on forms, the arguments after the question mark can indeed change based on input from the users. Path info is used for other information to be passed for the script (and indeed, you can use it for anything you want).

NEW TERM *Path information* is a way of passing extra information to a CGI script that is not as frequently changed as regular script arguments. Path information often refers to files on the Web server such as configuration files, temporary files, or the file that actually called the script in question.

To use path information, append the information you want to include to the end of the URL for the script, after the script name but before the ? and the rest of the arguments, as in the following example:

```
http://myhost/cgi-bin/myscript/remaining_path_info?arg1+arg2
```

When the script is run, the information in the path is placed in the environment variable PATH_INFO. You can then use that information any way you want to in the body of your script.

For example, say you have multiple links on multiple pages to the same script. You can use the path information to indicate the name of the HTML file that has the link. Then, after you finish processing your script, when you send back an HTML file, you can include a link in that file back to the page from which your readers came.

Creating Special Script Output

In the couple of examples you've created so far in this chapter, you've written scripts that output data, usually HTML data, and that data has been sent to the browser for interpretation and display. But what if you don't want to send a stream of data as a result of a script's actions? What if you want to load an existing page instead? What if you just want the script to do something and not give any response back to the browser?

Fear not; you can do these things in CGI scripts. This section explains how.

Responding by Loading Another Document

CGI output doesn't have to be a stream of data. Sometimes it's easier just to tell the browser to go to another page you have stored on your server (or on any server, for that matter). To send this message, you use a line similar to the following:

```
Location: ../docs/final.html
```

The Location line is used in place of the normal output; that is, if you use Location, you do not need to use Content-type or include any other data in the output (and, in fact, you can't include any other data in the output). As with Content-type, however, you must also include a blank line after the Location line.

The pathname to the file can be either a full URL or a relative pathname. All relative pathnames will be relative to the location of the script itself. This one looks for the document `final.html` in a directory called `docs` one level up from the current directory:

```
echo Location: ../docs/final.html
echo
```

NOTE

> You cannot combine `Content-type` and `Location` output. For example, if you want to output a standard page and then add custom content to the bottom of that same page, you'll have to use `Content-type` and construct both parts yourself. Note that you can use script commands to open up a local file and print it directly to the output; for example, `cat filename` sends the contents of the file `filename` as data.

No Response

Sometimes it may be appropriate for a CGI script to have no output at all. Sometimes you just want to take the information you get from the readers. You may not want to load a new document, either by outputting the result or by opening an existing file. The document that was on the browser's screen before should just stay there.

Fortunately, this procedure is quite easy. Instead of outputting a `Content-type` or `Location` header, use the following line (with a blank line after it, as always):

```
Status: 204 No Response
```

The `Status` header provides status codes to the server (and to the browser). The particular status of `204` is passed on to the browser, and the browser, if it can figure out what to do with it, should do nothing.

You'll need no other output from your script because you don't want the browser to do anything with it—just the one `Status` line with the blank line. Of course, your script should do something; otherwise, why bother calling the script at all?

NOTE

> Although `No Response` is part of the official HTTP specification, it may not be supported in all browsers or may produce strange results. Before using a `No Response` header, you might want to experiment with several different browsers to see what the result will be.

16

Scripts to Process Forms

Most uses of CGI scripts these days are for processing form input. Calling a CGI script directly from a link can execute only that script with the hard-coded arguments. Forms allow any amount of information to be entered by the readers of the form, sent back to the server, and processed by a CGI script. They're the same scripts, and they behave in the same ways. You still use Content-type and Location headers to send a response back to the browser. However, there are a few differences, including how the CGI script is called and how the data is sent from the browser to the server.

Form Layout and Form Scripts

As you learned yesterday, every form you see on the Web has two parts: the HTML code for the form, which is displayed in the browser, and the script to process the contents of that form, which runs on the server. They are linked together in the HTML code.

The ACTION attribute inside the <FORM> tag contains the name of the script to process the form, as follows:

```
<FORM ACTION="http://www.myserver.com/cgi-bin/processorscript">
```

In addition to this reference to the script, each input field in the form (a text field, a radio button, and so on) has a NAME attribute, which names that form element. When the form data is submitted to the CGI script you named in ACTION, the names of the tags and the contents of that field are passed to the script as name/value pairs. In your script, you can then get to the contents of each field (the value) by referring to that field's name.

GET and POST

One part of forms I didn't mention yesterday (except in passing) was the METHOD attribute. METHOD indicates the way the form data will be sent from the browser to the server to the script. METHOD has one of two values: GET and POST.

GET is just like the CGI scripts you learned about in the preceding section. The form data is packaged and appended to the end of the URL you specified in the ACTION attribute as argument. So, if your action attribute looks like

```
ACTION="/cgi/myscript"
```

and you have the same two input tags as in the previous section, the final URL might look like this:

```
http://myhost/cgi-bin/myscript?username=Agamemnon&phone=555-6666
```

Note that this formatting is slightly different from the arguments you passed to the CGI script by hand; this format is called URL encoding and is explained in more detail later in this chapter.

When the server executes your CGI script to process the form, it sets the environment variable QUERY_STRING to everything after the question mark in the URL.

POST does much the same thing as GET, except that it sends the data separately from the actual call to the script. Your script then gets the form data through the standard input. (Some Web servers might store it in a temporary file instead of using standard input; UNIX servers do the latter.) The QUERY_STRING environment variable is not set if you use POST.

Which one should you use? POST is the safest method, particularly if you expect a lot of form data. When you use GET, the server assigns the QUERY_STRING variable to all the encoded form data, and the amount of data you can store in that variable might be limited.

If you use POST, you can have as much data as you want because the data is sent as a separate stream and is never assigned to a variable. Additionally, the GET value has officially been deprecated in HTML 4.0 for internationalization reasons.

URL Encoding

URL encoding is the format that the browser uses to package the input to the form when the browser sends the input to the server. The browser gets all the names and values from the form input, encodes them as name/value pairs, translates any characters that won't transfer over the wire, lines up all the data, and—depending on whether you're using GET or POST—sends them to the server either as part of the URL or separately through a direct link to the server. In either case, the form input ends up on the server side (and therefore in your script) as gobbledygook that looks something like this:

```
theName=Ichabod+Crane&gender=male&status=missing&headless=yes
```

URL encoding follows these rules:

☐ Each name/value pair itself is separated by an ampersand (&).

☐ The name/value pairs from the form are separated by an equal sign (=). If the user of the form did not enter a value for a particular tag, the name still appears in the input, but with no value (as in "name=").

☐ Any special characters (characters that are not simple seven-bit ASCII) are encoded in hexadecimal preceded by a percent sign (%NN). Special characters include the =, &, and % characters if they appear in the input itself.

☐ Spaces in the input are indicated by plus signs (+).

Because form input is passed to your script in this URL-encoded form, you'll have to decode it before you can use it. However, because decoding this information is a common task, lots of tools are available for doing just that. You don't need to write your own decoding program unless you want to do something very unusual. The available decoding programs can do a fine job, and they might consider situations that you haven't, such as how to avoid having your script break because someone gave your form funny input.

I've noted a few programs for decoding form input later in this chapter, but the program I'm going to use for the examples in this book is called uncgi, which decodes the input from a form submission for you and creates a set of environment variables from the name/value pairs. Each environment variable has the same name as the name in the name/value pair, with the prefix WWW_ prepended to each one. Each value in the name/value pair is then assigned to its respective environment variable. So, for example, if you have a form with a name in it called username, the resulting environment variable uncgi creates is WWW_username, and its value is whatever the reader typed in that form element. After you've got the environment variables, you can test them just as you would any other variable.

You can get the source for uncgi from http://www.hyperion.com/~koreth/uncgi.html. Compile uncgi using the instructions that come with the source, install it in your cgi-bin directory, and you're ready to go.

Exercise 16.3: Tell me your name, Part 2.

Remember the form you created yesterday that prompts you for your name? Now you can create the script to handle that form. (The form is shown again in Figure 16.5, in case you've forgotten.) Using this form, you would type in your name and submit the form using the Submit button.

Figure 16.5.
The Tell Me Your Name form.

What if you don't type anything at the Enter your Name prompt? The script then sends you the response shown in Figure 16.6.

The input is sent to the script, which sends back an HTML document that displays a hello message with your name in it, as shown in Figure 16.7.

Modify the HTML for the Form

In the examples yesterday, you used a testing program called post-query as the script to call in the ACTION attribute to the <FORM> tag. Now that you're working with real scripts, you can modify the form so that it points to a real CGI script. The value of ACTION can be a full URL or a relative pathname to a script on your server. So, for example, the following <FORM> tag calls a script called form-name in a cgi-bin directory one level up from the current directory:

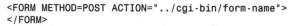

```
<FORM METHOD=POST ACTION="../cgi-bin/form-name">
</FORM>
```

Figure 16.6.
*The result of
the name form.*

Figure 16.7.
Another result.

If you're using uncgi to decode form input, as I am in these examples, things are slightly different. To make uncgi work properly, you call uncgi first and then append the name of the actual script as if uncgi were a directory, like this:

```
<FORM METHOD=POST ACTION="../cgi-bin/uncgi/form-name">
</FORM>
```

Other than this one modification, you don't need to modify the form at all. Now you can move onto the script to process the form.

The Script

The script to process the form input is a CGI script, just like the ones you've been creating up to this point in the chapter. All the same rules apply for Content-type headers and passing the data back to the browser.

The first step in a form script is usually to decode the information that was passed to your script through the POST method. In this example, however, because you're using uncgi to decode form input, the form decoding has already been done for you. Remember how you put uncgi in the ACTION attribute to the form, followed by the name of your script? When the form input is submitted, the server passes that input to the uncgi program, which decodes the form input for you, and then calls your script with everything already decoded. Now, at the start of your script, all the name/value pairs are available for you to use.

Moving on, print out the usual CGI headers and HTML code to begin the page:

```
echo Content-type: text/html
echo
echo "<HTML><HEAD>"
echo "<TITLE>Hello</TITLE>"
```

```
echo "</HEAD><BODY>"
echo "<P>"
```

Now comes the meat of the script. You have two branches to deal with: one to accuse the readers of not entering names and one to say hello when they do.

The value of the theName element, as you named the text field in your form, is contained in the WWW_theName environment variable. Using a simple Bourne shell test (-z), you can see whether this environment variable is empty and include the appropriate response in the output:

```
if [ ! -z "$WWW_theName" ]; then
    echo "Hello, "
    echo $WWW_theName
else
    echo "You don't have a name?"
fi
```

Finally, add the last bit of HTML code to include the "go back" link. This link points back to the URL of the original form (here, called name1.html, in a directory one level up from cgi-bin):

```
echo "</P><P><A HREF="../lemay/name1.html">Go Back</A></P>"
echo "</BODY></HTML>"
```

And that's all there is to this process. Learning how to create CGI scripts is the hard part; linking them together with forms is easy. Even if you're confused and don't quite have the process down, bear with me. You'll find lots more examples to look at and work through tomorrow.

Troubleshooting

Here are some of the most common problems with CGI scripts and how to fix them:

☐ The content of the script is being displayed, not executed.

Have you configured your server to accept CGI scripts? Are your scripts contained in the appropriate CGI directory (usually cgi-bin)? If your server allows CGI files with .cgi extensions, does your script have that extension?

☐ Error 500: Server doesn't support POST.

You'll get this error from forms that use the POST method. This error most often means that you either haven't set up CGI scripts in your server, or you're trying to access a script that isn't contained in a CGI directory (see the preceding bullet).

This error can also mean, however, that you've misspelled the path to the script itself. Check the pathname in your form, and if it's correct, make sure that your script is in the appropriate CGI directory (usually cgi-bin) and that it has a .cgi extension (if your server allows it).

☐ The document contains no data.

Make sure you included a blank line between your headers and the data in your script.

☐ Error 500: Bad Script Request.

Make sure your script is executable. (On UNIX, make sure you've added chmod +x to the script.) You should be able to run your scripts from a command line before you try to call them from a browser.

CGI Variables

CGI variables are special variables set in the environment when a CGI script is called. All these variables are available to you in your script to use as you see fit. Table 16.2 summarizes them.

Table 16.2. CGI environment variables.

Environment Variable	What It Means
SERVER_NAME	The host name or IP address on which the CGI script is running, as it appears in the URL.
SERVER_SOFTWARE	The type of server you're running—for example, CERN/3.0 or NCSA/1.3.
GATEWAY_INTERFACE	The version of CGI running on the server. For UNIX servers, this version should be CGI/1.1.
SERVER_PROTOCOL	The HTTP protocol the server is running. This protocol should be HTTP/1.0.
SERVER_PORT	The TCP port on which the server is running. It is usually port 80 for Web servers.
REQUEST_METHOD	POST or GET, depending on how the form is submitted.
HTTP_ACCEPT	A list of content-types the browser can accept directly, as defined by the HTTP Accept header.
HTTP_USER_AGENT	The browser that submitted the form information. Browser information usually contains the browser name, the version number, and extra information about the platform or extra capabilities.
HTTP_REFERER	The URL of the document that this form submission came from. Not all browsers send this value; do not rely on it.
PATH_INFO	Extra path information, as sent by the browser using the query method of GET in a form.

16

Environment Variable	What It Means
PATH_TRANSLATED	The actual system-specific pathname of the path contained in PATH_INFO.
SCRIPT_NAME	The pathname to this CGI script, as it appears in the URL—for example, /cgi-bin/thescript.
QUERY_STRING	The arguments to the script or the form input (if submitted using GET). QUERY_STRING contains everything after the question mark in the URL.
REMOTE_HOST	The name of the host that submitted the script. This value cannot be set.
REMOTE_ADDR	The IP address of the host that submitted the script.
REMOTE_USER	The name of the user that submitted the script. This value will be set only if server authentication is turned on.
REMOTE_IDENT	If the Web server is running ident (a protocol to verify the user connecting to you), and the system that submitted the form or script is also running ident, this variable contains the value returned by ident.
CONTENT_TYPE	In forms submitted with POST, the value will be application/x-www-form-urlencoded. In forms with file upload, the content-type will be multipart/form-data.
CONTENT_LENGTH	For forms submitted with POST, the number of bytes in the standard input.

Programs to Decode Form Input

The one major difference between a plain CGI script and a CGI script that processes a form is that, because you get data back from the form in URL-encoded format, you need a method of decoding that data. Fortunately, because everyone who writes a CGI script to process a form needs to decode, programs are available to do the job for you and to decode the name/value pairs into something you can more easily work with. I like two programs: uncgi for general-purpose use, and cgi-lib.pl, a Perl library for use when you're writing CGI scripts in Perl. You can, however, write your own program if the ones I've mentioned here aren't good enough.

You also can find programs to decode data sent from form-based file uploads, although fewer of them are available. At the end of this section, I mention a few that I've found.

uncgi

Steven Grimm's uncgi, a program written in C, decodes form input for you. You can get information and the source for uncgi from http://www.hyperion.com/~koreth/uncgi.html.

To use uncgi, you should install it in your cgi-bin directory. Make sure you edit the makefile before you compile the file to point to the location of that directory on your system; it will then be able to find your scripts.

To use uncgi in a form, you'll have to modify the ACTION attribute slightly in the FORM tag. Instead of calling your CGI script directly in ACTION, you call uncgi with the name of the script appended. So, for example, if you have a CGI script called sleep2.cgi, the usual way to call it is as follows:

```
<FORM METHOD=POST ACTION="http://www.myserver.com/cgi-bin/sleep2.cgi">
```

If you're using uncgi, you call it like this:

```
<FORM METHOD=POST ACTION=" http://www.myserver.com/cgi-bin/uncgi/sleep2.cgi">
```

> **NOTE**
>
> The uncgi program is an excellent example of how path information is used. The uncgi script uses the name of the actual script from the path information to know which script to call.

The uncgi program reads the form input from either the GET or POST input (it figures out which automatically), decodes it, and creates a set of variables with the same names as the values of each NAME attribute, with WWW_ prepended to them. So, for example, if your form contains a text field with the name theName, the uncgi variable containing the value for theName is WWW_theName.

If multiple name/pairs in the input have the same names, uncgi creates only one environment variable with the individual values separated by hash signs (#). For example, if the input contains the name/value pairs shopping=butter, shopping=milk, and shopping=beer, the resulting FORM_shopping environment variable contains butter#milk#beer. You must handle this information properly in your script.

cgi-lib.pl

The cgi-lib.pl package, written by Steve Brenner, is a set of routines for the Perl language to help you manage form input. It can take form input from GET or POST and put it in a Perl list or associative array. Newer versions can also handle file upload from forms. You can get information about (and the source for) cgi-lib.pl from http://www.bio.cam.ac.uk/cgi-lib/. If you decide to use the Perl language to handle your form input, cgi-lib.pl is a great library to have.

To use `cgi-lib.pl`, retrieve the source from the URL listed in the preceding paragraph, and put it in your Perl libraries directory (often `/usr/lib/perl`). Then in your Perl script itself, use the following line to include the subroutines from the library in your script:

```
require 'cgi-lib.pl';
```

Although `cgi-lib.pl` contains several subroutines for managing forms, the most important one is the `ReadParse` subroutine. `ReadParse` reads either GET or POST input and conveniently stores the name/value pairs as name/value pairs in a Perl associative array. In your Perl script, you usually call it as follows:

```
&ReadParse(*in);
```

In this example, the name of the array is `in`, but you can call it anything you want to.

Then, after the form input is decoded, you can read and process the name/value pairs by accessing the name part in your Perl script like this:

```
print $in{'theName'};
```

This particular example just prints out the value of the pair whose name is `theName`.

If multiple name/pairs have the same names, `cgi-lib.pl` separates the multiple values in the associative array with null characters (`\0`). You must handle this information properly in your script.

Decoding File Upload Input

Because form-based file upload is a newer feature requiring a different kind of form input, few programs will decode the input you get back from a form used to upload local files.

Recent versions of `cgi-lib.pl` handle file uploads very nicely, encoding them into associative arrays without the need to do anything extra to deal with them. See the home page for `cgi-lib.pl` at `http://www.bio.cam.ac.uk/cgi-lib/` for more information.

Another library for handling CGI data in Perl 5, `CGI.pl`, also deals with file uploads. See `http://valine.ncsa.uiuc.edu/cgi_docs.html` for details.

Decoding Form Input Yourself

Decoding form input is the sort of task that most people will want to leave up to a program such as the ones I've mentioned in this section. But, in case you don't have access to any of these programs, if you're using a system that these programs don't run on, or you feel you can write a better program, here's some information that will help you write your own.

The first thing your decoder program should check for is whether the form input was sent via the POST or GET method. Fortunately, this task is easy. The CGI environment variable REQUEST_METHOD, set by the server before your program is called, indicates the method and tells you how to proceed.

16

If the form input is sent to the server using the GET method, the form input will be contained in the QUERY_STRING environment variable.

If the form input is sent to the server using the POST method, the form input is sent to your script through the standard input. The CONTENT_LENGTH environment variable indicates the number of bytes that the browser submitted. In your decoder, you should make sure you read only the number of bytes contained in CONTENT_LENGTH and then stop. Some browsers might not conveniently terminate the standard input for you.

A typical decoder script performs the following steps:

1. Separate the individual name/value pairs (separated by &).

2. Separate the name from the value (separated by =).

   If you have multiple name keys with different values, you should have some method of preserving all those values.

3. Replace any plus signs with spaces.

4. Decode any hex characters (%NN) to their ASCII equivalents on your system.

Interested in decoding input from file uploads? The rules are entirely different. In particular, the input you'll get from file uploads conforms to MIME multipart messages, so you'll have to deal with lots of different kinds of data. If you're interested, you can find the specifications for file upload, which will explain more. See those specifications at ftp://ds.internic.net/rfc/rfc1867.txt.

Non-Parsed Headers Scripts

If you followed the basic rules outlined in this section for writing a CGI script, the output of your script (headers and data, if any) will be read by the server and sent back to the browser over the network. In most cases, this process will be fine because the server can then do any checking it needs to do and add its own headers to yours.

In some cases, however, you might want to bypass the server and send your output straight to the browser: for example, to speed up the amount of time it takes for your script output to get back to the browser, or to send data that the server might question back to the browser. For most forms and CGI scripts, however, you won't need a script to do this job.

CGI scripts that handle this procedure are called NPH (non-processed headers) scripts. If you do need an NPH script, you'll need to modify your script slightly:

☐ The script should have an nph- prefix—for example, nph-pinglaura or nph-fixdata.

☐ Your script must send extra HTTP headers instead of just the Content-type, Location, or Status headers.

The headers are the most obvious change you'll need to make to your script. In particular, the first header you output should be an HTTP/1.0 header with a status code, like this:

```
HTTP/1.0 200 OK
```

This header with the 200 status code means "everything's fine; the data is on its way." Another status code could be

```
HTTP/1.0 204 No Response
```

As you learned previously, this code means that no data is coming back from your script, so the browser should not do anything (such as try to load a new page).

A second header you should probably include is the Server header. There is some confusion over whether this header is required, but including it is probably a good idea. After all, by using an NPH script, you're trying to pretend you are a server, so including it can't hurt.

The Server header simply indicates the version of the server you're running, as in the following example:

```
Server: NCSA/1.3
Server: CERN/3.0pre6
```

After including these two headers, you must also include any of the other headers for your script, including Content-type or Location. The browser still needs this information so that it knows how to deal with the data you're sending it.

Again, most of the time you won't need NPH scripts; the normal CGI scripts should work just fine.

ISINDEX Scripts

To finish off the discussion on CGI, let me talk about ISINDEX searches. The use of the <ISINDEX> tag was the way browsers sent information (usually search keys) back to the server in the early days of the Web. ISINDEX searches are all but obsolete these days because of forms; forms are much more flexible both in layout and with different form elements, and also in the scripts you use to process them. Recognizing this, the HTML 4.0 has deprecated ISINDEX, recommending that INPUT be used instead. But because I'm a completist, I'll include a short description of how ISINDEX searches work here as well.

ISINDEX searches are CGI scripts that take arguments, just like the scripts you wrote earlier in this chapter to find out whether someone was logged in. The CGI script for an ISINDEX search operates in the following ways:

☐ If the script is called with no arguments, the HTML that is returned should prompt the readers for search keys. Use the <ISINDEX> tag to provide a way for the readers to enter these keys. (Remember, this was before forms were introduced.)

☐ When the readers submit the search keys, the ISINDEX script is called again with the search keys as the arguments. The ISINDEX script then operates on those arguments in some way, returning the appropriate HTML file.

The core of the ISINDEX searches is the <ISINDEX> tag. The <ISINDEX> tag is a special HTML tag used for these kinds of searches. <ISINDEX> doesn't enclose any text, nor does it have a closing tag.

So what does <ISINDEX> do? It "turns on" searching in the browser that is reading this document. Depending on the browser, this action may involve enabling a search button in the browser itself (see Figure 16.8). For newer browsers, it may involve including an input field on the page (see Figure 16.9). The readers can then enter strings to search for, and then press Enter or click on the button to submit the query to the server.

Figure 16.8.

A search prompt in the browser window.

Figure 16.9.

A search prompt on the page itself.

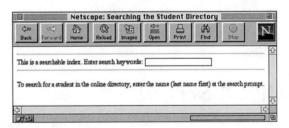

According to the HTML 2.0 specification, the <ISINDEX> tag should go inside the <HEAD> part of the HTML document. (It's one of the few tags that goes into <HEAD>, <TITLE> being the other obvious example.) In older browsers, where there was a single location for the search prompt, putting the tag here made sense because neither the search prompt nor the <ISINDEX> tag was actually part of the data of the document. However, because more recent browsers display the input field on the HTML page itself, being able to put <ISINDEX> in the body of the document is useful so that you can control where on the page the input field appears. (If it's in the <HEAD>, it'll always be the first thing on the page.) Most browsers will now accept an <ISINDEX> tag anywhere in the body of an HTML document and will draw the input box wherever that tag appears.

Finally, an HTML extension to the `<ISINDEX>` tag, introduced in HTML 3.2, allows you to define the search prompt. Again, in older browsers, the search prompt was fixed. (It was usually something confusing like "This is a Searchable index. Enter keywords.") The PROMPT attribute to `<ISINDEX>` allows you to define the string that will be used to indicate the input field, as in this example:

```
<P> To search for a student in the online directory,
enter the name (last name first):
<ISINDEX PROMPT="Student's name:   ">
```

Figure 16.10 shows the result of using this tag in Netscape.

Figure 16.10.

A Netscape search prompt.

`<ISINDEX>` is useful only in the context of an ISINDEX search. Although you can put it into any HTML document, it won't do anything unless a CGI script generated the HTML page to begin with.

Most of the time, creating HTML forms is a far easier way of prompting users for information.

Summary

CGI scripts, sometimes called server-side scripts or gateway scripts, make it possible for programs to be run on the server, and HTML or other files to be generated on the fly.

In this chapter, you reviewed all the basics of creating CGI scripts: both simple scripts and scripts to process forms, including the special headers you use in your scripts; the difference between GET and POST in form input; and how to decode the information you get from the form input. Plus you learned some extras about path information, URL encoding, ISINDEX searches, and the various CGI variables you can use in your CGI scripts. From here, you should be able to write CGI scripts to accomplish just about anything.

Q&A

Q What if I don't know how to program? Can I still use CGI scripts?

A If you have access to a Web server through a commercial provider, you might be able to get help from the provider with your CGI scripts (for a fee, of course). Also, if you know even a little programming, but you're unsure of what you're doing, you can find many examples available for the platform and server you're working with. Usually, these examples are either part of the server distribution or at the same FTP location. See the documentation that came with your server; it often has pointers to further help. In fact, for the operation you want to accomplish, there may already be a script you can use with only slight modification. But be careful; if you don't know what you're doing, you can rapidly get in over your head.

Q My Web server has a `cgi-bin` directory, but I don't have access to it. So I created my own `cgi-bin` directory and put my script there, but calling it from my Web pages didn't work. What did I do wrong?

A Web servers must be specially configured to run CGI scripts, and usually that means indicating specific directories or files that are meant to be scripts. You cannot just create a directory or a file with a special extension without knowing how your Webmaster has set up your server. Most of the time, you'll guess wrong, and your scripts will not work. Ask your Webmaster for help with installing your scripts.

Q My Webmaster tells me I can just create a `cgi-bin` directory in my home directory, install my scripts there, and then call them using a special URL called `cgiwrap`. You haven't mentioned this way of having personal `cgi-bin` directories.

A `cgiwrap` is a neat program that provides a secure wrapper for CGI scripts and allows users of public UNIX systems to have their own personal CGI directories. However, your Webmaster has to set up and configure `cgiwrap` specifically for your server before you can use it. If your Webmaster has allowed the use of `cgiwrap`, congratulations! CGI scripts will be easy for you to install and use. If you are a Webmaster and you're interested in finding out more information, check out `http://wwwcgi.umr.edu/~cgiwrap/`.

Q My scripts aren't working!

A Did you look in the section on troubleshooting for the errors you're getting and the possible solutions? In that section, I covered most of the common problems you might be having.

Q My Web provider won't give me access to `cgi-bin` at all. No way, no how. I really want to use forms. Is there any way at all I can do this?

A There is one way; it's called a Mailto form. With Mailto forms, you use a Mailto URL with your e-mail address in the ACTION part of the form, like this:

```
<FORM METHOD=POST ACTION="mailto:lemay@lne.com"> ... </FORM>
```

Then, when the form is submitted by your readers, the contents of the form will be sent to you via e-mail (or at least they will if you include your e-mail address instead of mine in the `mailto`). No server scripts are required to use this method.

This solution does pose a few major problems, however. The first is that the e-mail you get will have all the form input in encoded form. Sometimes you may be able to read it anyhow, but it's messy. To get around URL encoding, you can use special programs created just for Mailto forms; they will decode the input for you. Check out `http://homepage.interaccess.com/~arachnid/mtfinfo.html` for more information.

The second problem with Mailto forms is that they don't give any indication that the form input has been sent. There's no page to send back saying "Thank you. I got your form input." Your readers will just click Submit, and nothing will appear to happen. Because your readers get no feedback, they may very well submit the same information to you repeatedly. Including a warning to your readers on the page itself might be useful, to let them know that they won't get any feedback.

The third problem with Mailto forms is that they are not supported by all browsers, so your forms may not work for everyone who reads your page. Most of the major commercial browsers do support Mailto forms, however.

Q I'm writing a decoder program for form input. The last `name=value` pair in my list keeps getting all this garbage stuck to the end of it.

A Are you reading only the number of bytes indicated by the CONTENT_LENGTH environment variable? You should test for that value and stop reading when you reach the end, or you might end up reading too far. Not all browsers will terminate the standard input for you.

16

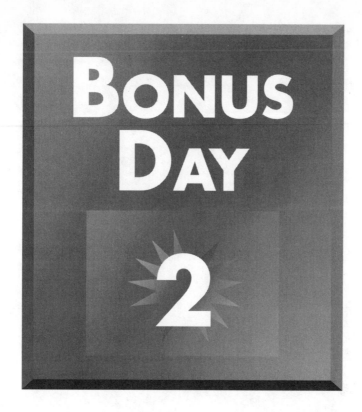

Cascading Style Sheets and Dynamic HTML

Chapter **17**

Making It All Dynamic

With the release of Netscape Communicator (which includes Navigator 4) and Microsoft Internet Explorer 4, both companies have introduced a set of extensions and new features that they have decided to call *Dynamic HTML*.

Dynamic HTML is something of a misnomer. It is not a single entity as is HTML 3.2, and it is not even a simple set of extensions to HTML. Instead, Dynamic HTML is a set of technologies ranging from HTML extensions to programming features designed to allow page authors to create more interactive pages that respond to the user's actions. In addition, Dynamic HTML is designed to enhance the designer's ability to control the appearance of the final document on the user's browser.

All these technologies could prove to be beneficial in producing technologically cutting-edge Web sites. However, there is a little hill to overcome: Netscape and Microsoft have different notions of what exactly Dynamic HTML is. While there are similarities, the two companies have independently created their own definitions of Dynamic HTML.

In this chapter we will take a look at Dynamic HTML, including the following topics:

☐ A review of the major features of both flavors of Dynamic HTML

☐ A look at common features in both browsers

☐ Positioning page elements in both browsers

☐ Using Dynamic Fonts in Netscape

Just What Is Dynamic HTML?

At its core, Dynamic HTML goes against the grain of HTML, which, as has been pointed out throughout the book, is a standard designed to be fully platform independent by being design independent. The reality is, though, that the Web has moved to the point where design can be as important or more important than platform independence—Dynamic HTML simply acknowledges this fact.

Without addressing the very question of whether Web pages should be created with visual appearance in mind, Dynamic HTML—in both its varieties—greatly enhances a Web author's ability to do so. (See Figure 17.1.)

Figure 17.1.

Dynamic HTML enhances authors' ability to design their pages.

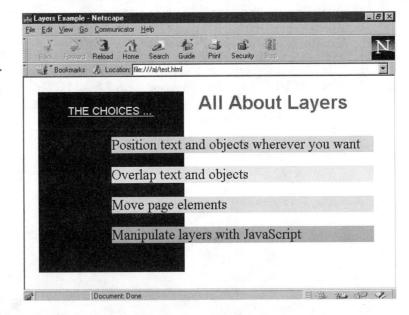

Unfortunately, Dynamic HTML seems like it may be more divisive than any major browser-specific extension to Web technology in the past. Both Microsoft and Netscape are highlighting their creations as they promote the upcoming releases of their new browsers, and in the process Web designers may be faced with tough decisions about whether or not to adopt any of these new features.

In order to make informed decisions, you need to have at least an awareness of the common, distinct features of the two company's implementations of Dynamic HTML.

Style Sheets: The Common Core of Dynamic HTML

Although many pieces of HTML differ between the two browsers, certain components are common to both. This is the best place to start our discussion of Dynamic HTML. So, just what do these two have in common? There are two main things:

☐ Cascading style sheets
☐ Finer control over the positioning of objects and the layout of pages

Cascading Style Sheets

If you followed the media frenzy surrounding the development of Netscape Communicator and Microsoft Internet Explorer 4, then you've probably heard references to style sheets and are asking yourself just what they are all about?

Well, the concept is simple, really.

Consider your word processor. Whether you write documents with Word, WordPerfect, or Lotus's WordPro, you have probably encountered style sheets of some sort. Style sheets allow you to define the default appearance of different parts of your document, and that is exactly the goal of cascading style sheets. With cascading style sheets, you can control the color and style of fonts, adjust white space, and so on.

Cascading style sheets are a standard defined by the World Wide Web Consortium (W3C), so you can expect to see them in more browsers than just Netscape's and Microsoft's offerings. We will be looking at cascading style sheets in detail in Chapter 18, "Stylizing Your Pages."

Object Positioning and Layout Controls

One of the central notions in Dynamic HTML is that authors have more control over the layout of their documents and can finely position objects on the page.

Both Netscape and Microsoft are committed to this notion and share some common approaches to this, including proposed extensions to cascading style sheets for positioning objects. Still, there are distinct differences between the two browsers: each have their unique ways to control object positioning.

We will look at object positioning—in both Netscape Communicator and Microsoft Internet Explorer—later in this chapter in the section titled "Positioning Objects."

17

The Way Microsoft Sees Things

Microsoft's approach to Dynamic HTML includes several unique features:

☐ Document Object Model

☐ Database features

☐ Multimedia controls

Let's look at each of these in turn.

The Document Object Model

The Document Object Model is at the core of Microsoft's approach to Dynamic HTML.

This object model provides the mechanisms by which you can script pages, make programming changes to styles and attributes of elements in the page, replace elements, and react to user events. Essentially, this is Internet Explorer 3's scripting environment on steroids. In Internet Explorer 3, Jscript and VBScript—the two scripting languages that shipped with the browser—could be used to script reactions to a limited set of user actions and could only dynamically change and update a limited number of page elements and a limited number of attributes of these elements.

The Document Object Model, though, allows programmers to work with all the objects in a Web page instead of only certain objects. Any scripting language supported by Internet Explorer 4, including Jscript and VBScript, can be used to create these scripts and programs.

The Document Object Model requires some programming skill and knowledge of either Jscript or VBScript; therefore, it is beyond the scope of this book. However, it is important to be aware that the model goes beyond any found in previous browsers that supported scripting, including Netscape 3 and Internet Explorer 3. It even goes beyond what Netscape has implemented in Netscape Communicator.

Database Features

In our discussion of CGI scripting in Chapter 16, "Beginning CGI Scripting," you learned that it was possible to integrate Web pages with up-to-date information out of a database system. This can be used to create online catalogs, reservation systems, or information repositories—basically anything that depends on up-to-date, organized information.

With this built-in data support, Microsoft expects that designers will be able to create pages that organize data on the fly, on the client system. This would effectively minimize network traffic and server requests because Internet Explorer's built-in database engine can do the job of sorting and organizing data once it is received from a server.

17

Internet Explorer includes a number of multimedia controls. These are essentially ActiveX controls that can be embedded in pages to provide animated images, stylized type, audio mixing, transition effects, and the movement of page elements or objects in a two-dimensional plane.

There are numerous Multimedia controls available with Internet Explorer 4.0:

- **Behaviors**: Provides special behaviors for controls and other page elements
- **Effects**: Applies a graphics filter to any item on a page
- **Hot Spot**: Makes regions of the screen clickable
- **Mixer**: Mixes multiple WAV audio files
- **Path**: Moves objects on a path
- **Sequencer**: Controls timing of events
- **Sprite**: Creates animations
- **Sprite Buttons**: Creates animated buttons
- **Structured Graphics**: Provides graphics that can be scaled and rotated

Object Positioning

This topic is pretty much self-explanatory. Dynamic HTML provides you with fine control over the exact placement of elements on a page; you have the ability to control which elements sit on top of, and possible obscure, other elements. Combined with scripting, this can provide a flexible way to move elements around on the page and to adjust the page as a user interacts with it.

Netscape Goes Its Own Way

Just as Microsoft has its own way of doing much of Dynamic HTML, so does Netscape. Here are the key features unique to Netscape:

- Layers
- JavaScript Style Sheets
- Dynamic Fonts

Layers

In Netscape Communicator, the layer feature provides a mechanism for finely controlling the positioning of objects. You can define overlapping layers of both transparent and opaque content, and using JavaScript you can move layers, hide them, and change their relationship with each other.

Figure 17.2 shows an example of the use of Netscape's layer feature with HTML text overlapping an inline image.

Figure 17.2.
HTML text placed over the "Juxta Publishing" logo.

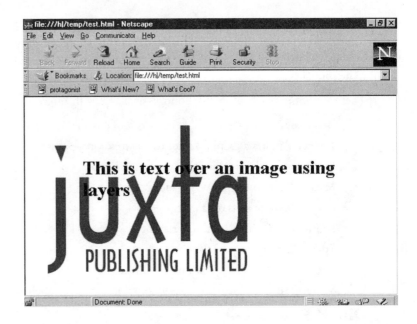

The details of using layers is discussed later in this chapter in the section titled "Positioning Objects."

JavaScript Style Sheets

Where Microsoft and Netscape both support cascading style sheets, Netscape adds an alternative: JavaScript Style Sheets. With JavaScript Style Sheets, each property in the style sheet is reflected in JavaScript. Thus, you can use JavaScript to define and manipulate properties of the style sheet just as the Document Object Model in Microsoft Internet Explorer allows you to use scripts to manipulate the properties of objects in a page.

JavaScript Style Sheets can define specific styles for any HTML element and can adjust page layout, including margins and fonts. We will look at JavaScript Style Sheets in the next chapter, "Stylizing Your Pages."

Positioning Objects

Now that you have a sense of what Dynamic HTML is all about, and some of the inconsistencies between Netscape and Microsoft in their approaches, let's take a look at one of the core capabilities of Dynamic HTML in both browsers: precise positioning of objects in the page.

With Communicator, Netscape has introduced the layers technology using its own set of HTML extensions tags. Microsoft, on the other hand, has opted to implement a proposed W3C extension to cascading style sheets to provide positioning capabilities.

Consider the example of the use of layers as shown in Figure 17.2: Using Netscape's layers technology means that the positioning is not applied in Internet Explorer, as shown in Figure 17.3.

Figure 17.3.

Using Netscape's layers technology means Internet Explorer 4 cannot position the affected elements.

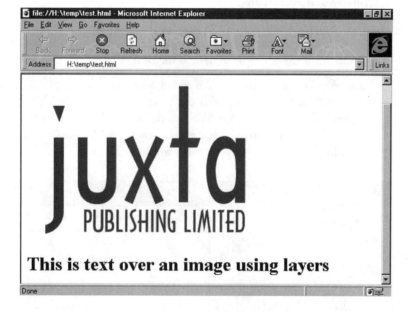

On the other hand, if you position using the extensions to cascading style sheets implemented by Microsoft, the positioning will work in Communicator, which also supports the extensions. Given this, it would seem unnecessary to ever use the Netscape layers system. However, the layers technology is easier to learn if you have never used style sheets, and it integrates well with Communicator's JavaScript environment. If you only have Netscape users viewing your pages, as might be the case with an intranet, you might consider using layers instead of cascading style sheets to position objects.

All this means that if you want to use these new positioning features, you need a firm understanding of both approaches so that you can consider the best ways to position elements for your needs. We'll start by looking at the Netscape approach, and then consider how Microsoft does things.

Netscape's Layers

Netscape has created three new tags that provide what is needed to create layers and position elements: <LAYER>, <ILAYER>, and <NOLAYER>.

Let's start by looking at the general concept behind layers. Layers exist in a parent-child relationship. That is, one layer can act as a container for another layer. When you create a document with the <BODY> tag, that effectively creates a container in which layers can be placed and manipulated.

When layers are created, they can be positioned based on the parent layer containing them or relative to the entire document window. Creating a layer in a document with no other layers treats the entire document as the container <LAYER>.

By way of example, Figure 17.4 shows how layers can be placed within each other in this parent-child relationship, with the parent containing the child. In this case, Layer B is contained within Layer A, which is contained within the document. Layer B's positioning can be specified relative to Layer A or relative to the document window. Layer A can be positioned relative to the document window.

Figure 17.4.

An example of layers containing other layers.

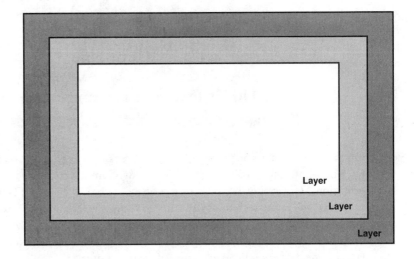

There are two types of layers available in Netscape: explicitly positioned layers and inline layers.

Explicitly positioned layers are created with the <LAYER> tag. With no attributes, the <LAYER> tag creates a layer that is positioned at the top-left corner of the container layer with the same width and height as the containing layer. The containing layer is transparent; that is, it has no background color or image, so the layer below shows through instead of a background.

Of course, creating a layer like the one just described would rarely be useful. Generally, you'll want to at least specify the position of the top-left corner of a layer. This is done using the LEFT and TOP attributes, which specify how many pixels away from the top-left corner of the containing layer a new layer should start.

Consider this example:

```
<HTML>
<HEAD>
<TITLE>Layer Example 1</TITLE>
</HEAD>
<BODY>
<IMG SRC="logo.gif">
<LAYER TOP=25 LEFT=25><H1>This text is in a layer positioned
25 pixels down and 25 pixels to the right of the main
document window's top-left corner.</H1></LAYER>
</BODY>
</HTML>
```

The results are displayed in Figure 17.5.

Figure 17.5.

A layer 100 pixels to the right and down from the document window's origin.

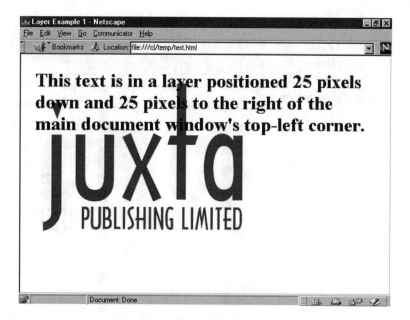

There are two things to notice in this example: First, the <LAYER> tag is closed with a </LAYER> tag. This is important to do in order to specify what portion of the document is to be displayed in the layer. If you didn't do this, the browser wouldn't know what you wanted in the layer and would incorrectly display the page. For instance, if you wanted to place a second logo immediately following the first and you added it after the layer definition, you would get something like this:

```
<HTML>
<HEAD>
<TITLE>Layer Example 1</TITLE>
</HEAD>
<BODY>
<IMG SRC="logo.gif">
<LAYER TOP=25 LEFT=25><H1>This text is in a layer positioned
25 pixels down and 25 pixels to the right of the main
document window's top-left corner.</H1></LAYER>
<IMG SRC="logo.gif">
</BODY>
</HTML>
```

As you can see in Figure 17.6, the first logo immediately precedes the second, and the placement of the logos is independent of the layer definition. But, if you leave out the closing </LAYER> tag, then the first image doesn't even get displayed, as shown in Figure 17.7. Basically, Navigator gets confused if you don't close the <LAYER> tag, so remember to always close it.

Figure 17.6.

The </LAYER> *tag is used to specify which content is displayed in a given layer.*

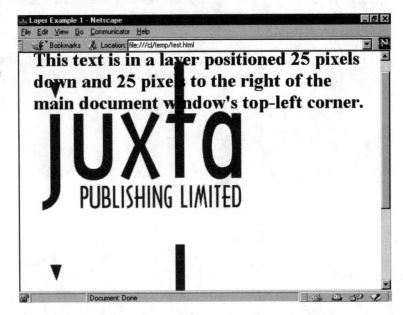

Figure 17.7.
Without the
</LAYER> tag, the
browser doesn't know
when the layer ends.

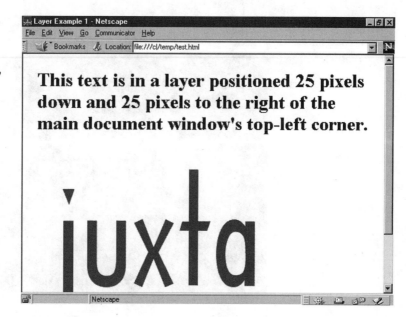

In addition to the </LAYER> tag in the example, it is important to notice that the layer has taken the default background appearance (transparent); therefore, the image shows through the layer wherever there are no elements displayed in the layer.

However, there will inevitably be cases where you want to be able to specify a background color or background graphic for a layer. This is done by using the BGCOLOR or BACKGROUND attributes of the <LAYER> tag. These attributes work in the same way as they do in the <BODY> tag.

For example, the following code creates a welcome page using a layer with a background graphic:

```
<HTML>
<HEAD>
<TITLE>Welcome to Landegg Academy</TITLE>
</HEAD>
<BODY BGCOLOR="black">
<LAYER TOP=100 LEFT=100 BACKGROUND="landegg.gif">
<DIV ALIGN=CENTER><FONT COLOR=black FONT="Arial" SIZE=7><STRONG>
Welcome to Landegg Academy on the World Wide Web
</STRONG></FONT></DIV>
</LAYER>
</BODY>
</HTML>
```

This produces results similar to Figure 17.8.

Figure 17.8.

Using a background image in a layer.

Notice, however, in the example that the layer doesn't produce the most attractive results. That's because, by default, the layer is free to stretch from the specified left and top position to the right side of the containing layer based on the layout of the content of the layer. The layer will be deep enough to contain the content of the layer. The design would be much nicer if the layer wasn't quite as wide, and if it left more black background from the document window showing at the right.

You can achieve this result using the WIDTH attribute. You can assign a number of pixels or a percentage value to the WIDTH attribute to fix the width of the layer. For instance, setting a value of 65% to the WIDTH attribute in the previous example produces results like those shown in Figure 17.9.

The HEIGHT attribute is similar to the WIDTH attribute, except that the default behavior is different. When you omit the WIDTH attribute, the default is to make the layer as wide as possible. Leaving out the HEIGHT attribute is different: the layer will be only as tall as is needed to display the content of the layer.

Figure 17.9.

Using the WIDTH *attribute to control the width of a layer.*

 NOTE

The WIDTH attribute doesn't work all of the time. If you specify a width for a layer that is narrower than a fixed-width element displayed in the layer (such as an image), then the layer's width will be expanded to fit the width of the element (unless, of course, that makes the layer wider than the containing layer, in which case it will be the maximum width possible). You need to keep this in mind when designing your layers. For instance, if you define a layer as 80% of the document window's width and then the user has a very narrow window open, the width of the layer may end up being larger than 80% of the window's width in order to adjust for the width of the layer's content.

There is one more attribute that helps you control the appearance of the layer and the content displayed in the layer. Consider the final result shown in Figure 17.9. The layer looks much better than it did at first, but there is still a small issue: the text is mighty close to the margins. It would look better if you could control the amount of space between the content of the frame and the edge of the frame—in other words, you want to be able to adjust any of the four margins of the frame.

This is done by using the CLIP attribute. CLIP may sound like a strange name for the attribute, but its name comes from the concept of clipping a rectangle—that is, the visible area of the layer. Unlike the WIDTH and HEIGHT or LEFT and TOP attributes, CLIP takes a set of four numbers, separated by commas, as a value. The values specify, in order, the space left over on the left, top, right and bottom of the layer. The left and right values actually indicate the respective edges of the visible rectangle as measured from the left of the frame, whereas top and bottom values are indicated relative to the top of the frame.

For instance, CLIP=10,10,100,100 would create a rectangle that is 10 pixels in from the left and top of the layer and has a right and bottom edge 100 pixels from the left and top edge of the layer. Figure 17.10 shows how this works. Similarly, CLIP=0,0,100,100 would leave no space at the left or top but would have the same right and bottom margins as the previous example (see Figure 17.11.)

Figure 17.10.

The visible rectangle for a frame is specified relative to the top and left sides of the layer.

If you want to leave no space on the top and left sides, there is a short form of the CLIP attribute that takes only two values for the right and bottom sides. Thus, CLIP=0,0,100,100 is the same as CLIP=100,100 and would match the diagram in Figure 17.11.

17

Figure 17.11.
No space is left at the top or left sides.

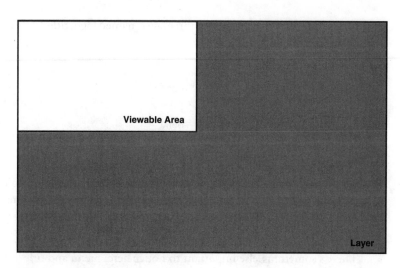

17

Naming Layers

As with frames and windows, you can name layers using either the NAME attribute or, in this case, the ID attribute (both are the same). By giving a name to a layer, you are making it possible to refer to a given layer in a JavaScript script as well as to refer to it in HTML—as you'll see in the next section when we discuss Z-orders. For instance, `<LAYER NAME="testlayer">` creates a layer named "testlayer."

Using Z-Orders

So far, you've seen how to create layers that overlap each other and are precisely placed relative to each other or absolutely relative to the top of the page.

However, there is more power to the layers feature. This comes from using the Z-order. *Z-order* refers to the order in which layers are stacked. By default, new layers appear on top of all existing layers. However, this behavior changes when you specify a Z-index, or the layer's position in the existing Z-order.

This can be done using one of three attributes: Z-INDEX, ABOVE, or BELOW.

ABOVE and BELOW function in a similar way. If you use the attribute ABOVE=somelayer, the new layer is placed immediately below the layer named somelayer—that is, somelayer is *above* the new layer. BELOW works in a similar way: BELOW=otherlayer says that the new layer goes immediately above otherlayer since otherlayer is *below* the new layer.

For example, if you have created three layers named logo, title, and menu, you can place them in the document as follows:

```
<LAYER NAME="logo">
    Some HTML
    <LAYER NAME="menu" BELOW="logo">
        Some HTML
    </LAYER>
    <LAYER NAME="title" ABOVE="menu">
        Some HTML
    </LAYER>
</LAYER>
```

This would create three layers with logo at the bottom, title in the middle, and menu on top: that's because logo is immediately below menu when menu is defined, and then we indicate menu should be immediately above title, pushing title in between the two previously defined layers.

There's something else important to notice here: menu and title are both defined inside of logo's <LAYER> and </LAYER> tags. What this does is indicate that logo is the container layer for both menu and title; in other words, what we have here are nested layers. Menu and title are nested inside of logo. In this way, if you specify placement of menu or title, it would be relative to logo in both cases.

The ABOVE and BELOW attributes are fairly simple, but this simplicity limits their usefulness. If you have numerous layers, it can be cumbersome to keep track of what layer sits where in the stack if you rely on ABOVE and BELOW.

This can be addressed by controlling the Z-order using the Z-INDEX attribute of the LAYER tag. With this attribute, you can specify the order of layers with integers. The higher the integer, the higher up in the pile the layer is, sitting on top of layers with lower numbers. Using negative numbers causes layers to be positioned below the container layer.

NOTE In Preview Release 3 of Netscape Communicator (available at press time), negative Z-INDEX values were not supported. They should be supported by the time the final release of Netscape Communicator is available.

Using Z-INDEX, you can re-create the earlier template of three nested layers:

```
<LAYER NAME="logo" Z-INDEX=1>
    Some HTML
    <LAYER NAME="menu" BELOW="logo" Z-INDEX=3>
        Some HTML
    </LAYER>
    <LAYER NAME="title" ABOVE="menu" Z-INDEX=2>
```

```
    Some HTML
  </LAYER>
</LAYER>
```

Obviously, it is easier to see which layer sits where by quickly glancing at the numerical Z-INDEX values. On the other hand, the ABOVE and BELOW example required careful attention to the layer names in order to realize what was happening.

Let's flesh out this template a bit to see exactly how the Z-order works. Let's start by adding colors, position attributes, and widths to the layers:

```
<LAYER NAME="logo" Z-INDEX=1 BGCOLOR=blue>
  LOGO LAYER
  <LAYER NAME="menu" Z-INDEX=3 TOP=100 BGCOLOR=cyan WIDTH=90%>
    MENU LAYER
  </LAYER>
  <LAYER NAME="title" Z-INDEX=2 TOP=50 BGCOLOR=red HEIGHT=150 WIDTH=80%>
    TITLE LAYER
  </LAYER>
</LAYER>
```

This produces results like those shown in Figure 17.12.

Figure 17.12.

Using the Z-order, you can control which layer is on top of which layer.

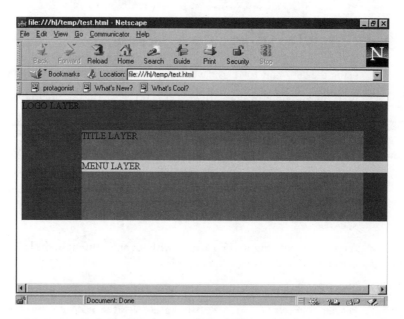

To get a better sense of how Z-order works, let's change the Z-INDEX value of the title layer to 4. What does this do? As you can see in Figure 17.13, the result is that the title layer now obscures the menu layer, except for the small rectangle hanging out at the right. The reason is that by changing the Z-INDEX of the title from 2 to 4, we move it above the menu, which has a Z-INDEX of 3.

Figure 17.13.
*What happens if you
change Z-indexes.*

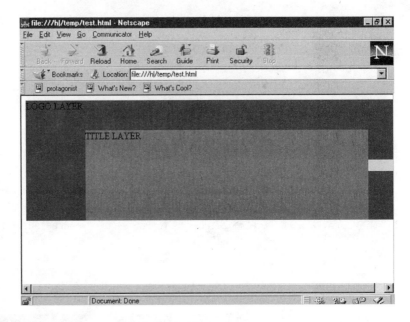

Absolute Positioning of Layers

So far, all the examples of layers that we have seen involve relative positioning of the layers using the LEFT and TOP tags: layers are positioned relative to their container or parent layer.

Netscape provides an alternative to LEFT and TOP in the form of the PAGEX and PAGEY attributes, which are used to specify the origin (or top-left corner) of the layer relative to the document window instead of the immediate parent layer. Of course, if the immediate parent layer of a layer is the document window, then PAGEX is the same as LEFT and PAGEY is the same as TOP.

Let's take a look at a small example of the difference between relative and absolute positioning. We'll start with a layer contained in the document window:

```
<LAYER TOP=100 LEFT=100 WIDTH=100 HEIGHT=100 BGCOLOR="black">
</LAYER>
```

As you can see in Figure 17.14, even without any content in the layer, this creates a page with a 100 by 100 pixel black square in it.

The following is a layer inside the layer with relative positioning:

```
<LAYER TOP=100 LEFT=100 WIDTH=100 HEIGHT=100 BGCOLOR="black">
   <LAYER TOP=20 LEFT=20 WIDTH=60 HEIGHT=60 BGCOLOR="cyan">
   </LAYER>
</LAYER>
```

As expected, this centers a layer with a cyan background in the middle of the first layer, as shown in Figure 17.15.

Figure 17.14.
Start with a layer.

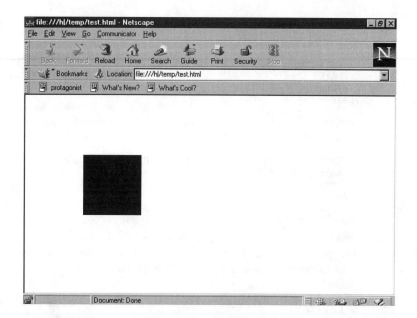

Figure 17.15.
A relatively positioned layer in another layer.

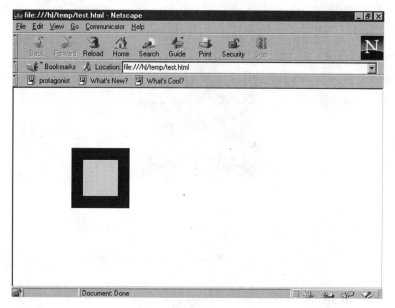

You could create the same result by replacing TOP and LEFT with the appropriate PAGEY and PAGEX values:

```
<LAYER TOP=100 LEFT=100 WIDTH=100 HEIGHT=100 BGCOLOR="black">
   <LAYER PAGEX=120 PAGEY=120 WIDTH=60 HEIGHT=60 BGCOLOR="cyan">
   </LAYER>
</LAYER>
```

However, what would happen if you change the value of PAGEX and PAGEY to place the cyan square outside the boundaries of the parent layer?

```
<LAYER TOP=100 LEFT=100 WIDTH=100 HEIGHT=100 BGCOLOR="black">
   <LAYER PAGEX=0 PAGEY=0 WIDTH=60 HEIGHT=60 BGCOLOR="cyan">
   </LAYER>
</LAYER>
```

As you'll notice in Figure 17.16, even though the second layer is nested in the first, by using PAGEX and PAGEY, it is no longer contained within the physical boundaries of the parent layer. But, the cyan layer needs to be displayed within the parent layer, so the parent layer extends to the left and top far enough to include the child layer.

Figure 17.16.

Positioning a layer with PAGEX and PAGEY outside the parent layer.

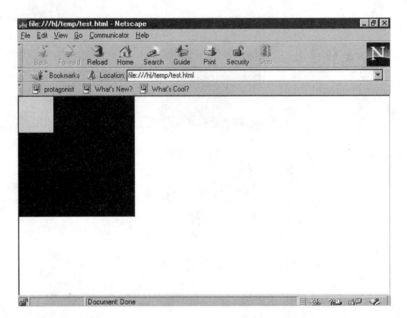

Similarly, if you adjust the child layer to be far to the right and bottom of the parent layer's boundary (for instance, PAGEX=250 and PAGEY=250), you get a result similar to Figure 17.17.

17

Figure 17.17.

Position a layer to the right and bottom of its parent.

Using External Source Files with Layers

In all the examples so far, we have used content specified in one file to create layers. However, layers can also contain content from external files using the SRC attribute of the layer tag.

Let's take a look at a simple example. We will create a page to display a daily special for an online towel store (I doubt there is one, but it sounds odd enough to try).

The page displays the daily special in a layer that obtains its content from an external HTML file called daily.html. In this way, you can edit daily.html each day without having to work with the whole file—this makes managing things a little easier.

The main document might look something like this:

```
<HTML>
<HEAD>
<TITLE>
Towels On-line
</TITLE>
</HEAD>
<BODY>
<H1 ALIGN=CENTER>TOWELS ON-LINE</H1>
<HR>
<LAYER TOP=150 SRC="daily.html">
</LAYER>
</BODY>
</HTML>
```

Next, the `daily.html` file needs to be created:

```
<H2>Today's Special:</H2>
<H3>Red Towels</H3>
All red towels are 25% -- today only. Order now!
```

When put all together, the results look something like Figure 17.18.

Figure 17.18.

Using the SRC *attribute.*

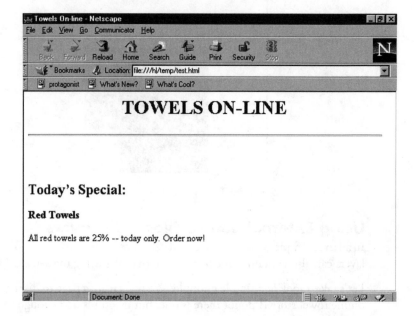

Notice that the `<LAYER>` tag is closed with `</LAYER>` even though there is no content in between the tags. This is still necessary. There are two reasons: If you want to specify any content after the layer, the browser needs to know where the layer ends, and layers can combine content from the SRC file with content coded directly in between the `<LAYER>` and `</LAYER>` tags.

When you do this, the content of the SRC file will be displayed before the content between the tags. Let's add a horizontal line below the content of `daily.html` using this technique:

```
<HTML>
<HEAD>
<TITLE>
Towels On-line
</TITLE>
</HEAD>
<BODY>
<H1 ALIGN=CENTER>TOWELS ON-LINE</H1>
<HR>
<LAYER TOP=150 SRC="daily.html">
```

17

```
<HR>
</LAYER>
</BODY>
</HTML>
```

Hiding and Showing Layers

One final attribute of the <LAYER> tag allows you to control the visibility of a given layer. The VISIBILITY attribute takes one of three possible values: SHOW, HIDE, or INHERIT.

SHOW and HIDE are pretty obvious: SHOW means the layer is displayed, HIDE means the layer is hidden. INHERIT, on the other hand, is not as obvious. What INHERIT does is indicate that the layer should inherit its visibility status from its parent container layer.

While it may not seem useful to be able to make a layer invisible with the HIDE attribute or to inherit visibility from the parent layer, these will become extremely useful when we look at scripting layers later in this chapter in the section titled "Manipulating Layers with JavaScript."

Inline Layers

Having looked at explicitly positioned layers using the <LAYER> tag, we need to take a look at inline layers and how they differ from explicitly positioned layers.

Inline layers are positioned relative to the current flow of the document where they appear. They are created using the <ILAYER> tag. For instance,

```
An in-line layer starts <ILAYER>here</ILAYER>
```

creates an inline layer that appears on the current line of text after the word *starts*. Notice that <ILAYER> takes a closing </ILAYER> tag, just as <LAYER> needs to be closed by the </LAYER> tag.

In many ways, using <ILAYER> and <LAYER> is very similar. They take exactly the same attributes, including NAME, TOP, LEFT, WIDTH, and HEIGHT. However, in the case of inline layers, TOP and LEFT specify position relative to the current position in the flow of the document.

This means that <ILAYER> can be used for several formatting purposes that previously had to be achieved through difficult workarounds.

Take the case where you want to indent the left side of a paragraph by 15 pixels. You could use

```
<DIV ALIGN=LEFT>
<P>This paragraph is not indented at all.</P>
<P><ILAYER LEFT=15>The first word is indented by 15 pixels
in this example which produces results like what you see here.
</ILAYER></P>
</DIV>
```

to produce the results shown in Figure 17.19.

Figure 17.19.

Using <ILAYER> to indent the left side of a paragraph.

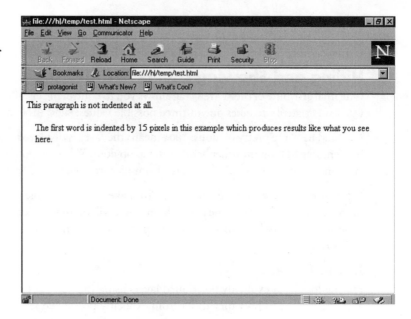

Similarly, the source code

```
See how we can move a <ILAYER TOP=5>word</ILAYER> five pixels down.
```

produces the results shown in Figure 17.20.

Figure 17.20.

<ILAYER> can be used to change the baseline of text.

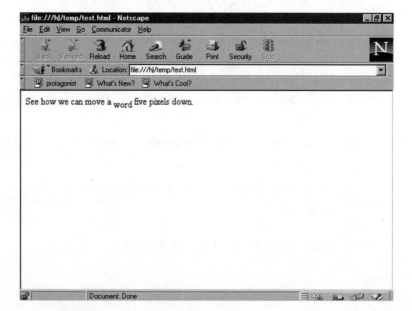

17

Dealing with Other Browsers

Before moving on to look at how to manipulate layers with JavaScript, let's consider how to cater to browsers that don't support Netscape's layers technology. If your layers document doesn't make use of any scripts, then the contents of your layers documents will load into other browsers because <LAYER> and <ILAYER>, which define the layers, will simply be ignored.

However, there are cases where this won't work: when you include a JavaScript script that depends on layers functionality and try to load it into a JavaScript-enabled browser without layers support, or when ignoring the <LAYER> or <ILAYER> tags will produce layouts that don't work for the content being presented. In these cases you need a way to provide alternative content for Netscape and other browsers, just as we did for frames using the <NOFRAMES> tag.

That's where the <NOLAYER> tag comes in. Any content between <NOLAYER> and </NOLAYER> will be ignored in Netscape Communicator or other future browsers that support layers. For example,

```
Layers Content
<NOLAYER>
    Non-Layer Content
</NOLAYER>
```

will display *Non-Layer Content* only on browsers that don't know how to handle layers. The problem here is that *Layers Content* will also be displayed by those browsers, minus the actual layers layout. Therefore, you need a way to hide the layers content from other browsers in a way that will allow Netscape, and other layers-capable browsers in the future, to display the layer's content.

Netscape's solution to the problem is conditional comments. Conditional comments allow you to provide a condition that indicates if the content of the comment should be evaluated as regular HTML by the browser. The structure of a conditional comment looks like this:

```
<--&{"&"};{test expression};
    Layers Content
-->
```

As you can see, the comment is opened with <-- and closed with -->, so they look like regular comments to non-layers browsers. The {*test expression*} portion is the key to making Netscape display the layer content.

So, what do you use for the test expression? The test expression really needs to be a JavaScript expression, and it needs to be one to see if the browser supports layers or not. Netscape suggests testing for the existence of the document.layers object because this will only exist in layers-capable browsers. Therefore, you want to test the expression `typeof document.layers == "object"`. This means that the final structure of a document for both layers and non-layers browser should be this:

```
<--&{"&"};{typeof document.layers == "object"};
   Layers Content
-->
<NOLAYER>
   Non-Layers Content
</NOLAYER>
```

> **NOTE**   Conditional comments are not supported in Preview Release 4 of Netscape Communicator. That's why there are no concrete examples in this section. Conditional Comments should be supported in the final release of Communicator.

Positioning Objects in Microsoft Internet Explorer

Learning how layers work in Netscape was a pretty exhausting session. The only difficulty with layers is that Netscape's main rival, Microsoft, doesn't support layers in the latest version of its browser, Internet Explorer 4.

Nonetheless, there are ways to position objects in Internet Explorer 4 in ways quite similar to the layers technology from Netscape. This is done with a proposed extension to the Cascading Style Sheet standard. This extension is supported by both Netscape and Microsoft and, in some ways, is an extension of the layers functionality.

> **NOTE**   The preview releases of both Netscape Communicator and Internet Explorer 4, available at press time, inconsistently and incompletely support these extensions. In fact, at times, Netscape seems to support some features better even though it is Microsoft who has been most vocal about supporting this technology.
>
> For this reason, many examples in this section are simple or may not work as expected. Patience is needed. When the final releases are out, support should be better in both browsers.

We won't get fully into the syntax and use of style sheets until the next chapter, but for now it is enough to know that you can define and name style sheets using the `<STYLE>` and `</STYLE>` tags:

```
<STYLE>
   Style sheet Definition
</STYLE>
```

These style sheets can then be applied to different page elements. Alternatively, you can define specific styles for elements using the `STYLE` attribute of many HTML tags.

You will see how both these techniques are used as we move through the examples in this section.

Let's start by getting a feel for what you can do with this approach to positioning. In many ways, we can do the same things we did with layers, but by using different commands, occasionally in different ways. You can position sections either relatively or absolutely. You can float elements and then allow text to flow around them, you can control the visibility of elements, and you can determine the Z-order of elements.

CSS Positioning Properties

The proposed positioning extensions to cascading style sheets implements the following nine properties:

- [ ] `position`: Establishes a new rectangular plane for layout. The property has three possible values—`absolute`, `relative`, or `static`.

- [ ] `left`: Defines the left edge of a rectangular pane for layout. Possible values include a length in pixels as an offset from the container's left edge, a percentage of the container's width, or `auto` (the default).

- [ ] `top`: Defines the top edge of a rectangular pane for layout. Possible values include a length in pixels as an offset from the container's top edge, a percentage of the container's height, or `auto` (the default).

- [ ] `width`: Specifies the width of a rectangular pane. Possible values include a length in pixels, a percentage of the container's width, or `auto` (the default).

- [ ] `height`: Specifies the height of a rectangular pane. Possible values include a length in pixels, a percentage of the container's height, or `auto` (the default).

- [ ] `clip`: Defines the part of an element that is visible without affecting layout. Any part of an element that is outside its clipping region is transparent. Take four values (`top`, `right`, `bottom`, `left`) as offsets from the element's origin, or `auto`, the default, which covers the entire element.

17

☐ overflow: Determines what happens when an element exceeds the specified height or width. Possible values are none, clip, and scroll.

☐ z-index: Specifies the Z-order of elements. Takes a positive or negative integer, or auto (the default value).

☐ visibility: Determines the initial display status of an element. Possible values are inherit, visible, and hidden.

It is immediately evident that there is a lot of similarity between these properties and the attributes of the <LAYER> tag, but these properties provide a few more options. For instance, with <LAYER> you couldn't specify what to do when the content didn't fit in the layer. Here, you have the flexibility to determine this with the overflow property.

NOTE   It is important to note that in the preview releases of both Netscape Communicator and Microsoft Internet Explorer 4, not all the properties are functional. For instance, setting overflow to clip in Internet Explorer doesn't do anything, and scroll doesn't work in either browser.

The easiest way to use these properties is as values in the STYLE attribute of an HTML tag. The most obvious place to use this attribute is in the <DIV> tag, with which you can surround a series of HTML statements and apply the style to all of them.

Consider this example:

```
<HTML>
<HEAD>
<TITLE>Style Sheet Positioning</TITLE>
</HEAD>
<BODY>
The following text is positioned using
Cascading Style Sheet properties ...
<DIV STYLE="position: absolute; top:100;
left:100; width:100; overflow:none;">
This text has been positioned in a 100 pixel
wide area offset by 100 pixels from the top
and left of the page.
</DIV>
</BODY>
</HTML>
```

This produces the results shown in Figure 17.21.

Figure 17.21.
Using the STYLE
attribute of the <DIV>
tag to position
elements.

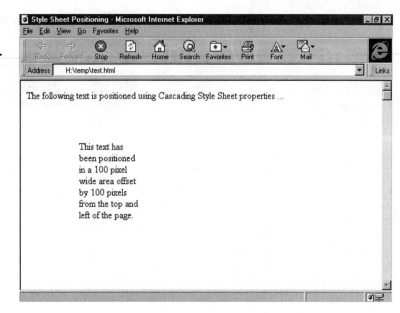

Immediately, you'll notice several interesting points about this example:

☐ The syntax for defining a position is simple: each property is separated from its value by a colon, and each property/value pair is followed by a semicolon.

☐ Absolute positioning is used. According to the specification, elements with absolute positioning are laid out without regard for their parent elements' dimensions or positions. Absolute positioned elements know nothing about each other and are placed relative to the document window.

☐ Setting overflow to none allows the rectangular pane to expand to display the entire contents of the element.

These observations raise certain issues. First, how do the other values of overflow work?

Let's take a look at overflow: clip. According to the specification, this means that the contents should be cut off at the boundary of the element's visible area as defined in the style. Netscape properly renders this. Internet Explorer doesn't. We see how this would be done in Netscape in Figure 17.22.

Figure 17.22.

Setting overflow to `clip` *cuts off the position text at the edges of the element's visible area.*

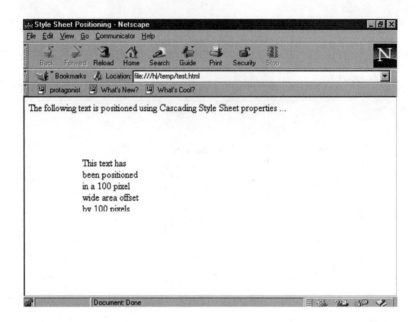

Next, we need to consider the difference between `absolute`, `relative`, and `static` positioning.

As you just saw, absolute positioning places an element relative to the document window, independent of all other elements. You'll be able to see this quite clearly if we overlap two elements partially:

```
<HTML>
<HEAD>
<TITLE>Style Sheet Positioning</TITLE>
</HEAD>
<BODY>
The following text is positioned using
Cascading Style Sheet properties ...
<DIV STYLE="position: absolute; top:100;
left:100; width:100; overflow:none;">
This text has been positioned in a 100 pixel wide
area offset by 100 pixels from the top and
left of the page.
</DIV>
<DIV STYLE="position: absolute; top:150;
left:100; width:100; overflow:none;">
This text has been positioned in a 100 pixel wide
area offset by 100 pixels from the top and
left of the page.
</DIV>
</BODY>
</HTML>
```

What we've done here is to repeat the <DIV> element twice, but the second time it is moved down by 50 pixels. The result is the mixed up text we see in Figure 17.23.

Figure 17.23.

With absolute positioning, the placement of elements is independent of all other elements in a page.

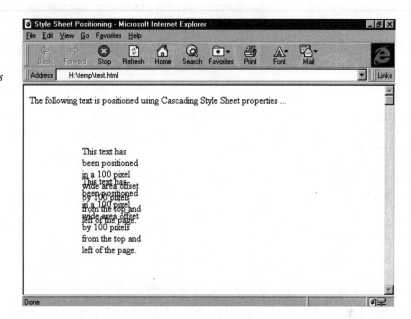

Relative positioning is somewhat different. Elements positioned this way are placed in the parent element in the flow of the HTML content. Thus, the element retains its natural formatting, but has some of the features of absolute positioned elements, such as a Z-order, visibility controls, and the ability to include child elements. In some ways this is like inline layers in Netscape Communicator.

With these relative positioned elements, you can apply the top, left, width, and height properties to offset the element from its natural position in the flow.

For instance, the following example demonstrates that you can shift text up or down or cut off words using these properties:

```
<HTML>
<HEAD>
<TITLE>Relative Positioning</TITLE>
</HEAD>
<BODY>
This text includes a
<SPAN STYLE="position: relative; top: -2">word</SPAN>
that is raise two pixels, another
<SPAN STYLE="position: relative; top: 3">word</SPAN>
that is lowered three pixels and yet another
<SPAN STYLE="position: relative; clip: 0 20 20 0;
overflow: clip">word</SPAN>
that is clipped.</BODY>
</HTML>
```

This produces Figure 17.24, as shown in Netscape Communicator.

Figure 17.24.

Relative positioning in Netscape Communicator.

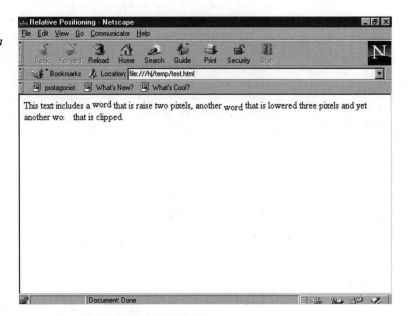

In this example, you'll notice the use of `<SPAN>` and `</SPAN>` to indicate the section that is being positioned. This is done because using `<DIV>` would indicate that the text should be positioned as a new paragraph, producing the results shown in Figure 17.25. We don't want this, so use `<SPAN>` instead, which defines the span without making it a separate paragraph.

Static positioning is the third positioning alternative in the cascading style sheets positioning proposal. According to the specifications from the World Wide Web Consortium, static positioning is identical to normally rendered HTML. Static positioning of elements means that they cannot be positioned or repositioned with scripts; there is no coordinate system created for child elements.

If you change the position to static in the previous example, you would end up with what appears to be a normal HTML document, as shown in Figure 17.26. This is the default behavior for the position property.

17

Figure 17.25.

Using <DIV> instead of <SPAN>.

Figure 17.26.

Static positioning: It's just plain old HTML.

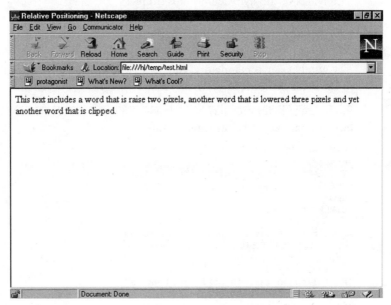

Using Named Styles

As you have noticed in the last few examples, always using the STYLE attribute to define the positioning of elements can clutter up your HTML code. Instead, you can use the <STYLE> and </STYLE> tags to define a set of styles and give them descriptive names that can be used later when assigning styles.

To do this, place a <STYLE> section at the top of your document:

```
<STYLE TYPE="text/css">
<!--
   Style definitions
-->
</STYLE>
```

There are two things to keep in mind when doing this. First, the HTML comments ensure that the style definitions won't be displayed in a browser that doesn't support styles. Second, the TYPE attribute of the <STYLE> tag has been used. This is because there are more than one type of style sheet system, and cascading style sheets is only one of the them. They all can be defined inside <STYLE> tags, so you need to tell the browser what type of style sheet you are defining.

The syntax of the style definition is simple:

```
#styleName1 { styleDefinition1 }
#styleName2 { styleDefinition2 }
etc.
```

The number sign is mandatory, and the style definition is the same thing you would include in the STYLE attribute of <DIV> or <SPAN>.

For instance, in the previous example where we positioned some text inside a 100 square pixel box, the page could be rewritten as this:

```
<HTML>
<HEAD>
<TITLE>Style Sheet Positioning</TITLE>
</HEAD>
<BODY>
<STYLE TYPE="text/css">
<!--
#smallbox { position: absolute; top:100;
➥left:100; width:100; overflow:none; }
-->
</STYLE>
The following text is positioned using
Cascading Style Sheet properties ...
<DIV ID="smallbox">
This text has been positioned in a 100 pixel
wide area offset by 100 pixels from the top
and left of the page.
</DIV>
</BODY>
</HTML>
```

What we've done is define the style immediately after the <BODY> tag and then applied it to the appropriate element by assigning the style to the <DIV> tag with the ID attribute.

Summary

This has been a big chapter, but hopefully you've gained a lot out of it. What have you learned?

We started by reviewing Dynamic HTML—those sets of extensions to the upcoming new browsers from Netscape and Microsoft. You saw how explicit positioning of objects, style sheets, font control, and more were part of both companies' definition of Dynamic HTML. At the same time, though, you learned that the two companies are taking different, and at times incompatible, approaches to this new concept.

The core of the chapter looked at one of the central features of Dynamic HTML: explicit two-dimensional positioning of objects on the page.

Netscape implements this using its layers technology—a set of HTML tags and JavaScript objects, properties, and methods that allow a page author to position and layer objects on the page as well as move them, hide them, and show them.

Microsoft takes a different approach in Internet Explorer, implementing a set of extensions to standard cascading style sheets (which you will learn more about in the next chapter) that provide similar functionality to the Netscape layers technology.

In the next chapter we will consider another central feature of Dynamic HTML: style sheets. Both Netscape Navigator and Microsoft Internet Explorer support cascading style sheets—a standard from the World Wide Web Consortium for specifying the appearance of HTML elements. Table 17.1 presents a quick summary of all the tags and extensions you've learned about in this chapter.

Table 17.1. HTML tags and style sheet properties from this chapter.

Tag or Property	Attribute	Use
<LAYER>		(Netscape extension) Specifies a layer of content.
	NAME	(Netscape extension) Name of the layer.
	ID	(Netscape extension) Name of the layer (same as NAME).
	LEFT	(Netscape extension) Left edge of layer in pixels from left edge of container.
	TOP	(Netscape extension) Top edge of layer in pixels from top edge of container.

continues

Table 17.1. continued

Tag or Property	Attribute	Use
	PAGEX	(Netscape extension) Left edge of layer in pixels from left edge of window.
	PAGEY	(Netscape extension) Top edge of layer in pixels from top edge of window.
	SRC	(Netscape extension) URL of file containing source content for layer.
	Z-INDEX	(Netscape extension) Specifies Z-order of layer.
	ABOVE	(Netscape extension) Specifies layer directly above current layer.
	BELOW	(Netscape extension) Specifies layer directly below current layer.
	WIDTH	(Netscape extension) Specifies width of the layer.
	HEIGHT	(Netscape extension) Specifies height of layer.
	CLIP	(Netscape extension) Specifies clipping rectangle of the layer.
	VISIBILITY	(Netscape extension) Indicates whether the layer is visible or hidden or inherits its visibility from its parent.
	BGCOLOR	(Netscape extension) Background color of the layer.
	BACKGROUND	(Netscape extension) Filename of background graphic for the layer.
	onMouseOver	(Netscape extension) Action to take when mouse pointer enters the layer.
	onMouseOut	(Netscape extension) Action to take when mouse pointer leaves the layer.
	onFocus	(Netscape extension) Action to take when layer gets focus.
	onBlur	(Netscape extension) Action to take when layer loses focus.
	onLoad	(Netscape extension) Action to take when the layer finishes loading.

17

Tag or Property	Attribute	Use
`<ILAYER>`		(Netscape extension) Specifies an in-line layer of content.
	`NAME`	(Netscape extension) Name of the layer.
	`ID`	(Netscape extension) Name of the layer (same as `NAME`).
	`LEFT`	(Netscape extension) Left edge of layer in pixels from left edge of container.
	`TOP`	(Netscape extension) Top edge of layer in pixels from top edge of container.
	`PAGEX`	(Netscape extension) Left edge of layer in pixels from left edge of window.
	`PAGEY`	(Netscape extension) Top edge of layer in pixels from top edge of window.
	`SRC`	(Netscape extension) URL of file containing source content for layer.
	`Z-INDEX`	(Netscape extension) Specifies Z-order of layer.
	`ABOVE`	(Netscape extension) Specifies layer directly above current layer.
	`BELOW`	(Netscape extension) Specifies layer directly below current layer.
	`WIDTH`	(Netscape extension) Specifies width of the layer.
	`HEIGHT`	(Netscape extension) Specifies height of layer.
	`CLIP`	(Netscape extension) Specifies clipping rectangle of the layer.
	`VISIBILITY`	(Netscape extension) Indicates if the layer is visible, hidden or inherits its visibility from its parent.
	`BGCOLOR`	(Netscape extension) Background color of the layer.
	`BACKGROUND`	(Netscape extension) Filename of background graphic for the layer.
	`onMouseOver`	(Netscape extension) Action to take when mouse pointer enters the layer.
	`onMouseOut`	(Netscape extension) Action to take when mouse pointer leaves the layer.

17

continues

Table 17.1. continued

Tag or Property	Attribute	Use
	onFocus	(Netscape extension) Action to take when layer gets focus.
	onBlur	(Netscape extension) Action to take when layer loses focus.
	onLoad	(Netscape extension) Action to take when the layer finishes loading.
<NOLAYER>		Specifies content to display in a non-layers browser.
position		(CSS extension) Specifies how an object should be positioned.
left		(CSS extension) Specifies left edge of an object.
top		(CSS extension) Specifies top edge of an object.
width		(CSS extension) Specifies width of an object.
height		(CSS extension) Specifies height of an object.
clip		(CSS extension) Specifies visible part of an object.
overflow		(CSS extension) Specifies what do when an object is larger than its viewable area.
z-index		(CSS extension) Specifies an object's Z-order.
visibility		(CSS extension) Specifies visibility of an object.

Q&A

Q Some people have told me to avoid layers because they work only with Netscape. Should I avoid them?

A There is no clear answer to this question. It is true that only Netscape Communicator, not even Netscape Navigator 3.0, supports layers. Having said this, that alone is not a reason to avoid layers. After all, if you are creating a page for a small audience, such as an intranet, where you can be fairly certain what browser people are viewing your pages with, then layers can be a useful tool. Also, remember that, at first, frames were a Netscape-only extension and many people warned against using them. Now, they are common and fairly widely supported.

If you want to use layers but have concerns, then use the <NOLAYER> tag and you shouldn't have too much of a problem.

Q **Is the difference between Netscape's and Microsoft's ideas about what Dynamic HTML is all that important?**

A One of the common views on the Net is that Dynamic HTML and the release of Internet Explorer 4 and Netscape Communicator could fracture HTML forever and that it will never be a standard afterwards. This would mean that the whole idea of developing pages using a standard that could then be viewed anywhere would collapse.

I'm a bit of an optimist. Every time the two companies have diverged, they have tended to converge afterwards. I think that will happen in this case as well, even if the differences are a bit larger this time around. The new technologies, in both browsers, are too significant to discount, and in the end, everything should settle down.

17

Chapter 18

Stylizing Your Pages

In the last chapter we focused on one of the two major components in both Microsoft's and Netscape's approach to Dynamic HTML: explicit, two-dimensional positioning of objects and elements within an HTML page.

In this chapter we are going to look at *style sheets*, the other major component endorsed by both companies. Although Microsoft and Netscape take different approaches to this concept, their idea behind style sheets is to provide the degree of design control afforded by numerous extensions to HTML (as well as HTML 3.2 and beyond), add a little more design control, and separate it from HTML itself. In other words, appearance (or style) would be separated from structure, thus helping HTML to do what it was always intended to do: define structure independent of appearance or browser.

In this chapter we'll look at the World Wide Web Consortium's approach to style sheets, called *cascading style sheets* (or CSS), which is supported by both Microsoft and Netscape in their new browsers.

The Concept of Style Sheets

The concept of style sheets is really quite simple. First, style rules define the layout, typographic, and design features of a document separate from the definition of the document's structure. Then, a document's structure is defined using standard HTML (the same as in the past). An author can then define preferred appearance and design using a style sheet: a set of rules, usually defined in a separate file, that a compliant browser uses to render the structured document defined with standard HTML.

In this way, a browser that doesn't support style sheets can still render the document as a standard HTML document and, because the author has separated the two, the standard HTML document should stand on its own without dependence on the style sheet. Another advantage of using style sheets is that as Web documents are increasingly viewed in non-standard ways, such as through audio players for the visually impaired or through other means where standard browser technology is inaccessible, the structured HTML document can still be rendered in a useful way without being affected by superfluous, and often confusing, HTML extension tags intended to provide visual layout in a browser.

Approaches to Style Sheets

Style sheets as a concept is not tied to a specific technology or definition. In the HTML world, there is one main standard known as cascading style sheets. This is a standard proposed by the World Wide Web Consortium (W3C), the parent organization that defines each new generation of standard HTML.

By using cascading style sheets, you can specify everything from typefaces for different HTML elements to font colors, background colors and graphics, margins, spacing, type style, and much more. Basically, any part of the visual appearance of your document can be defined with cascading style sheets. Then, in browsers that support this type of style sheet, including Netscape Communicator and Internet Explorer 4, these style definitions will be applied to the final appearance of the document.

NOTE   Another proposal for style sheets comes from the International Organization for Standardization. Called *Document Style Semantics and Specification Language*, this proposal addresses all of SGML—not just HMTL—but hasn't made headway into the HTML world as of the time this book was sent to press. However, because HTML is simply an application of SGML, it is important to be aware of this alternative to cascading style sheets. There may come the day when this type of style sheet is relevant to the HTML world.

18

Finally, as if having two possible standards-based approaches to style sheets weren't enough, Netscape has created it's own alternative version of style sheets. Just as Netscape has a layers alternative for positioning objects on a page while still supporting the emerging standard, Netscape also has its own JavaScript style sheets while continuing to support cascading style sheets.

This sounds like a confusing situation and, because this is a new technology, it is. However, as is the case with all new technologies, things will settle down, and the VHS of style sheets will emerge while the Betamax falls to the side.

Applying Style Sheets to HTML

The wonder of the whole style sheets idea is that it is flexible. The tags and attributes used to apply style sheets to HTML documents don't tie authors and browser makers to a single type of style sheet.

Instead, the W3C has defined a set of tags and attributes that can be used to apply any style sheet to a document. The basics of this are simple:

☐ A style definition can be applied to a particular tag using the STYLE attribute (as in `<DIV STYLE="style-definition">` or `<H1 STYLE="style-definition">`).

☐ A style definition can be created in between `<STYLE>` and `</STYLE>` (this should be in the header of the HTML document).

☐ A style sheet can be imported from an external file using `<LINK REL=stylesheet HREF="name-of-stylesheet-file">`.

The `<LINK>` tag needs a bit of explanation. This tag associates an external style sheet file with the current document. In this way, a consistent style for a site can be determined by the site manager and applied to documents created by any author in an organization.

To effectively use the tag requires an understanding of persistent, default, and alternate styles. First, here are the basics:

☐ Persistent styles are always applied regardless of the user's local selections.

☐ Default styles apply when a page is loaded but can be disabled by the user in favor of an alternate style.

☐ Alternate styles are provided as options for the user to choose (as opposed to the default style).

The REL attribute of the `<LINK>` tag controls some of this process. With REL=stylesheet, the styles that are loaded are persistent. By adding a TITLE attribute, as in

```
<LINK REL=stylesheet TITLE=some-title HREF="URL">
```

the style becomes a default style.

Changing `REL=stylesheet` to `REL=alternate stylesheet` creates an alternate style sheet with a different title.

In this way, you can create a persistent style that contains those definitions that have to be applied, regardless of what choices a user makes, as well as provide a default and one or more alternatives that supplement the persistent style.

In addition to providing ways to incorporate style sheets into HTML documents, the creation of style sheets has added some other tags and attributes. As you saw earlier, `STYLE` can be applied to most tags to create an element-specific style definition. In addition, the `ID` and `CLASS` attributes can be used to apply a named style, defined elsewhere in the header or a style sheet file, to a specific element, as in `<DIV ID="`*`id-name`*`">` or `<P CLASS="`*`class-name`*`">`.

The difference here is subtle. A class is a broadly defined style that defines properties for some or all elements in a document. Then the class can be applied to any element using the `CLASS` attribute. Only the style definitions for that element in the specified class will be applied to the element.

An `ID`, on the other hand, defines something that has a unique value over an entire document and is often used to override specific settings of a class for specific instances of an element.

The new `<SPAN>` tag provides a way to apply a style to a portion of text without a structural role (which, therefore, isn't contained within a specific HTML structural tag). This can be used to apply a style to the first letter or word of a document. Because `<SPAN>`, itself, has no effect on the text, only the style will affect the text's appearance.

Working with Cascading Style Sheets

Before getting down to the nitty gritty, let's discuss the whole "cascading" idea. Just what does it mean that this particular brand of style sheets is cascading? Clearly, there are no cascading waterfalls involved.

Cascading refers to the capability for style information from more than one source to be combined. For instance, an organizational style from an external file could be combined with document-specific styles defined within the document along with element-specific styles defined within an element's `STYLE` attribute. The cascading part of the picture comes into play because there is an ordered sequence to the style sheets: rules in later sheets take precedence over earlier ones.

Now you are ready to try your hand at using cascading style sheets. Cascading style sheets use a simple syntax for defining style properties.

Basically, the style for an element is defined using a list of property-value pairs, which looks something like this:

```
name: value; name: value; name: value; ...
```

The names in this case are the property names that are part of the CSS specification (this is what you will learn this chapter). The values are any legal values for the given property. These lists can be used in several ways to apply style to an element:

- [ ] In the STYLE attribute of an HTML tag (see Chapter 17, "Making It All Dynamic," for a discussion of positioning in Microsoft Internet Explorer 4).

- [ ] In a named class or ID in between the <STYLE> and </STYLE> tags (again, refer to the last chapter in the section on positioning objects with Internet Explorer).

- [ ] In a style definition for a particular type of HTML tag, again between <STYLE> and </STYLE>. This type of definition defines a style for all occurrences of a given HTML tag. For instance, you could define all occurrences of <H1> to display in red type.

Let's look at examples of each. Incorporating a style into a STYLE attribute is as simple as

```
<DIV STYLE="style-definition">
```

or

```
<H1 STYLE="style-definition">
```

The problem with this is that you need to define a style for each occurrence of an element, such as a paragraph, even if they all take the same style definition. You can get around this in two ways.

Your first choice is to apply a style to all elements of a given type. For instance, the following style sheet creates a style that is applied to all <IMG> tags in a document as well as another style for all <H3> tags in a document:

```
<STYLE TYPE="text/css">
IMG { style-definition }
H3 { style-definition }
</STYLE>
```

Notice the use of the TYPE attribute in the <STYLE> tag to indicate the use of cascading style sheets.

This approach means that your HTML code, itself, can be completely free of STYLE attributes. However, there are situations in which you will use given styles throughout a document but will want to explicitly identify when they are used. For example, you might have two different styles for the <DIV> tag depending on the paragraph, or you might have one style that is applicable to numerous tags (such as all headers). You can use named styles as an alternative approach:

```
<STYLE TYPE="text/css">
#id-name1 { style-definition }
#id-name2 { style-definition }
</STYLE>
```

18

Then, you could choose when to apply the styles using the ID attribute of an HTML tag, such as

```
<DIV ID="style-name1">
```

or

```
<LI ID="style-name2">
```

You can apply properties to specific elements within an ID by preceding the hash mark with an element name:

```
<STYLE TYPE="text/css">
#id-name1 { style-definition }
H1#id-name1 { style-definition }
</STYLE>
```

This example creates a definition for all elements and then adds specific information for just the <H1> element; it will take hold only when the ID is applied to the <H1> element.

The syntax for defining classes is similar:

```
<STYLE TYPE="text/css">
.class-name1 { style-definition }
H1.class-name1 { style-definition }
</STYLE>
```

There is one more important concept we should discuss before proceeding to the CSS properties: contextual selectors. Let's say you wanted to define a style for italic text that appears within a second-level heading. You want the style to apply to these cases but not to italic text anywhere else in the document. To achieve this, you use the following:

```
<STYLE TYPE="text/css">
H2 I { style-definition }
</STYLE>
```

This defines a style for any occurrence of <I> within an <H2> block.

The CSS properties can be grouped into several broad categories:

☐ Font appearance and style

☐ Background colors and images

☐ Text alignment

☐ Spacing

☐ Border appearance

☐ Miscellaneous (including scaling, text wrapping, and lists)

These groupings are my own because I find it useful to think in this way. The W3C has their own set of groupings in the huge CSS specification document.

In the next section of the chapter, we will look at some of the main properties and how to use them. There are too many to cover in a single section of a single chapter. If you need more information, you can find the complete specification of cascading style sheets on the Web at `http://www.w3.org/pub/WWW/TR/REC-CSS1`.

The preview releases of Internet Explorer 4 and Netscape Communicator do not fully implement the cascading style sheets properties. For this reason, we are looking at only selected properties, and even some of these do not work at the moment. Sorry, that's the Web.

Font Appearance and Style

Cascading style sheets have a strong collection of properties for defining font appearance. In fact, with cascading style sheets, page authors have more control than they had with the simplistic `<FONT>` tag in HTML.

Table 18.1 outlines the main properties for controlling font appearance.

Table 18.1. CSS font properties.

Property	Description
font-family	Sets font face. Possible values are a typeface name (such as Arial, Times, or Palatino) or one of five generic font names: SERIF, SANS-SERIF, CURSIVE, FANTASY, MONOSPACE.
font-size	Sets the font size in absolute, relative, or percentage terms.
font-style	Sets the font style as oblique, italic, or normal.
font-weight	Sets the font weight as normal, bold, bolder, or lighter.
font-variant	Sets the font to small-caps or normal.
font	Sets multiple font properties at once. Takes a list of values containing font-weight, font-size, font-style, font-family, and line-height (which you'll see later in this chapter).

continues

18

Table 18.1. continued

Property	Description
color	Sets the color of text as an RGB triplet or as one of 16 valid color names: AQUA, BLACK, BLUE, FUCHSIA, GRAY, GREEN, LIME, MAROON, NAVY, OLIVE, PURPLE, RED, SILVER, TEAL, WHITE, YELLOW.
text-decoration	Sets the font decoration as underline, overline, line-through, or blink.

There are a few things worth noting in this list:

☐ When you set the font family, using font-family, you can provide a comma-separated list of font names. If the system the browser is running on doesn't have a specified font, it moves on to the next font on the list. The W3C advises that a generic family name should be the last name in the list. The reason for this is that every browser will have a default font for a given generic family.

☐ When setting font size using font-size, absolute sizes are defined via a keyword such as xx-small, x-small, small, medium, large, x-large, or xx-large. These values map to specific font sizes in the browser. Relative sizes are relative to the font size of the parent element and can be defined as larger or smaller.

☐ Font weights are set on a scale of numerical values: 100, 200, 300, 400, 500, 600, 700, 800, and 900. The font-weight property can take either one of the values normal, bold, bolder, or lighter or one of the numbers. normal maps to 400 and bold maps to 700 on the numerical scale. bolder and lighter set the weight relative a parent element.

The following document highlights the effects of many of these properties:

```
<HTML>
<HEAD>
<TITLE>CSS Font Properties</TITLE>
</HEAD>
<BODY>
<SPAN STYLE="font-family: Arial">font-family: Arial</SPAN>
<SPAN STYLE="font-family: fantasy">font-family: fantasy</SPAN>
<HR>
<SPAN STYLE="font-size: xx-small">font-size: xx-small</SPAN>
<SPAN STYLE="font-size: medium">font-size: medium</SPAN>
<SPAN STYLE="font-size: xx-large">font-size: xx-large</SPAN>
<HR>
<SPAN STYLE="font-style: italic">font-style: italic</SPAN>
<HR>
<SPAN STYLE="font-weight: 100">font-weight: 100</SPAN>
<SPAN STYLE="font-weight: 500">font-weight: 500</SPAN>
<SPAN STYLE="font-weight: 900">font-weight: 900</SPAN>
```

```
<HR>
<SPAN STYLE="font-variant: normal">font-variant: normal</SPAN>
<SPAN STYLE="font-variant: small-caps">font-variant: small-caps</SPAN>
<HR>
<SPAN STYLE="text-decoration: underline">text-decoration: underline</SPAN>
<SPAN STYLE="text-decoration: overline">text-decoration: overline</SPAN>
<SPAN STYLE="text-decoration: line-through">
text-decoration: line-through</SPAN></BODY>
</HTML>
```

The results are shown in Figure 18.1 in Internet Explorer 4.

Figure 18.1.
Various CSS font properties.

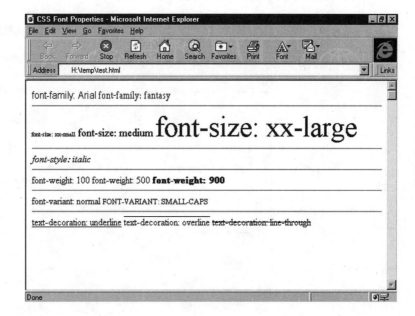

By applying these styles, it is possible to define a style sheet to create a document that is unique in appearance:

```
<HTML>
<HEAD>
<TITLE>More font property examples</TITLE>
<STYLE TYPE="text/css">
H1 {font: bold large monospace; text-decoration: overline underline; color: red}
LI {font-family: fantasy; font-size: medium; font-weight: 100;
font-variant: small-caps; color: blue}
</STYLE>
</HEAD>
<BODY BGCOLOR="aqua">
<H1>COMPUTER DOESN'T TURN ON?</H1>
<UL>
<LI>Check the power cord is plugged into the wall.
<LI>Check the power cord is plugged into the back of the computer.
<LI>Check the power switch is in the on position.
```

```
<LI>Check the monitor is plugged into the back of the computer.
<LI>Check the monitor is turned on.
</UL>
<HR>
<H1>STILL DOESN'T WORK?</H1>
<UL>
<LI>Call your vendor
</UL>
</BODY>
</HTML>
```

This produces the results shown in Figure 18.2.

Figure 18.2.

Defining a consistent appearance using style sheets.

Notice that in the header of the document a style sheet is defined between the `<STYLE>` and `</STYLE>` tags. This style sheet provides a set of style sheets for the `<H1>` tag and for the `<LI>` tag. In this way, any occurrence of the `<H1>` tag will apply the properties defined for the tag in the style sheet, and a similar thing happens with each occurrence of the `<LI>` tag that picks up the properties defined for it.

In this way, you can define the appearance of all the HTML elements in your document in one place, the style sheet, and then simply worry about basic HTML coding of the document, itself.

18

Background Colors and Images

In HTML you have basic control over the background appearance of a document: you can use BGCOLOR to set a background color of a document or BACKGROUND to set a background image. With tables, some browsers expanded on this by letting page authors apply backgrounds to individual cells in a table.

Well, in CSS you have even more control. There are six properties for controlling background. Also, because style sheets are applied on an element-by-element basis, you can have more than one background in a page. The six properties are outlined in Table 18.2.

Table 18.2. Background properties in CSS.

Property	Description
background-color	Sets a background color for an element. Possible values are a color name, RGB triplet, or transparent.
background-image	Sets the background image. The value should be the URL of an image or none.
background-repeat	Determines how a background image should be displayed. Possible values are repeat (repeat horizontally and vertically), repeat-x (repeat horizontally), repeat-y (repeat vertically), no-repeat (no repetition of the image).
background-attachment	Determines whether the background image is attached to the canvas or whether it scrolls with the document. Possible values are scroll and fixed.
background-position	Sets the initial position of a background image. Possible values are described later in this section.
background	A shorthand property that can take a combination of the five other properties' values.

It is fairly obvious that these properties provide more fine control over backgrounds and their appearance than HTML's limited tags and attributes.

Some of these properties require further comment. The W3C recommends that you set a background color to be used when a background image is unavailable.

Needing even more clarification, though, is the background-position property. Positioning of a background image is a little complex. Possible formats are keywords, placement in units, or placement by percentage. For example, you can combine top, center, bottom, left, and right to position a background image by using a pair of keywords such as top right, center left, and center (which means center center). Using percentages is a little different. A value

18

of A% B% means that the point A% across and B% down the image is placed directly at the point A% across and B% down the element. Thus, 0% 0% is the same as top left, and 100% 100% means bottom right.

Let's take a specific example: We are positioning a background image in a browser window. The image is 100 pixels by 100 pixels. The windows is 200 pixels by 200 pixels. If we use 10% 20% as the positioning information, here's what happens:

☐ The point 10% across and 20% down from the top left of the image is determined; this is, in other words, the pixel that is 10 pixels from the left and 20 pixels from the top.

☐ The point 10% across and 20% down from the top left of the image is determined; in other words, this is the pixel that is 20 pixels from the left and 40 pixels from the top of the image.

☐ The image is placed in the window so that these two points line up on top of each other.

Using a single percentage sets the horizontal value and defaults the vertical to 50%. Finally, using units such as centimeters, you can use 3cm 3cm to place the top left corner of the image offset by three centimeters down and to the right of the top-left corner of the element.

At the time of this book's publication, background images using CSS were not supported in either Netscape Communicator or Internet Explorer 4. For this reason, we can't really do an example. background-color does work in Internet Explorer, however, and can be used to set the background color for either the entire document or a specific element:

```
<HTML>
<HEAD>
<TITLE>CSS Background Colors</TITLE>
<STYLE TYPE="text/html">
#mainback {background-color: yellow}
#typeback {background-color: #000000; color: white}
</STYLE>
</HEAD>
<BODY ID="mainback">
<DIV ID="typeback">This is an example of a
background color for an element.</DIV>
<HR>
</BODY>
</HTML>
```

As you will notice in Figure 18.3, you can use CSS to apply background colors to the page as a whole (mainback is applied to the entire document) as well as to individual elements such as a paragraph of text (typeback is used in this case). Here, typeback also defines a font color with the color property so that the type will be visible against the black background color.

Figure 18.3.

Using background colors with cascading style sheets.

Text Alignment Properties in CSS

18

Cascading style sheets provide numerous properties that allow page authors to align text. These properties allow the type of fine typographic control users of word processors and desktop publishing applications have available to them but could not use on the Web.

The main text alignment properties are outlined in Table 18.3.

Table 18.3. Text alignment properties in CSS.

Property	Description
vertical-align	Sets the vertical alignment for an element relative to the parent element, the line the element is part of, or the line height of the line the element is contained in. Values of baseline, middle, sub, super, text-top, and text-bottom are relative to the parent element. top and bottom are relative to the line, itself. A percentage raises the baseline of the element above the baseline of the parent.
text-align	Sets the alignment of text within an element to left, center, right, or justify.
text-indent	Sets the indentation of the first line of formatted text in an element. The value can be either an absolute length or a percentage of the element width.

Support for these text-alignment properties is better implemented in the current preview releases of both Netscape's and Microsoft's browsers. Neither browser supports vertical-align at the moment and fully justifying text with text-align only works in Netscape Communicator.

However, left, center, and right alignment works as does text indentation. The following example shows the results of working with the text-align property:

```
<HTML>
<HEAD>
<TITLE>Text Alignment</TITLE>
</HEAD>
<BODY>
<DIV STYLE="text-align: left">This is an example of a
left-aligned paragraph. Notice how the text is ragged
on the right but aligned on the left. This property mimics
the actions of the ALIGN attribute of the DIV tag in HTML.</DIV>
<HR>
<DIV STYLE="text-align: right">This is an example of a
right-aligned paragraph. Notice how the text is ragged
on the left but aligned on the right. This property mimics
the actions of the ALIGN attribute of the DIV tag in HTML.</DIV>
<HR>
</BODY>
</HTML>
```

This produces the results shown in Figure 18.4.

Figure 18.4.

Text alignment using CSS.

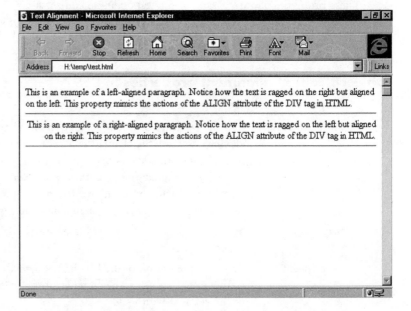

18

Of course, this isn't that amazing. You could do all of this before using the ALIGN attribute in numerous HTML tags, including <DIV> and <IMG>.

The text-indent property provides a more interesting capability. Many people complain that one of the flaws of HTML is that it is impossible to indent the first line of a paragraph using plain HTML. Of course, people have worked around this using various techniques, including placing small, transparent GIF images at the start of a line, but this approach causes strange results in some browsers, such as those that don't support transparent GIFs and text-based browsers such as Lynx.

With cascading style sheets you can now achieve flexible indentation of the first line of a paragraph using the text-indent property. As mentioned in Table 18.3, you can use two approaches to this: indentation can be an absolute length or a percentage of the element width.

NOTE

Netscape Communicator currently does not support the text-indent property.

Let's start with absolute lengths. You can use any of the standard measurement units supported in cascading style sheets:

```
<HTML>
<HEAD>
<TITLE>Text Indentations</TITLE>
</HEAD>
<BODY>
<DIV STYLE="text-indent: 0.5in">This paragraph is indented 0.5
inches on the first line. Using this technique we can achieve
layouts which look like those possible with Word Processors and
layout software.</DIV>
<HR>
<DIV STYLE="text-indent: 4cm">This paragraph is indented 4
centimeters on the first line. Using this technique we can
achieve layouts which look like those possible with Word
Processors and layout software.</DIV>
<HR>
<DIV STYLE="text-indent: 20px">This paragraph is indented 20
pixels on the first line. Using this technique we can achieve
layouts which look like those possible with Word Processors and
layout software.</DIV>
<HR>
</BODY>
</HTML>
```

As you can see in Figure 18.5, using absolute indentations allows you to have flexible and precise control over the size of an indentation.

18

Figure 18.5.

Text indentation can be achieved with style sheets.

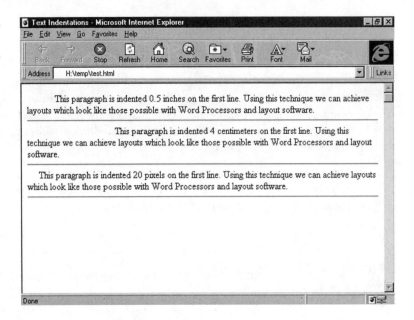

The only danger here is that if you choose a small indentation and the user has an extremely wide window, then the indentation may be insignificant. Similarly, a wide indent in a narrow window can create odd results, as shown in Figure 18.6.

Figure 18.6.

Take care when sizing indentations for paragraphs.

This can be addressed by using a percentage value for an indentation. For instance, setting text-indent to 10% creates an indentation that is 10 percent of the element's width. As you can see in Figure 18.7 and 18.8, the result is acceptable in the average window as well as in a narrow window.

Figure 18.7.

Using a percentage to set the indent width.

Figure 18.8.

Using percentages works in any window.

Spacing

After text alignment, another useful layout feature is the ability to control the spacing of page elements. This can range from controlling line spacing, word spacing, and letter spacing in text to setting the margins of elements and controlling white space in a document.

Table 18.4 highlights some useful spacing properties.

Table 18.4. Useful spacing properties.

Property	Description
word-spacing	Sets space to add to the default space between words. Possible values are an absolute length or normal (the default).
letter-spacing	Sets space to add to the default space between letters. Possible values are an absolute length or normal (the default).
line-height	Sets the distance between two line's baselines. A numerical value means the line height will be the font size multiplied by the number. A length value defines an absolute length. A percentage sets the height as a percentage of the default line size. You can also use normal, which sets the height to the default.
margin-top	Sets the top margin of an element. Can take a length, a percentage, or auto.
margin-right	Sets the right margin of an element. Can take a length, a percentage, or auto.
margin-bottom	Sets the bottom margin of an element. Can take a length, a percentage, or auto.
margin-left	Sets the left margin of an element. Can take a length, a percentage, or auto.
margin	Sets the margin of an element. Takes one to four values, which can be lengths, percentages, or auto.
padding-top	Sets the space between the top border and the content of an element. Can take a length, a percentage, or auto.
padding-right	Sets the space between the right border and the content of an element. Can take a length, a percentage, or auto.
padding-bottom	Sets the space between the bottom border and the content of an element. Can take a length, a percentage, or auto.
padding-left	Sets the space between the left border and the content of an element. Can take a length, a percentage, or auto.

Property	Description
padding	Sets the space between the border and the content of the element. Can take a length, a percentage, or auto.
white-space	Indicates how white space inside an element should be handled. Possible values are normal (white space is collapsed as with standard HTML), pre (just like the <PRE> tag), and nowrap (need to use to wrap).

These spacing properties give you a lot of control over layout. Let's start with letter-spacing, word-spacing, and line-height. Using these properties, you have good control over the appearance of text and paragraphs.

For instance, you could create a double-spaced paragraph using

```
line-height: 2
```

as shown in Figure 18.9.

NOTE

line-height, letter-spacing, and word-spacing are not currently supported in Netscape Communicator Preview Release 3.

 18

Figure 18.9.

Line spacing using line-height.

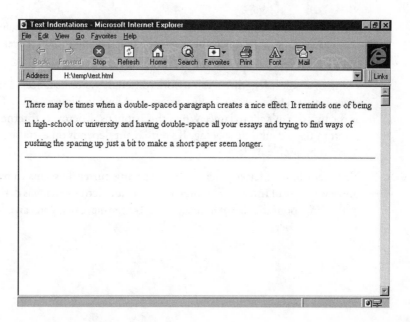

There may be times when a double-spaced paragraph creates a nice effect. It reminds one of being in high-school or university and having double-space all your essays and trying to find ways of pushing the spacing up just a bit to make a short paper seem longer.

What has happened here is a numerical value is used for `line-height`, which results in multiplying the font size by the value (in this case, 2). This means that increasing the font size increases the line spacing, as in Figure 18.10.

Figure 18.10.

Line spacing can be dependent on the font size.

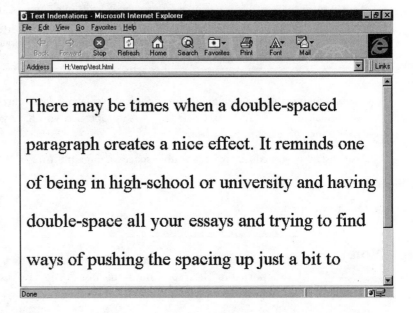

Using percentages, you get similar results. For instance, `line-height: 200%` has the same result as `line-height: 2` because it sets the line spacing to 200 percent of the default versus multiplying by 2—it's the same thing.

Using an absolute length as a value works differently. For instance, `line-height: 2cm` sets the space between baselines to 2 centimeters, as shown in Figure 18.11. This works fine as long as the text doesn't get to large. When this happens, Microsoft Internet Explorer will simply revert to the default line spacing. If your layout depends on extra space between lines, then this can be problematic.

Next, let's look at letter spacing (word spacing currently seems to have no effect with the preview release of Internet Explorer 4). By default, letter spacing is derived from information in the font about the size of letters. Using `letter-spacing`, you can add space to this default amount of space.

Figure 18.11.
Line spacing of 2 centimeters.

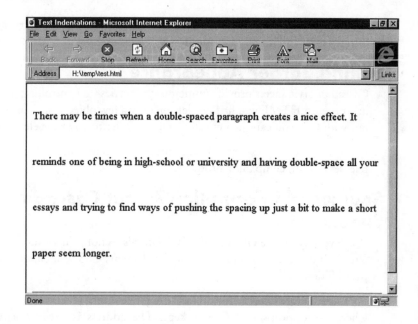

Figure 18.11.
Line spacing of 2 centimeters.

With just a few more CSS properties, you can create an effective masthead banner for a page like in Figure 18.12:

```
<H1 STYLE="letter-spacing: 0.3in; font-family: cursive;
font-weight: 900; color: yellow; background-color: black;
margin: 0.1in">HEADLINE</H1>
```

Figure 18.12.
A pretty headline.

18

When it comes to working with margins and padding and the white-space property, most things aren't working at press time in either Internet Explorer 4 or Netscape Communicator.

Setting Border Appearance

Cascading style sheets provide numerous properties for controlling the borders of elements in a page. In HTML you had borders on only a few objects, such as images and table cells, but with CSS you can theoretically apply a border to any page element.

Unfortunately, at press time, border properties seem noticeably absent from the preview releases of both companies' browsers.

Sources of Information About Cascading Style Sheets

We have only touched the surface of CSS in this section. This is mostly because it is too large a topic and because no browser really implements CSS well enough to dive deep into the possibilities.

If you want more information on cascading style sheets, you can find it at the W3C Web site, where a specification of CSS is kept. The address is http://www.w3.org/pub/WWW/TR/REC-CSS1.

Here are some other useful sources of information, as well:

☐ Quick Reference: http://webcom.net/~gmc/html/quick_ref.html
☐ Unfurling Style Sheets (article on ZD Internet Magazine's Web site): http://www.zdim.com/content/anchors/199704/28/1.html
☐ CSS Structure and Rules: http://www.htmlhelp.com/reference/css/structure.html
☐ W3C's CSS Home Page: http://www.w3.org/pub/WWW/Style/ (See Figure 18.13.)

18

Figure 18.13.

The World Wide Web Consortium's CSS home page.

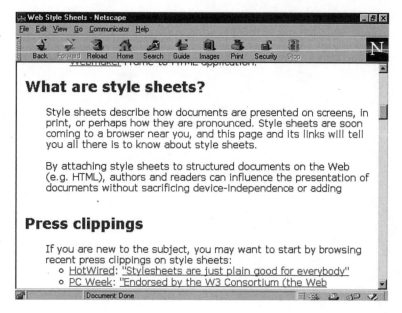

Q&A

Q How do I decide which type of style sheets to use? Having to make this choice just confuses me.

A Don't worry. You are not the only one who is confused by this choice. Basically, there are several approaches. If you are using styles to add some unique visual effects that aren't critical to your presentation, then you can choose whichever flavor you are most comfortable with. If you want the widest possible audience to be able to view the styles, you are best off using cascading style sheets because of the broader browser support at the moment.

Q I am confused by these background color and image properties. Why don't I just use tables and apply background images and colors to specific cells?

A You are absolutely correct that you can achieve some similar results using tables. The thing is this: Table tags have some problems. First, they are not strictly structural mark-up tags, so they cannot be rendered correctly in some browsers such as Lynx and spoken word browsers for the blind. This means that the text within the table can come out in the wrong order and will appear awful in these browsers. By using style sheets to achieve some of the same results, you can focus on strict structural mark-up of your document, which ensures that even on browsers not supporting style sheets, the document is at least clear and useable.

Appendixes

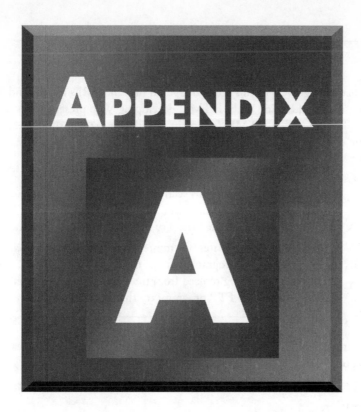

Sources for Further Information

Haven't had enough yet? In this appendix you'll find the URLs for all kinds of information about the World Wide Web, HTML, developing Web presentations, and locations of tools to help you write HTML documents. With this list you should be able to find just about anything you need on the Web.

> **NOTE**
>
> Some of the URLs in this section refer to FTP sites. Some of these sites may be very busy during business hours, and you may not be able to immediately access the files. Try again during non-prime hours.
>
> Also, some of these sites, for mysterious reasons, may be accessible through an FTP program, but not through Web browsers. If you are consistently getting refused from these sites using a browser, and you have access to an FTP program, try that program instead.

The sites are divided into the following categories and listed in alphabetical order under each category:

Access Counters
Browsers
Collections of HTML and WWW Development Information
Forms and Image Maps
HTML Editors and Converters
HTML Validators, Link Checkers, and Simple Spiders
Java, JavaScript, and Embedded Objects
Log File Parsers
Other
Servers and Server Administration
Sound and Video
Specifications for HTML, HTTP, and URLs
The Common Gateway Interface (CGI) and CGI Scripting
The Future of HTML and the Web
Tools and Information for Images
Web Providers
WWW Indexes and Search Engines

Access Counters

A good access counters tutorial
```
http://melmac.harris-atd.com/access_counts.html
```

Access counters without server programs
```
http://www.digits.com/
```

Digits for use in access counters
http://www.digitmania.holowww.com/

Net-Trak
http://net-trak.netrail.net/

Page Count
http://www.pagecount.com/

Jcount
http://www.jcount.com/

WebTracker
http://www.fxweb.holowww.com/tracker/

Internet Count
http://www.icount.com/

LiveCounter
http://www.chami.com/prog/lc/

Yahoo!'s list of access counters
http://www.yahoo.com/Computers/World_Wide_Web/Programming/Access_Counts/

Browsers

Arena (X)
http://www.w3.org/hypertext/WWW/Arena/

Amaya (X)
http://www.w3.org/Amaya/

Emacs-W3 (for Emacs)
http://www.cs.indiana.edu/elisp/w3/docs.html

A general list
http://www.w3.org/hypertext/WWW/Clients.html

Internet Explorer
http://www.microsoft.com/ie/

Lynx (UNIX and DOS)
http://www.cc.ukans.edu/about_lynx/

NCSA Mosaic (X, Windows, Mac)
http://www.ncsa.uiuc.edu/SDG/Software/Mosaic/NCSAMosaicHome.html

Netscape Navigator (X, Windows, Mac)
http://home.netscape.com/comprod/products/navigator/index.html

Netscape Communicator (X, Windows, Mac)

http://home.netscape.com/comprod/products/communicator/index.html

WinWeb (Windows) and MacWeb (Macintosh)

http://www.einet.net/EINet/WinWeb/WinWebHome.html

Collections of HTML and WWW Development Information

The Developer's JumpStation

http://oneworld.wa.com/htmldev/devpage/dev-page.html

The home of the WWW Consortium

http://www.w3.org/

The HTML Writer's Guild

http://www.hwg.org/

Netscape's HTML Assistance pages

http://home.netscape.com/assist/net_sites/index.html

The Repository

http://cbl.leeds.ac.uk/nikos/doc/repository.html

The Virtual Library

http://WWW.Stars.com/

The World Wide Web FAQ

http://www.boutell.com/faq/

Yahoo!'s WWW section

http://www.yahoo.com/Computers/World_Wide_Web/

Forms and Image Maps

Carlos' forms tutorial

http://robot0.ge.uiuc.edu/~carlosp/cs317/cft.html

Client-site image maps

http://ds.internic.net/internet-drafts/draft-seidman-clientsideimagemap-02.txt

File upload in forms

ftp://ds.internic.net/rfc/rfc1867.txt

HotSpots (a Windows image map tool)

http://www.cris.com/~automata/index.html

Image maps in NCSA

http://hoohoo.ncsa.uiuc.edu/docs/tutorials/imagemapping.html

Mapedit: A tool for Windows and X11 for creating Imagemap map files

http://www.boutell.com/mapedit/

Mosaic form support documentation

http://www.ncsa.uiuc.edu/SDG/Software/Mosaic/Docs/fill-out-forms/overview.html

The original NCSA forms documentation

http://hoohoo.ncsa.uiuc.edu/cgi/forms.html

Imaptool (Linux/X-Windows image map tool)

http://www.sci.fi/~uucee/ownprojects/

Map This (Windows image map creator)

http://galadriel.ecaetc.ohio-state.edu/tc/mt/

LiveImage (Windows-based image map tool)

http://www.mediatec.com/

Poor Person's Image Mapper (Web-based image map creation system)

http://zenith.berkeley.edu/~seidel/ClrHlpr/imagemap.html

Yahoo!'s forms list

http://www.yahoo.com/Computers_and_Internet/Internet/World_Wide_Web/
Programming/Forms/

HTML Editors and Converters

A list of converters and editors, updated regularly

http://www.w3.org/hypertext/WWW/Tools/

A great list of editors

http://www.yahoo.com/Computers_and_Internet/Software/Internet/World_Wide_Web/
HTML_Editors/

HTML Assistant Pro (Windows)

http://www.brooknorth.com/istar.html

HotDog (Windows)

http://www.sausage.com

WebEdit (Windows)

http://www.sandiego.com/webedit/

HTML Web Weaver and World Wide Web Weaver (Macintosh)

http://www.MiracleInc.com/

AsWedit (UNIX)
http://www.advasoft.com

SoftQuad HoTMetaL Pro (Windows, Macintosh, UNIX)
http://www.sq.com

Microsoft Front Page (Windows, Macintosh)
http://www.microsoft.com/frontpage/

HTML Editor (Macintosh)
http://dragon.acadiau.ca/~giles/HTML_Editor/Documentation.html

HTML Validators, Link Checkers, and Simple Spiders

The HTML Validator
http://www.webtechs.com/html-val-svc/

htmlchek
http://uts.cc.utexas.edu/~churchh/htmlchek.html

lvrfy (link checker)
http://www.cs.dartmouth.edu/~crow/lvrfy.html

MOMSpider
http://www.ics.uci.edu/WebSoft/MOMspider/)

Weblint
http://www.unipress.com/cgi-bin/WWWeblint

Yahoo!'s List of HTML Validation and HTML Checkers
http://www.yahoo.com/Computers/World_Wide_Web/HTML/Validation_Checkers/

Yahoo!'s List of Web Spiders and Robots
http://www.yahoo.com/Computers_and_Internet/Internet/World_Wide_Web/
Searching_the_Web/Robots__Spiders__etc__Documentation/

Java, JavaScript, and Embedded Objects

Gamelan, an index of Java applets
http://www.gamelan.com/

JavaScript author's guide
http://www.netscape.com/eng/mozilla/2.0/handbook/javascript/index.html

Netscape's information about Java

http://home.netscape.com/comprod/products/navigator/version_2.0/java_applets/

Netscape's information about JavaScript

http://www.netscape.com/comprod/products/navigator/version_2.0/script/

Sun's Java home page

http://www.javasoft.com/

Yahoo! Java directory

http://www.yahoo.com/Computers_and_Internet/Programming_Languages/Java/

Log File Parsers

getstats

http://www.eit.com/software/getstats/getstats.html

wusage

http://www.boutell.com/wusage/

Yahoo!'s List

http://www.yahoo.com/Computers/World_Wide_Web/HTTP/Servers/Log_Analysis_Tools/

Other

Tim Berners-Lee's style guide

http://www.w3.org/hypertext/WWW/Provider/Style/Overview.html

The Yale HyperText style guide

http://info.med.yale.edu/caim/manual/index.html

Servers and Server Administration

Access control in NCSA HTTPD

http://hoohoo.ncsa.uiuc.edu/docs/setup/access/Overview.html
http://hoohoo.ncsa.uiuc.edu/docs/tutorials/user.html
http://hoohoo.ncsa.uiuc.edu/docs/setup/admin/UserManagement.html

Apache (UNIX)

http://www.apache.org/

Avoiding robots

http://web.nexor.co.uk/mak/doc/robots/norobots.html

A

CERN HTTPD (UNIX)

http://www.w3.org/pub/WWW/Daemon/

JigSaw Server (Java)

http://www.w3.org/pub/WWW/Jigsaw/

Current list of official MIME types

ftp://ftp.isi.edu/in-notes/iana/assignments/media-types/media-types

MacHTTP and WebStar (Macintosh)

http://www.starnine.com/

Microsoft Internet Information Server (Windows NT)

http://www.microsoft.com/iis

NCSA HTTPD (UNIX)

http://hoohoo.ncsa.uiuc.edu/

NCSA Server Includes

http://hoohoo.ncsa.uiuc.edu/docs/tutorials/includes.html

NCSA winHTTPD (Windows 3.*x*)

http://www.city.net/win-httpd/

Netscape's Web servers (UNIX, Windows NT)

http://home.netscape.com/comprod/server_central

O'Reilly WebSite (Windows 95/NT)

http://website.ora.com/

Sound and Video

Audio Applications (commercial, bundled, shareware) for SGI Systems

http://reality.sgi.com/employees/cook/audio.apps/

AVI-Quick (Macintosh converter for AVI to Quicktime)
SoundHack (sound editor for Macintosh)
Sound Machine (sound capture/converter/editor for Macintosh)
SoundAPP (Macintosh sound converter)
Sparkle (MPEG player and converter for Macintosh)
WAVany (Windows sound converter)
WHAM (Windows sound converter)

http://www.shareware.com/code/engine/SearchOption?frame=none
(search for the program and platform you're interested in)

FastPlayer (Macintosh Quicktime player and "flattener")

ftp://ftp.ncsa.uiuc.edu/Mosaic/Mac/Helpers/fast-player-110.hqx

The Internet Underground Music Archive (IUMA)
http://www.iuma.com/

The MPEG FAQ
http://www.crs4.it/~luigi/MPEG/mpegfaq.html

QFlat (Windows QuickTime "flattener")
ftp://venice.tcp.com/pub/anime-manga/software/viewers/qtflat.zip

QuickTime information
http://quicktime.apple.com/

SmartCap (Windows Quicktime and AVI Converter)
ftp://ftp.intel.com/pub/IAL/Indeo_video/smartc.exe

SOX (UNIX and DOS sound Converter)
http://www.spies.com/Sox/

XingCD (AVI to MPEG converter)
Send mail to xing@xingtech.com or call 1-805-473-0145

Yahoo!'s video information
http://www.yahoo.com/Computers_and_Internet/Multimedia/Video/

Yahoo!'s sound information
http://www.yahoo.com/Computers/Multimedia/Sound/

Specifications for HTML, HTTP, and URLs

A

Frames
http://home.netscape.com/assist/net_sites/frames.html

The HTML 3.2 specification
http://www.w3.org/TR/REC-html32.html

The HTML 4.0 draft specification
http://www.w3.org/TR/WD-html40/

The HTTP specification
http://www.w3.org/hypertext/WWW/Protocols/HTTP/HTTP2.html

Information about HTTP
http://www.w3.org/pub/WWW/Protocols/

Mosaic tables

`http://www.ncsa.uiuc.edu/SDG/Software/XMosaic/table-spec.html`

Pointers to URL, URN, and URI information and specifications

`http://www.w3.org/hypertext/WWW/Addressing/Addressing.html`

The Common Gateway Interface (CGI) and CGI Scripting

An archive of CGI Programs at NCSA

`ftp://ftp.ncsa.uiuc.edu/Web/httpd/Unix/ncsa_httpd/cgi`

The CGI specification

`http://hoohoo.ncsa.uiuc.edu/cgi/interface.html`

`cgi-lib.pl`**, a Perl library to manage CGI and Forms**

`http://www.bio.cam.ac.uk/cgi-lib/`

An index to HTML-related programs written in Perl

`http://www.seas.upenn.edu/~mengwong/perlhtml.html`

A library of C programs to help with CGI deveopment

`http://wsk.eit.com/wsk/dist/doc/libcgi/libcgi.html`

The original NCSA CGI documentation

`http://hoohoo.ncsa.uiuc.edu/cgi/`

Un-CGI, a program to decode form input

`http://www.hyperion.com/~koreth/uncgi.html`

Yahoo!'s CGI list

`http://www.yahoo.com/Computers_and_Internet/Internet/World_Wide_Web/`
`CGI___Common_Gateway_Interface/`

The Future of HTML and the Web

Adobe Acrobat

`http://www.adobe.com/prodindex/acrobat/main.html`

General information about PDF

`http://www.ep.cs.nott.ac.uk/~pns/pdfcorner/pdf.html`

SHTTP information

`http://www.eit.com/creations/s-http/`

SSL information

`http://www.netscape.com/info/security-doc.html`

Cascading Style Sheets overview

http://www.w3.org/hypertext/WWW/Style/

JavaScript Style Sheets

http://developer.netscape.com/library/documentation/communicator/jsss/index.htm

VRML FAQ

http://vag.vrml.org/VRML_FAQ.html

VRML home site

http://vrml.wired.com/

Web security overview

http://www.w3.org/hypertext/WWW/Security/Overview.html

Yahoo!'s list on security, encryption, and authentication

http://www.yahoo.com/Computers_and_Internet/Security_and_Encryption/

Tools and Information for Images

Anthony's Icon Library

http://www.cit.gu.edu.au/~anthony/icons/index.html

Barry's Clip Art Server

http://www.barrysclipart.com/

Frequently Asked Questions about JPEG

http://www.cis.ohio-state.edu/hypertext/faq/usenet/jpeg-faq/faq.html

Frequently Asked Questions from comp.graphics

http://www.primenet.com/~grieggs/cg_faq.html

GIF Converter for Macintosh
Graphic Converter for Macintosh
LView Pro for Windows
Transparency for Macintosh

http://www.shareware.com/code/engine/SearchOption?frame=none
(search for the program and platform you're interested in)

giftrans

ftp://ftp.rz.uni-karlsruhe.de/pub/net/www/tools/giftrans.c

Some good information about transparent GIFs

http://melmac.harris-atd.com/transparent_images.html

Yahoo!'s clip art list

http://www.yahoo.com/Computers/Multimedia/Pictures/Clip_Art/

Yahoo!'s GIF list
http://www.yahoo.com/Computers/Software/Data_Formats/GIF/

Yahoo!'s PNG List
http://www.yahoo.com/Computers_and_Internet/Software/Data_Formats/
PNG__Portable_Network_Graphics_/

Yahoo!'s icons list
http://www.yahoo.com/Computers/World_Wide_Web/Programming/Icons/

Web Providers

An index from HyperNews
http://union.ncsa.uiuc.edu/HyperNews/get/www/leasing.html

Yahoo!'s List of Web Hosting Services
http://www.yahoo.com/Business_and_Economy/Companies/Internet_Services/
Web_Services/Hosting/

Yahoo!'s List of Directories of Internet Access Providers
http://www.yahoo.com/Business_and_Economy/Companies/Internet_Services/
Access_Providers/Directories/

The List (Worldwide list of Internet Providers)
http://thelist.iworld.com/

WWW Indexes and Search Engines

Alta Vista
http://www.altavista.digital.com/

Excite
http://www.excite.com

Lycos
http://www.lycos.com/

Web Crawler
http://www.webcrawler.com/

Yahoo!
http://www.yahoo.com/

InfoSeek
http://www.infoseek.com/

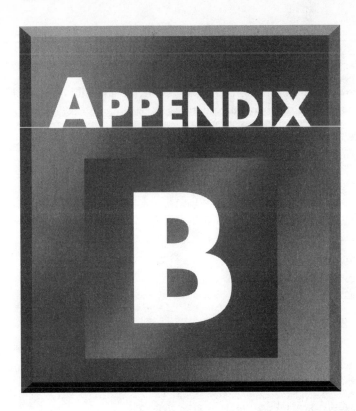

HTML 4.0 Quick Reference

HTML 4.0 is an ambitious attempt to meet the needs of Web developers worldwide, both casual and professional. This appendix provides a quick reference to all the elements and attributes of the language.

NOTE   This appendix is based on the information provided in the *HTML 4.0 Specification W3C Working Draft 8-July-1997*, which can be found at http://www.w3.org/TR/WD-html40/.

In order to make the information readliy accessible, this appendix organizes HTML elements by their function in the following order:

- ☐ Structure
- ☐ Text phrases and paragraphs
- ☐ Text formatting elements
- ☐ Lists
- ☐ Links
- ☐ Tables
- ☐ Frames
- ☐ Embedded content
- ☐ Style
- ☐ Forms
- ☐ Scripts

Within each section the elements are listed alphabetically and the following information is presented:

- ☐ Usage—A general description of the element
- ☐ Start/End Tag—Indicates whether these tags are required, optional, or illegal
- ☐ Attributes—Lists the attributes of the element with a short description of their effects
- ☐ Empty—Indicates whether the element can be empty
- ☐ Notes—Relates any special considerations when using the element and indicates whether the element is new, deprecated, or obsolete

NOTE Several elements and attributes have been *deprecated*, which means that although they're still supported, their further use is not recommended. The same or similar functionality is provided using new or alternate features.

NOTE HTML 4.0 introduces several new attributes that apply to a significant number of elements. These are referred to as %coreattrs, %i18n, and %events and are explained at the end of the appendix.

Following this, the common attributes (those with a % in front of them) and intrinsic events are summarized.

Structure

HTML relies upon several elements to provide structure to a document (as opposed to structuring the text within) as well as provide information that is used by the browser or search engines.

<BDO>...</BDO>

Usage	The bidirectional algorithm element is used to selectively turn off the default text direction.
Start/End Tag	Required/Required
Attributes	lang="..."—The language of the document.
	dir="..."—The text direction (ltr, rtl).
Empty	No
Notes	The dir attribute is mandatory.

<BODY>...</BODY>

Usage	Contains the content of the document.
Start/End Tag	Optional/Optional
Attributes	%coreattrs, %i18n, %events
	background="..."—Deprecated. URL for the background image.
	bgcolor="..."—Deprecated. Sets background color.
	text="..."—Deprecated. Text color.
	link="..."—Deprecated. Link color.
	vlink="..."—Deprecated. Visited link color.
	alink="..."—Deprecated. Active link color.
	onload="..."—Intrinsic event triggered when the document loads.
	onunload="..."—Intrinsic event triggered when document unloads.
Empty	No
Notes	There can be only one BODY and it must follow the HEAD. The BODY element can be replaced by a FRAMESET element. The presentational attributes are deprecated in favor of setting these values with style sheets.

B

Comments `<!-- ... -->`

Usage	Used to insert notes or scripts that are not displayed by the browser.
Start/End Tag	Required/Required
Attributes	None.
Empty	Yes
Notes	Comments are not restricted to one line and can be any length. The end tag is not required to be on the same line as the start tag.

`<DIV>...</DIV>`

Usage	The division element is used to add structure to a block of text.
Start/End Tag	Required/Required
Attributes	%coreattrs, %i18n, %events
	align="..."—Deprecated. Controls alignment (left, center, right, justify).
Empty	No
Notes	Cannot be used within a P element. The align attribute is deprecated in favor of controlling alignment through style sheets.

`<!DOCTYPE...>`

Usage	Version information appears on the first line of an HTML document and is a Standard Generalized Markup Language (SGML) declaration rather than an element.

`<H1>...</H1>` through `<H6>...</H6>`

Usage	The six headings (H1 is the uppermost, or most important) are used in the BODY to structure information in a hierarchical fashion.
Start/End Tag	Required/Required
Attributes	%coreattrs, %i18n, %events
	align="..."—Deprecated. Controls alignment (left, center, right, justify).
Empty	No
Notes	Visual browsers will display the size of the headings in relation to their importance, with H1 being the largest and H6 the smallest. The align attribute is deprecated in favor of controlling alignment through style sheets.

<HEAD>...</HEAD>

Usage	This is the document header, and it contains other elements that provide information to users and search engines.
Start/End Tag	Optional/Optional
Attributes	`%i18n`
	`profile="..."`—URL specifying the location of META data.
Empty	No
Notes	There can be only one HEAD per document. It must follow the opening HTML tag and precede the BODY.

<HR>

Usage	Horizontal rules are used to separate sections of a Web page.
Start/End Tag	Required/Illegal
Attributes	`%coreattrs, %events`
	`align="..."`—Deprecated. Controls alignment (`left`, `center`, `right`, `justify`).
	`noshade="..."`—Displays the rule as a solid color.
	`size="..."`—Deprecated. The size of the rule.
	`width="..."`—Deprecated. The width of the rule.
Empty	Yes

<HTML>...</HTML>

Usage	The HTML element contains the entire document.
Start/End Tag	Optional/Optional
Attributes	`%i18n`
	`version="..."`—URL of the document type definition specifying the HTML version used to create the document.
Empty	No
Notes	The version information is duplicated in the `<!DOCTYPE...>` declaration and therefore is not essential.

<META>

Usage	Provides information about the document.
Start/End Tag	Required/Illegal

B

Attributes	`%i18n`
	`http-equiv="..."`—HTTP response header name.
	`name="..."`—Name of the meta information.
	`content="..."`—Content of the meta information.
	`scheme="..."`—Assigns a scheme to interpret the meta data.
Empty	Yes

\<SPAN\>...\</SPAN\>

Usage	Organizes the document by defining a span of text.
Start/End Tag	Required/Required
Attributes	`%coreattrs, %i18n, %events`
Empty	No

\<TITLE\>...\</TITLE\>

Usage	This is the name you give your Web page. The TITLE element is located in the HEAD element and is displayed in the browser window title bar.
Start/End Tag	Required/Required
Attributes	`%i18n`
Empty	No
Notes	Only one title allowed per document.

Text Phrases and Paragraphs

Text phrases (or blocks) can be structured to suit a specific purpose, such as creating a paragraph. This should not be confused with modifying the formatting of the text.

\<ACRONYM\>...\</ACRONYM\>

Usage	Used to define acronyms.
Start/End Tag	Required/Required
Attributes	`%coreattrs, %i18n, %events`
Empty	No

\<ADDRESS\>...\</ADDRESS\>

Usage	Provides a special format for author or contact information.
Start/End Tag	Required/Required

Attributes	%coreattrs, %i18n, %events
Empty	No
Notes	The BR element is commonly used inside the ADDRESS element to break the lines of an address.

`<BLOCKQUOTE>...</BLOCKQUOTE>`

Usage	Used to display long quotations.
Start/End Tag	Required/Required
Attributes	%coreattrs, %i18n, %events
	cite="..."—The URL of the quoted text.
Empty	No

`<BR>`

Usage	Forces a line break.
Start/End Tag	Required/Illegal
Attributes	%coreattrs, %i18n, %events
	clear="..."—Sets the location where the next line begins after a floating object (none, left, right, all).
Empty	Yes

`<CITE>...</CITE>`

Usage	Cites a reference.
Start/End Tag	Required/Required
Attributes	%coreattrs, %i18n, %events
Empty	No

`<CODE>...</CODE>`

Usage	Identifies a code fragment for display.
Start/End Tag	Required/Required
Attributes	%coreattrs, %i18n, %events
Empty	No

`<DEL>...</DEL>`

Usage	Shows text as having been deleted from the document since the last change.
Start/End Tag	Required/Required

B

Attributes	%coreattrs, %i18n, %events
	cite="..."—The URL of the source document.
	datetime="..."—Indicates the date and time of the change.
Empty	No
Notes	New element in HTML 4.0.

<DFN>...</DFN>

Usage	Defines an enclosed term.
Start/End Tag	Required/Required
Attributes	%coreattrs, %i18n, %events
Empty	No

<EM>...</EM>

Usage	Emphasized text.
Start/End Tag	Required/Required
Attributes	%coreattrs, %i18n, %events
Empty	No

<INS>...</INS>

Usage	Shows text as having been inserted in the document since the last change.
Start/End Tag	Required/Required
Attributes	%coreattrs, %i18n, %events
	cite="..."—The URL of the source document.
	datetime="..."—Indicates the date and time of the change.
Empty	No
Notes	New element in HTML 4.0.

<KBD>...</KBD>

Usage	Indicates text a user would type.
Start/End Tag	Required/Required
Attributes	%coreattrs, %i18n, %events
Empty	No

`<P>...</P>`

Usage	Defines a paragraph.
Start/End Tag	Required/Optional
Attributes	`%coreattrs, %i18n, %events`
	`align="..."`—Deprecated. Controls alignment (`left`, `center`, `right`, `justify`).
Empty	No

`<PRE>...</PRE>`

Usage	Displays preformatted text.
Start/End Tag	Required/Required
Attributes	`%coreattrs, %i18n, %events`
	`width="..."`—The width of the formatted text.
Empty	No

`<Q>...</Q>`

Usage	Used to display short quotations that do not require paragraph breaks.
Start/End Tag	Required/Required
Attributes	`%coreattrs, %i18n, %events`
	`cite="..."`—The URL of the quoted text.
Empty	No
Notes	New element in HTML 4.0.

`<SAMP>...</SAMP>`

Usage	Identifies sample output.
Start/End Tag	Required/Required
Attributes	`%coreattrs, %i18n, %events`
Empty	No

`<STRONG>...</STRONG>`

Usage	Stronger emphasis.
Start/End Tag	Required/Required
Attributes	`%coreattrs, %i18n, %events`
Empty	No

B

_{...}

Usage	Creates subscript.
Start/End Tag	Required/Required
Attributes	`%coreattrs, %i18n, %events`
Empty	No

^{...}

Usage	Creates superscript.
Start/End Tag	Required/Required
Attributes	`%coreattrs, %i18n, %events`
Empty	No

<VAR>...</VAR>

Usage	A variable.
Start/End Tag	Required/Required
Attributes	`%coreattrs, %i18n, %events`
Empty	No

Text Formatting Elements

Text characteristics such as the size, weight, and style can be modified using these elements, but the HTML 4.0 specification encourages you to use style instead.

<B>...</B>

Usage	Bold text.
Start/End Tag	Required/Required
Attributes	`%coreattrs, %i18n, %events`
Empty	No

<BASEFONT>

Usage	Sets the base font size.
Start/End Tag	Required/Illegal
Attributes	`size="..."`—The font size (1–7 or relative, that is +3).
	`color="..."`—The font color.
	`face="..."`—The font type.

| Empty | Yes |
| Notes | Deprecated in favor of style sheets. |

`<BIG>...</BIG>`

Usage	Large text.
Start/End Tag	Required/Required
Attributes	%coreattrs, %i18n, %events
Empty	No

`<FONT>...</FONT>`

Usage	Changes the font size and color.
Start/End Tag	Required/Required
Attributes	size="..."—The font size (1–7 or relative, that is, +3).
	color="..."—The font color.
	face="..."—The font type.
Empty	No
Notes	Deprecated in favor of style sheets.

`<I>...</I>`

Usage	Italicized text.
Start/End Tag	Required/Required
Attributes	%coreattrs, %i18n, %events
Empty	No

`<S>...</S>`

Usage	Strikethrough text.
Start/End Tag	Required/Required
Attributes	%coreattrs, %i18n, %events
Empty	No
Notes	Deprecated.

`<SMALL>...</SMALL>`

Usage	Small text.
Start/End Tag	Required/Required
Attributes	%coreattrs, %i18n, %events
Empty	No

B

<STRIKE>...</STRIKE>

Usage	Strikethrough text.
Start/End Tag	Required/Required
Attributes	%coreattrs, %i18n, %events
Empty	No
Notes	Deprecated.

<TT>...</TT>

Usage	Teletype (or monospaced) text.
Start/End Tag	Required/Required
Attributes	%coreattrs, %i18n, %events
Empty	No

<U>...</U>

Usage	Underlined text.
Start/End Tag	Required/Required
Attributes	%coreattrs, %i18n, %events
Empty	No
Notes	Deprecated.

Lists

You can organize text into a more structured outline by creating lists. Lists can be nested.

<DD>...</DD>

Usage	The definition description used in a DL (definition list) element.
Start/End Tag	Required/Optional
Attributes	%coreattrs, %i18n, %events
Empty	No
Notes	Can contain block-level content, such as the <P> element.

<DIR>...</DIR>

Usage	Creates a multi-column directory list.
Start/End Tag	Required/Required
Attributes	%coreattrs, %i18n, %events
	compact—Deprecated. Compacts the displayed list.

Empty	No
Notes	Must contain at least one list item. This element is deprecated in favor of the UL (unordered list) element.

`<DL>...</DL>`

Usage	Creates a definition list.
Start/End Tag	Required/Required
Attributes	%coreattrs, %i18n, %events
	compact—Deprecated. Compacts the displayed list.
Empty	No
Notes	Must contain at least one `<DT>` or `<DD>` element in any order.

`<DT>...</DT>`

Usage	The definition term (or label) used within a DL (definition list) element.
Start/End Tag	Required/Optional
Attributes	%coreattrs, %i18n, %events
Empty	No
Notes	Must contain text (which can be modified by text markup elements).

`<LI>...</LI>`

Usage	Defines a list item within a list.
Start/End Tag	Required/Optional
Attributes	%coreattrs, %i18n, %events
	type="..."—Changes the numbering style (1, a, A, i, I), ordered lists, or bullet style (disc, square, circle) in unordered lists.
	value="..."—Sets the numbering to the given integer beginning with the current list item.
Empty	No

`<MENU>...</MENU>`

Usage	Creates a single-column menu list.
Start/End Tag	Required/Required
Attributes	%coreattrs, %i18n, %events
	compact—Deprecated. Compacts the displayed list.

B

	Empty	No
	Notes	Must contain at least one list item. This element is deprecated in favor of the UL (unordered list) element.

`<OL>...</OL>`

	Usage	Creates an ordered list.
	Start/End Tag	Required/Required
	Attributes	`%coreattrs, %i18n, %events`
		`type="..."`—Sets the numbering style (`1`, `a`, `A`, `i`, `I`).
		`compact`—Deprecated. Compacts the displayed list.
		`start="..."`—Sets the starting number to the chosen integer.
	Empty	No
	Notes	Must contain at least one list item.

`<UL>...</UL>`

	Usage	Creates an unordered list.
	Start/End Tag	Required/Required
	Attributes	`%coreattrs, %i18n, %events`
		`type="..."`—Sets the bullet style (`disc`, `square`, `circle`).
		`compact`—Deprecated. Compacts the displayed list.
	Empty	No
	Notes	Must contain at least one list item.

Links

Hyperlinking is fundamental to HTML. These elements enable you to link to other documents.

`<A>...</A>`

	Usage	Used to define links and anchors.
	Start/End Tag	Required/Required
	Attributes	`%coreattrs, %i18n, %events`
		`charset="..."`—Character encoding of the resource.
		`name="..."`—Defines an anchor.
		`href="..."`—The URL of the linked resource.

target="..."—Determines where the resource will be displayed (user-defined name, _blank, _parent, _self, _top).

rel="..."—Forward link types.

rev="..."—Reverse link types.

accesskey="..."—Assigns a hotkey to this element.

shape="..."—Enables you to define client-side imagemaps using defined shapes (default, rect, circle, poly).

coords="..."—Sets the size of the shape using pixel or percentage lengths.

tabindex="..."—Sets the tabbing order between elements with a defined tabindex.

Empty	No

\<BASE>

Usage	All other URLs in the document are resolved against this location.
Start/End Tag	Required/Illegal
Attributes	href="..."—The URL of the linked resource.
	target="..."—Determines where the resource will be displayed (user-defined name, _blank, _parent, _self, _top).
Empty	Yes
Notes	Located in the document HEAD.

\<LINK>

Usage	Defines the relationship between a link and a resource.
Start/End Tag	Required/Illegal
Attributes	%coreattrs, %i18n, %events
	href="..."—The URL of the resource.
	rel="..."—The forward link types.
	rev="..."—The reverse link types.
	type="..."—The Internet content type.
	media="..."—Defines the destination medium (screen, print, projection, braille, speech, all).
	target="..."—Determines where the resource will be displayed (user-defined name, _blank, _parent, _self, _top).
Empty	Yes
Notes	Located in the document HEAD.

B

Tables

Tables are meant to display data in a tabular format. Before the introduction of HTML 4.0, tables were widely used for page layout purposes, but with the advent of style sheets this is being discouraged by the W3C.

`<CAPTION>...</CAPTION>`

Usage	Displays a table caption.
Start/End Tag	Required/Required
Attributes	%coreattrs, %i18n, %events
	align="..."—Deprecated. Controls alignment (top, bottom, left, right).
Empty	No
Notes	Optional.

`<COL>`

Usage	Groups columns within column groups in order to share attribute values.
Start/End Tag	Required/Illegal
Attributes	%coreattrs, %i18n, %events
	span="..."—The number of columns the group contains.
	width="..."—The column width as a percentage, pixel value, or minimum value.
	align="..."—Horizontally aligns the contents of cells (left, center, right, justify, char).
	char="..."—Sets a character on which the column aligns.
	charoff="..."—Offset to the first alignment character on a line.
	valign="..."—Vertically aligns the contents of a cell (top, middle, bottom, baseline).
Empty	Yes

`<COLGROUP>...</COLGROUP>`

Usage	Defines a column group.
Start/End Tag	Required/Optional
Attributes	%coreattrs, %i18n, %events
	span="..."—The number of columns in a group.

B

width="..."—The width of the columns.

align="..."—Horizontally aligns the contents of cells (left, center, right, justify, char).

char="..."—Sets a character on which the column aligns.

charoff="..."—Offset to the first alignment character on a line.

valign="..."—Vertically aligns the contents of a cell (top, middle, bottom, baseline).

Empty	No

<TABLE>...</TABLE>

Usage	Creates a table.
Start/End Tag	Required/Required
Attributes	%coreattrs, %i18n, %events

align="..."—Controls alignment (left, center, right).

bgcolor="..."—Deprecated. Sets the background color.

width="..."—Table width.

cols="..."—The number of columns.

border="..."—The width in pixels of a border around the table.

frame="..."—Sets the visible sides of a table (void, above, below, hsides, lhs, rhs, vsides, box, border).

rules="..."—Sets the visible rules within a table (none, groups, rows, cols, all).

cellspacing="..."—Spacing between cells.

cellpadding="..."—Spacing in cells.

Empty	No

<TBODY>...</TBODY>

Usage	Defines the table body.
Start/End Tag	Optional/Optional
Attributes	%coreattrs, %i18n, %events

align="..."—Horizontally aligns the contents of cells (left, center, right, justify, char).

char="..."—Sets a character on which the column aligns.

charoff="..."—Offset to the first alignment character on a line.

valign="..."—Vertically aligns the contents of cells (top, middle, bottom, baseline).

Empty	No

`<TD>...</TD>`

Usage	Defines a cell's contents.
Start/End Tag	Required/Optional
Attributes	`%coreattrs`, `%i18n`, `%events`

axis="..."—Abbreviated name.

axes="..."—axis names listing row and column headers pertaining to the cell.

nowrap="..."—Deprecated. Turns off text wrapping in a cell.

bgcolor="..."—Deprecated. Sets the background color.

rowspan="..."—The number of rows spanned by a cell.

colspan="..."—The number of columns spanned by a cell.

align="..."—Horizontally aligns the contents of cells (left, center, right, justify, char).

char="..."—Sets a character on which the column aligns.

charoff="..."—Offset to the first alignment character on a line.

valign="..."—Vertically aligns the contents of cells (top, middle, bottom, baseline).

Empty	No

`<TFOOT>...</TFOOT>`

Usage	Defines the table footer.
Start/End Tag	Required/Optional
Attributes	`%coreattrs`, `%i18n`, `%events`

align="..."—Horizontally aligns the contents of cells (left, center, right, justify, char).

char="..."—Sets a character on which the column aligns.

charoff="..."—Offset to the first alignment character on a line.

valign="..."—Vertically aligns the contents of cells (top, middle, bottom, baseline).

Empty	No

`<TH>...</TH>`

Usage	Defines the cell contents of the table header.
Start/End Tag	Required/Optional
Attributes	`%coreattrs, %i18n, %events`

`axis="..."`—Abbreviated name.

`axes="..."`—axis names listing row and column headers pertaining to the cell.

`nowrap="..."`—Deprecated. Turns off text wrapping in a cell.

`bgcolor="..."`—Deprecated. Sets the background color.

`rowspan="..."`—The number of rows spanned by a cell.

`colspan="..."`—The number of columns spanned by a cell.

`align="..."`—Horizontally aligns the contents of cells (`left`, `center`, `right`, `justify`, `char`).

`char="..."`—Sets a character on which the column aligns.

`charoff="..."`—Offset to the first alignment character on a line.

`valign="..."`—Vertically aligns the contents of cells (`top`, `middle`, `bottom`, `baseline`).

Empty	No

`<THEAD>...</THEAD>`

Usage	Defines the table header.
Start/End Tag	Required/Optional
Attributes	`%coreattrs, %i18n, %events`

`align="..."`—Horizontally aligns the contents of cells (`left`, `center`, `right`, `justify`, `char`).

`char="..."`—Sets a character on which the column aligns.

`charoff="..."`—Offset to the first alignment character on a line.

`valign="..."`—Vertically aligns the contents of cells (`top`, `middle`, `bottom`, `baseline`).

Empty	No

`<TR>...</TR>`

Usage	Defines a row of table cells.
Start/End Tag	Required/Optional

B

Attributes	%coreattrs, %i18n, %events
	align="..."—Horizontally aligns the contents of cells (left, center, right, justify, char).
	char="..."—Sets a character on which the column aligns.
	charoff="..."—Offset to the first alignment character on a line.
	valign="..."—Vertically aligns the contents of cells (top, middle, bottom, baseline).
	bgcolor="..."—Deprecated. Sets the background color.
Empty	No

Frames

Frames create new "panels" in the Web browser window that are used to display content from different source documents.

<FRAME>

Usage	Defines a frame.
Start/End Tag	Required/Illegal
Attributes	name="..."—The name of a frame.
	src="..."—The source to be displayed in a frame.
	frameborder="..."—Toggles the border between frames (0, 1).
	marginwidth="..."—Sets the space between frame the border and content.
	marginheight="..."—Sets the space between the frame border and content.
	noresize—Disables sizing.
	scrolling="..."—Determines scrollbar presence (auto, yes, no).
Empty	Yes

<FRAMESET>...</FRAMESET>

Usage	Defines the layout of FRAMES within a window.
Start/End Tag	Required/Required
Attributes	rows="..."—The number of rows.
	cols="..."—The number of columns.

onload="..."—The intrinsic event triggered when the document loads.

onunload="..."—The intrinsic event triggered when the document unloads.

Empty   No

Notes   FRAMESETs can be nested.

`<IFRAME>...</IFRAME>`

Usage   Creates an inline frame.

Start/End Tag Required/Required

Attributes   name="..."—The name of the frame.

src="..."—The source to be displayed in a frame.

frameborder="..."—Toggles the border between frames (0, 1).

marginwidth="..."—Sets the space between the frame border and content.

marginheight="..."—Sets the space between the frame border and content.

scrolling="..."—Determines scrollbar presence (auto, yes, no).

align="..."—Deprecated. Controls alignment (left, center, right, justify).

height="..."—Height.

width="..."—Width.

Empty   No

`<NOFRAMES>...</NOFRAMES>`

Usage   Alternative content when frames are not supported.

Start/End Tag Required/Required

Attributes   None.

Empty   No

Embedded Content

Also called inclusions, embedded content applies to Java applets, imagemaps, and other multimedia or programattical content that is placed in a Web page to provide additional functionality.

<APPLET>...</APPLET>

Usage	Includes a Java applet.
Start/End Tag	Required/Required
Attributes	codebase="..."—The URL base for the applet.
	archive="..."—Identifies the resources to be preloaded.
	code="..."—The applet class file.
	object="..."—The serialized applet file.
	alt="..."—Displays text while loading.
	name="..."—The name of the applet.
	width="..."—The height of the displayed applet.
	height="..."—The width of the displayed applet.
	align="..."—Controls alignment (bottom, middle, top, left, right).
	hspace="..."—The horizontal space separating the image from other content.
	vspace="..."—The vertical space separating the image from other content.
Empty	No
Notes	APPLET is deprecated in favor of the OBJECT element.

<AREA>

Usage	The AREA element is used to define links and anchors.
Start/End Tag	Required/Illegal
Attributes	shape="..."—Enables you to define client-side imagemaps using defined shapes (default, rect, circle, poly).
	coords="..."—Sets the size of the shape using pixel or percentage lengths.
	href="..."—The URL of the linked resource.
	target="..."—Determines where the resource will be displayed (user-defined name, _blank, _parent, _self, _top).
	nohref="..."—Indicates that the region has no action.
	alt="..."—Displays alternative text.
	tabindex="..."—Sets the tabbing order between elements with a defined tabindex.
Empty	Yes

<IMG>

Usage	Uncludes an image in the document.
Start/End Tag	Required/Illegal
Attributes	`%coreattrs, %i18n, %events`
	`src="..."`—The URL of the image.
	`alt="..."`—Alternative text to display.
	`align="..."`—Deprecated. Controls alignment (`bottom`, `middle`, `top`, `left`, `right`).
	`height="..."`—The height of the image.
	`width="..."`—The width of the image.
	`border="..."`—Border width.
	`hspace="..."`—The horizontal space separating the image from other content.
	`vspace="..."`—The vertical space separating the image from other content.
	`usemap="..."`—The URL to a client-side imagemap.
	`ismap`—Identifies a server-side imagemap.
Empty	Yes

<MAP>...</MAP>

Usage	When used with the `AREA` element, creates a client-side imagemap.
Start/End Tag	Required/Required
Attributes	`%coreattrs`
	`name="..."`—The name of the imagemap to be created.
Empty	No

<OBJECT>...</OBJECT>

Usage	Includes an object.
Start/End Tag	Required/Required
Attributes	`%coreattrs, %i18n, %events`
	`declare`—A flag that declares but doesn't create an object.
	`classid="..."`—The URL of the object's location.
	`codebase="..."`—The URL for resolving URLs specified by other attributes.

B

`data="..."`—The URL to the object's data.

`type="..."`—The Internet content type for data.

`codetype="..."`—The Internet content type for the code.

`standby="..."`—Show message while loading.

`align="..."`—Deprecated. Controls alignment (`texttop`, `middle`, `textmiddle`, `baseline`, `textbottom`, `left`, `center`, `right`).

`height="..."`—The height of the object.

`width="..."`—The width of the object.

`border="..."`—Displays the border around an object.

`hspace="..."`—The space between the sides of the object and other page content.

`vspace="..."`—The space between the top and bottom of the object and other page content.

`usemap="..."`—The URL to an imagemap.

`shapes=`—Enables you to define areas to search for hyperlinks if the object is an image.

`name="..."`—The URL to submit as part of a form.

`tabindex="..."`—Sets the tabbing order between elements with a defined `tabindex`.

Empty	No

\<PARAM\>

Usage	Initializes an object.
Start/End Tag	Required/Illegal
Attributes	`name="..."`—Defines the parameter name.
	`value="..."`—The value of the object parameter.
	`valuetype="..."`—Defines the value type (`data`, `ref`, `object`).
	`type="..."`—The Internet media type.
Empty	Yes

Style

Style sheets (both inline and external) are incorporated into an HTML document through the use of the STYLE element.

<STYLE>...</STYLE>

Usage	Creates an internal style sheet.
Start/End Tag	Required/Required
Attributes	`%i18n`
	`type="..."`—The Internet content type.
	`media="..."`—Defines the destination medium (`screen`, `print`, `projection`, `braille`, `speech`, `all`).
	`title="..."`—The title of the style.
Empty	No
Notes	Located in the `HEAD` element.

Forms

Forms create an interface for the user to select options and submit data back to the Web server.

<BUTTON>...</BUTTON>

Usage	Creates a button.
Start/End Tag	Required/Required
Attributes	`%coreattrs, %i18n, %events`
	`name="..."`—The button name.
	`value="..."`—The value of the button.
	`type="..."`—The button type (`button`, `submit`, `reset`).
	`disabled="..."`—Sets the button state to disabled.
	`tabindex="..."`—Sets the tabbing order between elements with a defined `tabindex`.
	`onfocus="..."`—The event that occurs when the element receives focus.
	`onblur="..."`—The event that occurs when the element loses focus.
Empty	No

<FIELDSET>...</FIELDSET>

Usage	Groups related controls.
Start/End Tag	Required/Required
Attributes	`%coreattrs, %i18n, %events`
Empty	No

<FORM>...</FORM>

Usage	Creates a form that holds controls for user input.
Start/End Tag	Required/Required
Attributes	`%coreattrs, %i18n, %events`

`action="..."`—The URL for the server action.

`method="..."`—The HTTP method (`get`, `post`). `get` is deprecated.

`enctype="..."`—Specifies the MIME (Internet media type).

`onsubmit="..."`—The intrinsic event that occurs when the form is submitted.

`onreset="..."`—The intrinsic event that occurs when the form is reset.

`target="..."`—Determines where the resource will be displayed (user-defined name, `_blank`, `_parent`, `_self`, `_top`).

`accept-charset="..."`—The list of character encodings.

Empty	No

<INPUT>

Usage	Defines controls used in forms.
Start/End Tag	Required/Illegal
Attributes	`%coreattrs, %i18n, %events`

`type="..."`—The type of input control (`text`, `password`, `checkbox`, `radio`, `submit`, `reset`, `file`, `hidden`, `image`, `button`).

`name="..."`—The name of the control (required except for `submit` and `reset`).

`value="..."`—The initial value of the control (required for radio and checkboxes).

`checked="..."`—Sets the radio buttons to a checked state.

`disabled="..."`—Disables the control.

`readonly="..."`—For text password types.

`size="..."`—The width of the control in pixels except for text and password controls, which are specified in number of characters.

`maxlength="..."`—The maximum number of characters that can be entered.

`src="..."`—The URL to an image control type.

`alt="..."`—An alternative text description.

usemap="..."—The URL to a client-side imagemap.

align="..."—Deprecated. Controls alignment (left, center, right, justify).

tabindex="..."—Sets the tabbing order between elements with a defined tabindex.

onfocus="..."—The event that occurs when the element receives focus.

onblur="..."—The event that occurs when the element loses focus.

onselect="..."—Intrinsic event that occurs when the control is selected.

onchange="..."—Intrinsic event that occurs when the control is changed.

accept="..."—File types allowed for upload.

Empty	Yes

\<ISINDEX\>

Usage	Prompts the user for unput.
Start/End Tag	Required/Illegal
Attributes	%coreattrs, %i18n

prompt="..."—Provides a prompt string for the input field.

Empty	Yes
Notes	Deprecated.

\<LABEL\>...\</LABEL\>

Usage	Labels a control.
Start/End Tag	Required/Required
Attributes	%coreattrs, %i18n, %events

for="..."—Associates a label with an identified control.

disabled="..."—Disables a control.

accesskey="..."—Assigns a hotkey to this element.

onfocus="..."—The event that occurs when the element receives focus.

onblur="..."—The event that occurs when the element loses focus.

Empty	No

<LEGEND>...</LEGEND>

Usage	Assigns a caption to a FIELDSET.
Start/End Tag	Required/Required
Attributes	%coreattrs, %i18n, %events

align="..."—Deprecated. Controls alignment (top, bottom, left, right).

accesskey="..."—Assigns a hotkey to this element.

Empty	No

<OPTION>...</OPTION>

Usage	Specifies choices in a SELECT element.
Start/End Tag	Required/Optional
Attributes	%coreattrs, %i18n, %events

selected="..."—Specifies whether the option is selected.

disabled="..."—Disables control.

value="..."—The value submitted if a control is submitted.

Empty	No

<SELECT>...</SELECT>

Usage	Creates choices for the user to select.
Start/End Tag	Required/Required
Attributes	%coreattrs, %i18n, %events

name="..."—The name of the element.

size="..."—The width in number of rows.

multiple—Allows multiple selections.

disabled="..."—Disables the control.

tabindex="..."—Sets the tabbing order between elements with a defined tabindex.

onfocus="..."—The event that occurs when the element receives focus.

onblur="..."—The event that occurs when the element loses focus.

onselect="..."—Intrinsic event that occurs when the control is selected.

onchange="..."—Intrinsic event that occurs when the control is changed.

Empty	No

\<TEXTAREA>...\</TEXTAREA>

Usage	Creates an area for user input with multiple lines.
Start/End Tag	Required/Required
Attributes	`%coreattrs, %i18n, %events`
	`name="..."`—The name of the control.
	`rows="..."`—The width in number of rows.
	`cols="..."`—The height in number of columns.
	`disabled="..."`—Disables the control.
	`readonly="..."`—Sets the displayed text to read-only status.
	`tabindex="..."`—Sets the tabbing order between elements with a defined `tabindex`.
	`onfocus="..."`—The event that occurs when the element receives focus.
	`onblur="..."`—The event that occurs when the element loses focus.
	`onselect="..."`—Intrinsic event that occurs when the control is selected.
	`onchange="..."`—Intrinsic event that occurs when the control is changed.
Empty	No
Notes	Text to be displayed is placed within the start and end tags.

Scripts

Scripting language is made available to process data and perform other dynamic events through the `SCRIPT` element.

\<SCRIPT>...\</SCRIPT>

Usage	The `SCRIPT` element contains client-side scripts that are executed by the browser.
Start/End Tag	Required/Required
Attributes	`type="..."`—Script-language Internet content type.
	`language="..."`—Deprecated. The scripting language, deprecated in favor of the `type` attribute.
	`src="..."`—The URL for the external script.
Empty	No
Notes	You can set the default scripting language in the `META` element.

B

<NOSCRIPT>...</NOSCRIPT>

Usage	The NOSCRIPT element provides alternative content for browsers unable to execute a script.
Start/End Tag	Required/Required
Attributes	None
Empty	No

Common Attributes and Events

Four attributes are abbreviated as %coreattrs in the preceding sections. They are

- ☐ id="..."—A global identifier.
- ☐ class="..."—A list of classes separated by spaces.
- ☐ style="..."—Style information.
- ☐ title="..."—Provides more information for a specific element, as opposed to the TITLE element, which entitles the entire Web page.

Two attributes for internationalization (i18n) are abbreviated as %i18n:

- ☐ lang="..."—The language identifier.
- ☐ dir="..."—The text direction (ltr, rtl).

The following intrinsic events are abbreviated %events:

- ☐ onclick="..."—A pointing device (such as a mouse) was single-clicked.
- ☐ ondblclick="..."—A pointing device (such as a mouse) was double-clicked.
- ☐ onmousedown="..."—A mouse button was clicked and held down.
- ☐ onmouseup="..."—A mouse button that was clicked and held down was released.
- ☐ onmouseover="..."—A mouse moved the cursor over an object.
- ☐ onmousemove="..."—The mouse was moved.
- ☐ onmouseout="..."—A mouse moved the cursor off an object.
- ☐ onkeypress="..."—A key was pressed and released.
- ☐ onkeydown="..."—A key was pressed and held down.
- ☐ onkeyup="..."—A key that was pressed has been released.

Character Entities

Table B.1 contains the possible numeric and character entities for the ISO-Latin-1 (ISO8859-1) character set. Where possible, the character is shown.

NOTE Not all browsers can display all characters, and some browsers may even display different characters from those that appear in the table. Newer browsers seem to have a better track record for handling character entities, but be sure and test your HTML files extensively with multiple browsers if you intend to use these entities.

Table B.1. ISO-Latin-1 character set.

Character	Numeric Entity	Character Entity (if any)	Description
	&#00;–&#08;		Unused
	&#09;		Horizontal tab
	&#10;		Line feed
	&#11;–&#31;		Unused
	&#32;		Space
!	&#33;		Exclamation mark
"	&#34;	&quot;	Quotation mark
#	&#35;		Number sign
$	&#36;		Dollar sign
%	&#37;		Percent sign
&	&#38;	&amp;	Ampersand
'	&#39;		Apostrophe
(	&#40;		Left parenthesis
)	&#41;		Right parenthesis
*	&#42;		Asterisk
+	&#43;		Plus sign
,	&#44;		Comma
-	&#45;		Hyphen
.	&#46;		Period (fullstop)
/	&#47;		Solidus (slash)
0–9	0–9		Digits 0–9
:	&#58;		Colon

continues

Table B.1. continued

Character	Numeric Entity	Character Entity (if any)	Description
;	&#59;		Semicolon
<	&#60;	&lt;	Less than
=	&#61;		Equals sign
>	&#62;	&gt;	Greater than
?	&#63;		Question mark
@	&#64;		Commercial at
A–Z	A–Z		Letters A–Z
[	&#91;		Left square bracket
\	&#92;		Reverse solidus (backslash)
]	&#93;		Right square bracket
^	&#94;		Caret
–	&#95;		Horizontal bar
`	&#96;		Grave accent
a–z	a–z		Letters a–z
{	&#123;		Left curly brace
|	&#124		Vertical bar
}	&#125;		Right curly brace
~	&#126;		Tilde
	&#127;–Ÿ		Unused
			non-breaking space
¡	&#161;	&iexcl;	Inverted exclamation
¢	&#162;	&cent;	Cent sign
£	&#163;	&pound;	Pound sterling
¤	&#164;	&curren;	General currency sign
¥	&#165;	&yen;	Yen sign
¦	&#166;	¦ or &brkbar;	Broken vertical bar
§	&#167;	&sect;	Section sign
¨	&#168;	¨ or¨	Umlaut (dieresis)

Character	Numeric Entity	Character Entity (if any)	Description
©	©	©	Copyright
a	ª	ª	Feminine ordinal
‹	«	&laqo;	Left angle quote, guillemet left
¬	¬	¬	Not sign
-	­	­	Soft hyphen
®	®	®	Registered trademark
¯	¯	¯ or &hibar;	Macron accent
°	°	°	Degree sign
±	±	±	Plus or minus
2	²	²	Superscript two
3	³	³	Superscript three
´	´	´	Acute accent
µ	µ	µ	Micro sign
¶	¶	¶	Paragraph sign
·	·	·	Middle dot
¸	¸	¸	Cedilla
1	¹	¹	Superscript one
º	º	º	Masculine ordinal
›	»	»	Right angle quote, guillemet right
1/4	¼	&fraq14;	Fraction one-fourth
1/2	½	&fraq12;	Fraction one-half
3/4	¾	&fraq34;	Fraction three-fourths
¿	¿	¿	Inverted question mark
À	À	À	Capital A, grave accent
Á	Á	Á	Capital A, acute accent
Â	Â	Â	Capital A, circumflex accent

continues

B

Table B.1. continued

Character	Numeric Entity	Character Entity (if any)	Description
Ã	&#195;	&Atilde;	Capital A, tilde
Ä	&#196;	&Auml;	Capital A, dieresis or umlaut mark
Å	&#197;	&Aring;	Capital A, ring
Æ	&#198;	&AElig;	Capital AE dipthong (ligature)
Ç	&#199;	&Ccedil;	Capital C, cedilla
È	&#200;	&Egrave;	Capital E, grave accent
É	&#201;	&Eacute;	Capital E, acute accent
Ê	&#202;	&Ecirc;	Capital E, circumflex accent
Ë	&#203;	&Euml;	Capital E, dieresis or umlaut mark
Ì	&#204;	&Igrave;	Capital I, grave accent
Í	&#205;	&Iacute;	Capital I, acute accent
Î	&#206;	&Icirc;	Capital I, circumflex accent
Ï	&#207;	&Iuml;	Capital I, dieresis or umlaut mark
Ð	&#208;	Ð orĐ	Capital Eth, Icelandic
Ñ	&#209;	&Ntilde;	Capital N, tilde
Ò	&#210;	&Ograve;	Capital O, grave accent
Ó	&#211;	&Oacute;	Capital O, acute accent
Ô	&#212;	&Ocirc;	Capital O, circumflex accent
Õ	&#213;	&Otilde;	Capital O, tilde

Character	Numeric Entity	Character Entity (if any)	Description
Ö	`&#214;`	`&Ouml;`	Capital O, dieresis or umlaut mark
×	`&#215;`	`&times;`	Multiply sign
Ø	`&#216;`	`&Oslash;`	Capital O, slash
Ù	`&#217;`	`&Ugrave;`	Capital U, grave accent
Ú	`&#218;`	`&Uacute;`	Capital U, acute accent
Û	`&#219;`	`&Ucirc;`	Capital U, circumflex accent
Ü	`&#220;`	`&Uuml;`	Capital U, dieresis or umlaut mark
Ý	`&#221;`	`&Yacute;`	Capital Y, acute accent
Þ	`&#222;`	`&THORN;`	Capital THORN, Icelandic
β	`&#223;`	`&szlig;`	Small sharp s, German (sz ligature)
à	`&#224;`	`&agrave;`	Small a, grave accent
á	`&#225;`	`&aacute;`	Small a, acute accent
â	`&#226;`	`&acirc;`	Small a, circumflex accent
ã	`&#227;`	`&atilde;`	Small a, tilde
ä	`&#228;`	`&auml;`	Small a, dieresis or umlaut mark
å	`&#229;`	`&aring;`	Small a, ring
æ	`&#230;`	`&aelig;`	Small ae dipthong (ligature)
ç	`&#231;`	`&ccedil;`	Small c, cedilla
è	`&#232;`	`&egrave;`	Small e, grave accent
é	`&#233;`	`&eacute;`	Small e, acute accent

continues

B

Table B.1. continued

Character	Numeric Entity	Character Entity (if any)	Description
ê	ê	ê	Small e, circumflex accent
ë	ë	ë	Small e, dieresis or umlaut mark
ì	ì	ì	Small i, grave accent
í	í	í	Small i, acute accent
î	î	î	Small i, circumflex accent
ï	ï	ï	Small i, dieresis or umlaut mark
ð	ð	ð	Small eth, Icelandic
ñ	ñ	ñ	Small n, tilde
ò	ò	ò	Small o, grave accent
ó	ó	ó	Small o, acute accent
ô	ô	ô	Small o, circumflex accent
õ	õ	õ	Small o, tilde
ö	ö	ö	Small o, dieresis or umlaut mark
÷	÷	÷	Division sign
ø	ø	ø	Small o, slash
ù	ù	ù	Small u, grave accent
ú	ú	ú	Small u, acute accent
û	û	û	Small u, circumflex accent
ü	ü	ü	Small u, dieresis or umlaut mark
ý	ý	ý	Small y, acute accent
þ	þ	þ	Small thorn, Icelandic
ÿ	ÿ	ÿ	Small y, dieresis or umlaut mark

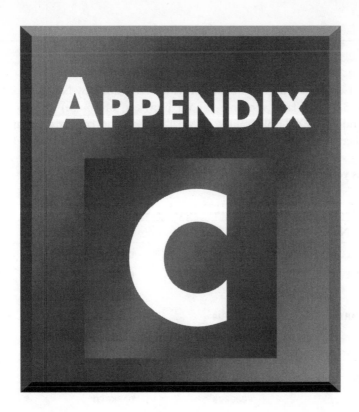

APPENDIX C

Colors by Name and Hexadecimal Value

Table C.1 contains a list of all the color names recognized by Navigator 2.0 and Internet Explorer 3.0 (and later versions of both browsers, of course) and also includes their corresponding HEX Triplet values. To see all these colors correctly, you must have a 256-color or better video card and the appropriate video drivers installed. Also, depending on the operating system and computer platform you are running, some colors may not appear exactly as you expect them to.

Table C.1. Color values and HEX triplet equivalents.

Color Name	HEX Triplet	Color Name	HEX Triplet
ALICEBLUE	#A0CE00	DARKGRAY	#A9A9A9
ANTIQUEWHITE	#FAEBD7	DARKGREEN	#006400
AQUA	#00FFFF	DARKKHAKI	#BDB76B
AQUAMARINE	#7FFFD4	DARKMAGENTA	#8B008B
AZURE	#F0FFFF	DARKOLIVEGREEN	#556B2F
BEIGE	#F5F5DC	DARKORANGE	#FF8C00
BISQUE	#FFE4C4	DARKORCHID	#9932CC
BLACK	#000000	DARKRED	#8B0000
BLANCHEDALMOND	#FFEBCD	DARKSALMON	#E9967A
BLUE	#0000FF	DARKSEAGREEN	#8FBC8F
BLUEVIOLET	#8A2BE2	DARKSLATEBLUE	#483D8B
BROWN	#A52A2A	DARKSLATEGRAY	#2F4F4F
BURLYWOOD	#DEB887	DARKTURQUOISE	#00CED1
CADETBLUE	#5F9EA0	DARKVIOLET	#9400D3
CHARTREUSE	#7FFF00	DEEPPINK	#FF1493
CHOCOLATE	#D2691E	DEEPSKYBLUE	#00BFFF
CORAL	#FF7F50	DIMGRAY	#696969
CORNFLOWERBLUE	#6495ED	DODGERBLUE	#1E90FF
CORNSILK	#FFF8DC	FIREBRICK	#B22222
CRIMSON	#DC143C	FLORALWHITE	#FFFAF0
CYAN	#00FFFF	FORESTGREEN	#228B22
DARKBLUE	#00008B	FUCHSIA	#FF00FF
DARKCYAN	#008B8B	GAINSBORO	#DCDCDC
DARKGOLDENROD	#B8860B	GHOSTWHITE	#F8F8FF

Color Name	HEX Triplet	Color Name	HEX Triplet
GOLD	#FFD700	MAGENTA	#FF00FF
GOLDENROD	#DAA520	MAROON	#800000
GRAY	#808080	MEDIUMAQUAMARINE	#66CDAA
GREEN	#008000	MEDIUMBLUE	#0000CD
GREENYELLOW	#ADFF2F	MEDIUMORCHID	#BA55D3
HONEYDEW	#F0FFF0	MEDIUMPURPLE	#9370DB
HOTPINK	#FF69B4	MEDIUMSEAGREEN	#3CB371
INDIANRED	#CD5C5C	MEDIUMSLATEBLUE	#7B68EE
INDIGO	#4B0082	MEDIUMSPRINGGREEN	#00FA9A
IVORY	#FFFFF0	MEDIUMTURQUOISE	#48D1CC
KHAKI	#F0E68C	MEDIUMVIOLETRED	#C71585
LAVENDER	#E6E6FA	MIDNIGHTBLUE	#191970
LAVENDERBLUSH	#FFF0F5	MINTCREAM	#F5FFFA
LEMONCHIFFON	#FFFACD	MISTYROSE	#FFE4E1
LIGHTBLUE	#ADD8E6	NAVAJOWHITE	#FFDEAD
LIGHTCORAL	#F08080	NAVY	#000080
LIGHTCYAN	#E0FFFF	OLDLACE	#FDF5E6
LIGHTGOLDENRODYELLOW	#FAFAD2	OLIVE	#808000
LIGHTGREEN	#90EE90	OLIVEDRAB	#6B8E23
LIGHTGREY	#D3D3D3	ORANGE	#FFA500
LIGHTPINK	#FFB6C1	ORANGERED	#FF4500
LIGHTSALMON	#FFA07A	ORCHID	#DA70D6
LIGHTSEAGREEN	#20B2AA	PALEGOLDENROD	#EEE8AA
LIGHTSKYBLUE	#87CEFA	PALEGREEN	#98FB98
LIGHTSLATEGRAY	#778899	PALETURQUOISE	#AFEEEE
LIGHTSTEELBLUE	#B0C4DE	PALEVIOLETRED	#DB7093
LIGHTYELLOW	#FFFFE0	PAPAYAWHIP	#FFEFD5
LIME	#00FF00	PEACHPUFF	#FFDAB9
LIMEGREEN	#32CD32	PERU	#CD853F
LINEN	#FAF0E6	PINK	#FFC0CB

C

continues

Table C.1. continued

Color Name	HEX Triplet	Color Name	HEX Triplet
PLUM	#DDA0DD	SLATEGRAY	#708090
POWDERBLUE	#B0E0E6	SNOW	#FFFAFA
PURPLE	#800080	SPRINGGREEN	#00FF7F
RED	#FF0000	STEELBLUE	#4682B4
ROSYBROWN	#BC8F8F	TAN	#D2B48C
ROYALBLUE	#4169E1	TEAL	#008080
SADDLEBROWN	#8B4513	THISTLE	#D8BFD8
SALMON	#FA8072	TOMATO	#FF6347
SANDYBROWN	#F4A460	TURQUOISE	#40E0D0
SEAGREEN	#2E8B57	VIOLET	#EE82EE
SEASHELL	#FFF5EE	WHEAT	#F5DEB3
SIENNA	#A0522D	WHITE	#FFFFFF
SILVER	#C0C0C0	WHITESMOKE	#F5F5F5
SKYBLUE	#87CEEB	YELLOW	#FFFF00
SLATEBLUE	#6A5ACD	YELLOWGREEN	#9ACD32

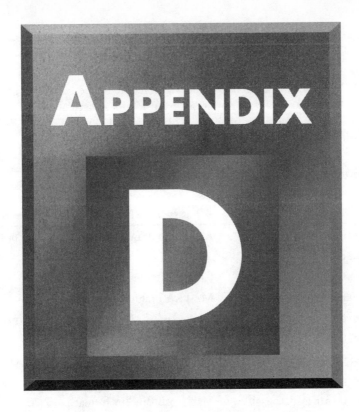

APPENDIX D

MIME Types and File Extensions

Table D.1 lists some the file extensions and MIME content types supported by many popular Web servers. If your server does not list an extension for a particular content type, or if the type you want to use is not listed at all, you will have to add support for that type to your server configuration.

Table D.1. MIME types and HTTPD support.

MIME Type	What It Is (If Noted)	File Extensions
application/acad	AutoCAD drawing files	dwg, DWG
application/arj		arj
application/clariscad	ClarisCAD files	CCAD
application/drafting	MATRA Prelude drafting	DRW
application/dxf	DXF (AutoCAD)	dxf, DXF
application/excel	Microsoft Excel	xl
application/i-deas	SDRC I-DEAS files	unv, UNV
application/iges	IGES graphics format	igs, iges, IGS, IGES
application/mac-binhex40	Macintosh BinHex format	hqx
application/msword	Microsoft Word	word, w6w, doc
application/mswrite	Microsoft Write	wri
application/octet-stream	Uninterpreted binary	bin
application/oda		oda
application/pdf	PDF (Adobe Acrobat)	pdf
application/postscript	PostScript	ai, PS, ps, eps
application/pro_eng	PTC Pro/ENGINEER	prt, PRT, part
application/rtf	Rich Text Format	rtf
application/set	SET (French CAD standard)	set, SET
application/sla	Stereolithography	stl, STL
application/solids	MATRA Prelude Solids	SOL
application/STEP	ISO-10303 STEP data files	stp, STP, step, STEP
application/vda	VDA-FS Surface data	vda, VDA
application/x-csh	C-shell script	csh
application/x-director	Macromedia Director	dir, dcr, dxr
application/x-dvi	TeX DVI	dvi
application/x-gzip	GNU Zip	gz, gzip

MIME Type	What It Is (If Noted)	File Extensions
application/x-mif	FrameMaker MIF Format	mif
application/x-hdf	NCSA HDF data file	hdf
application/x-latex	LaTeX source	latex
application/x-netcdf	Unidata netCDF	nc,cdf
application/x-sh	Bourne shell script	sh
application/x-stuffit	StuffIt Archive	sit
application/x-tcl	TCL script	tcl
application/x-tex	TeX source	tex
application/x-texinfo	Texinfo (Emacs)	texinfo,texi
application/x-troff	Troff	t, tr, roff
application/x-troff-man	Troff with MAN macros	man
application/x-troff-me	Troff with ME macros	me
application/x-troff-ms	Troff with MS macros	ms
application/x-wais-source	WAIS source	src
application/x-bcpio	Old binary CPIO	bcpio
application/x-cpio	POSIX CPIO	cpio
application/x-gtar	GNU tar	gtar
application/x-shar	Shell archive	shar
application/x-sv4cpio	SVR4 CPIO	sv4cpio
application/x-sv4crc	SVR4 CPIO with CRC	sv4crc
application/x-tar	4.3BSD tar format	tar
application/x-ustar	POSIX tar format	ustar
application/x-winhelp	Windows Help	hlp
application/zip	ZIP archive	zip
audio/basic	Basic audio (usually μ-law)	au, snd
audio/x-aiff	AIFF audio	aif, aiff, aifc
audio/x-pn-realaudio	RealAudio	ra, ram
audio/x-pn-realaudio-plugin	RealAudio (plug-in)	rpm
audio/x-wav	Windows WAVE audio	wav

continues

D

Table D.1. continued

MIME Type	What It Is (If Noted)	File Extensions
image/gif	GIF image	gif
image/ief	Image Exchange Format	ief
image/jpeg	JPEG image	jpg, JPG, JPE, jpe, JPEG, jpeg
image/pict	Macintosh PICT	pict
image/tiff	TIFF image	tiff, tif
image/x-cmu-raster	CMU raster	ras
image/x-portable-anymap	PBM Anymap format	pnm
image/x-portable-bitmap	PBM Bitmap format	pbm
image/x-portable-graymap	PBM Graymap format	pgm
image/x-portable-pixmap	PBM Pixmap format	ppm
image/x-rgb	RGB image	rgb
image/x-xbitmap	X Bitmap	xbm
image/x-xpixmap	X Pixmap	xpm
image/x-xwindowdump	X Window dump (xwd) format	xwd
multipart/x-zip	PKZIP archive	zip
multipart/x-gzip	GNU ZIP archive	gzip
text/html	HTML	html, htm
text/plain	Plain text	txt, g, h, C, cc, hh, m, f90
text/richtext	MIME rich text	rtx
text/tab-separated-values	Text with tab-separated values	tsv
text/x-setext	Struct-enhanced text	etx

MIME Type	What It Is (If Noted)	File Extensions
video/mpeg	MPEG video	mpeg, mpg, MPG, MPE, mpe, MPEG, mpeg
video/quicktime	QuickTime video	qt, mov
video/msvideo	Microsoft Windows video	avi
video/x-sgi-movie	SGI MoviePlayer format	movie
x-world/x-vrml	VRML Worlds	wrl

INDEX

MACMILLAN COMPUTER PUBLISHING USA

A VIACOM COMPANY

Technical ---- Support:

If you need assistance with the information in this book or with a CD/Disk accompanying the book, please access the Knowledge Base on our Web site at **http://www.superlibrary.com/general/support**. Our most Frequently Asked Questions are answered there. If you do not find the answer to your questions on our Web site, you may contact Macmillan Technical Support **(317) 581-3833** or e-mail us at **support@mcp.com**.

HTML 4 Unleashed

Rick Darnell, Michael Larson, et al.   *Covers HTML*

A comprehensive guide and reference to the foundation language of the World Wide Web, *HTML Unleashed* provides an exhaustive resource devoted to the language of Web development. *HTML Unleashed* will provide readers the information they need to grow with an ever-changing technology.

Covers all the latest proprietary extensions, including Microsoft's Active HTML and Netscape's JavaScript Stylesheets

Includes information on integrating HTML with other technologies such as Java and ActiveX

Details new HTML technologies such as the experimental "Cougar" specification, Cascading Style Sheets, and Extensible Markup Language (XML)

CD-ROM contains a wide variety of HTML development tools, a collection of examples from the authors, and two electronic books in HTML format

$49.99 USA/$70.95 CAN	*Accomplished–Expert*	*Internet/Web Publishing*	
1-57521-299-4	*1,100 pp.*	*7 3/8 x 9 1/8*	*7/1/97*

Laura Lemay's Guide to Sizzling Web Site Design

Molly Holzschlag   *Covers Web Site Design*

This book is more than just a guide to the hottest Web sites, it's a behind-the-scenes look at how those sites were created. Web surfers and publishers alike will find this book an insightful guide to some of the most detailed Web pages. The latest Web technologies are discussed in detail, showing readers how the technologies have been applied and how the readers can implement those features into their Web pages.

CD-ROM includes source code from the book, images, scripts, and more

$45.00 USA/$63.95 CAN	*Casual–Accomplished*	*Internet/Web Publishing*
1-57521-221-8	*400 pp.*	*7 3/8 x 9 1/8* *2/1/97*

Teach Yourself Java 1.1 in 21 Days, Second Edition

Laura Lemay & Charles Perkins   *Covers Java 1.1*

This updated bestseller is the definitive guide to learning Java 1.1. *Teach Yourself Java 1.1 in 21 Days, Second Edition* carefully steps you through the fundamental concepts of the Java language, as well as the basics of applet design and integration with Web presentations.

Learn the basics of object-oriented programming and Java development

Create stand-alone cross-platform applications

Add interactivity and animation to your Web sites by using Java applets

CD-ROM includes Sun's Java Developer's Kit 1.1; Sun's Java Developer's Kit 1.02 for Macintosh; and Sun's Bean Developer's Kit for Windows 95, Windows NT, and Solaris

$39.99 USA/$56.95 CAN	*New–Casual*	*Internet/Programming*
1-57521-142-4	*7 3/8 x 9 1/8*	*4/1/97*

Java 1.1 Unleashed, Third Edition

Michael Morrison et al.   *Covers Java 1.1*

Completely revised, updated, and expanded, this comprehensive reference provides users with all the information they need to master Java 1.1 programming, program advanced Java applets, and successfully integrate Java with other technologies.

Extensive coverage of Java 1.1, the Java extension APIs, JavaBeans, JavaOS, and more

CD-ROM contains Sun's JDK and other Java development tools

$49.99 USA/$70.95 CAN	*Accomplished–Expert*	*Internet/Programming*
1-57521-298-6	*1,400 pp.*	*7 3/8 x 9 1/8* *4/1/97*

Teach Yourself Great Web Design in a Week

Anne-Rae Vasquez-Peterson & Paul Chow   *Covers the World Wide Web*

This step-by-step, full-color tutorial is loaded with graphics, tables, diagrams, and examples of what to do—and what not to do—when designing Web pages. Users will master the fundamentals of good page design—from typography and layout to use of color and graphics—and learn how to apply them to the Web.

Provides Q&A sections, week-at-a-glance previews, and real-world exercises to make learning easy and fun

CD-ROM contains Internet Explorer 3.0, Microsoft ActiveX, and HTML development tools, ready-to-use templates, graphics, scripts, Java applets, and ActiveX controls

$49.99 USA/$70.95 CAN	*New–Casual*	*Internet/Web Publishing*	
1-57521-253-6	*400 pp.*	*7 3/8 x 9 1/8*	*4/1/97*

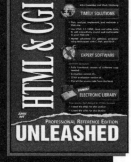

Web Publishing & Programming Resource Kit

Sams & Sams.net Development Groups   *Covers Web Publishing*

This seven-volume, 3,300-page Resource Kit has everything users need to program virtually anything for the World Wide Web. From HTML, Java, and JavaScript programming to CGI, Visual Basic Script, ActiveX, and advanced animations and multimedia, this must-have resource covers it all.

Three bonus CD-ROMs are loaded with more than two gigabytes of Web site development and maintenance tools, HTML templates, CGI scripts, Java applets and scripts, third-party graphics tools, multimedia utilities, and more

$149.99 USA/$209.95 CAN	*Accomplished*	*Internet/Web Publishing*	
1-57521-239-0	*3,300 pp.*	*7 3/8 x 9 1/8*	*5/1/97*

HTML 3.2 & CGI Unleashed, Professional Reference Edition

John December   *Covers HTML 3.2 and CGI*

This comprehensive professional instruction and reference guide for the World Wide Web covers all aspects of development processes, implementation, tools, and programming.

CD-ROM features coverage of planning, analysis, design, HTML implementation, and gateway programming

Covers the new HTML 3.2 specification, plus new topics such as Java, JavaScript, and ActiveX

Features coverage of planning, analysis, design, HTML implementation, and gateway programming

$59.99 USA/$84.95 CAN	*Accomplished–Expert*	*Internet/Programming*	
1-57521-177-7	*900 pp.*	*7 3/8 x 9 1/8*	*9/1/96*

Web Publishing Unleashed, Professional Reference Edition

William Stanek et al.   *Covers HTML, CGI, JavaScript, VBScript, ActiveX*

Web Publishing Unleashed, Professional Reference Edition is a completely new version of the first book, and it includes entire sections on JavaScript, Java, VBScript, and ActiveX, plus expanded coverage of multimedia Web development, adding animation, developing intranet sites, Web design, and much more!

Includes a 200-page reference section

CD-ROM includes a selection of HTML, Java, CGI, and scripting tools for Windows/Mac

$59.99 USA/$84.95 CAN	*Intermediate–Advanced*	*Internet/Web Publishing*	
1-57521-198-X	*1,200 pp.*	*7 3/8 x 9 1/8*	*12/1/96*

Add to Your Sams.net Library Today
with the Best Books for Internet Technologies

ISBN	Quantity	Description of Item	Unit Cost	Total Cost
1-57521-299-4		HTML 4 Unleashed (Book/CD-ROM)	$49.99	
1-57521-221-8		Laura Lemay's Guide to Sizzling Web Site Design (Book/CD-ROM)	$45.00	
1-57521-142-4		Teach Yourself Java 1.1 in 21 Days, Second Edition (Book/CD-ROM)	$39.99	
1-57521-298-6		Java 1.1 Unleashed, Third Edition (Book/CD-ROM)	$49.99	
1-57521-253-6		Teach Yourself Great Web Design in a Week (Book/CD-ROM)	$49.99	
1-57521-239-0		Web Publishing & Programming Resource Kit (7 Books/3 CD-ROMs)	$149.99	
1-57521-177-7		HTML 3.2 & CGI Unleashed, Professional Reference Edition (Book/CD-ROM)	$59.99	
1-57521-198-X		Web Publishing Unleashed, Professional Reference Edition (Book/CD-ROM)	$59.99	
		Shipping and Handling: See information below.		
		TOTAL		

Shipping and Handling: $4.00 for the first book, and $1.75 for each additional book. If you need to have it NOW, we can ship product to you in 24 hours for an additional charge of approximately $18.00, and you will receive your item overnight or in two days. Overseas shipping and handling adds $2.00. Prices subject to change. Call between 9:00 a.m. and 5:00 p.m. EST for availability and pricing information on latest editions.

201 W. 103rd Street, Indianapolis, Indiana 46290

1-800-428-5331 — Orders   1-800-835-3202 — FAX   1-800-858-7674 — Customer Service

Book ISBN 1-57521-336-2